International Higher Education's Scholar-Practitioners: bridging research and practice

International Higher Education's Scholar-Practitioners: bridging research and practice

Edited by
Bernhard Streitwieser
& Anthony C. Ogden

SYMPOSIUM
BOOKS

Symposium Books Ltd
PO Box 204, Didcot, Oxford OX11 9ZQ, United Kingdom
www.symposium-books.co.uk

Published in the United Kingdom, 2016

ISBN 978-1-873927-77-9

Printed and bound in the United Kingdom by Hobbs the Printers, Southampton
www.hobbs.uk.com

Contents

LEVERAGING THE SCHOLAR-PRACTITIONER: EDUCATION, RESEARCH, AND FUTURE OPPORTUNITIES

Acknowledgements

This volume would not have been possible without the keen insights and experiences of the many scholar-practitioners who have contributed to this volume. We are immensely grateful for their hard work, perseverance and infinite patience with us and are indebted and humbled by their leadership and dedication to advancing the field and practice of international education.

We would also like to thank our publisher, Roger Osborn-King, and all of his colleagues at Symposium Books for their guidance and willingness to take on this important and pressing issue.

Finally, we would like to acknowledge and express our gratitude to our respective families. Bernhard wishes to thank his wife, Mary Beth, and his children, Max and Lena, for putting up with far too much emailing and texting even on weekends and evenings and over the many hours he devoted to this book. Anthony would like to thank his partner, Takashi, for his patience, support and encouragement. Lastly, we wish to thank our 'day job' colleagues, whose unwavering support, encouragement and patience made this project manageable and in the end achievable.

Foreword

HANS DE WIT

Is there a scholar-practitioner debate in international higher education? As a result of my involvement in international higher education for close to forty years, I have always been intrigued by the debate about the assumed tension between scholars and practitioners, between research and practice, in international higher education. Maybe that fascination stems from my own career path, combining and crossing these lines on several occasions. It was therefore a good idea of the editors to write a book about this topic. Their invitation to write a foreword for this substantive publication made me reflect again on this issue, based on my personal experience as both a scholar and a practitioner.

Why are international educators so intrigued, and to a certain extent obsessed, by this issue? Is this topic unique to international higher education? Has the issue changed over the past two decades under the influence of globalization and internationalization in higher education? Can international higher education, or internationalization of higher education, be considered 'disciplines', and do they have a scholarly home, or does the strength of these areas lie more in their multidisciplinary dimensions? These questions come to mind when reading through the chapters of this book, which provide a variety of views, experiences and approaches with respect to these issues.

It is important to keep in mind that internationalization in higher education is a rather new phenomenon in the study of higher education. Until 25 years ago, it was mainly a practice, and that practice was rather marginal in higher education, and as a result of that, so, too, was the scholarly study devoted to it. If there was any scholarly work, it was minimal and embedded in the broader field of comparative and international education, and mainly done in the United States. And it is relevant to note that already then there was a debate between scholarly and practical orientation in the field of comparative and international education. International educators were seen more as practitioners, while comparative education was perceived as more scholarly, but even that distinction was not strict (de Wit, 2002, p. 105).

Twenty years ago, Ulrich Teichler wrote: 'Most of the research available on academic mobility and international education seems to be occasional, coincidental, sporadic and episodic' (1996, p. 341), Ten years later, he observed together with Barbara Kehm:

> Research on international dimensions of higher education has substantially expanded in recent years. Just as internationalisation in higher education has become clearly more multidimensional and multifaceted, so has research about internationalisation in higher education ... The thematic range, the disciplines and research domains contributing to it, and the modes of inquiry have become broader ... Altogether, research on internationalisation in higher education has become more strongly intertwined with research on other aspects – a fact that reflects the increasing mainstreaming of international aspects of higher education. (Kehm & Teichler, 2007, p. 269)

In the same year, I wrote: 'Internationalization of (higher) education has become more important on the policy agenda but also on the research agenda' (de Wit, 2007, p. 259).

What can we learn from these quotes on the debate about the relationship between scholarship and practice in international higher education? First, it is still a rather recent issue, in policy, practice and research. Second, the increase in policy and practice has stimulated the growth in scholarly attention and production in the field. Third, the field of international higher education has become broader and more diverse over the years, and by that also the scholarly focus. Fourth, multi- and interdisciplinary approaches are more relevant than a single disciplinary focus. Fifth, while internationalization has become more mainstream and comprehensive in policy and practice, its study has also become more intertwined with the broader field of international higher education. And finally, the roles of scholars and practitioners are not mutually exclusive, with an increasing number of practitioners doing scholarly work, while an increasing number of scholars are also engaged in policy and practice.

Let us look at the first group, the practitioners who do scholarly work. Even there the picture is complex. In the first place, the category of practitioners in international higher education is very broad and diverse. There are senior international officers (SIOs) who manage the policy and practice of international education, and there are international education officers who work in education abroad, foreign student advising, admissions, exchanges, etc. And they can work either in institutions of higher education (in itself a very broad and diverse category) or in a wide range of governmental entities, non-governmental organizations (NGOs) or businesses related to international higher education. Each of these functions requires different skills and competencies and has different scholarly needs and interests. In other words, one cannot put all international educators in the same basket, and the same applies to the research related to their work.

An interesting observation to make in this context is that most SIOs are coming from faculty ranks and have a PhD, and in many cases even a tenured faculty position, not in international higher education, but in a great variety of disciplines. Interestingly enough, an increasing number of other international education officers in the United States follow or have followed a graduate education program in the field of international education, and elsewhere (in particular in Europe) they have followed professional development courses in international education. One can question whether the education they receive in the field is always adequate, but certainly they get more training than their bosses, the SIOs.

What does that imply for the SIOs? On the one hand, as leading practitioners, they bring to their function their academic experience and background, which provide them with a scholarly mind and attitude which are useful for their work, and which also bring them recognition from the rest of senior management and the academic community. On the other hand, they lack specific knowledge of international higher education, in a field that is increasingly broad and more diverse and complex. Several among them, though – including a large group of the authors in this book and myself – have developed, over their years as SIOs, a research interest in international higher education and are publishing scholarly work on aspects of it. And in that work they bring their diverse scholarly knowledge with them.

Is the situation in the United States, where nearly all the authors in this book have their experience, different from the situation elsewhere in the world? In many aspects there is indeed a difference. In other parts of the world, SIOs either are tenured faculty with temporary functions as vice-presidents or vice-rectors of international relations who, as a result, do not have the motivation or time to focus on the study of international higher education, or they are practitioners with little or no research background, and as a result lack the academic knowledge and experience to do scholarly research. This last group accounts for the many solid institutional or programmatic case studies and evaluations of projects, programs and institutional strategies, which are still the main production in the field, but which lack a comparative and conceptual framework.

Looking back on my own professional development, many aspects mentioned in the book and also touched upon above are illustrative of the conspicuous relationship between scholarship and practice in international higher education. I started – like many SIOs – as a social anthropologist and sociologist, and was a teacher and researcher in Latin American studies. As a result of that academic background, I became an SIO and built up experience as a practitioner. Among other things, this resulted in my contribution to the founding of the European Association for International Education (EAIE). Ten years into my SIO function, older and wiser, I developed an interest in studying the meanings and rationales of the internationalization of higher education. I became a practitioner/scholar, which resulted in books, book chapters and journal articles, and in founding the *Journal of Studies in International Education*. Again, ten years later, I left the practitioner function of SIO and became a full-time scholar as a professor of internationalization of higher education, culminating in my current position as director/ professor of the Center for International Higher Education at Boston College.

What can we learn from the chapters in this book and the multifaceted relationship between scholarship and practice? As my personal experience also illustrates, there is not a strong dividing line between the two. But it is a fact that the field has become so complex, broad and varied that we can no longer rely on the unrelated academic background and experience of the faculty who take up SIO positions, or on the administrative skills and practical training that non-academic international education officers have acquired. There is an increasing need for professional development training at the graduate level, specific for international higher education, and there is an even greater need for academic research to feed policy and practice into the field. I hope that this message comes through by reading this book that, thanks to the work of its editors and authors, has provided an insight into the diverse and complex picture of policy, practice and research in international higher education.

References

de Wit, Hans (2002) *Internationalization of Higher Education in the United States of America and Europe: a historical, comparative, and conceptual analysis.* Westport, CT: Greenwood Press.

de Wit, Hans (2007) Ten Years of Editorial Policy of the *Journal of Studies in International Higher Education*: overview, challenges, and opportunities, *Journal of Studies in International Education*, 11(3/4), 251-259. http://dx.doi.org/10.1177/1028315307303533

Kehm, Barbara & Teichler, Ulrich (2007) Research on Internationalisation in Higher Education, *Journal of Studies in International Education*, 11(3/4), 260-273. http://dx.doi.org/10.1177/1028315307303534

Teichler, Ulrich (1996) Research on Academic Mobility and International Cooperation in Higher Education: an agenda for the future, in P. Blumenthal, C. Goodwin, A. Smith & U. Teichler (Eds) *Academic Mobility in a Changing World*, pp. 338-358. London: Jessica Kingsley.

PREFACE

International Higher Education's Scholar-Practitioners: bridging research and practice

BERNHARD STREITWIESER & ANTHONY C. OGDEN

International higher education is a complex phenomenon that involves many different activities, players, institutions and realities today. A wide range of stakeholders participate in making international higher education in all of its diverse forms possible. With the growth in the number of students who now engage in educational mobility and exchange, the increased size of the administrative cadre vital to supporting it and other internationalization activities, and the research foundation that has been built up around these and other phenomena, there are now many more players involved than ever before. However, when we look closely at international education activity, two distinct categories emerge: those who 'do it', and those who 'study it' – the *practitioners* and the *scholars*. Practitioners are viewed as those who facilitate international education activity by managing all the details necessary for ensuring successful mobility and exchange for students and staff. Scholars are viewed as those who study the phenomenon and publish research on its meaning and impact but are removed from daily practice. We give these two groups distinct names as if they operated in completely distinct orbits, but that dichotomy is simplistic and false: it excludes those hybrid scholar-practitioners or practitioner-scholars – neither necessarily precluding nor prioritizing the other – who routinely and actively engage in both kinds of activities.

We believe that the idea of the professional who spans both research and practice has for too long been largely overlooked by the academic and administrative structures governing US higher education. In international higher education writ large, there are now many who by the very nature of their engagement clearly bridge both areas. It is these bridge builders this book has set out to explore and profile.

With this volume, we have aimed to satisfy two primary objectives: to open a much-needed dialogue exploring the notion of the scholar-practitioner in international higher education; and to develop a reference for the growing number of international education graduate programs established to train the next generation in our field and profession. The intellectual discussions in each chapter take different approaches to exploring the meaning of the scholar-practitioner, while the final chapter shares each contributor's unique personal story and professional pathway to becoming a scholar-practitioner. We chose to structure the book this way with the hope of inspiring both our peers and our students to appreciate the many different international educator profiles and realize how urgent broad thinking and the liberal utilization of a wide skill set has become. An underlying message of this volume is to caution against international education graduate programs facilitating a linear approach to work in our field and profession. Rather than seeing students enter and leave a program with an unchallenged, single-minded focus, we hope the collective intellectual arguments and personal essays presented in this volume will inspire all of us to realize our full potential to work broadly in the field and to utilize our wide skill set to enhance current practices, question traditional beliefs, and dare us to be even more innovative.

This book addresses numerous questions, and undoubtedly raises new ones, as well it should. Some of the topics the chapters address include understanding who scholar-practitioners of international higher education are and how those with clearly defined roles in international education (e.g. SIOs, directors of education abroad or international scholar and student services offices, managers of large institutions or foundations, faculty, graduate students) view the role of the scholar-practitioner. Contributing authors question what role, if any, the scholar-practitioner should have among the faculty ranks, especially given that jobs once strictly defined as 'practitioner' now often require PhD-level credentials. Others discuss the role of the scholar-practitioner by institution type or discipline and what future scholar-practitioners need to know. To some extent, all chapters look to the future of international higher education and what will be required of scholar-practitioners.

This volume brings together the critical voices of many senior, mid-level and junior colleagues in our community who are reflecting deeply on the many and unique roles in this field and profession and how they intersect with the notion of the scholar-practitioner. In a conscious effort to represent these diverse perspectives, we have included chapters from both long-term and well-established voices in the field as well as those who are emerging scholar-practitioners. The contributors include education abroad professionals, international student and scholar professionals, senior international officers, key leaders from influential professional associations and private organizations, and seasoned observers of the field. These thought leaders have all shared their critical views and some of the paradigms of practice they have developed over time.

While our intention as editors was not to advocate for a particular position, role or set of activities the scholar-practitioner has or should have in any given context, we felt it important to note that as editors we also bring our own perspectives on the role of the scholar-practitioner in international higher education. Ogden is a self-identified scholar-practitioner who takes the perspective that his professional success is closely tied to his ability to effectively use research and scholarship to guide practice and similarly to leverage practice to inform the direction and scope of future research. Streitwieser began his career as an international education practitioner but felt frustrated with how little reflection and research was expected in his daily work. Today in his role as a faculty member he finds himself excited to help students appreciate how combining a research framework with the lessons from practice are essential skills to succeed in this age of accountability. Together, we hope this book will provide a platform for understanding these and other perspectives.

The volume is divided into four major sections. Following a foreword by Hans de Wit that lays out the broad mandate to engage in an exploration of the notion of the scholar-practitioner, the first section of the volume includes chapters that introduce the scholar-practitioner in international higher education in historical and present-day perspective. The section begins with an introductory discussion by the volume's editors of the defining features of the scholar-practitioner in international higher education. Chapter 2 then explores the dichotomy of the terms 'practitioner' and 'scholar' and presents a new action agenda based on the confluence of three critical and interrelated factors. Chapter 3 begins a historical overview by highlighting the most notable scholar-practitioners of international education, reaching back to the early trailblazers. Chapter 4 digs yet deeper into history by highlighting the earliest years of international education scholarship and the significant roles that scholar-practitioners have played in shaping the direction of the field and profession over time. This chapter identifies many of the early efforts where scholar-practitioners had a significant impact on the field and follows the growth and development of the scholar-practitioner over time.

The second section provides context-specific chapters related to the scholar-practitioner in the profession of international education. Chapter 5 provides the perspective of a senior international officer (SIO) on the place and potential of the scholar-practitioner in the academy in particular. Chapter 6 frames the education abroad professional as a transdisciplinary scholar-practitioner and explores a working definition of the term 'education abroad scholar-practitioner' as a way to conceptualize a transdisciplinary approach to the field and practice of education abroad. The chapter addresses a complex set of dilemmas through dialogue and synthesis between and among disciplines and administrative units. Chapter 7 focuses on international student and scholar services (ISSS) professionals and suggests that increasing pressures to ensure federal immigration regulatory compliance have forestalled them from more fully embracing the role of the scholar-practitioner in any effective way. Chapter 8 examines the role of international educators in small and one-person international education offices and the unique challenges they face balancing their dual roles as practitioners and scholars. Chapter 9 unpacks the voices of scholar-practitioners in the community college context and challenges the stereotype of community colleges as being only practitioner oriented. The final chapter in the section, chapter 10, provides an association's perspective on an emerging type of scholar-practitioner who is at the forefront of quality assurance in international education and engages in scholarly activity thorough researching and becoming grounded in industry standards, best practices and data related to student outcomes.

The third section consists of personal essays and narratives that are intimately related to the role of the scholar-practitioner in advancing international education scholarship and practice. In chapter 11, Bruce La Brack provides an overview of his pioneering role in advancing ongoing orientation programming. Elizabeth Brewer in chapter 12 reflects on her own path as a 'late-blooming' scholar-practitioner to craft advice for newcomers who are entering the profession and negotiating their place within institutions engaged in internationalization. In chapter 13, Richard Slimbach shares his insightful critique of how higher education more broadly has failed to escape the runaway costs, the marginal learning and the absence of an ultimate *why* that bedevils US higher education and internationalization activity. In chapter 14, Michael Woolf provides an insightful and critical perspective on role of the education abroad scholar-practitioner in navigating the intersections of curriculum integration, intercultural learning and benchmarking. In chapter 15, Gregory Light provides a critical reflection on the practice of international education from the perspective of a parallel academic practice focused on the promotion of innovative learning and teaching. In chapter 16, the final chapter in the section, Jane Edwards proposes a model for using research informed by a range of disciplines and applied to topics of significance to international educators to illustrate the essential and productive connections between scholarship and practice in international education.

The final section of the volume consists of instructional chapters that are related to the education and training of scholar-practitioners in relation to the future of international higher education. Chapter 17 positions intercultural competency as the foundation for scholar-practitioners of international education. Chapter 18 focuses on the range of graduate education programs in the United States that are utilizing different approaches to prepare scholar-practitioners as future international education leaders. Chapter 19 focuses on the research landscape of international higher education and proposes useful strategies for finding, organizing and evaluating research. Chapter 20 provides a perspective on the ways that the roles and experiences of scholar-practitioners may evolve in the future in light of current realities and in the face of ongoing challenges and opportunities to expand and strengthen this unique function in international higher education.

Following the twenty chapters, the book finishes with a collection of brief personal narratives that share the diverse pathways each contributor has taken to becoming a scholar-practitioner of international higher education today. Through these personal narratives, this final section exemplifies our core premise that scholar-practitioners are actively contributing to and leading the advancement of the field and profession of international higher education.

In inviting these thought pieces and essays, we have set out to create an academic, intellectual and broad analysis of the scholar-practitioner as he or she is seen in our field and profession. We hope that higher education administrators, researchers, faculty, teachers, policy makers, graduate students and observers of international higher education generally will find this book useful in furthering their exposure to pertinent topics and positions related to the internationalization of higher education and the advancement of both the field and the profession of international higher education.

CHAPTER 1

Heralding the Scholar-Practitioner in International Higher Education

BERNHARD STREITWIESER & ANTHONY C. OGDEN

SUMMARY US higher education institutions are generally staffed by two categories of professional employees: the *scholars*, or faculty, who analyze, write, and teach about a particular area of study and its implications, and the *administrators*, who manage the education enterprise and make scholarship and instruction possible. This has also been the pattern in the large and growing profession of international higher education, which includes education abroad, international student exchange, and institutional internationalization among other activities increasingly important in a context of domestic and global competition. In many cases, however, this perceived division is misleading. A hybrid group of *scholar-practitioners* now exists that works primarily in administrative capacities but also contributes important analysis and reflection on the nature and impact of their practice through disseminating scholarship in the field. This chapter reviews the development of the scholar-practitioner, situates this hybrid professional in today's higher education context, and proposes a model and definition for the scholar-practitioner's role in international higher education. The chapter concludes by suggesting that the academic and administrative structures governing higher education today should reimagine the unique potential of these hybrid professionals as international higher education develops as a profession and an important area of scholarship.

Introduction

This introductory chapter heralds the prominence and potential of the scholar-practitioner in the field and profession of international higher education. In doing so it seeks to launch a much-needed conversation about the perception and reality of this new kind of hybrid professional.

The changing structure of higher education institutions has led to new models and profiles of professionals today that go beyond the traditional labels of either *administrator* or *scholar*. In US higher education now, the numbers of core research faculty responsible for research and scholarship have been shrinking while a much broader classification of so-called *alternative-academics* or *third-space professionals* has been growing. While this development in itself is an area of concern for many in higher education, our primary focus in this chapter is to present a new way to think about a holistic integration of third-space professionals and research faculty within the context of a changing higher education environment.

Many of these new hybrid professionals possess high-level academic credentials, sophisticated research training, and aspirations to disseminate their work much like their faculty colleagues do, but they find themselves stationed in administrative positions. These professionals seek ways to bridge dedicated administrative work with scholarly engagement and inquiry in order to help shape their emerging field. Although we intentionally advocate for scholar-practitioners and the positive attributes we believe they bring to advancing the professional and scholarly profile of international higher education today, the model of scholar-practitioner synergy we propose will be useful to administrators and faculty alike in illustrating the benefits of greater synergy between practice and scholarship.

In this chapter we use the terms *field* and *profession* deliberately in discussing scholar-practitioners. We see our collective work in international higher education as further establishing the contours of what is becoming a recognizable area of scholarship. However, what makes the emerging role of the scholar-practitioner of international higher education perhaps a difficult one to grasp is that there is not yet a formally recognized international education profession or discipline. Although there are no formal criteria, an academic discipline is generally well defined and broadly recognized throughout higher education. While international education as a field of research is surely expanding, few would readily identify international education as a discipline. Many in this volume refer to a 'profession of international education' and the 'international education professional' and, although there are certainly positive trends toward the professionalization of international education, more needs to happen for this to meet generally accepted criteria for a profession. However, increasingly, those operating within international education have come to accept the idea of a field of international education research and scholarship and to embrace a burgeoning profession that has an established code of ethics and recognizable competencies.

Today, the very nature of the activity of international higher education produces a steady stream of rich quantitative and qualitative data. Analyzing these data requires skills in evaluation, assessment, and how to use a variety of theoretical lenses and methodologies. Thoughtful professionals who facilitate internationalization, education abroad, and international student exchange, among other activities, are well positioned to disseminate their reflections and analysis through an increasing number of established academic journals, publishers, and online platforms that now exist. Yet their administrative positions often do not give them opportunities or time to fully engage in their field in a scholarly way. We believe that this dynamic is changing, however, as international education becomes a recognized area of research informed and enriched by the many reflective practitioners who are working in the field today and who strive to disseminate their knowledge through the many public and peer-reviewed media now available.

This chapter discusses the context of US higher education which has led to the development and need for an engaged scholar-practitioner professional today; it then proposes a definition for the scholar-practitioner that is specific to the international higher education context and discusses its implications; and it concludes by advocating that the academic and administrative structures governing US higher education should reimagine, re-evaluate, and discover this unique group of hybrid scholar-practitioners and the potential they bring to further developing the international education enterprise writ large.

The Evolving Nature of Higher Education

Since the early 1990s, increasing numbers of observers of higher education have called for change in the bifurcated view of scholar/faculty and practitioner/administrator. The title of this volume endorses that idea through the metaphor of 'bridging'. Other contributors to this book have invoked similar language: finding 'crosswalks' between research and practice (see the chapter by Hudzik); rejecting the 'arrested development' that a bifurcation causes (Light); or melding insider-practitioner status with outsider-scholar objectivity (Hunter and Rumbley). All of these authors advocate for a new paradigm that values fluidity between scholars/faculty and practitioners/administrators, and that fits better in the modern university environment and the broader intellectual workplace.

Philip Altbach, who has written prolifically about comparative international higher education, contends that in the US higher education system, the academic administration – what he terms the 'administrative estate' – has grown faster than any other sector of the academy. Del Favero and Bray (2015) have argued that research on the faculty–administrator relationship and its role within higher education governance structures, however, 'is disjointed and haphazard and has yet to be taken up by scholars in a serious way. One gets a general sense from the higher education literature of a relationship that is at the very least challenging, and at the extreme is adversarial and conflict-laden' (2015, para. 2). For Altbach, the development of the administrative estate has been driven primarily by a demand for increased accountability in university governance from federal and state levels, accrediting agencies, and boards of trustees and university presidents (2007, p. 14). We would add to this, concerned parents and students as fee-paying constituents. However, while the academy has become larger and more complex, it has also been chronically slow to adapt to modern times (Kerr, 2001). As a result, traditional beliefs about status, hierarchy, and position are not always in step with this rapidly changing university environment. Traditional faculty is still seen primarily as the intellectual force of higher education, while administrators are still seen as the workforce, to put the differences most bluntly.

Recent growth in higher education enrollments has compelled universities to hire more administrators than ever before in crucial management roles at many different levels. The growth of international education activities – including student and staff mobility, international partnerships, dual degree programs, and branch campuses, among other factors – has contributed to this trend. With faculty primarily seen as serving the teaching and research functions of the institution, the expansion of the academy has also led to a greater managerial group of professionals who hold increasing power in the modern university system, where the traditional dynamic of faculty control over governance has gradually become diminished (Altbach, 2007).

In higher education broadly, there are now many new 'alternative academic career paths' (Altbach, 2007, p. 15) that go beyond the traditional role of the tenured professor, who in some institutions is becoming a minority. Other types of faculty now hold titles like clinical professor, research professor, or professor of practice, or have roles that combine academic and administrative obligations. Furthermore, the expanding group of part-time faculty and adjunct professors who are on contract appointments or paid on a course-by-course basis without benefits or other protections has also weakened the traditionally clear lines between which positions constitute the 'research cadre' on campus and which do not. Many of these faculty members are now hired for their applied knowledge and their ability to bridge scholarship and practice. The number of traditional core faculty today only comprises about one-fifth of the entire academic population (Altbach, 2007, p. 16; June, 2012).

There is no doubt that the so-called administrative estate has become increasingly crucial to the successful operation of higher education institutions. By now, given the demands of a changed academy, many mid- and higher-level administrators also possess higher-order credentials and terminal degrees. This has happened for numerous reasons. The movement toward higher education for the masses has introduced more administrative complexity and a need for more specialized offices with trained personnel. The needs and expectations of today's students and parents have also created a demand for higher-order skills in managers charged with caring for students' academic and psychosocial well-being, especially in institutions where high tuition rates come with accompanying high service expectations. As indicated above, cost-cutting measures and less public funding have also meant fewer openings for faculty-line positions. As a result, those coming out of graduate schools who traditionally would have pursued faculty posts have become 'blended professionals' (Whitechurch, 2009), 'third-space professionals' (Whitechurch, 2013) or 'alt-ac' (alternative-academic) professionals (Bickford & Whisnant, 2013; Kim, 2015). While some who find themselves in these positions characterize the situation as highly dissatisfying and out of sync with their credentials and aspirations, it has become a new reality (Bousquet, 2015).

Where international higher education as a growing activity is concerned, universities now must employ full-time professionals who are trained in a variety of areas, including legal and accounting issues, program management, health and safety compliance, international risk management, visa and immigration services, and other needs. Study Abroad Offices and International Student and Scholar Services Offices (among similar names) are primarily staffed by student advisors, program developers, and managers who are versed in logistical issues, health and safety procedures, orientation programming, and other roles that relate directly to educating students abroad and integrating visiting students into the home campus. Traditionally these offices have dealt less directly with faculty, who may interact with them primarily on curricular issues or on faculty-directed education abroad programs. According to Altbach, 'Administrators have little direct relationship to the professoriate and do not owe their jobs to the faculty. They have become a new "estate" of the university – a self-perpetuating group central to the operation of the institution' (2007, p. 14).

In most cases, these offices are increasingly strapped for personnel, and their workloads far exceed their capacity (see the chapters by Beaudin and Berends, by Austell, and by Reinig). With growing student interest in education abroad and rapidly rising enrollments of international students in the USA, these offices have needed to hire or work closely with experts who have higher-level training in legal affairs, health services, communication, student learning and development, enrollment management, and other critical administrative competencies. This change has meant that the 'pendulum of authority in higher education has swung from the academics to managers and bureaucrats' (Altbach et al, 2010, p. 89). The impact of this on the academy has been significant.

In her research on the evolving identities of higher education professional staff, Whitechurch describes blended professionals as those who are 'increasingly being recruited to dedicated appointments that spanned both professional and academic domains' (2009, p. 3). With the expansion of higher education over time, this class has not only grown, but their status has evolved and their roles have become more complex and critically important. The 'third space' – what Whitechurch terms 'the space between professional and academic spheres of activity' (2013, p. xii) – has led to a context in which 'the boundaries between professional and academic spheres of activity are becoming blurred' (Whitechurch & Law, para. 1). In this scenario, the concept of service has become 're-oriented towards one of partnership with academic colleagues, students and external agencies' (Whitechurch, 2013, p. xii). In the evolving higher education context, these developments appear to be occurring without being explicitly articulated or acknowledged. This book is a response to that development as manifested in the field and profession of international higher education.

Career Pathways of International Education Scholar-Practitioners

The essays collected for this volume come from senior international officers, education abroad and international student and scholar professionals, key leaders from influential professional associations and private organizations, and seasoned scholars from around the world to profile and share the reflections of the wide breadth of scholar-practitioners working in the field today. Many of the contributors have entered international education positions either vertically through education, training and career advancement or laterally from faculty positions, related professions, and administrative appointments. These profiles illustrate the scholar-practitioners in the current context of international education work and help explain the need to rethink the organizational structure and culture of international education within higher education more broadly.

While international experiences and proficiency in other languages may have once been adequate credentials to launch a career in international education, an increasing number of career-bound international educators are coming up through the ranks (see the chapter by Brewer). These prospective international educators are now arriving with appropriate graduate education and training, made possible in part by the growing number of sophisticated graduate programs in international higher education (Urias et al, 2007). In their chapter in this volume, Woodman and Punteney explain that many of these programs have been established to meet the growing demand for leaders in international higher education. Program curricula have been shaped by emerging trends in international higher education, and many clearly articulate goals to prepare graduate students for careers that engage both scholarship and practice.

To be sure, prospective employers are increasingly seeking candidates with specialized graduate education and preparation (Dessoff, 2006; Urias et al, 2007; Mueller & Overmann, 2014). For example, the Forum on Education Abroad has conducted a number of membership surveys to better understand the various pathways for careers in international education. In a 2013 survey, the Forum on Education Abroad found that more than half of the respondents had a master's degree and another 27% had a doctorate (PhD or EdD). Professional degrees, such as the MBA or JD, were held by 6% of the respondents. Fewer than 70% reported having some proficiency in a second language, and only about half had lived abroad (Forum on Education Abroad, 2013). In a similar study, the Association of International Education Administrators (AIEA) conducted a membership survey of Senior International Officers (SIOs) and found that 81% held a doctoral or professional degree (AIEA, 2014).

In 2015, NAFSA: Association of International Educators released its list of the necessary competencies for success in the field of international education (NAFSA, 2015). Presented as the basic building blocks of the international education profession, the list is intended to define the professional knowledge, skills, and abilities expected of international education professionals, regardless of their area of specialization or role. The tool is organized into four key professional practice areas – comprehensive internationalization, education abroad, international education enrollment, and international student and scholar services – as well as cross-cutting competencies, which describe the shared skills and knowledge needed across all international education domains. There are a number of major competencies within each professional practice area, and each is organized to reflect three main functions: direct service, management, and strategy and policy. Although research and scholarship do not emerge as distinct competencies, the document repeatedly mentions that to fulfill each competency, one must identify, access, utilize, and contribute relevant research and scholarship. In almost areas, one must at least be familiar with relevant research, theory, and scholarship.

While many come to international education positions with specialized education and professional training in international education and seek advancement through promotion and reassignment, often from one institution to the next, others are strategically recruited from related professions or the faculty ranks. Tenured faculty members and others who come into international education laterally more often than not are recruited for international education leadership positions. In the aforementioned 2014 Association of International Education Administrators survey of Senior International Officers, three-quarters of respondents held faculty positions. The majority of SIOs (61%) have been in their positions for five years or less, and nearly all (91%) reported that knowledge of international issues in higher education is by far the most valued characteristic. Although the majority of SIOs have been engaged in international education for less than five years, their chief responsibilities are partnerships and linkages, representing the institution in institutional dealings, and strategic planning for internationalization. Herein lies a major challenge for career international educators.

Many career international educators work in administrative positions but have qualifications on par with their more secure tenured faculty or senior colleagues who came from the faculty to assume the most senior leadership posts. Though this cadre of scholar-practitioners may work in predominantly administrative capacities, they rely on advanced academic training and are often working alongside tenured faculty members on all facets of educational delivery, including program design, evaluation and assessment. They are hired for their scholarly credentials, called upon for their knowledge and expertise, and generally engaged in various forms of teaching, research and service.

Some of these professionals are in their posts by choice because they prefer managerial and administrative work, while others who once aspired to faculty positions have been channeled into more tenuous part-time or short-term employment because of institutional cost-saving and restructuring measures. Some of these professionals may have hit a glass ceiling: despite having academic qualifications and scholarly abilities similar to their faculty colleagues, they are stuck in administrative roles and regarded as mere administrators (a point reinforced in some of the chapters in this volume). In these positions it remains difficult to advance or switch tracks upward into an academic career, particularly if the environment does not regard them as scholarly contributors. These professionals may be permanently stationed in administrative positions that offer less intellectual flexibility and protection than that enjoyed by their faculty counterparts. Despite these constraints, we see more and more of them thinking reflectively about their work and projecting their intellectual voices through actively publishing, commenting on key issues in public forums, presenting at conferences, and being leading lights for the development of the profession and field of international education.

Introducing the Scholar-Practitioner

Since the early 1980s, public discourse has increasingly recognized and welcomed the scholar-practitioner as a new kind of scholarly professional in higher education. A sizeable and growing body of literature now explores various forms of scholarly practice from multiple disciplinary perspectives. There is a journal dedicated exclusively to studying scholar-practitioners, the *Scholar Practitioner Quarterly,* and the concept has been extensively discussed in professional publications, including the *Chronicle of Higher Education* and *Inside Higher Ed.* Research on this topic initially emerged from the management and human resource development literature, and from medicine, clinical psychology, law, and the STEM (science, technology, engineering, and mathematics) fields (McClintock, 2004; Schwandt & Shashkin, 2014). Discussions of the notion are ongoing in many fields, from psychology and nursing to business and education (Banks et al, 2007; Scully-Russ et al, 2013). Yet a simple and widely accepted definition has not emerged in any of these disciplines. Instead, articulation of the concept depends more on the particular area of study in which it resides. The place and role of these professionals within the academy is also a point of contention. Wasserman and Kram (2009), in a study of 25 self-identified scholars and practitioners, asked, 'What can practitioners offer scholars and scholars offer practitioners in order to foster collaborations that elevate and articulate what we are learning as we do this work in the world? These are critical questions that we have not yet answered' (p. 33). In the emerging field and profession of international education, the idea of the scholar-practitioner has intellectual and practical resonance but has not yet been broadly defined or widely discussed.

Three influential texts emerged between the 1980s and early 2000s that reimagined how practice could be thought about, how scholarship could be reconsidered, and how scholarship and practice could function in greater harmony. Some of the authors of these texts commented on each other's work in their own writings and discussed its implications for their own developing ideas around scholarship and practice (Boyer, 1990; Schön, 1995; McClintock, 2001). Together these three important intellectual arguments articulate some of the critical elements that are relevant for understanding a scholar-practitioner profile today.

In his 1983 book, *The Reflective Practitioner: how professionals think in action,* Donald Schön cautioned against what he saw as a general 'widening rift between the universities and the professions, research and practice, thought and action' (p. viii). Within universities he saw an even stiffer dichotomy separating science and scholarship from practitioners 'who wish to gain a better understanding of the practical uses and limits of research-based knowledge, or to help scholars who wish to take a new view of professional action' (p. viii). Schön therefore advocated for research into the kind of thinking that underlies and helps explain the way professionals carry out their work, and asked questions like, 'What is the kind of knowing in which competent practitioners engage? How is professional knowing like and unlike the kinds of knowledge presented in academic textbooks, scientific papers, and learned journals? In what sense, if any, is there intellectual rigor in professional practice?' (p. viii). Schön urged inquiry and action to be seen as combined activities and gave concrete wording to the essentially simple idea that one's work does not merely happen out of habit or mechanical routine. Rather, successful and meaningful practice, he felt, depends on personal deliberation and careful reflection, or as Osterman (1990) put it, 'a challenging, focused and critical assessment of one's own behavior as a means towards developing one's own craftsmanship' (p. 134).

While Schön's work focused on how practice needs to become more reflective, Ernest Boyer's ground-breaking 1990 book, *Scholarship Reconsidered: priorities of the professoriate,* emphasized how scholarship must better align with practice. Boyer argued that scholarship needed to be seen in broader terms, which he outlined in four distinct but interrelated activities: the scholarship of *discovery*, of *integration*, of *application*, and of *teaching*. Although Boyer's study addressed faculty and not administrators per se, he stressed that faculty needed to rethink their 'service' work in order to better bridge theory and practice (Glassick, 2000), so that research could become more effective in addressing societal problems and benefit a wider public (Beattie, 2000; Glass et al, 2011). As Boyer observed, 'When you get tenure in the school of education, it is not to go out and work with children in the schools, but to do another research project' (Boyer, 1996, p. 132). Boyer cautioned that the distinctions between scholarship and practice should not constrict the application of research to addressing practical needs.

The third contribution that has advanced our understanding of the scholar-practitioner is Charles McClintock's 2004 introduction of the Scholar-Practitioner Model. This model brought together elements of Schön's notion of reflective practice with Boyer's notion of the scholarship of practice. McClintock urged scholar-practitioners to employ research and practice in complementary ways that could bridge a deep understanding of theory and methods and complementary skills in evaluation and measurement. To document the effectiveness of their work, McClintock argued, scholar-practitioners needed the skills to 'draw upon knowledge from multiple sources', including theory, case studies of best practices, and a clear understanding of 'values-based maxims and morals' (p. 396). He felt that the ideal or 'wise' scholar-practitioner should be able to 'abstractly, efficiently, and creatively interpret information from their everyday work' (p. 396) and frame situations from multiple perspectives, propose competing hypotheses, and identify evidence that could test alternative explanations (McClintock, 2001).

McClintock's model is particularly relevant to international education and the work of serving students in that he emphasized the importance of practitioners having the most reliable knowledge informed by study and research in order to accurately understand and serve their clients' needs. McClintock pointed out that practitioners are often at the forefront of interpreting immediate changes and developments in a particular context and are therefore better positioned to respond quickly than researchers, who need more time for analysis. 'Practitioner work occurs within institutional settings that provide continual economic, societal, and ethical challenges that research knowledge can guide only at a very general level', he wrote (2004, p. 395). This part of McClintock's model is particularly important, in that scholar-practitioners require a deep understanding of theory and methods – not the surface-level mechanistic or routine functions sometimes attributed to them – in order to engage in evaluation and measurement that allows them to document the true effectiveness of their work.

The idea common to Schön, Boyer and McClintock is that practice, if it is reflective, and scholarship, if it is applicable, can and must become conjoined activities rather than remaining separate domains. Schön validated the work of practitioners by embedding the idea – indeed the requirement – that constant and critical self-reflection is a prerequisite for improving practice. Boyer encouraged faculty to think about how theoretical work, intended to advance knowledge, must also help address pressing societal needs for the mutual enrichment of the academy and those outside of it. Finally, McClintock insisted that if practice is to be ethical, purposeful, and valuable to its beneficiaries, it must also be based on an intimate understanding of context and buttressed by the most reliable knowledge that comes from research, reflection, data, and study. It is important for international educators to question if their work in facilitating and advancing their field and profession is indeed grounded in these rigorous conditions articulated by Schön, Boyer, and McClintock.

In related work we see as relevant to international higher education that has continued to consider and refine the notion of the scholar-practitioner, Ruona and Gilley (2009) provide a useful typology that groups scholar-practitioners into four distinct categories. *Atheoretical practitioners* lack the educational qualifications, professional affiliations, and theoretical grounding relevant to their workplace. *Practitioners* have basic mastery of knowledge common in their field, engage with colleagues and scholarly resources to learn more, and use their field's terminology to appropriately converse with key stakeholders. *Reflective practitioners* understand their field, use its terminology authoritatively, and leverage that understanding to reflect critically on their practice and seek out scholarly resources to further improve their work. Finally, *scholarly practitioners* not only understand their field, converse with authority, and use scholarly sources to improve their daily practice, but also actively conduct research, publish in refereed journals, attend conferences, and disseminate their thinking in order to actively advance their profession (Ruona and Gilley, 2009, p. 441). Given all of the players involved in international education, there is undoubtedly room for many levels and types of professionals. Those who begin as atheoretical practitioners, perhaps as student interns or first-time advisors fresh from their own education abroad experiences, will ideally mature into reflective practitioners and eventually become fully fledged scholar practitioners.

In light of the increasing activity in international higher education, the demand has intensified for universities to have competently trained professionals who constantly develop, innovate, and improve their work. There is little time for practitioners, per Ruona and Gilley's definition, to stagnate at an entry level. An important implication of McClintock's model is that the skills of the practitioner/administrator are not by default less rigorous or more superficial and/or mechanistic than the attributes of the scholar/faculty; the skill sets are different but not necessarily at odds with one another. Rather, practitioners can contribute importantly to the intellectual development of their fields and professions, and scholar-practitioners bring the potential to build bridges of collaboration with their academic colleagues. Indeed, in today's academy, where new hybrids of faculty and administrators contribute to the intellectual and administrative life of the institution, the fluidity of these roles reinforces Boyer's notion of the scholarship of practice as being especially relevant (Fear & Sandmann, 2001).

In this regard, the definition of scholar-practitioners provided by Short (2006) is instructive: they are professionals who 'ground their practice in research and theory, they are champions of research and theory in the workplace and in professional associations, they conduct research, and they disseminate findings from their own research and practice. They are partners with academics and with other practitioners' (p. 261). A similar definition also comes from an influential commentator on the international higher education landscape, Michael Smithee. In his commentary, Smithee calls for scholar-practitioners to have a wide range of skills that are not so far off from those customarily expected of faculty and academic researchers. Smithee describes the international educator as one who 'conducts research, teaches, trains, counsels, investigates, utilizes, and disseminates knowledge and information in the form of concepts, procedures, processes, and skills' (Smithee, 2015a). He argues that international educators need to adopt a 'mindset which incorporates the ideal, to practice in a way that garners the respect of those in academia, not just those in the field of international education' (Smithee, 2015b). The critical part of Smithee's definition is that international educators must see themselves as researchers who disseminate knowledge, not merely as practitioners who facilitate mobility and exchange.

We realize that Short's characterization of a 'partnership' with academics may trouble some faculty if it suggests that they relinquish control over the intellectual development of their disciplines and now work shoulder to shoulder with non-tenured administrators. That is not our suggestion. Rather, we argue that those who work with a reflective mindset in administrative positions bring a specialized knowledge and skilled expertise to improving work that will strengthen the purpose, functions, and outcomes of activity in their field. The added value that scholar-practitioners can bring – the very idea of a productive 'partnership' instead of a rivalry or intractable hierarchical relationship between administrators and academics – should be seen as a positive development, rather than one that threatens to rob faculty of their traditional right to steer the intellectual creativity of the academy.

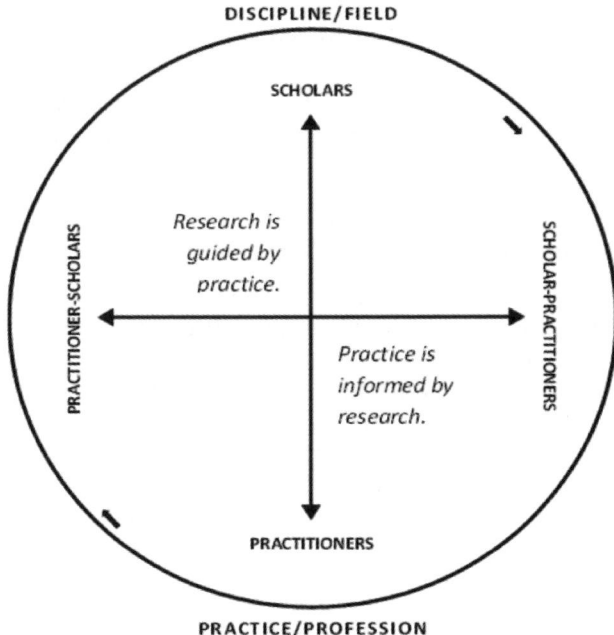

Figure 1. The scholar-practitioner.
Source: Derived in part from the work of Boyer (1990), Schön (1995), and McClintock (2001).

In today's higher education institutions many are needed to make the enterprise successful. Scholars and practitioners may no longer be as far apart as the traditional faculty–administrator dichotomy has dictated. The standards set by the commentators cited above that espouse various ideals of a scholar-practitioner profile all assume sophisticated intellectual skills that demonstrate various forms of intelligence; an understanding of theory; the ability to engage in research, measurement, and analysis; and a passion for sharing their knowledge through scholarly dissemination. These are similar skills to those we readily expect of faculty but so far have less often demanded of administrators.

Derived in part from the work of Boyer (1990), Schön (1995), and McClintock (2001), Figure 1 illustrates the interconnectedness we see in how scholars and practitioners in higher education can work in tandem. At the top of the circle, scholars are invested in advancing their academic disciplines and scholarly fields of research. At the bottom, practitioners are similarly invested in advancing their professions. Along the sides, the scholar-practitioners or practitioner-scholars depict the relationship between the faculty/scholars and administrator/ practitioners. Here, the work of practitioners is informed by research and in turn the scholarship or the direction of the research is guided by the needs or questions coming from practice. The two sets of intellectual activities work in harmony, with each benefiting and influencing the direction of the other.

An adaptation of this model appears in the following section to illustrate the scholar-practitioner in international higher education activity specifically (see Figure 2).

The Scholar-Practitioner in International Higher Education

In this chapter, and in the sum of the articles we have collected for the volume, we strive to herald the scholar-practitioner within international higher education and shed light on the role that these individuals bring to advancing the scholarship and practice of our field and profession. While practitioners make international education possible and scholars have taken up the study of international education as a line of scholarly inquiry, the scholar-practitioners of international higher education by the very nature of their work bridge both areas. They leverage existing research and scholarship to inform practice and share the collective aim of scholars to advance the theoretical and empirical foundations of the field.

To advance this understanding, we propose the following definition of the scholar-practitioner in international higher education.

The scholar-practitioners of international higher education are collaborative educators who engage in the research process and use and disseminate their knowledge and information in the form of concepts, procedures, processes, and skills for the benefit of those who are engaged in international education. While they do not necessarily need to maintain an active research agenda, it is important that they understand, utilize, and facilitate research directions.

Scholar-practitioners of international education do not view research and scholarship as a burden or an addition to an already demanding workload. Rather, they take the perspective that professional success is closely tied to the ability to effectively identify, access, and utilize research and scholarship to inform practice. It is important to scholar-practitioners of international higher education to challenge untested claims and avoid casual assumptions, especially in light of the absence or inclusive nature of the existing research (Ogden et al, 2014). It is important that research supports and provides a foundation for making decisions. Although scholar-practitioners of international education may not necessarily engage in research or maintain active research agendas, they sponsor and support research by providing time, personnel, and/or other resources to advance these efforts. They recognize the potential gap between scholarship and practice and seize opportunities to leverage the practice to inform the direction and scope of future research.

Figure 2 illustrates the interaction between the field of international education and the international education profession.

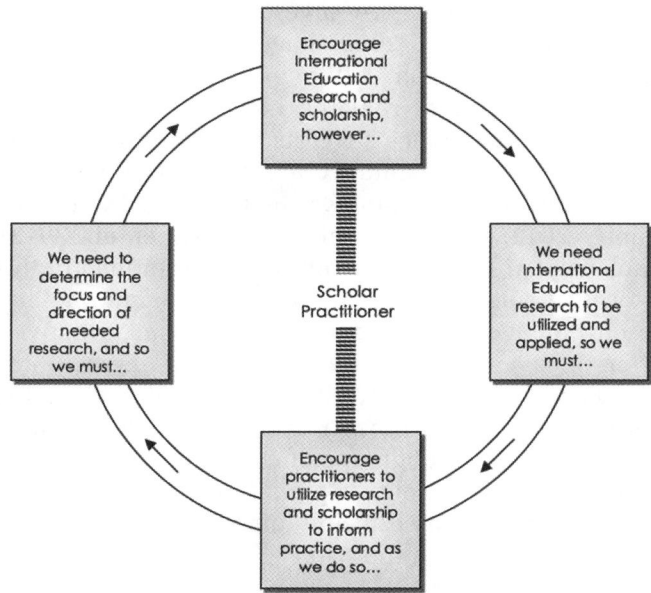

Figure 2. The International Education scholar-practitioner.
Source: The style and flow of this illustration were inspired by Trompenaars and Hampden Turner (1998).

From the top, researchers are encouraged to pursue research on international education; however, that research should have direct application to practice, as Boyer advocated. International education practitioners should be familiar with existing literature and utilize findings to inform and enhance practice, as McClintock advised in his model. In turn, practitioners should engage scholars in pursuing areas of needed research, reflecting on their understanding of problems in practice to help inform inquiry, operationalizing McClintock's ideal. The scholar-practitioner of international education can bridge these areas through this iterative process of practice and research informing one another. Important to this model is to understand the context in which today's scholar-practitioners work in US higher education institutions, as that context determines both the limitations and opportunities they will have. As scholars of international education are increasingly expected to pursue lines of inquiry with direct professional application, so too are international education professionals increasingly seen as knowledge area experts who are familiar with the existing research and can be called upon to engage competently in scholarly practice.

For example, among many more we could cite, as US institutions direct more attention to documenting practices that maximize student success, higher education researchers are investigating the extent to which high-impact experiences (Kuh, 2008) have a causal impact on retention and persistence to graduation. Although the research on the impact of education abroad programs remains inconclusive (Ogden & Streitwieser, 2016), preliminary evidence suggests that education abroad participants do have higher four- five- and six-year graduation rates and that minority students may have even higher graduation rates (Malmgren & Galvin, 2008; Hamir, 2011; O'Rear et al, 2012; Xu et al, 2013). Education abroad scholar-practitioners will want to stay informed of this ongoing research in order to use preliminary findings to inform their promotion and outreach practices and program development initiatives. Aware of self-selection bias and the many factors that increase the likelihood of a student participating in education abroad, the education abroad scholar-practitioner can help inform researchers in determining effective methodologies and how to align specific program components with desired outcomes. All in all, the scholar-practitioner is engaged in a complex process that bridges scholarship and practice and ensures a healthy symbiotic relationship between the two.

Conclusion

Within the academic establishment, the number of those who are classified exclusively as core research faculty is arguably shrinking while the number of scholar-practitioners, whose positions and work bridge scholarship and practice, is growing. The lines between scholar and practitioner are continuing to blur, as the recognition of scholar-practitioners is growing ever more vibrant.

The challenge for higher education will be to re-evaluate and reimagine systems and structures that welcome and embrace the potential of these non-faculty employees who have faculty-level competencies and potential. The existing paradigm, which has often marginalized this 'administrative estate' as somehow less capable, must be upended. Much is lost when personnel in this estate are less valued or less empowered to use their intellectual training and skills to engage in research, evaluation, writing, publishing, teaching, and other rigorous work that is traditionally expected only of faculty. Scholar-practitioners are eager to share and make evident their knowledge and expertise and to contribute intellectually to their fields by presenting, engaging within academia, and publishing in their field and beyond. Allowing, and indeed encouraging them, to do this will require important changes in the current reward structures, hiring practices, and budgeting priorities that exist (Choudaha & Streitwieser, 2014).

The momentum in recent decades toward the internationalization of higher education has begun to reveal new opportunities for scholar-practitioners of international higher education. As these hybrid professionals are increasingly required to have scholarly credentials, pursue active research agendas, and engage in various forms of teaching, research, and service, the existing paradigm within contemporary higher education will need to expand in ways that more systematically recognize, value, and incentivize their presence and contributions. As the authors in this book emphasize, these scholar-practitioners play a significant role in aligning the scholarship and profession of international education, which in turn advances comprehensive internationalization of our very institutions.

Acknowledgements

The authors would like to thank Julia Storberg-Walker and Nancy Kober for their helpful comments on earlier drafts.

References

Altbach, P.G. (2007) *Tradition and Transition: the international imperative in higher education*. Rotterdam: Sense.

Altbach, P.G., Reisberg, L. & Rumbley, L.E. (2010) *Trends in Global Higher Education: tracking an academic revolution*. Rotterdam: Sense.

Association of International Education Administrators (AIEA) (2014) *A Survey on Senior International Officers: individual and institutional profiles*. Durham, NC: AIEA.

Banks, C.H., Wang, J., Zhang, W. & McLean, L. (2007) Human Resource Development Scholar-Practitioners: connecting the broken divide of research and practice. http://files.eric.ed.gov/fulltext/ED504766.pdf

Beattie, D.S. (2000) Expanding the View of Scholarship: Introduction, *Academic Medicine*, 75(9), 871-875. http://dx.doi.org/10.1097/00001888-200009000-00006

Bickford, D.M. & Whisnant, M. (2013) A Move to Bring Staff Scholars out of the Shadows, *Chronicle of Higher Education*, November 25.

Bousquet, M. (2015) A PhD Should Result in a Tenure Track Job, Not an Al-Ac One (essay), *Inside Higher Ed*, October 20.

Boyer, E.L. (1990) *Scholarship Reconsidered: priorities of the professoriate.* Princeton, NJ: Carnegie Foundation for the Advancement of Teaching.

Boyer, E.L. (1996) From Scholarship Reconsidered to Scholarship Assessed, *Quest 48*, 129-139. http://dx.doi.org/10.1080/00336297.1996.10484184

Choudaha, R. & Streitwieser, B. (2014) How Do We Assess the Impact of Internationalization? *University World News*, October 3. http://www.universityworldnews.com

Del Favero, M. & Bray, N. (2015) The Faculty–Administrator Relationship: partners in prospective governance?, *Scholar-Practitioner Quarterly*, Fall. https://www.questia.com/read/1G1-146073793/the-faculty-administrator-relationship-partners-in

Dessoff, A. (2006) Master's Degrees: a key to your career?, *International Educator*, Jan./Feb., 36-43.

Fear, F.A. & Sandmann, L.R. (2001) The 'New' Scholarship: implications for engagement and extension, *Journal of Higher Education Outreach and Engagement,* 7(1 & 2), 29-39.

Forum on Education Abroad (2013) *Preliminary Report: 2013 Institutional and Program Resources Survey: individual member response data.* Carlisle, PA: Forum on Education Abroad.

Glass, C.R., Doberneck, D.M. & Schweitzer (2011) Unpacking Faculty Engagement: the types of activities faculty members report as publicly engaged scholarship during promotion and tenure, *Journal of Higher Education Outreach and Engagement*, 15(1), 7-29.

Glassick, C.E. (2000) Boyer's Expanded Definition of Scholarship, the Standard for Assessing Scholarship, and the Elusiveness of the Scholarship of Teaching, *Academic Medicine*, 75(9), 872-880. http://dx.doi.org/10.1097/00001888-200009000-00007

Hamir, H.B. (2011) Go Abroad and Graduate On-time: study abroad participation, degree completion, and time-to-degree. PhD dissertation, University of Nebraska–Lincoln. http://world.utexas.edu/forms/abroad/barclay-dissertation.pdf

June, A.W. (2012) Adjuncts Build Strength in Numbers: the new majority generates a shift in academic culture, *Chronicle of Higher Education*, November 5.

Kerr, C. (2001) *The Uses of the University.* Cambridge, MA: Harvard University Press.

Kim, J. (2015) 5 Misunderstandings about Alt-Ac Salaries, *Inside Higher Ed*, May 3.

Kuh, G.D. (2008) High-impact Educational Practices: what they are, who has access to them, and why they matter. American Association for Colleges & Universities. http://www.aacu.org/leap/hips

Malmgren, J. & Galvin, J. (2008) Effects of Study Abroad Participation on Student Graduation Rates: a study of three incoming freshman cohorts at the University of Minnesota, Twin Cities, *NACADA Journal*, 28(1), 29-42. http://dx.doi.org/10.12930/0271-9517-28.1.29

McClintock, C. (2001) Spanning Boundaries of Knowledge and Organization: collaborations for mind and management in higher education, *Organization*, 8(2), 351-359. http://dx.doi.org/10.1177/1350508401082018

McClintock, C. (2004) Scholar Practitioner Model, in A. Distefano, K. Rudestam & R. Silverman (Eds) *Encyclopedia of Distributed Learning*, pp. 393-397. Thousand Oaks, CA: SAGE.

Mueller, S.L. & Overmann, M. (2014) *Working World: careers in international education, exchange, and development.* Washington, DC: Georgetown University Press.

NAFSA: Association of International Educators (2015) *NAFSA International Education Professional Competencies.* Washington, DC: NAFSA.

Ogden, A. & Streitwieser, B. (2016) A Concise Overview of Research on US Education Abroad, in D. Velliaris & D. Coleman-George (Eds) *Handbook of Research on Study Abroad Programs and Outbound Mobility.* Adelaide: IGI Global Press.

Ogden, A., Streitwieser, B. & Crawford, E. (2014) Empty Meeting Grounds: situating intercultural learning in US education abroad, in B. Streitwieser (Ed.) *Internationalization of Higher Education and Global Mobility.* Oxford: Symposium Books.

O'Rear, I., Sutton, R.L. & Rubin, D.L. (2012) The Effect of Study Abroad on College Completion in a State University System. http://glossari.uga.edu/wpcontent/uploads/downloads/2012/01/Glossari-Grad-Rate-Logistic-Regressions-040111.pdf

Osterman, K.F. (1990) Reflective Practice: a new agenda for education, *Education and Urban Society*, 22, 133-152. http://dx.doi.org/10.1177/0013124590022002002

Ruona W.E.A. & Gilley, J.W. (2009) Practitioners in Applied Professions: a model applied to human resource development, *Advances in Human Resource Development*, 11(4), 438-453.

Schön, D.A. (1983) *The Reflective Practitioner: how professionals think in action.* New York: Basic Books.

Schön, D.A. (1995) Knowing-in-Action: the new scholarship requires a new epistemology, *Change*, Nov.–Dec., 27-34.

Schwandt, D. & Shashkin, M. (2014) The Co-evolving Nature of Human and Organizational Sciences: a theory–practice imperative, in David Schwandt, Ellen Scully-Russ & Kathleen Crowley (Eds) *Human Interactions, Processes, and Contexts: reflections on the past and envisioning the future.* Bloomington, IN: Author House.

Scully-Russ, E., Lehner, R. & Shuck, B. (2013) A Scholar-Practitioner Case Approach: implications for advancing theory and research through informed practice, *Advances in Developing Human Resources*, 15(3), 243-251.

Short, D.C. (2006) HRD Scholar-Practitioners: a definition and description of core activities, in F.M. Nafukho & H.C. Chin (Eds) *AHRD Conference Proceedings*, pp. 258-264. Bowling Green, OH: AHRD.

Smithee, M. (2015a) 7/8 – What is an International Educator? And This Brings Us To? Blog series, July 26. https://www.linkedin.com/pulse/Part-78-What-International-Educator-Brings-Us-Michael-Smithee-edd?articleId=6031111917831991296

Smithee, M. (2015b) 8/8 – What is an International Educator? A Mindset: looking forward. Blog series, Aug. 8. https://www.linkedin.com/pulse/88-What-International-Educator-Mindset-Looking-Michael-Smithee-edd

Trompenaars, F. & Hampden-Turner, C. (1998) *Riding the Waves of Culture: understanding diversity in global business*, 2nd edn. New York: McGraw-Hill.

Urias, D., Deardorff, D. & Heyl, J.D. (2007) Standards of Quality for Master's Degree Level Programs in International Education: ensuring quality and effectiveness, in *Atlas of International Student Mobility*. Washington, DC: Institute of International Education.

Wasserman, I.C. & Kram, K.E. (2009) Enacting the Scholar-Practitioner Role: an exploration of narratives, *Journal of Applied Behavioral Science*, 45(1), 12-38.

Whitechurch, C. (2009) The Rise of the Blended Professional in Higher Education: a comparison between the UK, Australia and the United States, *Higher Education*, 58(3), 407-418.

Whitechurch, C. (2013) *Reconstructing Identities in Higher Education: the rise of third space professionals.* London: Routledge.

Xu, M., de Silva, C.R., Neufeldt, E. & Dane, J. (2013) The Impact of Study Abroad on Academic Success: an analysis of first-time students entering Old Dominion University, Virginia, 2000-2004, *Frontiers: The Interdisciplinary Journal of Study Abroad*, 23, 90-103.

CHAPTER 2

Internationalization Practitioners and Scholarship: dichotomies and crosswalks

JOHN K. HUDZIK

SUMMARY The scholar-practitioner discussion in internationalization is shaped considerably by three overarching factors: the historical but evolving notion of what counts for scholarly stature and utility within the higher education enterprise; the diversifying state of scholarship and practice in higher education internationalization; and considerations of who can conduct legitimate internationally oriented research and scholarship. These three factors interact. The chapter grounds discussion in the literature and experience of engaged scholarship and the scientist-practitioner model used in clinical and applied psychology for over seventy years, and in other professions. Ernest Boyer's typology of scholarship provides a way to think about the widening diversity of internationalization scholarship and roles for both practitioners and scholars. The terms 'practitioner' and 'scholar' are often used in a way that creates a false dichotomy. There are both intellectual and practical reasons for breaking down the artificial dichotomy when applied to internationalization scholarship. Following discussion of the meaning of 'practitioner' in internationalization, attention shifts to developing job expectations and skill sets of so-called practitioners in order to conduct research and scholarship under the models of engaged scholarship and Boyer's typology. An action agenda to start the process is outlined.

The scholar-practitioner discussion in internationalization is shaped considerably by three overarching factors. First is the historical but evolving notion of what counts for scholarly stature and utility within the higher education enterprise. Second is the diversifying state of scholarship and practice in higher education internationalization under its more comprehensive and strategic forms. The third concerns who conducts legitimate research and scholarship; particularly, the roles of practitioners in internationalization scholarship. These three factors interact to provide opportunity for thinking more widely about scholarship: what should count as legitimate subject matter of research and scholarship in internationalization, who can contribute to it and what 'rules for scholarship' apply.

Within the broader context of these three issues, this chapter's aim is toward re-imagining the scholarship and research roles of practitioners of internationalization (e.g. program directors, coordinators, advisors, administrators and other staff within the international office and its program units, and some internationally oriented support staff in departments and schools who are typically not seen as qualified, nor hired to engage in scholarship and research).

Evolving Landscapes of Scholarship in Academe

Intellectually and conceptually there are evolving views in higher education which challenge dichotomous thinking of pure vs. applied research and scholarship; discovery for the sake of knowledge vs. application; academic disciplines vs. professional programs; training vs. education; and disciplinary vs. trans-disciplinary modes of inquiry and research. Most, if not all, of these are false dichotomies if the term 'versus' is taken literally. A more updated view of valued research and scholarship is moving to a bigger tent to make room for a blending of all these dimensions, as well as incorporating legitimately varied expectations for outcomes from research and scholarship. This produces a more flexible environment for defining the roles of practitioners and scholars for research and practice in internationalization.

It is fair to say that the engagement paradigm helps to lead this widening view in research – variously labelled as, for example, 'publicly engaged scholarship' (Glass et al, 2011), 'engagement scholarship' (Fitzgerald & Simon, 2012), 'systemic engagement' (McNall et al, 2015), 'mode 2' scholarship (Gibbons et al, 1994) and 'knowledge co-production' (Hudzik & Simon, 2012). All of these models or approaches seek to blend knowledge discovery with application; all are implicit or explicit about the world of academe and the world of the practitioner being co-contributors to legitimate scholarship. A so-called triple helix model (Etzkowitz, 2008) blends traditional university-based autonomous search for knowledge (mode 1) with knowledge production that is context and inter-disciplinary problem-solving driven (mode 2), and with industry and government partners in setting research priorities and expectations for outcomes.

There are aspects of the 'triple helix strands' in the contemporary drivers of scholarship for higher education internationalization:

(1) traditional faculty and departmental scholarship in, for example, comparative politics, international relations, cultural anthropology, international economics; (2) emergent and expanding applications relating to active learning and problem-solving work in, for example, mobility, international development and problem solving, cross-cultural learning, and internationalizing curricula; and (3) policy goals and financial support of governments and interests of the private sector in internationalizing workforce development, gaining access to global cutting-edge knowledge, and building position in global markets. It is the building of crosswalks for these three strands that is part of the scholar-practitioner discussion for internationalization and that also is part of many contemporary critiques of higher education.

The idea of reciprocal collaboration in knowledge creation between 'scientist-practitioner' was adopted by the American Association of Applied Psychology in the mid-1940s based in part on the work of David Shakow (1969). A basic feature of the scientist-practitioner model is a relationship between, on the one hand, empirical research and theoretical modeling which produces generalizable knowledge and theory and, on the other hand, having experience gained from applying theory and knowledge to reshape basic theory and knowledge. The blending of scholarship aimed at basic knowledge with its application is what Donald Stokes (1997) calls 'use-inspired basic research', in which he identifies Pasteur's research as a principal example. It includes a search for fundamental knowledge but connected to considering how such knowledge can be used.

Use-inspired scholarship has appeal for thinking about scholarship in internationalization, because contemporary higher education internationalization is not an end in itself but rather a means to many ends and purposes. While understanding international and global factors and dynamics is of intellectual interest on its own for many, it is the myriad potential applications such knowledge has for improving the outcomes of higher education's teaching, research and service core missions in a twenty-first-century global environment that is justifying the growth in time and expense being allocated to it.

In political and policy arenas, recent critiques of the higher education enterprise focus on documenting practical outcomes of learning and research: documenting what Johnny or Susie have learned or can now do; whether they are able to get study-relevant jobs; whether higher education is contributing to building a workforce needed for a twenty-first-century global environment; whether research and scholarship solve societal problems on local and global scales; whether higher education outcomes create new ideas with applications, markets, or employment opportunities, and so forth (e.g. Miller 2006; Kehm & Teichler, 2007; Arum & Roska, 2011; Kehm, 2011; McPherson et al, 2009; Mehaffy, 2012; Erkkila & Piironen, 2013).

Internationalization will not escape pressure to demonstrate valued outcomes from, for example, mobility, internationalizing curricula, seeking international students, building cross-border partnerships, and so forth. This is potentially fertile ground for research collaborations between academic units with their knowledge and theory creation and scholarly interests and practitioners in variously configured international offices supporting mobility, active learning abroad, problem-solving applications and so forth.

A Diversifying Scholarship Connected to Internationalization

Much scholarship and practice in internationalization is still evolving and emerging as a field of inquiry and application. The concept of internationalization is also moving to a larger tent to incorporate comprehensive and strategic approaches to higher education internationalization and to more systemically interrelate the well-established with the emergent areas of scholarship and inquiry (Hudzik, 2015). The terms 'established' and 'emergent' scholarship are used for heuristic purposes rather than to reflect a neat and clean division per se.

Established Areas of Scholarship

There are established fields of inquiry that have a reasonably sizeable scholarly literature, such as comparative politics, which typically has a disciplinary/departmental home; international development studies, which tend to be inter- and trans-disciplinary by nature; some aspects of regional studies (typically transdisciplinary); international relations (either discipline or school based); some aspects of cross-cultural studies and knowledge with a somewhat eclectic mix of academic homes but often associated with departments and programs in the humanities and languages or in academic units studying culture and ethnicity, such as in anthropology or sociology; and in education examining, for example, multi-cultural and culture-based learning environments, substance and pedagogies.

Other examples from the past have been under the microscope. Part of the critique of Title VI area study centers (whether fair or not, and partly ideologically based) was that many of these centers were populated with scholars from traditional disciplines such as political science, anthropology, sociology, history and economics, where the principal interest was developing cross-cultural and comparative knowledge, language acquisition and deep knowledge of other cultures. The critique was that there was a general absence of using that knowledge for development and practical problem solving. Many area centers evolved, however, to include within their core faculty membership those from 'professional' programs (such as in community development, agriculture and food systems, environmental programs, public health, business and education) who engaged abroad for purposes of societal development and problem solving. These area centers offered a setting to blend disciplinary and professional subject matter expertise with knowledge of social, historical, cultural and value dimensions of other societies. The effort to blend is still evolving and was and remains somewhat problematic – pitting learning about other cultures and societies for its own sake against applying that knowledge to practical problem-solving applications.

Emergent Areas of Scholarship

Other areas of scholarship under the internationalization tent are more recent and emergent, such as in internationalizing curricula, mobility, examining institutional and organizational change forced by internationalization, and conducting outcome assessment scholarship relating to internationalization. These more recent and emergent areas of inquiry have not been an easy fit with the more traditional and narrow definition of 'high'-status scholarship within the academy. Even the more well-established forms of internationally oriented scholarship have not always found an easy home in institutions where departments and schools are largely domestically focused and oriented.

Practitioner Roles in Internationalization Scholarship?

Practitioners and Scholars

Universities are full of somewhat dubious distinctions over who does research and what kinds of research, and who doesn't or shouldn't. Research and scholarship is commonly assumed to be done by regular tenure stream faculty and sometimes by faculty or others on research appointments. Their credentials typically require the terminal degree (PhD or equivalent) and their research technical and substantive skills have been vetted and assessed as a condition of employment. Their job descriptions give higher priority (often the highest) to conducting research and producing scholarship. Practitioners in internationalization (e.g. program directors, coordinators, advisors, administrators and other staff within the international office and its units, or some internationally oriented support-staff positions in departments and schools) may or may not have the terminal degree, and more often don't. They have not been vetted for their research skills as a part of the hiring process, nor is research and scholarship a core part of the job description.

These differences, taken as a whole, historically differentiate the practitioner and scholar on two key dimensions. First, there is the assumption that practitioners by and large aren't hired to conduct research, or produce scholarship, and are not rewarded for doing it.

Second, practitioners are not typically extensively trained or educated in research techniques and methods and therefore are not considered knowledgeable and experienced in designing and conducting research that meets the scientific (qualitative, quantitative or theoretical) knowledge-creation standards of academe. (Of course, don't call attention to the fact that a lot of faculty research falls short of the scientific standard.)

Nonetheless, these two dimensions reinforce one another to the point that practitioners who were neither hired for nor generally considered educated and skilled in the research enterprise are looked upon as second-class citizens in the realm of scholarship and research. Yet, in many of the more recent areas of potential research and scholarship in internationalization, these practitioners sit on top of a potential gold mine of data and perspective – for example, in programs of mobility, internationalizing curricula, cross-cultural learning, integration of international student and scholars, and administrative support of international development work. The potential gold mine is where basic theory, knowledge and beliefs about international learning, research and theoretical models are put into practice. As was the case in clinical psychology decades ago, it is time to recognize the potential for enhancing basic knowledge and theory with lessons from their application.

Scholarship quality remains a requirement regardless of who does it or what kinds of purposes are behind the scholarship. This suggests not only thinking more broadly about who has scholarship roles to play, but an action agenda that will further enhance the quality of scholarship that practitioners in internationalization can produce.

Institutional Structures to Mediate Role Dichotomies

From personal experience as a senior international officer (SIO) and also from discussions at numerous institutions in the US and elsewhere, the two hemispheres of scholarship in internationalization (established and emergent) are not systematically interconnected in part because the fields of practice in mobility, curriculum internationalization, and some aspects of inter-cultural relations were administratively and intellectually housed in international relations/programs offices (or organizationally adrift and isolated) while the other areas of more traditional scholarship noted above tended to be housed in the 'academic side' of the institution (in departments, schools and interdisciplinary centers).

Adding to division and also differential stature is the implicit and often explicitly stated view (still pervasive) that international offices are service and support units while the academic units do the intellectual stuff, particularly valid scholarship. It is not uncommon to have both sides engage in a kind of rock throwing, with elements of practitioners believing 'they don't understand us, nor the value of what we do' while those in traditional scholar/faculty roles often see practitioners as mainly application technicians, or without sound intellectual, conceptual or theoretical foundations or valid empirical evidence supporting the outcomes of what they practice. As a result, collaborations between the two sides often never get off the ground or can be tense, unproductive, or demeaning.

There is evidence that some of the administrative and structural divisions are beginning to ameliorate through crosswalks built partly through an evolving concept of the SIO (Senior International Officer) and partly because of the infusion of internationalization into the core missions of higher education.

'SIO' is not a homogeneous concept. At some institutions, and historically, the SIO is in charge of mobility and perhaps the ESL program, as well as perhaps recruitment of international students and their support. The SIO in these circumstances is often without a secure academic home/appointment and without faculty background or status; additionally, there is typically little if any scholarship expected of these SIOs, or from units and individuals reporting to them (however, even without expectations, many such SIOs and some of their staff have engaged in scholarship over the last several decades).

However, at a growing number of institutions, the SIO position has responsibilities expanding beyond these areas to include direct, shared or collaborative leadership responsibilities for programs relating to area and thematic international study centers, broad-based inter-institutional cross-border partnerships, international development activity, and advising senior institutional leadership on internationalization across all key missions of teaching, research and service. Under these circumstances, the SIO becomes an institution-wide officer for internationalization, connecting across all areas of practice and scholarship. It is more likely to find SIOs in these positions also having departmental and faculty homes, and a track record of scholarly engagement.

There are also growing areas of connections and crosswalks owing to the infusion of international activity into key institutional missions. These opportunities include the following:

1. As education abroad expands, one successful strategy at many institutions involves curricular integration of education abroad, which brings academic units and their faculty together with mobility programs and their staffs to strengthen the intellectual and learning connectivity of education abroad to departmental majors and curriculum. There are obvious opportunities for collaborative scholarship related to learning.

2. International development activity not only engages service and research missions but increasingly international development is being refashioned from one-way assistance models into two-way co-production of knowledge and learning across borders, which impacts both curricular and research paradigms, and may serve to 'internationalize' domestic engagement scholarship.

3. Internationalizing the curriculum forces bridge building between those engaged in intercultural learning and languages with faculty and courses substantively defined by the academic disciplines and professional programs.

4. As international students become more plentiful and visible, their integration into the campus living and learning environments has also begun to empower more forthright consideration of their intellectual contribution to the learning environment of departments and their majors.

5. As institutions take a strategic interest in developing cross-border, inter-institutional partnerships in research, their research priorities and capacities become influenced by cross-cultural and cross-border perspectives. There are opportunities in this for collaborations and applications between internationalization support offices and academic departments.

Integrating Models of Scholarship in Academe and Internationalization

The engagement, scientist-practitioner and triple helix models provide paradigms to conceptualize research and scholarship in higher education internationalization. For example, government through funding and policy has encouraged international engagement for national and policy objectives and industry has awakened to the importance of international knowledge and perspective in a twenty-first-century global market place and for 'job-ready' graduates. Both government and industry have become stakeholders of internationalization with certain expectations for documenting outcomes. Other stakeholders in higher education have diverse motivations for internationalization such as improved access to global sources of cutting-edge knowledge and partnerships, developing an informed citizenry and workforce for a global environment, enhancing the global standing of the higher education institution, and promoting peace and mutual understanding, to name only some. The independent search for knowledge and truth in a global environment remains a core and valued premise of higher education. Hence, the 'triple helix' of university and its stakeholders, government, and industry defining practice and scholarship in internationalization has a certain reality.

What is emerging is a much larger tent of what can count as research and scholarship with status within the higher education institution. A very forthright and highly influential construction of such a larger tent was laid out by Ernest Boyer (1990). Boyer's typology (basic categories in italics below has implications for research and scholarship relating to internationalization:

- *Original research called the 'scholarship of discovery' that advances knowledge* (e.g. identifying and modeling the antecedents, cause and factors of peace and conflict. Or, some of the classic and more contemporary literature in international relations, studies of war and peace, and comparative policies are examples.)

- *Synthesis and integration of knowledge and information across disciplines and topics*, or, as Boyer pointed out, searching for larger meanings and more comprehensive understandings by pooling knowledge across disciplinary understandings (e.g. blending knowledge from several disciplinary perspectives to understand and shape larger global forces and events, such as global warming, communicable disease and conflict – putting together perspectives from, for example, community development, political, social, educational, value and cultural systems, behavioral and policy sciences, economic, and basic and applied science disciplines and programs). There are connections for this type of global scholarship to curricular, research and service missions.

- *The scholarship of engagement or application* (e.g. international development problem solving related to safe and sustainable food supply, clean water, environmental recovery, and health, to name some of the issues that require an intermingling of knowledge and practice from the natural and biological sciences, the social and behavioral sciences, values, ethics, and cross-cultural understandings, to name a few). There are many good examples of scholarship, research and discovery in international development where the focus, while on solving problems that afflict human kind, is also contributory to basic knowledge. An area of scholarship not well developed but fertile is the degree to which (and how) internationalizing curriculum, learning, research and service missions actually contributes to key stakeholder needs such as for government, industry, graduates, communities and so forth.

- *The systematic study of teaching and learning* (e.g. pedagogy, process and content and outcomes involving internationalization of teaching and learning and curricula, learning and other outcomes from an internationalized curriculum, mobility, language acquisition, cross-cultural studies). This has become a fairly popular area for research and scholarship in internationalization in recent years, and one in which internationalization practitioners are beginning to stake out territory.

As one looks through this typology it should be clear that these various 'types' of scholarship and research are linked, often building on and cross-informing one another. It is not sensible to think of one being better than another or one being scholarship and the other not; rather, each has different purposes in mind, but the purposes can become linked along with a wider view of who contributes. To be fair, this kind of view remains contested terrain in certain higher education quarters, but at least it is contested and building toward a more diverse appreciation of scholarship with different motivations, purposes and contributors.

The State of Scholarship in Higher Education Internationalization Practice

The focus of the remainder of this chapter is on the emergent or newer areas of scholarship relating to internationalization. The traditional pecking order of what counts and what is given high stature in the ivy halls is not a uniformly friendly environment for scholarship on internationalization of many kinds – although the more established topics of international scholarship have a better fit than the emerging forms and topics noted earlier. There are many reasons for this.

- The relatively newer scholarship interests relating to internationalization include mobility, internationalizing curricula and learning, integration and support of international students and scholars and cross-cultural learning and practice. They are ones that can, and do, involve practitioners in the international office (e.g. units supporting education abroad, international students and scholars, inter-cultural relations, and curriculum and learning, and perhaps units supporting international development problem solving).
- The emergent interests of scholarship and research suffer in institutional academic visibility, stature and marginalization because of their newness and their 'separateness'. Additionally, there is no readily recognizable disciplinary home, nor the appearance of a profession associated with internationalization per se. It lives in a multi- and trans-disciplinary state, without a readily recognizable systematic body of knowledge or tested theory, and with a paucity of programs to support development and credentialing of scholars (practitioner or faculty).
- The present body of research and scholarship in the newer areas of research interest is fairly elementary and of uneven and often questionable quality. For example, recent assessments of scholarship relating to education abroad illustrate research design and research practice inadequacies which create further difficulties in an academic environment. Difficulties and shortcomings when

applied to 'outcome' assessment research and scholarship include, for example:

–The measurement of inputs and outputs treated either implicitly or explicitly as measures of outcomes. There are practical reasons why data collection focuses on input and output data – they are easier to obtain, while outcome data are more costly or simply unavailable. The constraint is real, but the misrepresentation of what actually has been collected is problematic.

– Limited sample size and heavy reliance on case studies question the representativeness and generalizability of findings and conclusions, even when outcomes are being measured.

– Reliance on self-reported or opinion-based data rather than on more objective hard data. For example: asking students whether 'they thought they learned something' on a program versus actually testing learning (e.g. pre–post paper–pencil tests, or pre–post skill tests).

– Lax statistical standards, or inappropriate use of statistical measures limits the validity and reliability of findings (e.g. the use of parametric statistics with non-parametric data).

– The absence of theoretical underpinnings makes it difficult to establish and explain cause-and-effect relationships.

A recent annotated bibliography of sources of research on education abroad impacts and outcomes assembled by the Forum on Education Abroad (2012) is populated by research commonly displaying one or more of these shortcomings. While the shortcomings are typical, they reflect in part the challenges of conducting useful scholarship in the practice fields of internationalization. The usual challenges include unavailability of sufficient subjects or adequate samples, or lack of access to objective data, human subjects regulations and others limiting access to subjects or on using forms of experimental design, absence of theoretical grounding, and so forth (also see Hudzik & Stohl, 2009; Vande Berg et al, 2012; Hudzik, 2015).

These 'omissions' don't sit well with the dominant culture of scholarship in higher education, nor in expectations related to 'professionalizing' practice. But it is precisely the expanding time, money and effort being allocated to the internationalization of all higher education missions that require attention to the contributions practitioners can make to scholarship, particularly if there are opportunities for them to become quality contributions in research and discovery.

The Ideal vs. Reality. A reality guiding design of research and scholarship is to find a balance between the ideal and what is possible or practical in a given situation. Rarely does actual research meet the scientific ideal, particularly in the social, behavioral, learning and policy sciences (the worlds inhabited by much of the realm of internationalization scholarship). The objective is to do the best possible under circumstances and constraints but also recognize resulting limitations in what can be validly and reliably concluded. Those who conduct research have a responsibility to optimize design within constraints but also to point out limitations imposed by those constraints. That said, if the quality of scholarship in internationalization is to improve, especially that of enhancing the roles and contributions of practitioners, systematic attention needs to be devoted to enhancing the role of practitioner as scholar.

An Action Agenda to Enhance Practitioner Scholarship

It is limiting and counterproductive to ignore the potential roles and contributions of practitioners in scholarship. By encouraging their contributions, rather than ignoring or discouraging them, research is likely to advance in diversity and value. This will not be accomplished simply by wishing for it; there are several actions to help move such an effort forward. Attention has to be devoted to developing research models and methodologies that enhance and relate to practitioner scholarship contributions to understanding internationalization. The knowledge and skill base of practitioners who are conducting research needs to be further developed. A more diversified notion of scholarship that counts within internationalization needs to be recognized, much as within higher education generally. Some items for action to move such an agenda forward could include:

- Encourage development of graduate master's and PhD programs relating to higher education internationalization that build relevant research knowledge and skills, particularly within the newer areas of internationalization scholarship. The emergence of PhD programs (and possibly master's programs) in higher education internationalization such as at UCSC Milan, and others being contemplated, will help. So will the development of master's and PhD tracks or options in colleges of education such as at Michigan State University and elsewhere that help connect basic research skills to internationalization research topics through relevant thesis and dissertation topics.
- The professional associations for international educators (e.g. NAFSA, AIEA, EAIE, IEAA, the Forum) need to contribute to continuing professional development opportunities for membership.
  – One way to start is offering workshops, or perhaps a professional development series, that enhance practitioner research knowledge and skills related to internationalization. This should go beyond the present show-and-tell sessions often labelled 'research roundtables' which, although of value, merely update attendees on current

research and findings, but do not significantly develop knowledge and skills relating to research design and methodologies in the practical world.
– Workshops and fellowships could focus on practical challenges and means of conducting research and developing scholarship interests among attendees.– The development of research agenda for the profession of internationalization would help identify the key issues needing scholarship and research in the interest of building a reputable body of knowledge to support a profession.

- As faculty become more engaged in international activity and scholarship of their own, there is advantage for institutions as well as professional associations of international educators to encourage faculty/practitioner modes of collaboration much as was done in clinical and applied psychology decades ago. The same associations, as noted above, could also use their diverse membership to develop interest in collaborations between faculty and certain academic departments and professional programs with internationalization practitioners – both of which groups are members of these organizations.
- The key journals of scholarship in international education should develop journal 'research notes' sections which are short and focused pieces helping to develop wider awareness of knowledge and skills for conducting research relating to internationalization, particularly that of blending the scholar-practitioner worlds.
- Institutions should give thought to revising job descriptions and raising expectations/criteria for some practitioner positions to permit, encourage, or give the expectation to engage in research and scholarship in their area of practice. This is not unlike some of the models and expectations of those in clinical positions in the medical and allied health fields.
- In the same way that much of the research and scholarship of internationalization is beneficially inter- and trans-disciplinary, so ways should be found, perhaps under encouragement and support of the newer and more expansive SIO models, to team faculty and practitioners to jointly engage in scholarship around their programming efforts.

Summary

Just as the divide between scholar and practitioner has historical roots in higher education, so do developments over the last several decades recognizing the role and value that collaborations between scholars and practitioners can have in developing new knowledge and practical applications. Engagement models of higher education (e.g. engaged scholarship, co-production, mode 2 scholarship, and the 'triple helix' model) pursue compatible outcomes across goals of independent scholarship, applications across higher education missions, and connections to the priority needs and objectives of societies, government and economies. In effect the higher education environment is evolving to accommodate the roles that practitioners can play in scholarship and breaking down many false dichotomies between practitioners and scholars in this regard.

Scholarship relating to internationalization is also diversifying and developing to enhance the opportunity for meaningful knowledge generation by practitioners, particularly in newer areas of research, such as around the substance, methods and outcomes of mobility, internationalizing curricula, cross-cultural learning and skill building, and others. Practitioners in the arena of internationalization have access to a potential gold mine of data and perspective which can help inform and fill out models and theories of internationalization, just as has been the case in clinical fields such as clinical psychology.

With the opportunity for practitioner engagement in scholarship comes the responsibility to conduct solid research and scholarship. As discussed, there are shortcomings in the present state of the art in newer areas of internationalization scholarship, as well as established areas. Some of these shortcomings are attributable to inherent challenges in conducting research on internationalization. Some, however, result from a set of challenges that can be ameliorated if attention is paid to improving knowledge and skills relating to producing sound (i.e. valid and reliable) findings in the field. Some suggestions mentioned for attending to this include building supportive academic structures in higher education for practitioner scholarship, enhancing opportunities for practitioners to develop their research knowledge and skills, and giving recognition to practitioner research and scholarship. In addition, there are roles for the journals and professional associations in higher education internationalization to build and develop these capacities within and for an emerging profession.

References

Arum, J. & Roska, J. (2011) *Academically Adrift: limited learning on college campuses.* Chicago: University of Chicago Press.

Boyer, E.L. (1990) Scholarship Reconsidered: priorities of the professoriate. Princeton, NJ: Carnegie Foundation for the Advancement of Teaching.

Erkkilä, T. & Piironen, O. (2013) Shifting Fundaments of European Higher Education Governance: competition, ranking, autonomy and accountability, *Comparative Education*, 50(2), 177-191.
http://dx.doi.org/10.1080/03050068.2013.807643

Etzkowitz, H. (2008) *The Triple Helix: university-industry-government innovation in action.* New York: Routledge. http://dx.doi.org/10.4324/9780203929605

Fitzgerald, H.E. & Simon, L.A.K. (2012) The World Grant Ideal and Engagement Scholarship, *Journal of Higher Education Outreach and Engagement*, 16(3), 33-56.

Forum on Education Abroad (2012) Bibliography of Outcomes Assessment Studies in Education Abroad (October 2012) http://www.forumea.org/research-outcomes-reviewsypnosis2011.cfm (accessed on 22 March 2014).

Gibbons, M., Limoges, C., Nowotny, H. & Schwartzman, S. (1994) *The New Production of Knowledge: the dynamics of science and research in contemporary societies.* Thousand Oaks, CA: SAGE.

Glass, Chris R., Doberneck, Diane M. & Schweitzer, John H. (2011) Unpacking Faculty Engagement: the types of activities faculty members report as publicly engaged scholarship during promotion and tenure, *Journal of Higher Education Outreach and Engagement*, 15(1), 7-30.

Hudzik, John K. (2015) *Comprehensive Internationalization: institutional pathways to success.* Abingdon: Routledge.

Hudzik, J. & Simon, L.K. (2012) From a Land-grant to a World-grant Ideal: extending public higher education to a global frame, in D. Fogel & E. Malson-Huddle (Eds) *Precipice or Crossroads? Where America's Great Public Universities Stand and Where they are Going Midway through their Second Century.* Albany: SUNY Press.

Hudzik, J. & Stohl, M. (2009) Modeling Assessment of Outcomes and Impacts from Internationalization, in H. de Wit (Ed.) *Measuring Success in the Internationalization of Higher Education.* Amsterdam: European Association for International Education (EAIE).

Kehm, B. (2011) Research on Internationalisation in Higher Education. Paper presented at the International Higher Education Congress: New Trends and Issues, Istanbul, Turkey.

Kehm, B.M. & Teichler, U. (2007) Research on Internationalisation in Higher Education, *Journal of Studies in International Education*, 11, 260-273. http://dx.doi.org/10.1177/1028315307303534

McNall, M.A., Barnes-Najor, J.V., Brown, R.E., Doerneck, D.M. & Fitzgerald, H.E. (2015) Systemic Engagement: universities as partners in systemic approaches to community change, *Journal of Higher Education Outreach and Engagement*, 19(1), 7-32.

McPherson, P., Schulenburger, D.E., Gobstein, H., Keller, C. (2009) Competitiveness of Public Research Universities and Consequences for the Country: recommendations for change, in National Association of State Universities and Land-Grant Colleges Discussion Paper.

Mehaffy, G. (2012) Challenge and Change, *EDUCAUSE Review*, 47, 25-42.

Miller, C. (2006) A Test of Leadership: charting the future of US higher education. Washington, DC: Department of Education.

John K. Hudzik

Shakow, David (1969) *Clinical Psychology as Science and Profession: a forty-year odyssey*. Chicago: Aldine.

Stokes, D.E. (1997) *Pasteur's Quadrant: basic science and technological innovation*. Washington, DC: Brookings Institution Press.

Vande Berg, M., Paige, R.M. & Lou, K.H. (Eds) (2012) *Student Learning Abroad: what our students are learning, what they're not, and what we can do about it*, 1st edn. Sterling, VA: Stylus Publishing.

CHAPTER 3

The Emergence of the Scholar-Practitioner Identity in International Education: a 25-year review

JOHN D. HEYL

SUMMARY International educators have struggled over the years with how to develop their field as an academic discipline – and thus with identifying an appropriate research and methodological agenda – and with how to inform their scholarship with the diverse range of actual practice of international programs on campus, through provider organizations or professional networks. Despite this tension – or perhaps cause of it – a growing cohort of international education (IE) professionals see scholarly contributions as part of their professional responsibilities. This chapter identifies a group of international educators – some offering more personal statements, some social science–based studies, some compilations of institutional research – who helped shape the scholar-practitioner identity in the field over the past twenty-five years.

Introduction

There are several reasons why trying to name leading scholar-practitioners in international education is such a challenging – and possibly misguided – task. First, international education (IE) – unlike early childhood education, or even comparative education – is not (yet) a recognized academic discipline. This means that, among other things, the range of what counts as scholarship in the field remains quite wide and open to many styles of research and commentary (Streitwieser et al, 2012; also Krishnan, 2009).

Second, compounding the fragile nature of the field of IE as a scholarly discipline is the fact that leading practitioners have come from highly diverse backgrounds, many doctorally trained but not in IE itself – more commonly in an established humanities or social science discipline. Only in recent years has it become possible to receive doctoral training in IE, most commonly as a concentration in higher education leadership. Meanwhile, those producing scholarship in the field may hold positions in academic departments such as cultural studies, foreign language, business, anthropology or education – but they may just as likely be full-time practitioners in international offices who are closer to IE participants and relevant IE data – or may not be campus-based at all.

Third, this review inevitably leaves out many scholar-practitioners who have made important contributions to the field through their encouragement of other colleagues to pursue a research topic, their own insights to authors of manuscripts in development, or their writing on specialized topics that do not surface in this broad-brushed, US-centric treatment.

Despite these obstacles, this chapter attempts to chart a path of leading scholar-practitioners in international education over the past twenty-five years. This period has been chosen because, on the one hand, it coincides with the emergence of what might be called a scholarly agenda in the field, and, on the other, it covers the period of the author's direct involvement in the field. This review thus tells both a professional and highly personal tale. Along the way, we will meet Pathfinders, Strategists, Comparativists, Networkers and Digital Voices in international education.

Pathfinders

For those international education leaders who came out of an academic discipline into a practitioner-dominated field – either through some kind of joint appointment or, as in the case of this author, by giving up academic tenure in an established discipline and venturing into a new profession distinct from that of college professor but still campus-based – it was inevitable that these practitioner-administrators would want to identify – or help build – a scholarly underpinning for their new profession. Formerly scholar-teachers; they wanted to become scholar-practitioner *pathfinders* for the future of IE.

Several of the leading figures in international education in the 1980s came from Europe and were academic transplants who, not surprisingly, wanted their new area of practice to acquire academic legitimacy. These include Josef Mestenhauser (1926-2015), a political refugee from post-war Czechoslovakia to the University of Minnesota, and Burkart Holzner (1931-2014), an academic transplant from West Germany to the University of Pittsburgh.

Josef Mestenhauser was a law student in Prague when the Communist takeover took place in 1948; he protested those events and was imprisoned and beaten. Escaping Czechoslovakia in 1949, he subsequently landed a position at the University of Minnesota and earned a PhD in political science there in 1960. While working on his doctoral program, he served as an international student advisor, eventually directing that office and subsequently serving as director of Minnesota's Office of International Education from 1986 to 1992, before returning to the Department of Educational Policy and Administration as professor until 2000. He served as President of NAFSA in 1987-88. Significantly, in a 2009 curriculum vitae, Mestenhauser listed 'Application of Learning Concepts and Theories to International Education' and 'The Nature and Structure of Professionalism in International and Intercultural Education' as two of his chief scholarly interests. His papers and presentations reflect a continuing interest in the professional standing of international education practice – 'Are We Professionals, Semi-Professionals, or Dedicated Good Guys?' (1976); 'Internationalization of the Disciplines' (1987); 'The Concept of International Education' (1990) (Mestenhauser, 2009) – leading to a commitment to a systems theory approach to international education. As he wrote in his professional memoir, 'because international education is a system, the issues we face are not problems of separate parts, but of the system and its organization' (Mestenhauser, 2011). Appropriately, Mestenhauser's main contribution to the IE literature was a compilation on campus internationalization focusing on the curriculum (Mestenhauser & Ellingboe, 1998).

Burkart Holzner had written on social theory, social psychology and the sociology of knowledge in Germany prior to coming to the University of Pittsburgh in 1960 in the Department of Sociology. He maintained a deep interest in how social science knowledge interacts with policy-makers, co-editing *Realizing Social Science Knowledge* (Vienna, 1983), based on a conference honoring Paul Lazarsfeld, the renowned Viennese-born sociologist. Holzner served as director of Pittsburgh's University Center for International Studies from 1980 to 2000 and helped found the Association of International Education Administrators (AIEA) in 1982, serving as its 7th president in 1990-91. He was a dynamic administrator, building an array of federally funded National Resource Centers at Pittsburgh. He lectured internationally and established numerous global partnerships but also worked locally in helping to found the Pennsylvania Council for International Education (PACIE) (University of Pittsburgh, 2014). It was typical of Holzner's thinking that he could help compile a guidebook to local/state initiatives in international education as well as a grand-scale analysis of global trends in the early twenty-first century (Holzner & Dinneman, 1988; Holzner & Holzner, 2006).

The founding of AIEA in 1982 led to a series of initiatives that bridged scholarship, practice and government policy. Among these was the movement toward articulating a research agenda for the field. Barbara Burn (1926-2002), director and then associate provost of International

Programs at the University of Massachusetts Amherst (1968-2002), president of NAFSA (1982-83) and the 11th president of AIEA (1994-95), led much of this conversation (Fitzgibbons, 2002). One recalls Burn standing up at many a conference session in which anecdotal evidence was offered as evidence of a particular trend – 'These are all very interesting stories, but where is the research to back this up?' she would ask. She herself authored or co-authored a considerable ream of scholarship, much of it focusing on education abroad, foreign language study, single-country and comparative analyses and broader higher education issues (e.g. Burn, 1973, 1982; Carlson et al, 1990). In 1995 Burn chaired a group of leading scholars, campus practitioners and government program administrators to produce a report, *A Research Agenda for the Internationalization of Higher Education in the United States* (Burn & Smuckler, 1996). Over the next twenty years international educators, especially in the United States, had a roadmap for their own scholarly ambitions.

To recognize their contributions as both scholars and practitioners, all three – Mestenhauser, Holzner and Burn – two genial Europeans and one sometimes acerbic American – have had annual lecture series named in their honor. They were truly institutional, professional and conceptual pathfinders.

Strategists

Campus-based international educators most often function as *middle managers* at colleges and universities. They are directors or executive directors of an international office and, more recently, vice provosts/vice presidents of international/global engagement/affairs/education (Heyl, 2007). In these roles, IE leaders – perhaps more than other middle managers – reflect on how to broaden their influence on campus, both up and down the organization chart and across administrative silos while serving institutional missions of teaching, research and service. They become *strategists*.

A strategic perspective from the IE 'trenches' was provided by Jack Van de Water, long-time SIO (1976-2002) at Oregon State University, in three articles in *International Educator* (Van de Water, 1997, 2000, 2006; see also Van de Water, 2015). Van de Water's ideas on SIO leadership achieved wide circulation and launched an entire IE conversation on what came to be called *comprehensive internationalization*. But Van de Water's contributions were based more on reflections from a long and successful career of IE leadership and less on social science analysis.

More recently, this perspective gained extended treatment by John Hudzik in *Comprehensive Internationalization: institutional pathways to success* (Hudzik, 2015). This volume is in part conceptual (Part I) and in part based on diverse case studies of internationalization (Part II).

Hudzik's home university, Michigan State University, where he served as SIO under President Peter McPherson (1993-2004), is featured among the case studies. In this way, this study weds the scholar and practitioner approach to IE that has been so characteristic of IE scholarship over the years. Hudzik served as president of both AIEA (2002-03) and NAFSA (2009-10).

Much of the IE scholarship in the past decade has made reference to a widely cited definition of *internationalization* presented by Jane Knight in a 2004 article in the *Journal of Studies in International Education* (*JSIE*) (Knight, 2004). Serving as SIO at Ryerson University (Toronto, Canada) and earning five degrees from five different institutions in three countries has given Knight an unusual intellectual and experiential framework in which to understand transnational educational flows of all kinds. Her most recent work focuses on international education *hubs* – 'where a country is building and positioning itself as an attractive and acknowledged center of education, training, knowledge production, and innovation activities' (Knight, 2014).

Comparativists

There is a rich tradition of the study of comparative systems of education and higher education, best represented in the United States by the *Comparative Education Review* (*CER*), published since 1957 by the Comparative and International Education Society and the University of Chicago Press. But the purview of *CER* has always been very broad, encompassing education at all levels and focusing on education systems outside the United States and on national systems of educational policy. Likewise, *Comparative Education*, a UK-based journal founded in 1964 and published by Routledge, focuses on theoretical, conceptual and development issues. Neither of these journals, however, focuses on issues of special interest to the IE practitioner, such as global learning, student and faculty mobility and institutional leadership issues.

Many IE scholar-practitioners could be included in this tradition within the context of the just-mentioned foci. Jane Knight has already been mentioned and has contributed substantially to this perspective, especially with her conceptual work on various patterns of internationalization and her writing on African higher education (Knight & Teferra, 2008; Knight & Sehoole, 2013). Her work on *hubs* focuses on comparative developments in Southeast Asia, the Gulf states and southern Africa. Knight is one of the most published and most globally visible IE professionals in the past decade.

In addition, Philip Altbach, former editor of *CER* and director of Boston College's Center for International and Higher Education (CIHE; 1994-2015), wrote and edited multiple works on domestic (US) higher education, along with comparative studies, bibliographies and reference works (e.g. Altbach, 1979, 1998). In the course of his academic career, Altbach has had appointments in a variety of departments, including education, policy studies, sociology, Indian studies and information and library studies. At CIHE, Altbach edited *International Higher Education* (*IHE*) and sponsored conferences and publications on international education. Meanwhile, he authored or edited many volumes, ranging from Asian and Latin American higher education to issues involving a critique of the privatizing of higher education worldwide (Altbach & Balán, 2007; Altbach et al, 2012).

Altbach's successor at CIHE (in 2015), Hans de Wit, also mentioned above, is likewise clearly in this tradition. De Wit led the international affairs offices at both the Amsterdam University of Applied Sciences and the Università Cattolica del Sacro Coure in Milan, Italy, and published his doctoral dissertation comparing international education strategies in the United States and Europe (de Wit, 2002). He is a co-founder and past president (1994) of the European Association for International Education (EAIE). He has written on the internationalization of Latin American higher education and on global student mobility (de Wit et al, 2005; de Wit et al, 2008). As an editor, he has pulled together experts around the world to provide the reader with a genuinely global and comparative perspective. This was particularly apparent in his role co-editing the *SAGE Handbook of International Higher Education* (Deardorff et al, 2012).

Simon Marginson, shaped by the Australian experience in international education, has joined this highly productive cohort of comparativists with work that transcended the Australian case. He is now professor of International Higher Education and director of the Centre for Higher Education Futures at University College London, while retaining his position as Fellow at the University of Melbourne, his alma mater. Marginson writes frequently in the popular press on education issues, from the public/private divide in higher education to the impact of globalization on higher education and creativity in the knowledge economy. His comparative work has focused on international student security, higher education in the Asia Pacific and, more recently, STEM education globally (Marginson et al, 2010; Marginson et al, 2011; Freeman et al, 2015). International recognition of his work is reflected, for example, in his election to the Academia Europaea (the Academy of Europe) and in his selection to deliver the Clark Kerr Lecture at the University of California (2014) – the first non-American to be so honored.

Networkers

With the emergence of IE professional associations in the 1980s, including AIEA and EAIE, it was inevitable that leadership-based organizations, such as the American Council on Education (ACE), would take up issues focusing on international education.

Madeleine Green joined ACE in 1974, where she directed the ACE Fellows program (1978-1990) before leading the Center for Leadership Development (1987-2000) and then the Center for International and Institutional Initiatives (2001-2006) and International Initiatives (2006-2010). Involved early on in leadership issues, Green helped launch a series of monographs on institutional change. Focusing more directly on campus internationalization, she co-edited a series on internationalization in a variety of settings, from community colleges to comprehensive universities (e.g. Green, 2005; Green & Siaya, 2005). Green worked with an experienced team of co-authors, well networked with campus leaders across the United States, to produce status reports on internationalization that were both conceptual and application oriented. More recently, Green has published monographs for NAFSA that discuss issues involving assessment of global learning and update an earlier national mapping exercise (Green, 2012, 2015; see also, Green et al, 2008).

Darla Deardorff, executive director of AIEA since 2005, has likewise made substantial contributions as scholar-practitioner through a combination of social science–based research, case studies and edited volumes, as well as practitioner-based training and consulting. Much of Deardorff's own scholarship focuses on intercultural competence, the subject of her doctoral dissertation (Deardorff, 2004, 2006, 2009). As lead editor of the *SAGE Handbook of International Higher Education* (Deardorff et al, 2012), she managed an ambitious project that broadened the discussion of internationalization well beyond issues of intercultural competence to include institutional leadership, global trends, internationalization at home, cross-border delivery, student mobility and futuristic speculations. Recently, she has focused on the challenges of assessment in IE (Deardorff, 2015).

Academic vice president of the Council on International Education Exchange (CIEE) from 2005 to 2012, Michael (Mick) Vande Berg has led research studies to explore the role that US education abroad, whether by direct enrollment or mentored sojourn, can play in student gains in intercultural learning. His research supported the transformation in program management from a teaching-centered to a learning-centered experience and asked how education abroad can maximize its impact on a diverse range of student participants (Vande Berg et al, 2009). The Georgetown Consortium study, which involved almost 1300 students from 190 US institutions studying in 61 programs abroad, was pathbreaking for the range of global learning dimensions investigated. Subsequently, Vande Berg collaborated on an even wider application of learning theories to education abroad (Vande Berg et al, 2012).

John D. Heyl

Provocateurs

Some IE scholar-practitioners are perhaps better known as *provocateurs*. Chief among these is Michael Woolf, who is Deputy President for Strategic Development and Chief Academic Officer at CAPA International Education, an education abroad provider organization, and who follows very much in the tradition of Barbara Burn (see above). Woolf's unique background among IE leaders includes academic study in American Studies, a stint with the BBC and leadership roles with a number of education abroad entities, including the Foundation for International Education (FIE), Syracuse University Abroad, CIEE and CAPA. He has repeatedly jarred the international education field out of any latent complacency with, for example, his critique of 'authenticity' in education abroad: 'The pursuit of authenticity is an unlovely combination of futility and delusion' (Woolf, 2014); or of 'global citizenship': 'The concept of the "global citizen" is obviously an oxymoron – we are citizens of a country and we are not citizens of the global: the "globe" is a very fractured and divided place' (Woolf, 2010, p. 50). Somewhat notoriously, he has described US study in developing world locations ('nontraditional study abroad') as 'closer to pornography than it is to education' (Woolf, 2013). But in addition to these shots across the bow of IE, Woolf has co-edited CAPA's insightful occasional publications on such topics as cosmopolitanism, career integration, nationhood, the city as text and the study of war (Woolf & Gristwood, 2015). As with the best in IE scholarship, these publications combine challenging conceptual writing with telling case studies.

An early issue of *JSIE* (Spring 2000) featured an article by Peter Scott, then vice chancellor at Kingston University in London. With much of IE discussing Thomas Friedman's *The Lexus and the Olive Tree* (Friedman, 1999), Scott offered an early take on the impact of globalization on higher education. Scott articulated what many IE professionals felt at the dawn of the new century – that the university, where most were based, was losing its leadership in international education to several non-university actors – so-called corporate universities, government agencies, provider organizations and other non-profit and charitable entities. Scott is included here because he represents both a campus-based leader overseeing university adaptations to globalization and a powerful editorial voice globally (Scott, 1998). As a campus leader questioning past approaches to IE, he belongs alongside other campus leaders, such as Peter McPherson at Michigan State University, Sanford Ungar at Goucher College, David Maxwell at Drake University, Julio Leon at Missouri Southern State University and John Sexton at New York University, who, often as *provocateurs* on their own campuses, have overseen new approaches to internationalizing their institutions (Heyl, 2014).

Hans de Wit has identified with several of the scholar-practitioner roles sketched in this chapter – strategist, comparativist, networker – and *provocateur*. He has repeatedly warned of relying on widely accepted 'traditions' within the IE community, rather than truly innovating with a clear sense of the goal of one's practice. In a widely read short piece appearing in *IHE* (Winter 2011), de Wit and Uwe Brandenburg wrote of 'The End of Internationalization'. Only somewhat tongue in cheek, they asserted that 'internationalization has become the white knight of higher education, the moral ground that needs to be defended, and the epitome of justice and equity' (p. 15). An extension of Peter Scott's theme of a decade earlier, de Wit and Brandenburg argued that IE practitioners were losing their way by not asking the right questions about their field and their own activities: 'We should carefully reconsider our preoccupation with instruments and means [student exchanges/mobility/recruitment, degree portability, curriculum integration] and rather invest a lot more time into questions of rationales and outcomes' (p. 17). These issues continue to resonate among IE scholar-practitioners today.

Expanded Publishing Venues: new options for the IE scholar-practitioner in an age of globalization

Two professional journals debuted in the mid-1990s that provided important new outlets for research-based IE inquiry. *Frontiers: The Interdisciplinary Journal of Study Abroad* first appeared in 1995 as the academic journal of the recently formed Forum on Education Abroad, based at Dickinson College (Carlisle, PA). 'Intentionally interdisciplinary in scope', *Frontiers* sought to 'provide the field of education abroad [with] an intellectual charge' (www.frontiersjournal.com/index.htm). The journal has published several special issues, including a two-volume history of US study abroad (Hoffa, 2007; Hoffa & DePaul, 2010). Brian Whalen, president and CEO of the Forum, is also the editor of *Frontiers*, although *Frontiers* maintains editorial autonomy from the Forum. Since 2013, *Frontiers* has been published exclusively online as an open-access journal. Education abroad has, in fact, attracted some of the most ambitious IE research, much focusing on assessing cultural learning in education abroad. Many of the authors noted in this chapter – and elsewhere in this volume – have published in *Frontiers* (e.g. de Wit, 1995; Ogden, 2007-2008; Comp, 2010).

The inaugural issue of the *JSIE* in spring 1997 signaled a watershed in the evolution of the IE scholar-practitioner. Although several scholarly or semi-scholarly outlets had been available to IE practitioners over the years – including NAFSA's *International Educator*, the *Comparative Education Review*, *International Higher Education* (which debuted in 1995), *Frontiers* (see above) and Occasional Papers series sponsored by provider and exchange organizations – these did not meet the increasing demand, both within and without IE, for social science- and evidence-based research across the broad field of IE practice. From the beginning, as CIEE President Stevan Trooboff noted in his prefatory comments, *JSIE* wanted to stimulate research in the field as a way to 'establish, maintain and support a standard of academic and professional excellence that will serve us all and help raise the field to its full potential' (Trooboff, 1997). Implicit in these comments was the perceived need for a publishing venue that crossed academic, social science and practitioner lines. Under the editorship of Hans de Wit, beginning with the second year of publication, *JSIE* committed itself 'primarily to the publication of research articles, critical essays and book reviews' and to forgoing most semi-scholarly material (de Wit, 1998). Under de Wit's editorship – concluded in 2015 when he became the director of the Center for International Higher Education in the Lynch School of Education at Boston College (USA) – *JSIE* became the premier journal among IE practitioners.

In addition to new journals focusing on IE scholarship, several publishing houses began to build a catalog on international education from the mid-1990s on. Chief among these was SAGE, which has a long history of interest in publishing resources for teaching and research – mainly focusing on social science research and reference works, engineering and medicine. With the advance of globalization at the turn of the century, however, SAGE accelerated its publishing in IE. By 2015, the list of SAGE books and journals in IE was extensive, including several cited in this chapter (e.g. *JSIE*; Deardorff, 2009; Deardorff et al, 2012). Even more recently, Stylus (Sterling, Virginia), Sense (Rotterdam) and Symposium Books (Oxford, UK) have issued important works in the field, again including some cited here (e.g. Altbach 2005; de Wit et al, 2008; Brewer & Cunningham, 2009; Vande Berg et al, 2012; Knight & Sehoole, 2013; Brewer & Savicki, 2015; Deardorff, 2015). These newer entrants into IE publishing joined others, such as Routledge, Greenwood and Oryx, with even longer commitments to the field. With publishing venues expanding in which the scholar-practitioner could share research and commentary, the scholar-practitioner in IE has gained additional access to print and thereby greater visibility.

Digital Voices

The world of the Internet – especially self-authored websites, blogs, e-databases and e-publications – has created even newer outlets for the scholar-practitioner in IE. CAPA's occasional e-publications have been mentioned above. The range of this activity, in the nature of the Internet, is too broad to be surveyed here. One might cite David Comp's International Higher Education Consulting blog (ihec.doc.blogspot.com), a mix of personal accounts and professional commentary and interviews

– mainly focusing on education abroad (Comp's doctoral dissertation [Comp, 2013] focused on the National Security Education Program (NSEP) service requirement). This author's IELeaders.net focuses on issues and topics of special interest to senior IE leaders.

Other websites focus on core themes in IE, offer research data or compile bibliographical materials. Bruce La Brack's *What's Up with Culture* website (www2.pacific.edu/sis/culture/) focuses on helping students make 'successful cultural adjustments both before going overseas and upon returning home from studying abroad' and includes rich bibliographical resources for students, teachers and trainers. Rahul Choudaha, Chief Knowledge Officer at World Education Services (WES), leads a team of researchers that regularly distributes data-rich reports on global student mobility (www.wes.org/ras/reports). Stuart Hughes, senior librarian at the Australian Council for Educational Research (ACER), posts a searchable database of IE publications since 1990 for IDP Education (www.idp.com/researchdatabase) that represents a massive open-source repository of diverse publications and conference presentations in the field.

IE-focused professional associations are also active in providing digital views and resources. NAFSA, Forum and ACE digital publications have been mentioned above. In addition, AIEA's issue briefs, presidential and provosts' perspectives, occasional papers and survey summaries suggest the range of e-publications now common in the field. Elizabeth Brewer has not only contributed her own expertise in liberal arts learning and education abroad (Brewer & Cunningham, 2009; Brewer & Monahan, 2011; Brewer & Savicki, 2015), but, as chair of AIEA's Editorial Committee, has also co-written occasional papers (Brewer & Brockington, 2013; Brewer et al, 2015) and expanded the range of commentary offered by the AIEA website (www.aieaworld.org/publications). In addition, Brewer led the updating of AIEA's 1996 research agenda monograph with a continuing series of e-publications (see www.aieaworld.org/research-agenda).

Conclusion

Three features appear to characterize the outlook of the IE scholar-practitioner as it continues to evolve.

First, the recognition that institutional context matters means that a rigid definition of terms remains elusive and perhaps counterproductive. Hence, terms like *comprehensive internationalization*, *global citizenship*, *intercultural competence/global competence* and the *international university* remain necessarily context specific, despite the efforts of some scholars to generate more generally applicable frameworks. De Wit concludes: 'I'm afraid that more and more universities in the future will refer, in their mission statements and policies, to the fact that they are an international university, without clearly explaining what they mean by it' (de Wit, 2015). International educators recognize that context is critical to understanding the pace and hallmarks of internationalization in a specific institutional setting (Merkx & Nolan, 2015). In this sense, the IE practitioner vies with the IE scholar over the boundaries of generalizations in the field.

Second, much of IE scholarship is collaborative, dictated in part by the inevitable limitations on an individual researcher's knowledge of diverse topics within IE and diverse systems of higher education globally. Thus, many of the scholar-practitioners mentioned in this chapter and this volume have collaborated with each other to bring distinctive strengths and expertise together to focus on a particular topic. Moreover, even when individual scholar-practitioners have acquired a special area of expertise, typically rooted in their earlier academic training, they often branch out into other areas, applying theory to practice more broadly in IE. Thus, the categories employed in this chapter – Pathfinders, Strategists, Comparatists, Networkers, Digital Voices – are not mutually exclusive or even well demarcated. It is perhaps a special feature of IE as a still-evolving field of inquiry that the walls separating the various IE subfields – and those between IE and more established disciplines – are highly permeable, and scholar-practitioners are welcome to breach them with whatever analytical tools are available.

Third, much of IE scholarship, even when it is grounded in the experience of the practitioner, is speculative and future oriented. What, after all, will be the impact of new technologies on global learning? How will global conflicts reshape student and scholar mobility? What role will political corruption and cybertheft play in undermining transnational partnerships? What role will the privatization of higher education globally have on support for international collaboration (Deardorff et al, 2012, chapters 24, 25)? These are a few of the many unanswered questions that loom in the future for higher education in general and international higher education in particular. Thus, as Knight has observed regarding the 'far-fetched idea' of the *Edu-glomerate*, 'Edu-glomerates may sound like science fiction and a long way from today's reality. A couple of decades ago, the same could have been said about branch campuses or education hubs or even MOOCs. Stay tuned – the only constant these days in international education is innovation' (Knight, 2015, p. 119).

As mentioned at the outset of this chapter, any attempt to identify a Who's Who among scholar-practitioners in international education is bound to fail – at least in the limited framework of this chapter. What is certain is that two arcs in higher education – the institutional drive to become more internationally engaged, and the availability of venues through which IE professionals can share experience and analysis – are both rising. This will mean that the number and diversity of IE scholar-practitioners will increase in the years ahead. Whether and how this increased scholar-practitioner activity will (re)shape the future of higher education globally are still open questions. It will surely make that future more informed, self-critical – and interesting!

References

Altbach, P.G. (1979) *Comparative Higher Education: research trends and bibliography*. Los Altos, CA: Mansell.

Altbach, P.G. (1998) *Comparative Higher Education: knowledge, the university, and development*. Norwood, NJ: Ablex.

Altbach, P.G. (2005) *The Global Future of Higher Education and the Academic Profession: the BRICS and the United States; private higher education a global revolution*. Boston: Sense.

Altbach, P.G. & Balán, J. (Eds) (2007) *World Class Worldwide: transforming research universities in Asia and Latin America*. Baltimore: Johns Hopkins University Press.

Altbach, P.G., Reisberg, L., Yudkevich, M., Androuschchak, G. & Pacheco, I.F. (Eds) (2012) *Paying the Professoriate: a global comparison of compensation and contracts*. New York: Routledge.

Brandenburg, U. & de Wit, H. (2011) The End of Internationalization, *International Higher Education*, 62 (Winter), 15-17.

Brewer, E. & Brockington, J. (2013) International Education Self-studies and External Reviews. October. Durham, NC: Association of International Education Administrators (AIEA). https://aiea.memberclicks.net/assets/docs/Issue_Briefs/aiea_issuebrief_2013sept-%20op.pdf

Brewer, E., Charles, H. & Ferguson, A. (2015) Strategic Planning for Internationalization in Higher Education. February. Durham, NC: Association of International Education Administrators (AIEA). http://aiea.memberclicks.net/assets/docs/OccasionalPapers/occasional%20paper-%20strategic%20planning%20in%20a%20university%20context%202015.pdf

Brewer, E. & Cunningham, K. (Eds) (2009) *Integrating Study Abroad into the Curriculum: theory and practice across the disciplines*. Sterling, VA: Stylus.

Brewer, E. & Monahan, M. (Eds) (2011) Study Abroad and the City, *Frontiers: The Interdisciplinary Journal of Study Abroad*, 20 (Spring) Special Issue.

Brewer, E. & Savicki, V. (Eds) (2015) *Assessing Study Abroad: theory, tools, and practice*. Sterling, VA: Stylus.

Burn, B.B. (1973) Comparisons of Four Foreign Universities, in J.A. Perkins (Ed.) *The University as an Organization*, pp. 79-103. New York: McGraw-Hill.

Burn, B.B., with Opper, S. (1982) Internationalizing Higher Education in Sweden: the development of a national priority, *European Journal of Education*, 17(1), 49-58. http://dx.doi.org/10.2307/1503039

Burn, B.B. & Smuckler, R. (Eds) (1996) *A Research Agenda for the Internationalization of Higher Education in the United States*. Pullman, WA: Association of International Education Administrators (AIEA).

Carlson, J., Burn, B.B., Useem, J. & Yachimowicz, J. (1990) *Study Abroad: the experience of American undergraduates*. Westport, CT: Greenwood.

Comp, D. (2010) Germany as a Study Abroad Destination for US Students in STEM Disciplines, *Frontiers*, 19 (Fall–Winter), 191-203.

Comp, D. (2013) The National Security Education Program and its Service Requirement: an exploratory study of what areas of government and for what duration national security education program recipients have worked. Unpublished doctoral dissertation, Loyola University of Chicago. http://ecommons.luc.edu/luc_diss/509

Deardorff, D.K. (2004) Internationalization: in search of intercultural competence, *International Educator*, (Spring), 13ff.

Deardorff, D.K. (2006) Identification and Assessment of Intercultural Competence as a Student Outcome of Internationalization, *Journal of Studies in International Education*, 10(3) (Fall), 241-266.

Deardorff, D.K. (Ed.) (2009) *The SAGE Handbook of Intercultural Competence*. Thousand Oaks, CA: SAGE.

Deardorff, D.K. (2015) *Demystifying Outcomes Assessment for International Educators: a practical approach*. Sterling, VA: Stylus.

Deardorff, D.K., de Wit, H., Heyl, J.D. & Adams, T. (Eds) (2012) *SAGE Handbook of International Higher Education*. Thousand Oaks, CA: SAGE.

de Wit, H. (1995) Education and Globalization in Europe: current trends and future developments, *Frontiers*, 1 (Fall), 28-53.

de Wit, H. (1998) Editorial, *Journal of Studies in International Education*, 2(1) (Spring), 1. http://dx.doi.org/10.1177/1028315398002001001

de Wit, H. (2002) *Internationalization of Higher Education in the United States of America and Europe: a comparative, historical, and conceptual analysis*. Westport, CT: Greenwood Press.

de Wit, H. (2015) Is the International University the Future for Higher Education?, *International Higher Education*, 80 (Spring), 7.

de Wit, H., Agarwal, P., Elmahdy Said, M., Sehoole, M.T. & Sirozi, M. (Eds) (2008) *The Dynamics of International Student Circulation in a Global Context*. Boston: Sense.

de Wit, H., Jaramillo, I.C., Knight, J. & Gacel-Ávila, J. (Eds) (2005) *Higher Education in Latin America: the international dimension*. New York: World Bank. http://dx.doi.org/10.1596/978-0-8213-6209-9

Fitzgibbons, D.J. (2002) Burn Remembered as a Leader in International Education, *Campus Chronicle*, XVII(23), 1 March. http://www.umass.edu/pubaffs/publications/chronicle/archives/02/03-01/burn.htm

Freeman, B., Marginson, S. & Tytler, R. (Eds) (2015) *The Age of STEM: educational policy and practice across the world in science, technology, engineering and mathematics*. New York: Routledge.

Friedman, T. (1999) *The Lexus and the Olive Tree: understanding globalization.* New York: Farrar, Straus & Giroux.

Green, M. (2005) *Internationalization in Comprehensive Universities.* Washington, DC: American Council on Education (ACE).

Green, M. (2012) *Measuring and Assessing Internationalization.* Washington, DC: NAFSA. http://www.nafsa.org/wcm/Product?prodid=381.

Green, M. (2015) *Mapping the Landscape: accreditation and the international dimensions of US higher education.* Washington, DC: NAFSA. http://www.nafsa.org/wcm/Product?prodid=438

Green, M., Luu, D. T., & Burris, B. (Eds.) (2008) *Mapping Internationalization on U.S. Campuses.* Washington, DC: American Council on Education (ACE).

Green, M. & Siaya, L. (2005) *Internationalization in Community Colleges.* Washington, DC: American Council on Education (ACE).

Heyl, J.D. (2007) *The Senior International Officer (SIO) as Change Agent.* Durham, NC: Association of International Education Administrators (AIEA).

Heyl, J. D. (2014) IE Provocateurs. 20 May. http://www.ieleaders.net/archive.html

Hoffa, W.W. (2007) A History of US Study Abroad: beginnings to 1965, *Frontiers: forum on education abroad*, Special Issue.

Hoffa, W.W. & DePaul., S.C. (Eds) (2010) A History of US Study Abroad: 1965– Present, *Frontiers: forum on education abroad*, Special Issue.

Holzner, B. & Dinniman, A. (Eds) (1988) *Education for International Competence in Pennsylvania.* Pittsburgh, PA: University Center for International Studies.

Holzner, B. & Holzner, L. (2006) *Transparency in Global Change: the vanguard of the open society.* Pittsburgh, PA: University of Pittsburgh Press.

Hudzik, J.K. (2015) *Comprehensive Internationalization: institutional pathways to success.* New York: Routledge.

Knight, J. (2004) Internationalization Remodeled: rationales, strategies and approaches, *Journal of Studies in International Education*, 8(1) (Spring), 5-31.

Knight, J. (Ed.) (2014) *International Education Hubs: student, talent, knowledge-innovation models.* New York: Springer. http://dx.doi.org/10.1007/978-94-007-7025-6

Knight, J. (2015) International Universities: misunderstandings and emerging models? *Journal of Studies in International Education*, 19(2) (May), 107-121.

Knight, J. & Sehoole, C. (Eds) (2013) *Internationalization of African Higher Education: towards achieving the MDGs.* Boston: Sense.

Knight, J. & Teferra, D. (Eds) (2008) *Higher Education in Africa: the international dimension.* Chestnut Hill, MA: Center for International Higher Education, Boston College.

Krishnan, A. (2009) *What are Academic Disciplines?* Southampton: ESRC National Centre for Research Methods. eprints.ncrm.ac.uk/783/1/what_are_academic_disciplines.pdf

Marginson, S., Kaur, S. & Sawir, E. (Eds) (2011) *Higher Education in the Asia-Pacific: strategic responses to globalization*. New York: Springer. http://dx.doi.org/10.1007/978-94-007-1500-4

Marginson, S., Nyland, C., Sawir, E. & Forbes-Mewett, H. (2010) *International Student Security*. Cambridge: Cambridge University Press. http://dx.doi.org/10.1017/CBO9780511751011

Merkx, G. & Nolan, R. (Eds) (2015) *Internationalizing the Academy: lessons of leadership in higher education*. Cambridge, MA: Harvard Education Press.

Mestenhauser, J.A. (2009) Curriculum Vitae. http://www.global.umn.edu.

Mestenhauser, J.A. (2011) *Reflections on the Past, Present, and Future of Internationalizing Higher Education – Discovering Opportunities to Meet the Challenges*. Minneapolis: University of Minnesota. Kindle edn: Loc. 3021/4247.

Mestenhauser, J.A. & Ellingboe, B.J. (Eds) (1998) *Reforming the Higher Education Curriculum – Internationalizing the Campus*. Phoenix, AZ: Oryx Press.

Ogden, A. (2007-2008) The View from the Veranda: understanding today's colonial student, *Frontiers*, 15 (Fall/Winter), 35-55.

Scott, P. (Ed.) (1998) *The Globalization of Higher Education*. Buckingham: Open University Press.

Scott, P. (2000) Globalisation and Higher Education: challenges for the 21st century, *Journal of Studies in International Education*, 4(1) (Spring), 3-10.

Streitwieser, B., Le, E. & Rust, V. (2012) Research on Study Abroad, Mobility, and Student Exchange in Comparative Education Scholarship, *Research in Comparative and International Education*, 7(1), 5-19. http://dx.doi.org/10.2304/rcie.2012.7.1.5

Trooboff, S. (1997) Welcome Letter from the President, *Journal of Studies in International Education*, 1(1) (Spring), vi. http://dx.doi.org/10.1177/102831539700100101

University of Pittsburgh, University Center for International Studies (UCIS) (2014) In Memoriam: Burkart Holzner, PhD, Former UCIS Director. http://www.ucis.pitt.edu/main/news-events/holzner-remembered.

Vande Berg, M., Connor-Linton, J. & Paige, R.M. (2009) The Georgetown Consortium Project: interventions for student learning abroad, *Frontiers*, 18 (Fall), 1-75.

Vande Berg, M., Paige, R.M. & Lou, K.H. (Eds) (2012) *Student Learning Abroad: what our students are learning, what they're not, and what we can do about it*. Sterling, VA: Stylus.

Van de Water, J. (1997) Gaps in the Bridge to the Twenty-first Century: the customer is always right, *International Educator*, Spring, 10ff.

Van de Water, J. (2000) The International Office: taking a closer look, *International Educator*, (Spring), 30ff.

Van de Water, J. (2006) Lessons Learned: Musings on a 30-Year Career in International Education, *International Educator*, January–February, 57ff.

Van de Water, J. (2015) International Education Leadership: reflections on experience, in G. Merkx & R. Nolan (Eds) *Internationalizing the Academy:*

lessons in leadership in higher education, 37-52. Cambridge, MA: Harvard Education Press.

Woolf, M. (2010) Another Mishegas: global citizenship, *Frontiers*, 19 (Fall–Winter), 47-60.

Woolf, M. (2013) Politics-and-Poverty Tourism: the lure of study in developing countries, *Chronicle of Higher Education*, 13 August. http://www.chronicle.com/blogs/worldwise/politics-and-poverty.

Woolf, M. (2014) Study Abroad: the problem with seeking 'authenticity'. 5 March. http://www.capaworld.capa.org.

Woolf, M. & Gristwood, A. (2015) 'Ain't Gonna Study War No More': the lost agenda in education abroad. Occasional Publications, No. 4, May. http://www.capa.org/publications

CHAPTER 4

A Historical Overview of International Education Scholarship and the Role of the Scholar-Practitioner

DAVID COMP

SUMMARY Knowledge production within the field of international education in the United States has increased significantly since the end of World War II. This chapter identifies key events and ideas throughout this history when research and other scholarly pursuits have been discussed and debated to demonstrate the growth and development of the scholar-practitioner within the field of international education. The approach taken in this historical overview with regard to the definition of 'research' and the role of the scholar-practitioner within the field of international education involves numerous activities towards the goal of advancing knowledge in both practical and theoretical ways. This chapter predominately highlights scholarship on academic mobility both to and from the United States, especially in the early decades after World War II, but it should be noted that there are many other areas of focus within the field where scholar-practitioners focus their scholarship, such as on foreign credential evaluation and methodology, foreign higher education systems, intercultural competency, comprehensive campus internationalization, branch campuses, strategic international partnerships, and the economic impact of international education.

International education has a long and intriguing history dating back to ancient times, and in the United States international educational pursuits can be traced back to colonial times. As international educational activities have developed and grown over time, in particular since the end of World War II, so has interest in international education as a focus of scholarly inquiry. While the question about whether or not international education can be considered an academic discipline has been discussed among scholars and practitioners in the field, there is no doubt that scholarly inquiry on international education issues has grown in both scope and sophistication over the decades (Tewksbury, 1949; Flack, 1987; Useem & Useem, 1987; Mestenhauser, 2012; Heyl, 2013). This chapter will not seek to answer this academic discipline debate nor will it highlight the works of early and influential comparative education scholars such as Sir Michael Sadler, Isaac Kandel, William Brickman or George Bereday. Instead, this chapter identifies key events and ideas throughout this history when research and other scholarly pursuits have been discussed and debated to demonstrate the growth and development of the scholar-practitioner within the field of international education over time, with particular attention paid to the decades after World War II.

This chapter shares a similar perspective and definition of the term 'research' with the late Barbara Burn. Burn, in her essay honoring Jack Egle and his leadership at the Council on International Educational Exchange, clarifies her view of what research is within the field of international education and states that

> [research] involves a variety of activities, sometimes resulting in well-footnoted scholarly treatises, sometimes advancing knowledge of an issue or phenomenon in ways more practical than pedantic. The research and evaluation encouraged by CIEE has tended to be more issue-oriented than academic, more practical than theoretical, and ... aimed not at 'knowledge as its own end', but at 'knowledge for use'.
> (Burn, 1994, p. 58)

To be sure, the traditional view of 'research' is discussed and is the focus of much of the historical review in this chapter, especially in the early decades after World War II, but other types of scholarly work also fit into this historical overview. Over time, research in the field of international education has transitioned from the more empirical and scientific to more practical and issue oriented, and the scholar-practitioner has played a significant role in this shift.

The Interwar Years (1919-1939)

Shortly after the end of World War I the Institute of International Education (hereinafter referred to as IIE) was established, with support of the Carnegie Endowment, on 1 February 1919. Duggan (1920) declared in his first annual report of the director that the general aim of the new IIE was:

[to] develop international good will by means of educational agencies, and for its specific purpose to act as a clearinghouse of information and advice for Americans concerning things educational in foreign countries and for foreigners concerning things educational in the United States. (p. 2)

During its first year of operation, the IIE cooperated with the French High Commission and published a booklet entitled *Opportunities for Higher Education in France*, and began work on a companion booklet for foreign students seeking to study in the United States (Duggan, 1920, p. 11). Additionally, Duggan (1920) highlighted in his annual report plans for the IIE to issue an occasional bulletin in order to inform educational authorities in the United States on issues and developments in the international field. By 1921, the IIE distributed its first survey to institutions of higher education in the United States in an effort to standardize the assessment of incoming foreign students (Institute of International Education, n.d.).

While the IIE was establishing its first reciprocal student exchange program between Czechoslovakia and the United States in 1922 a bold new international educational plan was taking shape at the University of Delaware (Institute of International Education, n.d.). In 1923, the University of Delaware launched the Delaware Foreign Study Plan, which is considered to be the first education abroad program offered by an institution of higher education in the United States (Institute for Global Studies, University of Delaware, n.d.). The University of Delaware sent a total of 902 students on Junior Year Abroad programs between 1923 and 1948 (Institute for Global Studies, University of Delaware, n.d.). By 1926, Smith College followed and began sending student groups to Paris on Junior Year Abroad programs, and in 1930 Smith began a Junior Year Abroad program in Madrid, followed by a program in Florence, Italy in 1931 (Walton, 2005; Hoffa, 2007; Contreras, 2015). By 1939, all Junior Year Abroad programming at Smith College was terminated for the duration of World War II.

The new Junior Year Abroad programs and exchange programs established by the IIE provided new educational research opportunities. In 1930, the IIE conducted a survey entitled 'A Decade of International Fellowships: a survey of the impressions of American and foreign ex-fellows' (Hewlett, 1930). A second study that was conducted during the 1930s but received wider distribution via the *Modern Language Journal* was by Roxana Holden. Holden's 1934 study entitled 'Ten Years of Undergraduate Study Abroad' analyzed statistics and statements from alumni of the first ten years of the Junior Year Abroad programs (Holden, 1934). With the interruption of international educational activities during World War II, scholarly activities in this area also took a break, but these early scholarly endeavors set the stage for what was to come.

David Comp

The Development of International Education as a Field and the Idea of the Scholar-Practitioner (1945-1959)

As the dust settled across Europe and in the Pacific at the conclusion of World War II a new global reality faced the United States. The United States was no longer able to maintain its isolationist position in the new Cold War environment it was now confronting. A new focus on creating a globally competent and engaged citizenry began to gradually take shape across the higher education landscape in the United States. As a direct response to the devastation of World War II, freshman United States Senator J. William Fulbright of Arkansas introduced legislation to the United States Congress in September 1945 to sponsor international exchange programs for faculty and students between the United States and foreign countries. The Fulbright Act (Public Law 584; 79th Congress) initiated a long and successful history of international educational and cultural exchange between the United States and the rest of the world. The foreign language and educational components of later legislation such as the US Information and Educational Exchange Act of 1948 (also referred to as the Smith-Mundt Act), amendments to the Mutual Security Act of 1952, and the National Defense Education Act (NDEA) of 1958 were consolidated into the Mutual Educational and Cultural Exchange Act of 1961 (also referred to as the Fulbright-Hays Act). The Fulbright-Hays Act represents the flagship international educational exchange policy and program of the United States today. This period also saw the revival of Junior Year Abroad programs at many colleges and universities, as well as other types of international educational exchange programming and partnerships across the United States. The increase of international educational opportunities for faculty, students and professionals presented both challenges and opportunities for both scholars and practitioners who were engaged in such activities.

As the expansion of international educational exchanges progressed during the late 1940s into the 1960s there were several notable developments outside of federal government funding and legislation that advanced the research and scholarly activities of the field. The Council on Student Travel (its name changed to CIEE [Council on International Educational Exchange] in 1966) was founded in 1947 in an effort to help restore and assist with international educational activities and student travel after World War II. In March of 1951, the Council on Student Travel announced additional goals of its organization, with one of its new objectives being the development of standards and another to 'assist with or conduct research that will clarify the conditions under which educational travel could most effectively contribute to international understanding and education' (Hoffa, 2007, p. 203). While the first international student advisor position in the United States was appointed in 1908 at the University of Illinois, the National Association of Foreign Student Advisers (today known as NAFSA: Association of

International Educators) was founded in 1948 as a means of encouraging the professional development of the college and university officials who were advising the 25,000 foreign students studying in the United States after World War II (Jenkins, 1973, p. 11; Jenkins, 1979; NAFSA, n.d. a, b). Both the Council on Student Travel and the National Association of Foreign Student Advisers played a significant role in advancing international education in the United States, and over time they have enhanced and expanded their mandates to be leading organizations that have contributed greatly to and advanced the research and activities of the scholar-practitioner.

The mid-1950s also saw three major conferences held in the United States focused on international exchange. In late 1953, the Board of Foreign Scholarships (today known as the J. William Fulbright Foreign Scholarship Board) requested that the Committee on International Exchange of Persons of the Conference Board of Associated Research Councils hold a conference of senior-level individuals experienced in international exchanges to discuss policy and administrative matters pertaining to international exchanges (Committee on International Exchange of Persons of the Conference Board of Associated Research Councils, 1956, p. iv). The conference was held in Princeton, NJ from 2 to 4 December 1954 and is often referred to as the 'Princeton Meeting'. During his address at the Princeton Meeting focusing on research developments on the exchange of persons, Ralph L. Beals (1956) of the University of California, Los Angeles summed up the state of research and stated:

> research on exchange of persons is a relatively new field.
> Published materials are at a minimum, but a comprehensive
> research inventory prepared for the Social Science Research
> Council's Committee on Cross-Cultural Education ... reveals
> substantial and growing activity ... a considerable amount of
> publication may be expected in the near future, but
> unfortunately a significant proportion of the research is in the
> form of reports to government agencies and offices, and in
> many cases is not readily available for examination. Much of
> the research done so far is evaluative ... the studies already
> done indicate clearly that the problems of international
> exchange, although presenting methodological difficulties, are
> thoroughly amenable to research ... the results not only will
> prove immensely valuable to the understanding of the
> processes and results of international exchange of persons, but
> they often provide new and exciting ways of testing and
> extending our skills and knowledge in the social sciences.
> (pp. 53, 62)

The following year the IIE organized a National Conference on Exchange of Persons, held from 23 to 25 February 1955 in New York City. Approximately 750 people registered for the conference, with representation from 32 states across the United States, the District of Columbia, the Commonwealth of Puerto Rico and seven countries. One of the eight conference workshop sessions entitled 'Studying the Results of Exchange' provided background papers that summarized the current research and highlighted some of the hypotheses based on the research (IIE, 1955, p. 45). The workshop noted that research in this field was in its infancy and that few studies had been published, yet there was considerable in-depth discussion on various studies and recommendations for future research were made. Of specific note, it was suggested during this workshop that 'the application of research at universities may best be accomplished by associating those responsible for foreign students with the research programs, and by keeping research relevant to local problems' (IIE, 1955, p. 49). Following the success of the National Conference on Exchange of Persons in 1955 the IIE, in cooperation with 117 other organizations, held the Second National Conference on Exchange of Persons in Chicago on 5-7 December 1956. The speaker of the third plenary session entitled 'How can Research Findings Improve Exchange of Persons Programs?' was John Useem from the Department of Sociology and Anthropology at Michigan State University. In his talk, Useem highlighted three distinguishing features that characterized the present relation between social research and exchange programs:

> 1. There is a new social climate within international exchange organizations which is generally favorable to research and receptive to the findings of research.
> 2. Over the past decade we have been accumulating a fund of relevant knowledge, and currently we have under way or in blueprint a series of promising studies that will add to our sum of useful knowledge.
> 3. More than in any other international enterprise, exchange programs have available a fairly substantial body of information to draw upon, and the scientists have a higher prospect of their findings being used. (IIE, 1955, pp. 34-35)

Useem's talk is of particular interest and relevance to the development of the scholar-practitioner. Specifically, Useem felt it was appropriate to direct the remainder of discussion to a lengthy examination of the working relationships between social scientists conducting the research and the administrators of the exchange programs. Useem noted four major patterns of working relationships between social scientists and exchange program administrators. Concepts such as 'shared thinking' and the 'free exchange of ideas between staff and scientists' were highlighted. He even suggested that one of the patterns of working relationships consists of arrangements for a 'staff man' with the technical skills to assume the primary responsibilities for the gathering of facts, operational research or evaluation research and that administrators should work closely with researchers in the design of research studies so the inquiry 'deals with genuine administrative problems, concentrates on salient factors and assembles the sorts of information most needed in forthcoming decisions (IIE, 1955, pp. 34-37). By the end of the 1950s international education activities had gained significant momentum and attention, and a modest literature base was being established. While the direction of the field of international education was being shaped by leaders in the academy, government, foundations and the leadership from the international education organizations of the day, the concept of the scholar-practitioner within the field began to emerge.

The Growth and Professionalization of the Field of International Education and the Emergence of the Scholar-Practitioner (1960-1980)

The field of international education in the 1960s was still very much in its early developmental stage. The growing numbers of international students, scholars and faculty coming to the United States and the increased flow of US students and faculty overseas demonstrated the continued need to organize large-scale national conferences and colloquiums in order to bring together leaders in the field and to discuss important topics and issues related to international exchange. However, during this period we begin to see more specialized conferences and other high-level meetings focusing on more narrow and specific areas and topics within the field. While participation in these high-level gatherings was still dominated by senior academics and those with influence on international education policy, more opportunities presented themselves for administrators in the field of international education not only to participate but also to contribute to the dialogue. In many instances, based on their long-term professional work in the field coupled with their knowledge and understanding of the research and literature available, international education administrators often found themselves as the expert in the room, and the scholar-practitioner was able to add a much-needed perspective and voice to the conversation. Additionally, opportunities arose for scholar-practitioners to produce and advance knowledge in the field as publishing opportunities began to become more available.

In 1960, there were two significant conferences that highlighted the challenges of evaluating the study abroad experience of US undergraduates as well as the need for the development of standards in the field. On 14-16 January 1960 a national conference was held at

Mount Holyoke College entitled *Academic Programs Abroad: an exploration of the assets and liabilities* that brought together a select group of high-level academics, including many college and university presidents, deans and faculty, federal and foundation staff and several key program providers to discuss concerns with the state of study abroad and the proliferation of new study abroad program offerings (Bullard, 1960; Hoffa, 2007, pp. 241-248; Comp & Merritt, 2010, pp. 455-456; Contreras, 2015, pp. 112-114). As a follow-up to address the concerns that had been voiced and continue the dialogue on standards development that began at the Mount Holyoke Conference, the Association of American Colleges, the Council on Student Travel, the Experiment in International Living and the IIE hosted the National Conference on Undergraduate Study Abroad in Chicago in October 1960 (Bullard, 1960; Murray, 1965, p. 2; Hoffa, 2007, pp. 241-248; Comp & Merritt, 2010, pp. 455-456; Contreras, 2015, pp. 112-114). In his summary and report on the National Conference on Undergraduate Study Abroad, Stephen Freeman (1961) outlined 12 findings, including a focus on evaluating the results of study abroad for the student, the institution and the nation (Freeman, 1961; Bowman, 1987). As the 1960s progressed, opportunities for international education administrators to publish and present scholarly works to advance the research and knowledge base of the field opened up and it is during this decade that we see the rise and influence of international education scholar-practitioners.

As previously mentioned, Ralph L. Beals (1956) summed up the state of research on international exchanges during the 1954 Princeton Meeting and noted that a majority of the research on exchanges was in the form of reports to government agencies and offices and was not easily accessible to international education administrators and offices (pp. 53, 62). By the early-to-mid-1960s this was changing as more research and scholarly literature was being produced and distributed by organizations such as the National Association of Foreign Student Advisers and the Council on Student Travel to international education administrators and offices who were able to start building their own libraries as they advanced in their own professional and scholarly endeavors. The National Association of Foreign Student Advisers published and distributed the NAFSA Studies and Papers Professional Grant Reports to its members during the 1960s and allowed scholar-practitioners like Werner Warmbrunn to author NAFSA Studies and Papers Professional Grant Reports no. 4, entitled 'Observations of Education and Exchange in Asia: a report of a study trip, September to December, 1960', which was published in 1961 (Warmbrunn, 1961). Warmbrunn served as a foreign student adviser and director at Bechtel International Student Center at Stanford University from 1952 to 1964 before being invited by Pitzer College's president to help design the academic programs for the college and develop its community (Leo Baeck Institute, 2012). The Council on

Student Travel also capitalized on the opportunity to produce and distribute scholarly literature to the field and began publishing its Occasional Papers on International Educational Exchange series in 1965. The Council on International Educational Exchange has published 32 Occasional Papers on International Educational Exchange from 1965 to 2010. The Occasional Papers series focused on a variety of international education exchange subjects, with particular attention paid to US students abroad. The first part of Occasional Paper No. 2 by William Allaway, who was director of the Education Abroad Program of the University of California at the time of publication, wrote a paper entitled 'The Many-faceted Job of the Overseas Academic Program Director', with notes on the various responsibilities overseas program directors must perform, and stated that 'we must further keep in mind the diverse roles which the staff must serve: 1. as a scholar, in teaching and research' (Allaway, 1965, p. 3). While a majority of the research in the field focused on US students studying abroad, there were a large number of scholars and practitioners who turned their attention to researching the experiences of international students in the United States.

On 30-31 March 1967 the National Liaison Committee on Foreign Student Admissions (comprised of the American Association of Collegiate Registrars and Admissions Officers, the College Entrance Examination Board, the Council on Graduate Schools in the United States, the IIE and the National Association for Foreign Student Affairs) organized a colloquium held at Wingspread in Racine, Wisconsin focusing on foreign graduate students in the United States. Following the success of this colloquium, the National Liaison Committee held a second colloquium at Wingspread focusing on 'The Foreign Graduate Student: priorities for research and action' (Jameson, 1971). A total of seven recommendations emerged from this second Wingspread colloquium, with two of the recommendations highlighting the need for a more complete annual census of foreign students that provides data beyond what are provided in Open Doors to include the financial aid that foreign students receive. Another recommendation to come out of the colloquium deliberations was a need to make the data collected by various projects and publications, such as the consultations of the NAFSA Field Service Program and the Open Doors data relating to the selection and admissions procedures, more fully available for further analysis by others (Jameson, 1971, pp. 64-65). It should be noted that there was no representation by international education administrators from institutions of higher education that participated in the colloquium proceedings other than a few Directors of Admissions and an Associate Dean for International Exchange at this 1970 Wingspread colloquium. In 1974, another Wingspread colloquium was held and focused on the foreign undergraduate student in the United States.

As the field of international education grew over the decades one finds numerous examples of documented collaborations among international educational exchange organizations in the form of joint efforts to advance the field. In many respects, these inter-associational collaborations were scholarly endeavors. Such collaborations continued to flourish into the 1970s and 1980s, and one can find numerous examples of scholar-practitioners from across the international higher education landscape participating in and taking leadership positions in a variety of collaborative projects and initiatives. Examples of such inter-associational collaborations as well as individual association working groups where international education scholar-practitioners were involved include but are not limited to the following:

1. The Joint AACRAO/NAFSA Task Force on US Study Abroad
2. The CIEE Committee on Evaluation
3. The NAFSA Committee on Research and Evaluation
4. The Joint AACRAO/NAFSA Workshop Committee
5. The NAFSA Task Force on Faculty Involvement
6. International Society for Educational, Cultural and Scientific Interchanges (ISECSI)
7. The Joint Task Force on Data Collection (AACRAO, IIE, NAFSA)
8. The Research Committee of the International Educational Exchange Liaison Group (CEEB, IIE, IREX, NAFSA, AFS, FAA, CGS, NAS)
9. The International Research Opportunities Board of the SSCR (ACLS, CIES, USCIA, IREX, NSF, OE, SSRC, NEH)
10. The International Committee for the Study of Educational Exchange
11. The Inter-Associational Committee on Data Collection (AACRAO, IIE, NAFSA/SECUSSA)
12. The NAFSA Task Force on Standards and Responsibilities
13. The NAFSA Task Force on Standardized Reporting on US Undergraduate Study Abroad Programs at British Universities
14. The NAFSA Publications Task Force of the NAFSA Section on US Students Abroad (SECUSSA)

The identity and reputation of numerous scholar-practitioners came to light as a result of their work on and contributions to these and other committees and task forces and their influence and impact is still felt in the field of international education today.

The Scholar-Practitioner in the Field of International Education (1980-2000)

Building upon the momentum of research and scholarship in the field of international education, scholar-practitioners continued to lead and advance knowledge production in the field during the 1980s through 2000. While conferences and inter-associational collaborations continued to grow and flourish during this period, a variety of new avenues and technologies emerged and helped advance the production and distribution of new knowledge in the field. An excellent example of the work of the International Society for Educational, Cultural and Scientific Interchanges (listed above), and pertinent to the current discussion on the scholar-practitioner within the field of international education, was their co-sponsorship with the German Academic Exchange Service (DAAD) of the US-German Conference on Research on Exchanges held on 24-28 November 1980 in Bonn, Germany. What made this conference quite special, aside from the fact that it was an international conference focused on international exchanges, was that for the first time this conference intentionally brought together both scholars and practitioners 'to devote their energies and expertise to a common purpose: to establish and develop a dialogue between the "two cultures" – public administration and academic research – for the mutual benefit of both and, in particular, of all those engaged in controlled exchange programs' (DAAD, 1987, p. i). The delegates also agreed to continue this important dialogue at future conferences, as seen in the continued engagement between practitioners and research scholars during the Seminar on Cross-cultural Orientation Programs held in Minneapolis from 31 October to 3 November 1984 (International Society for Educational, Cultural, and Scientific Interchanges, 1985, p. 3). It was noted in the Bonn conference recommendations that one of the three areas of concern of the delegates was the relationship between research and practice and the relationship of researchers to practitioners, and that it needed improvement (DAAD, 1987, pp. 266 & 269). Several guidelines were offered to help improve the situation, such as practitioners identifying their needs to researchers and researchers involving practitioners in the definition and conduct of research studies (DAAD, 1987, p. 269). Littmann (1987) suggested that a significant portion of research is generated by self-interest of the institutions and that accountability is a driving force behind many authors and in particular for administrators (p. 195). Littmann (1987) does acknowledge that 'research on educational exchange – like all research – has a very strong personal component and scholarly interest or individual edification may prompt research just as much as professional interest' (p. 197). That said, finding time to conduct research or engage in scholarly activities while managing professional and administrative responsibilities is a significant challenge. Althen (1981) argues that while there is a plethora of printed literature available on intercultural communication, only scholars are expected to keep up to date and current whereas practitioners in international education have so many responsibilities that they don't have enough time to consult and digest even the smallest amount of the intercultural communication literature (pp. 1-2).

The 1980s and 1990s saw the arrival of several new publications that provided international education administrators with timely and digestible information relevant to the field, as well as research articles and other valuable scholarship. Additionally, these new publications provided an outlet for the scholar-practitioner to submit their scholarly work for publication. The following list highlights some of the more prominent publications available to scholar-practitioners:

1. The Occasional Papers Series in International Education – *Journal of the Association of International Education Administrators*
2. *International Educator* by NAFSA: Association of International Educators
3. *International Education Forum* – a publication of the Association of International Education Administrators
4. *Transitions Abroad* – the Magazine of International Travel and Life
5. *World Education News & Reviews* (*WENR*) by World Education Services
6. *International Higher Education* – quarterly publication of the Boston College Center for International Higher Education
7. *Frontiers: the Interdisciplinary Journal of Study Abroad*
8. *Journal of Studies in International Education*

Additionally, opportunities for scholar-practitioners to present and discuss their work have become more and more abundant. Associations such as NAFSA: Association of International Educators, Council on International Educational Exchange and the Association of International Educators have held annual conferences and are perhaps the three largest venues in the United States for scholar-practitioners to engage other scholar-practitioners in the field. An example of the scholar-practitioner influence in the field is observed in the formation of the Committee on Underrepresented Groups in Overseas Programs by the Council on International Educational Exchange in 1988. Building on that momentum, the Council on International Educational Exchange focused the theme of its 1990 annual conference in Charleston, South Carolina on *International Education: broadening the base of participation*. This further led to the publication of *Black Students and Overseas Programs: broadening the base of participation*, which highlighted many of the key papers presented at the conference. Jon Booth, Chair of the Committee on Underrepresented Groups in Overseas Programs and Director of the International Study and Travel Center at the University of Minnesota, notes that it was the hope of the committee that the book would be thought-provoking and a useful guide, and said that it welcomed reactions and suggestions, extending an offer to others to become part of the effort (Booth, 1991, ix). To be sure, these three associational conferences were not the only viable options for scholar-practitioners during this period to present and discuss their scholarship, but they were perhaps the most well known.

The Scholar-Practitioner as the Leading Knowledge Producer in the Field of International Education (2000-Present)

The rise and influence of the scholar-practitioner in the field of international education is perhaps best observed in the 2000s to the present day. The growth and development in the field of international education has been quite dramatic during this period of time and the opportunities for scholar-practitioners to be engaged and advance knowledge in the field are so plentiful that only a cursory overview is provided. In fact, the following developments are the result of scholar-practitioners in the field.

Forum on Education Abroad

Conceived in 2000 by education abroad leaders, the Forum on Education Abroad was incorporated by 2001, with the first annual conference held in Santa Fe, New Mexico in November 2004. It has focused on the development of standards of good practice for the field of education abroad, data collection, research and advocacy, and, over the last several years, has undertaken program assessment and quality improvement. The Forum on Education Abroad seeks contributions from members, and the opportunities for scholar-practitioners to become engaged and contribute are numerous. An example of this is demonstrated in the publication of *A Guide to Outcomes Assessment in Education Abroad* edited by Mell Bolen. This joint project of the Forum on Education Abroad and *Frontiers: The Interdisciplinary Journal of Study Abroad* afforded the opportunity for scholar-practitioners to contribute to this important and timely publication.

The Forum on Education Abroad has also partnered with the American Institute for Foreign Study (AIFS) and the AIFS Foundation and established the AIFS/AIFS Foundation Special Collection hosted at Dickinson College, which serves as a historical archive and depository of education abroad historical materials (Forum on Education Abroad, n.d. a). As a complement to and in collaboration with the AIFS/AIFS Foundation Special Collection, the Forum on Education Abroad has initiated the Forum Storytellers project in an effort to collect the oral history of senior leaders in the field (Forum on Education Abroad, 2015).

Teaching, Learning and Scholarship Knowledge
Community of NAFSA: Association of International Educators

As NAFSA: Association of International Educators reorganized in the mid-2000s to move away from professional sections to a knowledge community structure, the teaching, learning and scholarship knowledge community emerged as a place where scholar-practitioners are welcomed and can find a home to feed their interest in the scholarly side of the field. This knowledge community is made up of the following three networks: Intercultural Communication & Training (ICT); Internationalizing Teaching, Learning and Curriculum (ITLC); and Research & Scholarship (RS). An interesting project to come out of the work of the Research & Scholarship network was the online *Global Studies Literature Review* project, with issue number 1 issued in April 2010. The *Global Studies Literature Review* 'addresses a convergence of interests between the professional field of international education and the academic fields of international studies and international education' and provides scholar-practitioners with the opportunity to conduct book reviews from literature from the field of international education.

Data Collection

During her tenure as chair of the Section on US Students Abroad (SECUSSA) of NAFSA: Association of International Educators, Kathy Sideli initiated the National Data Collection Initiative through the IIE and SECUSSA in 1999. On 18 March 2008 the IIE hosted a new advisory group meeting for the Open Doors survey focusing on study abroad. This advisory group consisted of staff from NAFSA, members of NAFSA's Education Abroad Data Collection Sub-Committee, staff from the Forum on Education Abroad, as well as members of the Forum Data Committee. Key discussion points generated from the meeting include: increasing survey penetration; calculating participation rates; increased funding; reporting international students; and a survey of non-credit activities abroad (Cerosaletti, 2008).

Annotated Education Abroad and
International Student Research Bibliographies

In an effort to keep current and document the research literature on education abroad, various updates have been made to the *Research on US Students Abroad: a bibliography with abstracts*, edited by Henry Weaver in 1989. Updated bibliographies, maintained online by the Center for Global Education and Gary Rhodes, have been completed by Maureen Chao, David Comp and Albert Biscarra with support from Val Rust. The research literature focusing on international students in the United States has also received attention in the mid-2000s with the compilation of 559 pieces of scholarly literature into the *Annotated Bibliography of Research on International Students in the US* by Kristin Tamblyn in cooperation with David Comp (Tamblyn, n.d.).

A Research Agenda for the Internationalization of Higher Education in the United States

In 2015, the Editorial Committee of the Association of International Education Administrators initiated a series of publications that will build upon and expand on its 1996 publication *A Research Agenda for the Internationalization of Higher Education in the United States*. The first installment was prepared by Anthony Ogden and focuses on a research agenda for education abroad. Ogden also presented this work at the 2015 annual Council on International Educational Exchange conference held in Berlin.

Conclusion

The late Josef Mestenhauser was a leading scholar and theorist in the field of international education who had a long career as a scholar-practitioner, and his impact on the field is significant. In an email communication sent by Mestenhauser to several colleagues in the field he expressed concerns about certain literature and stated:

> I have championed the concept of professionalism in my job here, in NAFSA and elsewhere, and especially during my own presidency. One of the main features of professionalism is command of knowledge, practical and theoretical – I have always placed emphasis on the theoretical aspects because practice emerges from them ... we are reinforcing the idea that NAFSANs are primarily practitioners, who need only to know a few 'skills' that they use in their practice. The way things are going, according to the global trends, is that these aspects are important only at the entry level positions. If these semi-professionals want to rise higher in their profession, the higher they go, the less they will need these entry level skills, and the more they will depend on their ability to think conceptually and theoretically. (J. Mestenhauser, personal communication, 7 March 2013)

Mestenhauser's words highlight the importance of the scholar-practitioner in the field of international education. As the field has grown and developed over the decades, the opportunities for scholarly engagement available to practitioners have grown substantially and the impact that so many scholar-practitioners have had on the field is immeasurable.

References

Allaway, W.H. (1965) The Many-faceted Job of the Overseas Academic Program Director. Occasional Paper on International Education Exchange no. 2. New York: Council on Student Travel.

Althen, A. (1981) *Learning across Cultures: intercultural communication and international educational exchange.* Washington, DC: National Association for Foreign Student Affairs.

Beals, R.L. (1956) The Exchange of Persons: research developments, in *Educational Exchanges: aspects of the American experience*, pp. 53-62. Report of a conference sponsored by the Committee on International Exchange of Persons of the Conference Board of Associated Research Councils, Princeton, NJ, 2-4 December 1954. Washington, DC: National Academy of Sciences–National Research Council.

Bolen, M.C. (Ed.) (2007) *A Guide to Outcomes Assessment in Education Abroad.* Carlisle, PA: Forum on Education Abroad/*Frontiers: The Interdisciplinary Journal of Study Abroad.*

Booth, J. (1991) Introduction, in *Black Students and Overseas Programs: broadening the base of participation*, pp. vii-ix. New York: Council on International Educational Exchange. http://dx.doi.org/10.1017/cbo9780511720666.002

Bowman, J.E. (1987) Educating American Undergraduates Abroad: the development of study abroad programs by American colleges and universities. CIEE Occasional Paper on International Educational Exchange no. 24, November. New York: Council on International Educational Exchange.

Bullard, D.A. (1960) Academic Programs Abroad: an exploration of their assets and liabilities. Report of a special conference at Mount Holyoke College, South Hadley, MA. New York: Institute of International Education.

Burn, B.B. (1994) The Council's Role in Research, in C.J. Ping (Ed.) *The Power of Educational Exchange: essays in honor of Jack Egle*, pp. 57-64. New York: Council on International Educational Exchange.

Burn, B. & Smuckler, R.H. (1995) A Research Agenda for the Internationalization of Higher Education in the United States: recommendations and report. New York: Association of International Education Administrators.

Cerosaletti, G. (2008) IIE Convenes Advisory Group for Open Doors Study Abroad Survey. Message posted to NAFSA Advising & Recruitment in Education Abroad Network, 23 April.

Committee on International Exchange of Persons of the Conference Board of Associated Research Councils (1956) Educational Exchanges: aspects of the American experience. Report of a conference sponsored by Committee on International Exchange of Persons of the Conference Board of Associated Research Councils, Princeton, NJ, 2-4 December 1954. Washington, DC: National Academy of Sciences–National Research Council.

Comp, D. & Merritt, M. (2010) Qualitative Standards and Learning Outcomes for Study Abroad, in W.W. Hoffa & S. DePaul (Eds) *A History of US Study*

Abroad: 1965 to present, pp. 451-489. Carlisle, PA: Forum on Education Abroad/*Frontiers: The Interdisciplinary Journal of Study Abroad*.

Contreras, Jr., E. (2015) Rhetoric and Reality in Study Abroad: the aims of overseas study for US higher education in the twentieth century. Unpublished doctoral dissertation, Harvard Graduate School of Education, Cambridge, MA.

DAAD (1987) *Research on Exchanges*. Proceedings of the German-American conference at Wissenschaftszentrum, Bonn, 24-28 November 1980. Bonn: German Academic Exchange Service (DAAD).

Duggan, S.P. (1920) The Institute of International Education: first annual report of the director, bulletin no. 1. New York: Institute of International Education.

Flack, M.J. (1987) International Educational, Cultural and Scientific Interchange, in DAAD (Ed.) *Research on Exchanges*. Proceedings of the German-American conference at Wissenschaftszentrum, Bonn, 24-28 November 1980, pp. 1-6. Bonn: German Academic Exchange Service (DAAD).

Forum on Education Abroad (n.d.) AIFS/AIFS Foundation Education Abroad Special Collection. http://apps.forumea.org/SpecialCollection.cfm

Forum on Education Abroad (2015) Forum Storytellers. http://www.forumea.org/forum-storytellers

Freeman, S.A. (1961) Transplanted Students: a report on the national conference on undergraduate study abroad. New York: Institute of International Education.

Hewlett, T. (1930) A Decade of International Fellowships: a survey of the impressions of American and foreign ex-fellows. June. New York: Institute of International Education.

Heyl, J.D. (2013) Is International Education a Discipline? 22 May. https://aieablog.wordpress.com/2013/05/22/is-international-education-a discipline/

Hoffa, W.W. (2007) A History of US Study Abroad: beginnings to 1965. Carlisle, PA: Forum on Education Abroad/*Frontiers: The Interdisciplinary Journal of Study Abroad*.

Holden, R. (1934) Ten Years of Undergraduate Study Abroad, *Modern Language Journal*, 19(2), 117-122.

Institute for Global Studies, University of Delaware (n.d.) Study Abroad: our history. http://www.udel.edu/global/studyabroad/information/brief_history.html

Institute of International Education (IIE) (n.d.) A Brief History of IIE. http://www.iie.org/Who-We-Are/History

Institute of International Education (IIE) (1955) Report on the National Conference on Exchange of Persons, 23/24/25 February 1955. New York: Institute of International Education.

International Society for Educational, Cultural, and Scientific Interchanges (1985) *Bulletin of International Interchanges*, 22 (April). New York: AFS International/Intercultural Programs.

Jameson, S.C. (1971) The Foreign Graduate Student: priorities for research and action. A colloquium held at Wingspread, Racine, WI, 16-17 June 1970. New York: College Entrance Examination Board.

Jenkins, H.M. (1973) NAFSA and the Student Abroad: a silver anniversary review. Washington, DC: National Association for Foreign Student Affairs.

Jenkins, H.M. (1979) Looking through the History and Future of the National Association for Foreign Student Affairs: a glance back, a glimpse forward. Washington, DC: National Association for Foreign Student Affairs.

Leo Baeck Institute (2012) *Guide to the Werner Warmbrunn Collection 1885-2006*. Center for Jewish History, New York. http://findingaids.cjh.org/?pID=1452168

Littmann, U. (1987) Research in International Exchange – Why? In DAAD (Ed.) *Research on Exchanges*. Proceedings of the German-American conference at Wissenschaftszentrum, Bonn, 24-28 November 1980, pp. 194-197. Bonn: German Academic Exchange Service (DAAD).

Mestenhauser, J. (2012) Foreword, in D.K. Deardorff, H. de Wit, J.D. Heyl & T. Adams (Eds) *The SAGE Handbook of International Higher Education*, pp. vii-viii. Thousand Oaks, CA: SAGE.

Murray, J.R. (1965) Academic Study Abroad: its present status. CIEE Occasional Paper on International Educational Exchange no. 5. New York: Council on International Educational Exchange.

NAFSA: Association of International Educators (n.d. a) The History of NAFSA: Association of International Educators. http://www.nafsa.org/Learn_About_NAFSA/History/

NAFSA: Association of International Educators (n.d. b) Global Studies Literature Review. http://www.nafsa.org/Resource_Library_Assets/Networks/RS/Book_Reviews / Global_Studies_Literature_Review/

Ogden, A. (2015) Toward a Research Agenda for US Education Abroad. Association of International Education Administrators. http://www.aieaworld.org/assets/docs/research_agenda/ogden_2015.pdf

Tamblyn, K. (n.d.) *Annotated Bibliography of Research on International Students in the US*. http://webpages.charter.net/ktamblyn/Bibliography.htm

Tewksbury, D.G. (1949) International Education as a Foundations Discipline, *History of Education Journal*, 1(1) (Autumn), 21-24.

Useem, J. & Useem, R. (1987) Generating Fresh Research Perspectives and Study Designs for International Exchanges among the Highly Educated, in DAAD (Ed.) *Research on Exchanges*. Proceedings of the German-American conference at Wissenschaftszentrum, Bonn, 24-28 November 1980, pp. 24-58. Bonn: German Academic Exchange Service (DAAD).

Walton, W. (2005) Internationalism and the Junior Year Abroad: American students in France in the 1920s and 1930s, *Diplomatic History*, 29(2), 255-278. http://dx.doi.org/10.1111/j.1467-7709.2005.00473.x

Warmbrunn, W. (1961) Observations of Education and Exchange in Asia: a report of a study trip, September to December, 1960. NAFSA Studies and Papers

Professional Grant Reports no. 4, June. New York: NAFSA Association of Foreign Student Advisers.

Weaver, H.D. (Ed.) (1989) *Research on US students Abroad: a bibliography with abstracts.* New York: Council on International Educational Exchange, Education Abroad Program, University of California, Institute of International Education and National Association for Foreign Student Affairs. http://globaledresearch.com/

CHAPTER 5

The Benefits and Limits of Scholarship and Self-expression among International Education Professionals

DONNA SCARBORO

SUMMARY Among the most contested and significant issues in the field of international education is how best to prepare future professionals and leaders for the field. Among the skills and characteristics typically assumed to come with hiring a professor into an administrative role are academic strengths, such as the ability to mount research to determine the best answer to a question, the ability to convince others about the policies or activities indicated by the answer, the ability to organize and present complex information for non-experts, and a concern for issues affecting society. Whether and how individuals who exhibited such traits and abilities in academic life drew on them when adapting to their roles as managers is debated. This chapter explores how much effacement of the academic persona and how much adoption of the managerial persona are appropriate. But does specific, professional, graduate education narrowly aimed at specific skills of higher education or international education management attract and form the leaders we need? Or is the deep dive into a traditional academic subject? Do we now need to reverse-engineer international education managers to be more scholarly, as we have previously reverse-engineered academics into managers?

Introduction

The assumption behind the idea of a scholar-practitioner is this: that a career of service to and within academia might also have in it a search for the answers to burning questions. It might have, embedded in the practice or service of administration, episodes of exploration, discovery and experimentation. Indeed, at times these episodes might gain sufficient continuity to reveal an arc of work worth disseminating. Such a result is inherently hoped for in the central practices and experiences of scholars. What is its place in the work of an administrator?

Most universities in the early days of adaptation to globalized higher education appointed managers of international programs out of the faculty, drawing on people who were trained as researchers and classroom teachers and who brought with them assumptions about discovery and learning but perhaps few assumptions about management. In these circumstances, the shift into a new profession – the adaptation to being a 'practitioner' of international education – came with no operating instructions and with no bright lines that declared the life of teaching and research to be over. Throughout the ensuing challenges of administrative careers, the expectations and support for the scholar were often well preserved. The profession benefited from the curiosity, diligence and personal authority of many promising and established academics. Did these individuals over time become good managers, despite the lack of early training and orientation to office work? No doubt results were mixed.

It is instructive to look at areas of university administration outside the senior international officer (SIO) line, to see if the same trajectories have applied in recent history. For instance, at one time faculty members in the United States personally managed recruitment and admissions, critical university business now handled primarily by a professional class – at least at the undergraduate level. We in the United States are familiar with the career path of an individual who moves through undergraduate admissions from the shop floor to a position as dean or director. The time when faculty personally handled the task is forgotten. The modern undergraduate admissions profession evolved as the complexity of higher education increased in the US context. Admissions work became specialized and sufficiently demanding that faculty members could not continue on both paths – that of teacher/researcher and that of manager/admissions officer. With time, the effect of professionalization in the field of admissions became its own contributor to an inter-university arms race, with increasing competition leading to ever more sophisticated needs and requirements in specific management skills for admissions: marketing, budgeting, cost projections, personnel, IT, social media, and a hospitality function that includes training tour guides, arranging accommodation, and influencing planning for the appearance and upkeep of the campus.

While many have objected that today's university is mysteriously overloaded with administrative positions, external demands are a major driver. Admissions is just one area where this is true. Another is compliance. Yet another is generally termed 'accountability', which covers financial, legal, research and curricular areas. The external demands for accountability are now so outsized in comparison with fairly recent times that managerial structures and preparation are under duress to respond. This is true despite the observation that the process of meeting the requirements of quality assurance schemes 'is a bureaucratic process quite removed from either the student learning or creative research process, which, it is argued, lie at the heart of quality in higher education' (Harvey & Newton, 2007, p. 226).

In some countries, leaders of internationalization are on a path more like that of the current US undergraduate admissions officer. No extensive academic background is required, no research and teaching expected, and progress to the top jobs goes through the administrative rather than the faculty track. In the United States, a similar pattern may be emerging, particularly in recent decades when preparation through master's and PhD programs specifically aimed at developing managers of internationalization has taken root. In other words, the SIO position may be professionalized in a way that distinguishes it from preparation expected of the faculty, just as the undergraduate admissions leader's position has been for some time.

Higher education has never existed in a bubble but has changed according to the economic and cultural environment. Institutions naturally choose not to give up the effort to survive in a competitive climate, and they have therefore met the challenges – or struggled to meet them – with increased hiring of professional staff and appointment of division leaders who bring specific skills to meet the burdens and joys of ever-rising expectations and the challenges of rivals from all sides. Once these career paths become predictable avenues to satisfying work, a segment of students exposed to the work naturally find it interesting, and, in a circular motion driven by the competitive foundations of the surrounding culture in which higher education inevitably rests, there is now a sufficient market base of people seeking preparation *from* the university for work *in* the university.

Master's degrees and PhDs in higher education abound. They are not a US phenomenon only, and of course they are not aimed solely at the example of admissions work I have described above. The plethora of professionals on campus offering student services, data management, IT services, financial management and support for research all have attracted their share of individuals with graduate preparation specifically for the work. And to the extent that the graduate degrees have resulted in landing promising jobs, the cycle is fueled further by the success of the pioneer institutions offering them. We are creating ever-larger generations of well-prepared practitioners who are not oriented to teaching and research.

So, historically, we have moved from a time when academics-turned-managers were 'accidental tourists' in administration to a time when institutions cannot afford to support tourists as managers of their critical business. The stakes are too high, or so we increasingly seem to believe. And yet, we continue to see provosts, vice provosts and others drawn directly from faculty ranks and given whatever 'add-on' training might help them carry out demanding 'practitioner' duties. In some areas – internationalization and diversity come to mind – preparation specific to the office is increasingly accepted as a norm; in others – vice-presidents for research and deans and provosts, for instance – a lifetime academic career (with flourishes of administrative duty as chair or associate dean) is the signal preparation.

There is an acknowledged bifurcation in this picture between the academic-turned-administrator and the administrator pursuing an anticipated career as a practitioner, with the latter increasingly achieving a master's or even a PhD degree specific to university administration as a key credential. These two types of professionals work side by side in harmony or not, as do others in their combinations of preparation and background. But with these obvious lineaments drawn, we can begin to pay attention to some of the many nuances that may be relevant to one central question: what preparation is most helpful to those aspiring to careers in international education and to the institutions that need their contributions?

International Higher Education as
Scholarly Concern vs. Administrative Task

We might do well at this point to bracket another area of discussion by noting that graduate degrees in higher education are by no means exclusively aimed at management careers. Higher education is a phenomenon of modern life that merits scholarly attention – and international education is a highly visible and attractive area of study. The scholarly questions that drive many of the careers of PhDs and others in the field of education may be every bit as big and burning as scholarly pursuit of any topic that affects human endeavor. For the moment, however, I am curious about preparation for management in higher education – in other words, preparation for administration.

I am not separating these big, scholarly research interests from the minds and hearts of practitioners, but for the moment I am not examining the academic career path of those whose research interests lie in exploring, measuring or imagining higher education's effectiveness or its global reach from the scholarly perspective of an academic's office. Rather, I am exploring the practitioner's preparation in order to ask: is a scholarly background helpful to the practitioner? If so, what form should it take and how would it fit into preparation for active management in a complex institution?

To return to my analogy, I looked at the historical development of admissions professionals in higher education as a counterpoint to the generation of international administrators who were pulled from faculty ranks. It is important now to make a distinction between the development of a professional class in admissions and the same phenomenon in international education. Consider, as a beginning, the curricular prominence of the two. Admission to university is not an item that appears in university curricula. It is an outcome of one's earlier education but not the substance of the education. While there is a great deal to learn and teach regarding access to higher education through the admission process, we do not have an expectation that our undergraduate or graduate students will spend time on the subject en masse.

The same is not true of international education. The goals of international education are woven into activities affecting research, community engagement, faculty promotion, teaching and curriculum throughout the modern university. Students are expected to learn substantively about global issues and about cultures other than their own, and they are often encouraged to leave their own physical campus expressly to engage with cultures and geographies outside their national boundaries (Whitehead, 2015). Similarly, when we speak of the value of bringing international students to our campuses, we frequently cite the global perspectives they provide. And much of the management effort on many research-active campuses is in trying to align functions such as human resources (HR) and accounting with the day-to-day needs of researchers who must function professionally in a foreign environment to accomplish their work, while depending on an essential stream of support from their home institutions. In other words, internationalization is at the core of more than the functional or operational offices through which it may be administered. It affects the curriculum, student services, research, community relations, risk management, hiring and funding. It affects the draw and position of the institution, its reach and its footprint. In some respects, the administrative support for comprehensive internationalization is more akin to that associated with diversity and inclusion: no one owns it; everyone owns it. It is a core value because of the nature of the world in which the university sits.

Other forces pressing the university to professionalize its international leadership, along with the rank and file, come from changes in higher education worldwide (Deardorff et al, 2012; Streitwieser, 2014). Philip Altbach (Bassett & Maldonaldo-Maldonaldo, 2014, pp. 29-30) has ably shown that massification around the world has led to more diverse profiles of institutions within a given region. The intersection of this burgeoning manifestation of supply and demand with global mobility has produced an identity crisis for many institutions. For one thing, competition is no longer a phenomenon within the confines of a national system or even within the confines of a shared local language. The advent of English as an international calling card in higher education means that countries where the populace speaks another language may rapidly be converting many of their academic offerings to English so as to compete directly with peers in English-speaking countries.

Institutions also lost their place-bound assumptions of audience or market, meaning that a university or college in New York may have competitors from San Francisco or from Tokyo within shouting distance. Distance education and the evolving practice of putting brick-and-mortar outposts in communities far from the original home of the institution mean increasing pressure to address the challenges at the front door and to provide strategies to build campuses in new locations or break into new markets through distance learning. These are familiar currents, but it is as well to sort them in light of the management demand they represent. We have professionalized and increased our management capacity because for many universities the choice was to ramp up the management game or succumb to the brutal affronts of the higher education market. Altbach adds an important dimension:

> [A] global knowledge economy emerged that placed emphasis on the 'top' of the higher education system – universities and other institutions with the infrastructures and capabilities to deal with a globalized economy and the research and training needs of highly qualified professionals. These elite institutions often hire staff from an international labor market and educate students from many countries. (Bassett & Maldonaldo-Maldonaldo, 2014, p. 30)

These faculty members at the 'top' of the system not only represent global talent, they also know global talent from experience, having been educated in other 'top' institutions abroad, and they seek global talent in colleagues and students, thereby driving the motivations ever higher to participate in a global rather than a local, regional or national education and research network.

Other forces, such as struggles for resources and access, may push back against the global aspirations of institutions. But globalization is not abating and neither will the internationalization of universities. Given these trends and forces, what preparation is most helpful to those aspiring to careers in international education? What previous experience should be expected by those seeking to fill leadership positions in the field? And to what extent does a faculty member's background vs. a professional degree and management career in higher education provide advantages for the institution's leadership team? Is there reason to regret or resist the professionalization of international education leadership, in that it represents a byway that sidesteps a life of reflection, research, and writing in a scholarly field?

These are valuable questions both for hiring and for education offered toward work in the profession. Where we once allowed the 'accident' of a willing and capable academic to make the leap into a management position at the epicenter of the university's internationalization, we may now be making an equally accidental and even less intentional determination that preparation through an applied, professional degree for higher education is adequate to lead in an academic institution. Neither position is ideal. No one who has been in the field for long will have missed the many stories of failed leadership resulting from the assumption that teaching and scholarship in a foreign language or international business (or any other academic subject) are preparation to lead the institution wisely or to manage a staff productively. The ramp-up in skills from classroom to university administrative office takes real time, and there are losses along the way that are avoidable with appropriate background through experience in management. Another way to put this is to say that a history of successful management in higher education is the best possible evidence that an individual will be a successful manager in higher education.

At the same time, we have also seen failures of leadership that come about because an individual underestimates the difference between managing academic business and managing another type of business. Jane Knight, in the process of considering the definition of internationalization in higher education, helps to shed light on the shortcomings of applying market values to an academic enterprise:

> Central to this discussion is not how one defines internationalisation but rather what are the fundamental values underpinning it? The critical question is whether internationalisation has evolved from what has been traditionally considered a process based on the values of cooperation, partnership, exchange, mutual benefits, and capacity building to one that is increasingly characterized by competition, commercialization, self-interest and status building. Have the values related to economic political and status-related rationales trumped the importance and values related to academic and social-cultural purposes and benefits of higher education internationalization? (Bassett & Maldonaldo-Maldonaldo, 2014, p. 80)

If the answer is *yes, market values have trumped academic and altruistic purposes*, we might well be asking a far more fundamental question: who can save the university? And saving the university might itself take two contradictory forms: who can bring in more resources and compete in the 'status-related' marketplace vs. who can bring back the 'social-cultural' purpose of institutions that have drifted – or been forced – away from their scholarly mission?

Here precisely we come to the dilemma of management in international education. Demand for success in international recruitment aims toward one type of preparation, with much to be learned from the most sophisticated undergraduate (and graduate) admissions teams. Demand for comprehensive internationalization points toward another: an ability to rally disparate forces throughout the university in a single embrace of specific change in response to external reality. In this model, the peers of international educators would be senior diversity officers (SDOs). SIOs and SDOs both seek to reimagine management structures to align them both with the immediate needs of an institution (enrollment management; risk management; legal compliance; supplemental programming) and with the long-term adaptation of the institution's practice to its values (justice, knowledge, citizenship).

Conclusion

I conclude by pleading for a both/and model of forming young practitioners and identifying leaders in international education. My both/and conclusion allows me to accomplish three important things: bow respectfully to members of the profession who successfully made the leap from academic life to administrative roles or who may do so in the near future; rally those academic departments with graduate curricula aiming at university administration to keep the scholarly path wide and inviting for students; and urge aspiring SIOs to maintain their scholarly interest and commitment, whatever form they take.

Deep consideration of fraught issues is the right background for all forms of leadership in higher education. Equipping an entrant into this field with no more than the veneer of management techniques or management study will serve no one well. Fortunately, and thanks to the drive and determination of a generation that has thrived on technology and globalization and therefore seen its limits, students themselves are asking for the opportunity to explore the meaning in their experiences. However pragmatic and practitioner-oriented the rhetoric of experiential education may be, the underground force that nourishes it is the force of an exploration of meaning, both personal and social.

For example, MBA programs, under the downward pressure of a shrinking market for the degree and the upward pressure of the longings of the generation filling the graduate classroom, have increasingly turned to social entrepreneurship as a sister study to mergers and acquisitions. Why? Because students and young professionals want applied knowledge, but they want to apply it in a meaningful context. It is true as well of aspiring SIOs. They want to know the guts of internationalization, and they want to know how to steer their institutions away from the Scylla of financial harm and the Charybdis of social irrelevance. Without scholarly experience that enables them to seek out meaning behind the available data, young practitioners are sold a thin garment, in the guise of management skills, that will not last an institutional winter. Richard Bolden and colleagues at Exeter University in the UK stated the reality clearly when summarizing their research on academic leadership conducted across twenty-three institutions:

> [A]cademics respond to leadership that supports their values and identities. University managers who are anxious to encourage high levels of performance would be best to step back from mechanistic managerial approaches, and to emphasise instead the values associated with academic excellence. (Bolden et al, 2012, p. 44)

There is very good news here: SIOs are best selected from among those with ideas and the persistence to explore their ideas. SIOs are best selected from those who can put evidence together in a persuasive and well-supported form. And finally, SIOs who are committed to the pursuit of the social values of higher education as well as to responsible management will serve both masters better. Not only is it unnecessary for a leader in higher education to shed his or her personal or scholarly passion for a dispassionate managerial mask, it is against best practice. We who follow the path of the SIO role do best when we bring a scholar's devotion to a chosen aspect of our field (or any field) into play with the orientation of the entrepreneur and CEO.

References

Bassett, R. & Maldonado-Maldonado, A. (Eds) (2014) *The Forefront of International Higher Education: a festschrift in honor of Phillip G. Altbach.* Dordrecht: Springer.

Bolden, R., Gosling, J., O'Brien, A., et al (2012) *Academic Leadership: changing conceptions, identities and experiences in UK higher education.* London: Leadership Foundation for Higher Education & Exeter University.

Deardorff, D., Heyl, J., De Wit, H. & Adams, A. (Eds) (2012) *The SAGE Handbook of International Education.* Thousand Oaks, CA: SAGE.

Harvey, L. & Newton, J. (2007) Transforming Quality Evaluation: moving on, in D. Westerheidjen, B. Stensaker & M.J. Rosa (Eds) *Quality Assurance in Higher Education: trends in regulation, translation and transformation.* Dordrecht: Springer. http://dx.doi.org/10.1007/978-1-4020-6012-0_9

Streitwieser, Bernhard (Ed.) (2014) *Internationalisation of Higher Education and Global Mobility.* Oxford: Symposium Books.

Whitehead, Dawn Michelle (2015) Liberal Education, *Association of American Colleges and Universities*, 1(3) (Summer). http://www.aacu.org/liberaleducation/2015/summer/whitehead

CHAPTER 6

The Education Abroad Practitioner as Transdisciplinary Scholar

GISELDA BEAUDIN & LOUIS BERENDS

SUMMARY A transdisciplinary approach seeks to address complex global problems through dialogue and synthesis between and beyond disciplines. This in-between space represents the potentiality of transformation and can become a focal point for societal, cultural or pedagogical change. Education abroad practitioners in the United States are uniquely situated in a transdisciplinary space between practice and scholarship, and internal and external constituencies. Some practitioners, or rather scholar-practitioners, take advantage of this ambiguous role and actively produce scholarship while still engaging in the practice of education abroad. Since education abroad is itself transdisciplinary and much of the work is academic in nature, education abroad scholar-practitioners (EASPs) are extremely well positioned to steward the field of education abroad, develop lasting relationships with faculty and external partners, and imagine new solutions to evolving issues. However, there are many complex barriers preventing practitioners from becoming and remaining EASPs, from limited resources to limited venues for scholarship. Despite these challenges the EASP is perfectly positioned to thrive in spaces of transdisciplinarity and be a conduit between academic and administrative silos. This chapter argues that given the power inherent in a transdisciplinary approach, more education abroad practitioners should be encouraged and supported to become and remain education abroad scholar-practitioners.

The traditional structure of higher education in the United States discourages integrative approaches to teaching, research and learning (AAC&U, 2002, p. 16). Faculty are trained in discrete disciplines, and scholarship that challenges the borders between disciplines is often met with suspicion or with vigorous academic counterarguments. However, there are scholars and organizations advocating for a more transdisciplinary approach to scholarship, learning and teaching (AAC&U, 2002; Weld & Trainer, 2007; Brint et al, 2008; Jacob, 2015). A transdisciplinary approach seeks to address complex global problems through dialogue and synthesis between and beyond disciplines. 'It [transdisciplinarity] occasions the emergence of new data and new interactions from out of the encounter between disciplines ... [It] aims to open all disciplines to that which they share and to that which lies beyond them' (Nicolescu, 2002, p. 149). Transdisciplinarity is distinct from interdisciplinarity, which also draws connections and synthesizes knowledge from disparate fields, but does not disrupt the borders delineating academic silos or create the potential for new, integrated approaches. This difference is important since a transdisciplinary approach is situated in a space of liminality. First used by anthropologists to describe the moment or space in the middle of a ritual or process, the term 'liminal' describes any ambiguous space that is neither beginning nor end. This in-between space represents the potentiality of transformation. The concept of liminality has also been explored by critical theorists such as Elizabeth Grosz and Deleuze and Guattari (Deleuze & Guattari, 1987; Grosz, 1995). In their constructs, the liminal becomes a focal point for societal, cultural or even ontological change. Being in-between allows for transformation in a way that fixed and defined spaces do not. Thus transdisciplinarity, which occurs in the liminal spaces between and beyond disciplines, is crucial – only in the in-between can we find the space to imagine new solutions and create new pedagogies. If institutions expect to prepare successful and engaged citizens as many claim to do (Connecticut College, 2004; Rollins College, 2014), then a transdisciplinary approach is necessary. Scholar-practitioners working in education abroad (EA) are uniquely positioned to model this collective and transdisciplinary responsibility for student learning and development.

The Education Abroad Practitioner
vs. the Education Abroad Scholar-Practitioner

The education abroad practitioner (EAP) is any person working in the setting of international higher education who is associated in some way with outgoing international activities of students, staff and/or faculty. EAPs work in higher education in many different stages of their careers and in numerous settings that range from entry-level to senior international officers (SIOs), and from community colleges and other post-secondary institutions to third-party provider organizations.

As shown in Figure 1, EAPs, while normally situated within the domain of the practitioner or professional, are also uniquely positioned between and among a range of interrelated constituencies, both internal and external, and professional and academic. EAPs work with internal constituencies across the campus or organization and must be fluent in the 'languages' of faculty, administrators, professional staff, and students.

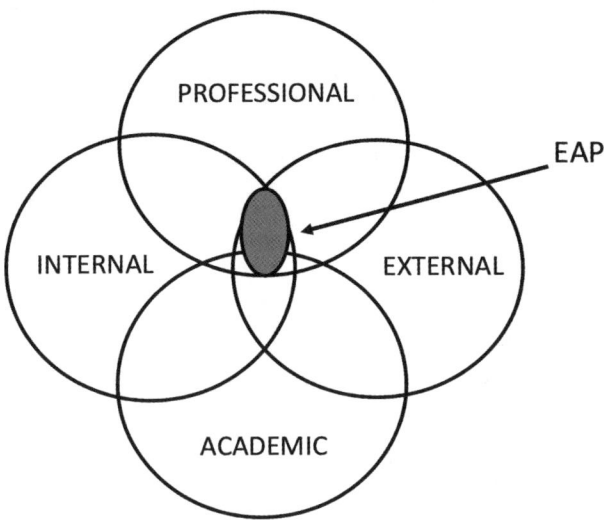

Figure 1. The placement of the education abroad practitioner (EAP).

Meanwhile, EAPs are continually navigating the external environment of collaborations with exchange partners, providers, and governmental and non-governmental organizations. While most of these relationships are about academic programs, interactions between an institution and an education abroad organization are often funneled through representative or liaison communications that simultaneously address the administrative activities and policy side while also incorporating more academic components. EAPs also work in academic spaces – that is, with their faculty colleagues and within academic affairs, both internally and externally. Faculty remain critically important and are central constituents for education abroad advocacy and all the practices, policies and procedures therein. In addition, EAPs must work in professional or practitioner spaces, with staff who are internal colleagues and with colleagues in the professional community of EA that spans many organizations and intellectual boundaries (i.e. NAFSA, the Forum on Education Abroad, the Association of International Education Administrators, etc.). As Figure 1 demonstrates, there is an overlap of academic and professional, both externally and internally (a scholar who works for a third-party provider or an on-campus staff member who also teaches). The EAP is perpetually between spaces, in the nexus between these overlapping spheres, straddling multiple boundaries, designations and responsibilities.

Although all EAPs are working to varying degrees in a transdisciplinary way and across numerous sectors of education abroad, they may have little to no knowledge of their value as both practitioner *and* scholar and may self-identify as one or the other depending on their background and awareness of themselves. While EAPs may inherently interact with the academic and scholarly aspects of education abroad, they are not as fully aware of their scope, influence and positionality, and do not engage in scholarly work. For EAPs to truly function as education abroad scholar-practitioners (EASPs) they must actively engage in academic spaces to imagine new solutions and creative alternatives within the practitioner platform.

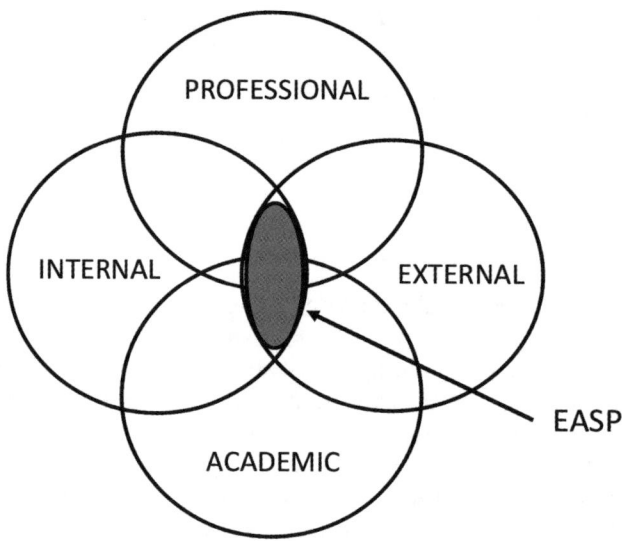

Figure 2. The placement of the education abroad scholar-practitioner (EASP).

An EASP can be any individual who works in US higher education and education abroad programming and services, but also actively and consciously straddles the divide between a practitioner and a scholar. The daily job functions of both EAPs and EASPs generally entail working closely with students, staff and/or faculty throughout the academic year for any activities and policies that relate to activities abroad. However, while the EAP works within academic spaces, as Figure 1 illustrates, the EASP works not just in academic spaces but as an academic or scholar (see Figure 2). Unlike the EAP, the EASP regularly engages with academic scholarship (research, writing, presenting) in addition to practicing within the field of EA. For example, the EASP may teach, advise and/or conduct research outside his/her daily administrative roles and responsibilities. An EASP does not need to hold an advanced degree, but is rather a person who can be categorized by the roles and responsibilities of working in the complex, dynamic and multi-faceted field of EA. In addition, the academic work of the EASP is often itself transdisciplinary since it draws both from academic knowledge in one or more fields and from the experience of working in EA.

The Case for the EASP

EA is inherently transdisciplinary, both an academic discipline and a professional field, combining traits of both kinds of thinking and doing and in the process embracing its own form of praxis. Successful EASPs must be able to understand and impact student learning in and out of the classroom, while still managing the logistics of complex programs, mitigating risk, overseeing staff, and establishing policies and procedures to support student mobility. EA involves both traditional academic learning (i.e. classroom based with faculty) and experiential learning, and EASPs must be able to understand, engage with, and impact both kinds of learning. In other words, EASPs must be able to function in a transdisciplinary space. In addition, knowledge of current education abroad and related scholarship is crucial to enacting best practices and impacting student learning – both of which EASPs need in order to justify and explain their practice.

EASPs must work successfully with a wide variety of faculty, whose perspectives on EA can vary greatly even within a single college or university. The EASP is well positioned to engage in critical conversations around how education abroad is (or should be) envisioned, implemented and/or revamped. Nationally, the increase in faculty-directed programs and short-term programs appears to be significantly correlated and the EASP should be a key player when navigating logistical and academic considerations that may involve curriculum integration, independent research and other significant academic components and projects. A successful EASP must develop longstanding relationships with faculty and with academic departments since faculty, unlike staff and even higher administration, are typically the most static constituency on campus. Clearly, an EASP with experience working in the academic sphere (teaching, research, presentations, writing, etc.) will be more effective in building these critical relationships both internally and externally.

How external college and university partnerships thrive (or flounder) in the nebulous space that is the transdisciplinarity in international higher education is a particularly interesting question given the growth of third-party providers and non-institutional organizations that produce or engage in academic teaching, writing and research. While nothing new, collaborations and partnerships between US higher education institutions and third-party providers and exchange partners for the purposes of expanding education abroad programming are fluid processes, and increasingly so with a 'marketplace' that continues to shift and expand. Given the complexity of higher education, coupled with institutional norms that impact education abroad policy on the subjective level, EASPs are well prepared to interact and collaborate with providers and exchange partners while navigating their own, seemingly in-flux, US host institutions. EASPs can navigate this successfully within a specific organizational structure, culture and leadership approach because they are used to functioning in nebulous places. Furthermore, EASPs can develop and articulate an EA strategic vision that requires relationship and partnership building across administrative and academic boundaries.

The growth in the number of non-traditional education abroad experiences (Institute of International Education, 2014) including internships, service-learning and research also emphasizes the transdisciplinary. These forms of experiential learning resist categorization into a particular academic field and are not always credit-bearing. While an internship or research project might be focused on one field, the work requires mobility: students engaged in such initiatives are expected to synthesize knowledge and skills from a range of fields and experiences. Such experiences are considered high-impact practices: they enhance student learning and development (Kuh, 2008), and they emphasize the importance of the transdisciplinary by mimicking real-world experiences where knowledge and skills are not organized into discrete units. Higher education institutions that have a long history of service-learning (the University of Michigan and Cornell University, for example) have documented the impact of such programs on students and the communities in which they operate (Kiely, 2005). This is true as well of institutions that focus on credit-bearing programs that involve student research, such as the School for International Training (SIT) and the School for Field Studies (SFS). Such institutions have always considered experiential learning academic, regardless of the associated credit. EASPs engage in this same kind of experiential transdisciplinary learning: experiences in daily practice impact scholarship, which changes practice, and generates further critical inquiry and research. This means that the EASP understands the value of both kinds of learning and can build both into programs and strategic plans.

Regardless of the program type, students abroad are expected to learn across borders; that is, students on an engineering program in China are expected not only to learn the content relevant to the course, but also to learn about Chinese culture, to reflect on their own identity and culture, perhaps even to develop skills such as cross-cultural communication, resiliency and confidence. In addition, education abroad programs might be co-led by faculty from different departments or by faculty from departments distinct from the students on the program, who may also represent a multi-disciplinary group. There is an inherent breakdown of borders in the process of student learning abroad. Education abroad students will hopefully venture into contact zones during their time abroad, liminal spaces where they will encounter others in genuine ways, be displaced from the familiar and therefore able to learn more, to transform. EASPs, who speak from their own experience in the liminal, expect their students to step off the colonial veranda (Ogden, 2007-08) and learn from being in-between.

In order to engage fully with different constituencies and best support the complex territories of education abroad programs, partnerships and learning, EASPs must engage in similar trans-academic/professional relationships and behaviors. An EASP must draw from a range of knowledge and experiences and venture outside specific disciplinary territories in order to be successful. EASPs should explore liminal spaces and be challenged to do work that feels unfamiliar, work that pushes at disciplinary boundaries and breaks down the false dichotomy between the professional and the academic.

Becoming an EASP

Despite the fact that the EAP is situated in a transdisciplinary space and EA itself is a transdisciplinary endeavor, there are significant challenges preventing EAPs from becoming and remaining EASPs. First and foremost, the professionalization of the field of international education (IE) has a complex impact on EAPs and EASPs. IE professionals currently in the field for 15 to 20 years entered the field through numerous channels – namely, through academic appointments or, in many cases, via the Peace Corps. Over the course of the past twenty years, there has been an exponential growth in the number of US-based master's and doctoral graduate programs that focus on international education in some capacity (Dessoff, 2006). While some programs may be more entrenched in theoretical foundations (history, philosophy, and/or sociology of education) and require a thesis, dissertation or capstone project, others are increasingly catering to real-world experiences and require an internship or practicum. Meanwhile, Doctor of Education (EdD) programs cater to the scholar-practitioner specifically in order to bridge the divide between academic and professional work. Additionally, the number of graduate programs in comparative and international education (CIE) can be measured by the content and sheer number of introductory courses being taught around the United States and abroad (Wiseman & Matherly, 2009). Holding a master's degree in IE (or a related field) is increasingly a minimum requirement for entry-level positions. Eighty-one percent of senior international officers (SIOs) hold PhDs (Kwai, 2015) and many such SIO positions require a terminal degree. This places IE graduate programs in a unique position to prepare the next generation of professionals within the competitive landscape of international graduate higher education. Furthermore, it brings to the fore the importance of training a rising generation of scholar-practitioners with the transdisciplinary skill set that is pivotal to the growth and sustainability of the IE field and practice.

These changes could bring a diverse set of practitioners to the field – with varied backgrounds and a range of degrees – and might enhance the transdisciplinary practice of EA and increase the number of EASPs working within the field. On the other hand, the focus on graduate programs in IE or related fields could narrow the diversity of EAPs and reduce the possibilities for transdisciplinary growth and innovation. The emphasis in some programs on practice has already resulted in more EAPs, whose experience creating scholarly work is limited. This then may reduce the common ground among and between practitioners or push the field of EA away from scholarship and toward the practice or professional aspects of the field.

The second challenge preventing EAPs from becoming or remaining EASPs is that many EA offices are understaffed and/or lack resources. Most practitioners have limited time in their schedules to devote to scholarship and even finding time to read publications or attend conferences (and attend sessions instead of meetings!) can be difficult. Getting students out and back safely and successfully is the non-negotiable work of an EA office, which means that scholarship for most practitioners must be squeezed in around the edges of a full-time position. With the pressure to increase numbers of students going abroad and concerns about liability driving any student travel, including student organizations, athletic trips and service-learning, toward the EA office, the workload for most practitioners has been on the rise. Many EAPs are thus tasked with managing the seemingly expansive landscape of volunteer and or service-based opportunities abroad. Overseeing such non-credit-bearing programs also convolutes the role of the EAP since it moves the EA office further away from the purely academic. In the end, many EASPs engage in scholarship outside of their normal workload and hours, which not everyone is able, expected, or encouraged to do.

Also complicating the issue for many practitioners is the traditional divide on most campuses between faculty and staff. While faculty must be engaged in scholarship, staff are not expected to be scholars. The exception to this is, of course, faculty who serve in administrative roles within EA, but even in these cases, either the faculty member remains a scholar and is not very involved with the daily ('practitioner') work of EA or the expectation for active scholarship is reduced due to the administrative responsibilities. The same is true of EASPs with PhDs who, despite their scholarly credentials, are expected to function primarily as a practitioner. As suggested above, some EAPs have not had much opportunity to produce scholarship during graduate school.

Additionally, the particular leadership and management style at the specific institution or organization can also pose significant challenges for the EAP striving to become an EASP. Many institutions lack a clear strategy for internationalization and/or may have decentralized international structures. This can result in limited resources for the EAP, further divides between the EAP and faculty engaged in internationalization, and lack of knowledge about the work of EA and its unique transdisciplinary nature.

Another challenge lies in the limited spaces for presentation and publication available to EASPs. While there are the several aforementioned professional organizations for international education, the format of many conferences sponsored by these organizations tends to put the focus on practical needs (i.e. meetings with exchange partners and third-party providers) and practice (i.e. sessions about types of programs, assessment methods, working with millennial students, etc.). The professional role of EASPs in the NAFSA context most certainly aligns with the education abroad knowledge community (KC), but also increasingly so with the teaching, learning and scholarship KC. The Forum on Education Abroad appears to be gaining in popularity, particularly among EASPs, as indicated by the growth in attendance over the past five years and the application of theoretical framing within many sessions that expands professional development for the EASP. Less popular within the EA US-based community are the more academic organizations such as the Comparative and International Education Society (CIES), the Association for the Study of Higher Education (ASHE) and the American Educational Research Association (AERA). While CIES has many opportunities for the EASP community to engage – namely, through the Higher Education Special Interest Group (the second-largest special interest group [SIG]) – there appears to be limited awareness of CIES resources among the vast majority of EASPs and hence a divide between the scholar and practitioner communities. Adding to this challenge are the limited resources available at many institutions for travel to conferences. For practitioners who cannot travel, the spaces for scholarly engagement are reduced to the few publications in the field. To combat these challenges, all professional organizations related to international education should examine issues related to education abroad and consider expanding options and spaces for meaningful professional and academic engagement in a strategic, collaborative and inclusive way that is in touch with the EASP roles and responsibilities.

Conclusion

Ultimately, since education abroad practitioners work in a liminal space between the academic and the professional, and education abroad is itself inherently transdisciplinary, it is imperative that more practitioners become aware of their scholarly intersections: that education abroad practitioners become education abroad scholar-practitioners. Education abroad has the potential to model a different approach to higher education, an approach that dismantles the structures of academic fields and recognizes that the most impactful learning happens in the intangible in-between. Education abroad scholar-practitioners could model for their colleagues and their students a transdisciplinary way of thinking *and* doing. This shift will only occur if more practitioners are empowered and given the opportunity to become scholars, and if more scholar-practitioners are recognized and rewarded for their roles within higher and international education internally, on campuses and in organizations, and externally, particularly in professional organizations and publications. As scholar-practitioners ourselves, we must work together to create spaces where practice and theory muddle in a mix of disciplines and where the transdisciplinary holds sway.

References

American Association of Colleges and Universities (AAC&U) (2002) *Greater Expectations: a new vision for learning as a nation goes to college.* Washington, DC: American Association of Colleges and Universities.

Brint, S.G., Turk-Bicakci, L., Proctor, K. & Murphy, S.P. (2008) Expanding the Social Frame of Knowledge: interdisciplinary degree-granting fields in American colleges and universities, 1975-2000, *Review of Higher Education*, 32(2), 155-183. http://dx.doi.org/10.1353/rhe.0.0042

Connecticut College (2004) Mission Statement. https://www.conncoll.edu/at-a-glance/mission–values/

Deleuze, G. & Guattari, F. (1987) *A Thousand Plateaus: capitalism and schizophrenia*, trans. B. Massumi. Minneapolis: University of Minnesota Press.

Dessoff, A. (2006) A Key to your Career? Master's Degrees, *International Educator*, January-February. Washington, DC: NAFSA: Association of International Educators.

Grosz, E. (1995) *Space, Time and Perversion*. New York: Routledge.

Institute of International Education (2014) Non-credit Work, Internships, and Volunteering Abroad, 2011/12-2012/13. Open Doors Report on International Educational Exchange. http://www.iie.org/opendoors.

Jacob, J.W. (2015) Interdisciplinary Trends in Higher Education, *Palgrave Communications*, 1. http://dx.doi.org/10.1057/palcomms.2015.1

Kiely, R. (2005) A Transformative Learning Model for Service-learning: a longitudinal case study, *Michigan Journal of Community Service Learning*, 12(1), 5-22.

Kuh, G.D. (2008) *High-impact Educational Practices: what they are, who has access to them, and why they matter*. Washington, DC: American Association of Colleges and Universities.

Kwai, C.K. (2015) A Survey on Senior International Officers, their Institutions and Offices. Association of International Education Administrators (AIEA) Annual Conference, Washington, DC, February.

Nicolescu, B. (2002) *The Manifesto of Transdisciplinarity*, trans. K. Voss. Albany: State University of New York Press.

Ogden, A. (2007-08) The View from the Veranda: understanding today's colonial student, *Frontiers: The Interdisciplinary Journal of Study Abroad*, 15, 35-55.

Rollins College (2014) Mission Statement. http://www.rollins.edu/about-rollins/mission/index.html

Weld, J. & Trainer, J. (2007) A Faculty Interdisciplinary Institute as Liberator from Stifling Disciplinary Mythology, *College Teaching*, 55(4), 157-163. http://dx.doi.org/10.3200/CTCH.55.4.157-163

Wiseman, A.W. & Matherly, C. (2009) The Professionalization of Comparative and International Education: promises and problems, *Research in Comparative and International Education*, 4(4), 334-355. http://dx.doi.org/10.2304/rcie.2009.4.4.334

CHAPTER 7

Scholar-Practitioners and the ISSS Professional

DAVID B. AUSTELL

SUMMARY The scholar-practitioner is an ideal which is enormously difficult for the international student and scholar services (ISSS) professional to aspire to, even among those who have been trained as doctoral-level academics. There are many significant impediments which force research and writing to the end of the ISSS professional's priority list. Among these are impediments which go to the very heart of what it is to be an ISSS professional – how these talented individuals are perceived by their institutions and by the government of the United States, and how they are prepared, academically and professionally, for their tasks as ISSS practitioners. The work of ISSS professionals is intense, time-consuming and relentless. Approximately 90-95% of their work currently focuses on the arcana of federal immigration regulatory compliance, endeavors that occur within a politically charged homeland security environment that is entirely unforgiving of compliance mistakes. Despite their effectiveness in dealing with the multi-task frenzy of these work realities, ISSS professionals on the front lines of service provision have not often been able additionally to embrace the role of the scholar-practitioner in any systematically effective way reflective of a comprehensive ISSS research agenda. This chapter focuses on the work demands and challenges which often forestall the inclusion of 'scholar-practitioner' in the typical ISSS professional's job description. Perceptions and identities of ISSS professionals are examined to explore goodness-of-fit with the scholar-practitioner ideal. Factors that impede the development of ISSS professionals into scholar-practitioners are identified, and means of overcoming these impediments are presented.

Introduction

Professionals working in the area of international student and scholar services (ISSS) engage in a very high-stakes game. The skills required to be effective in this work are manifested (after long study and ongoing effective practice) in the ISSS professionals' *mastery* of complex federal visa regulations; their *apprehension* of myriad potential visa violations, non-compliances and simple human errors; their *application* of this knowledge base to the particular advising needs of international clients; their *creation* of transparent and accurate solutions to these challenges; the flawless *execution* of their work while remaining culturally sensitive international educators; and perhaps greatest of all, their *dedication* to their work's key context, the field of international education. Moreover, *all* of these endeavors occur within a politically charged homeland security environment that is entirely unforgiving of compliance mistakes. In reality, the work of ISSS professionals is intense, time-consuming and relentless; approximately 90-95% of their work focuses on the arcana of federal immigration regulatory compliance.

Despite their effectiveness in dealing with the multi-task frenzy of these work realities, ISSS professionals on the front lines of service provision have not often been able to embrace the role of the scholar-practitioner, defined as 'a person who concurrently contributes to the field through research that leads to knowledge generation, and through active effective practice in the field' (Colwill, 2012), in any systematically effective way reflective of a comprehensive ISSS research agenda. It is clear that the role of the scholar-practitioner has gained enormous traction in professional life since its first appearance as the Vail model in 1973, and it has grown far beyond its initial context as a framework for practicing psychologists undergirding their practical work experiences with ongoing scholarly research. Whereas this model has effectively spread into many other academic and professional fields, and more recently into the highly specialized endeavors of international education, the sub-field of international student and scholar services has not yet widely embraced the role of scholar-practitioner among ISSS professionals. ISSS professionals are certainly not alone, since 'many fields … struggle with a gap between academic theory and professional practice' (Colwill, 2012). This is, however, particularly true in the ISSS environment where theory (such as it is) stems from an outmoded model of the ISSS professional which needs to be modernized in light of the realities of the new service model in the twenty-first century.

The scholar-practitioner is an ideal which is enormously difficult for ISSS professionals to aspire to, even among those practitioners who have been trained as doctoral-level academics (a fact which is often enormously frustrating to the individual). This is only in part due to the lack of an elusive will to write (addressed later in this chapter). More to the point are the many significant impediments which bump research and writing to the end of the ISSS professional's priority list. Among these are impediments which go to the very heart of what it is to be an ISSS professional; how these talented individuals are perceived by their institutions and by the government of the United States; and how they are prepared, academically and professionally, for their tasks as ISSS practitioners.

Despite significant challenges, ISSS professionals *must* embrace the role, identity and functions of the scholar-practitioner in order to address the current dearth of research regarding the ISSS work environment and the experiences and challenges of ISSS clients. It is the ISSS professional who is best able to identify potential research areas, whether technical or cultural, and address the subtleties of each. If ISSS professionals do not take on the role of the ISSS scholar-practitioner, then who will? The answer is *no one*, and ISSS-related research and generation of new knowledge in ISSS will simply not be done, to the detriment and impoverishment of the field. The gauntlet has been thrown down. ISSS professionals must now take it up.

International Student and Scholar Services: the current context

The ISSS professional is an anomalous creature in higher education. She does not fit neatly into student service professional paradigms, and she conducts her work in a fashion that is not closely paralleled in other types of academic administration. By rough analogy, her work is similar to that engaged in by university compliance specialists (for example, in deemed export control, or in the administration of federal contracts and grants) in its exhaustive attention to federal regulations. Moreover, the work is conducted within an overlay of intense cultural diversity present in the most diverse possible clientele, the university's international community of students, faculty and research scholars (a reality which is akin to the diversity-sensitive professional lives of student affairs personnel). Added to this is the overarching post-9/11 context of homeland security in which the federal government places increasingly strict compliance responsibilities on the institutions themselves related to the maintenance of visa statuses of international students and scholars (amounting essentially to ongoing unfunded federal mandates from the US Department of Homeland Security [USDHS]).

On campus, the ISSS professional is typically known as either an International *Student* Adviser, or an International *Faculty and Scholar* Adviser, or perhaps some combination of the two. The USDHS most often refers to the ISSS professional as a Designated School Official (DSO) – in other words, a university staff member who has been approved by the institution and by the USDHS to issue, sign and maintain international student visa documents, the I-20 (the visa application form for students entering the US in F-1 visa classification), and the DS-2019 (the J-1 visa application form issued by a Responsible Officer, or an Alternate Responsible Officer as designated by the US Department of State). There was a time prior to 9/11 when the typical ISSS professional engaged in both visa-related activities and programming activities supportive of students' acculturation and well-being, even developing programmatic opportunities for them to share stories and cultural information about their home countries. Especially among comprehensive research universities hosting large numbers of international students and scholars, this type of generalist is disappearing.

The huge majority of the ISSS professional's time, as much as 90-95% in large university settings, is now spent on institutional federal compliance requirements: immigration advising, the related processing of immigration documents, and the demands of reporting data essentially in real-time to the USDHS via the federal Student and Exchange Visitor Information System (SEVIS). Although programming is still carried out by ISSS professionals, the resulting programs are most often immigration/visa related. Cultural and acculturation programming has thus become a collaborative effort involving the international office, individual academic schools or departments, and professionals in the institution's student affairs division.

Institutionally, the professional 'status' of the ISSS professional is a *giddy thing*. In general, professional status derives from 'a set of philosophical assumptions, a specific body of knowledge, a code of ethics, a domain of concern, aspects of practice, and the use of legitimate tools' (Jebril, 2008, p. 35). This observation fits the anomalous ISSS professional very well. The philosophical assumption of the ISSS practitioner is firmly rooted in the vision of Senator William Fulbright (D/Arkansas) that international education increases cooperation among the peoples of the world (Fulbright, 2009). The specific body of knowledge is the ISSS practitioner's mastery of the arcana of federal immigration regulations; NAFSA: Association of International Educators provides a far-reaching Code of Ethics adhered to by ISSS professionals; the institutionally based communities of international students, faculty members and researchers comprise the domain of concern; highly complex standard operating procedures related to the many immigration processes which are the purview of ISSS practitioners constitute aspects of practice; and the US Code of Federal Regulations (especially volumes 8 and 22) and many other reference materials comprise the use of legitimate tools. Nonetheless, the status of the ISSS professional is quirky and rooted in identity and community perception, which are often at odds with each other (this is addressed more fully below).

In a perfect world, the status of the ISSS professional would be very high indeed, given the realities of the skill-sets and competencies required. For example, NAFSA recently published extensively detailed guidelines for the ISSS professional (NAFSA, 2015) covering scores of competencies spanning the minutiae of SEVIS regulatory compliance, 'glocal' advocacy, and complex and demanding communications with stakeholders (federal, state, city governments, campus community, surrounding community). In his now-classic volume, Gary Althen states:

> The [ISSS professional's] position is unique. While it is normally at a rather low level in the institutional hierarchy, it demands high levels of knowledge, sensitivity, judgement, tact, and operational effectiveness on the part of its incumbents. It is linked to nearly all parts of the educational institution, and ... is highly responsive to contemporary developments elsewhere in the country and around the world. [ISSS professionals] ... are often called upon to help foreign students make decisions that have lifelong implications.
> (Althen, 1983, p. 7)

In essence, ISSS professionals are gatekeepers who are given sufficient institutional authority to develop and maintain an immigration compliance program that is critical to the institution. Moreover, these gatekeepers monitor and implement changes in the federal regulations which are the constant reality of their work. ISSS gatekeepers are often the point persons for official governmental visits to campus from the US Immigration and Customs Enforcement (USICE) (and its Counterterrorism and Criminal Exploitation Unit, the CTCEU), as well as for visits from the FBI and other enforcement and intelligence agencies (Berger et al, 2015).

On a day-to-day basis, the post-9/11 professional life of the ISSS professional is stressful and intense. Since compliance with federal regulations dealing with the presence of international students and scholars is of key importance to the US Congress and, therefore, to USDHS and its sub-agency, the USICE, as well as to other enforcement agencies (e.g. the FBI), ISSS professionals have become the compliance focal points for the institution in all matters related to immigration concerns. Their actions have huge potential impact on individual internationals and on the institution as well. In short, ISSS professionals run with a fast and high-profile crowd, and engage in a business that constitutes very high institutional risk. The USDHS has continually demonstrated that, where international students and scholars are concerned, there is no margin of error related to visa compliance: USDHS has zero-tolerance for advising, processing and compliance errors. Moreover, there is essentially a lack of steady state in the regulatory world of the ISSS professional. Regulations change quickly and often (essentially, regulatory fluidity), and practitioners must master new regulatory language and develop new standard operating procedures supportive of the new regulations. Information must then be passed to their clientele who are often distressed, or, at the very least, concerned about the constancy of regulatory change. For the typical ISSS professional, the hours are long (nights and weekends are common) and remuneration is typically insufficient given the criticality of the work. It is small wonder that the role of ISSS scholar-practitioner is embraced so seldom among these talented and dedicated folk.

The ISSS Scholar-Practitioner: challenges and inhibitors

It is important to understand seven key challenges and inhibitors which commonly prevent ISSS professionals from embracing the role of the scholar-practitioner:

1. *Institutional perceptions of the ISSS professional's institutional role, and the ISSS professional's own perception of his role and identity.* In general, ISSS professionals are not trained as academics (though there are increasing numbers of PhDs surfacing in ISSS leadership), and they are not perceived as such by the academic community. This is exacerbated if ISSS professionals are institutionally located within the university's student affairs division. ISSS practitioners are most often seen institutionally as specialized administrators ('visa specialists'). This perception runs the gamut from positive and benevolent (ISSS practitioners as extremely skilled and sympathetic problem-solvers) to its very negative doppelgänger (the ISSS practitioner as bureaucrat, apparatchik and road-blocker). The 'mere administrator' perception has not been helped by the recent tendency, especially in the large research universities, for ISSS practitioners to focus almost entirely on federal immigration compliance, while other colleagues around campus focus on cultural and social programs for international students. In contrast, ISSS practitioners overall see themselves as *international educators*, 'globalists' who have an intense experiential simpatico with their student and scholar clients, and as masters of their technical duties related to federal compliance. ISSS practitioners generally do *not* see themselves as academics or researchers; and at the risk of being stereotypical, they are not hired by their institutions to be such; more often than not, research and academic writing is simply not a part of their job descriptions. Therefore, both the institutional perception and the personal perception of the ISSS practitioner's role are strong inhibitors of the scholar-practitioner persona among ISSS practitioners.

2. *The issue of prioritization in the context of an extremely time-consuming and work-intensive list of compliance priorities.* ISSS professionals work in a high-risk environment where a great deal is at stake – for example, the eligibility of the institution to continue importing internationals (and the associated potential loss of revenue) if an institution is federally sanctioned for egregious immigration violations; the continued presence of individual internationals who are meeting federal compliance requirements, and who are thus safe from USDHS criticism and related life disruptions; and even the personal livelihoods and career paths of clients and practitioners. Where can the

practitioner find time in an already frenetic and stressful workday to conduct research and write? Even among ISSS practitioners who are trained as academics, writing papers of any sort, much more so research and academic writing generated for publication, is very easily consigned to the bottom of the work pile. To illustrate, ISSS practitioners' desks can be seen as constantly 'on fire', with the practitioners putting out the hottest compliance blazes first. If an immigration crisis involving a VIP client, for example, constitutes solar fusion, then writing academic papers based on original research constitutes a walk in the garden in the cool of the day (and ISSS professionals are rarely at liberty to take such walks). A central question is thus exposed by this inhibitor: is there goodness-of-fit between the ISSS professional and the scholar-practitioner?

3. The lack of a systematic ISSS research agenda. The overall field of international education has embraced research and the generation of new knowledge in the field – for example, through the activities of NAFSA: Association of International Educators, and the Association of International Education Administrators (AIEA). In actual fact, however, research and writing in the ISSS sub-field has taken a back seat to research generated in other sub-fields – for example: comparative international education, the efficacy of study abroad, student life issues, global policy development, experiential/perceptual studies of foreign and domestic students engaging in international education activities, and the internationalization of the academic curriculum. These areas tend to have focused overall research agendas where research fuels even more research. Writing does appear in the ISSS sub-field, but its tendency (often of necessity) is toward the topic *du jour* – for example, abrupt and difficult changes in immigration regulations; emergencies involving visa issuance abroad; and crises related to homeland security concerns. Moreover, this type of writing is not always appropriate for peer-review journals. With no systematic research agenda set, ISSS scholar-practitioners, where they exist, will not engage in research writing so much as in journalism (important, but not the widest scope for the scholar-practitioner). In a review of literature and practice in the ISSS environment (spanning the years 1960 to 2014), Krishna Bista noted that 'there were only two books ... five research articles ... and nine doctoral dissertations ... that particularly focused on international student advising' (Bista, 2015). In the overall context of international education, ISSS-related research and writing appears fragmented, limited, ad hoc.

4. The lack of widespread research collaborations with other practitioners, academics government agencies and legal community for purposes of research and writing. Research and academic writing collaborations are performance based and demanding; they require commitment and time-sensitivity. The challenges of ISSS work priority directly affect the ability of an ISSS practitioner to face the demands of research.

5. *The lack of ISSS leadership in professional organizations articulating the development of a systematic ISSS research agenda as a critical need.* As a general rule, ISSS leaders in professional organizations have not stressed the criticality of research based on the development of a systematic research agenda.

6. *The lack of ISSS professionals trained as academic researchers and writers.* The great majority of ISSS professionals have completed bachelor's and master's degrees, the academic focuses of which are extremely diverse. JDs, PhDs and other terminal degrees are neither standard nor predominate in the ISSS sub-field. It is often the case that ISSS professionals, even having completed bachelor's and master's degrees, still do not possess the quantitative and qualitative skills needed to engage in original publishable research.

7. *The lack of a will to write.* A writer is not a writer *unless he writes.* As in any art, writing is an act of will. If the will to write has been abandoned, the scholar-practitioner latent in the ISSS professional will never surface. In part, this has to do with energy management. There *is* such a thing as too much work, and whipping a dead horse is no one's idea of fun. Simply 'adding on' the work of the scholar-practitioner is unwise and potentially harmful. ISSS professionals are not known for their acumen related to life-balance. Nonetheless, her best work cannot be done when the ISSS scholar-practitioner is exhausted and mired in the nights-and-weekends trap which will cause the will to write to vanish like vapor.

Meeting Challenges and Overcoming Inhibitors

Despite the sobering challenges which inhibit ISSS professionals from becoming ISSS scholar-practitioners, ISSS professionals *must* become adept in the research skills needed to generate new knowledge in the field, and must become pragmatic consumers of research in order to utilize newly generated knowledge informing and guiding ISSS best practices. There is no easy solution to the challenges and inhibitors identified above. The ISSS professional embracing the role of the scholar-practitioner operates in the constant presence of uncertainty in the endeavor. She might often wonder if the work is worth the effort; if it will actually add to the practical/professional lives of colleagues in the sub-field; if her skill-set is up to the task of writing for publication. Research guarantees neither publication nor audience. Essentially in this regard, the ISSS scholar-practitioner pursues knowledge production for its own sake with the optimistic hope that an audience will both surface and benefit from her efforts. These efforts need not be made by stumbling in the dark. Returning to the six skill-areas manifested by the effective

ISSS professional, guidance emerges related to the development of the ISSS scholar-practitioner.

1. Mastery. This characteristic is well known to the ISSS professional who masters the body of federal regulations governing the presence of international students and scholars in the United States. Going forward as a scholar-practitioner, she must further master: (a) *the existing literature* related to ISSS research in a general sense, and especially any research which might be of specific interest to her own research interests; (b) *the skill-set* required for generating publishable research (developing essential collaborations with professional, governmental and academic colleagues who have quantitative or qualitative skill-sets she might be lacking); and (c) *collaborative leadership skills and consensus-building* in order to develop an overall research agenda in the ISSS sub-field.

2. Apprehension. By engaging in the work of the scholar-practitioner, the ISSS professional apprehends (discerns) the inhibiting nature of perception – in other words, how his professional role is perceived by the campus community – and actively moves to change this perception; the 'mere administrator' or 'visa specialist' must be subsumed by the new ISSS persona of scholar-practitioner. Moreover, the ISSS scholar-practitioner apprehends the need for an overall research agenda, and perceives critical research questions within the context of this agenda – for example:

(a) Related to their work in federal immigration compliance, to what extent do ISSS professionals experience the following:

- Percentage of applications for immigration benefits approved by USDHS?
- Percentage of applications for immigration benefits denied by USDHS? What was the reason for the denial?
- Percentage of applications returned to the ISSS professional from USDHS with requests for additional support documentation (*request for evidence*, or RFE)? What specific type of additional information was requested in the RFE?
- Are there standards/best practices related to applications approved/denied/RFE'd?

(b) Since ISSS offices are increasingly consumed with tasks related to federal immigration compliance, to what degree are institutional divisions of student affairs beginning to offer specialized programs related to international students' acculturation needs while in the United States? What types of programs are being developed? How are program leaders/facilitators trained?

(c) To what degree are academic colleges or schools within universities (e.g. a School of Engineering, or a School of Business) beginning to offer specialized programs related to international students within the college/ school? What types of programs are being developed? How are program leaders/facilitators trained?

(d) To what degree are ISSS offices adopting the new service model inclusive of *inbound* immigration services, comprehensive *outbound* immigration services for anyone in the campus community traveling abroad under the auspices of the institution, *relocation* services for faculty members on assignment abroad, as well as tax and HR services related to global travel?

(e) How do international students adjust to life in the United States and to the academic life of their institutions? Are there best practices which assist with this process?

(f) What are the specific effects, positive and negative, of international student enclaves that are nationality based?

(g) How do international students from nations which are at odds with each other (e.g. Korea/China, Greek Cyprus/Turkish Cyprus, many African tribal 'nations') interact while present in US colleges and universities? Are there institutional opportunities for 'difficult conversations' and for effective and productive interactions and relationships to develop?

(h) To what extent do international students experience emotional difficulties while in the United States? What are the natures of these difficulties? Do the students make use of available counseling services? Are there significant differences among nationalities, gender, academic levels or age?

(i) US faculty members often struggle with how to best engage international students in their classes, especially when the students represent very different pedagogical backgrounds. Are there best practices related to academic engagement for international students? Are there significant differences among nationalities, gender, academic levels?

(j) What are specific difficulties experienced by American students who have international instructors or professors?

(k) What are specific difficulties experienced by international instructors/professors who have American students as well as a diverse mixture of other nationalities in their classes?

3. Application. ISSS professionals (aspiring scholar-practitioners) must apply their professional talents, expertise, experience and labor in pursuit of their research projects and the writing-up of results. Moreover, the ISSS scholar-practitioner must suggest applications of the research findings to specifics of ISSS professional life. To this end, the ISSS professional must be a regular *consumer* of research conducted in the ISSS field in order for the research to inform decision-making on the ground.

4. Creation. On one level, the creative process is a mystery. It is intertwined intimately with the Muse, with the divine spark, with inspiration. On another level, the creation (for example, of new knowledge) is a matter-of-fact and practical exercise that nonetheless requires reflection, solidifying of ideas, capturing these ideas whenever they emerge (essentially recorded in the form of field notes; a Moleskine notebook is a must-have at all times), fleshing out the initial ideas and concepts to researchable goals, and developing an appropriate project design.

5. Execution. In contrast with the neon-rush of face-time with the Muse (in the processes of creation), the execution of a project is perhaps the most mundane aspect of the work of the ISSS scholar-practitioner. It involves active discipline, dogged determination, and ongoing effort in often small increments forward which lead to the completion of a research project. Specifically, you cannot be a researcher unless you do the work of research; you cannot be an academic writer unless you write.

6. Dedication. For the ISSS professional, dedication to the ISSS sub-field of international education is a commonality. To be effective as an ISSS scholar-practitioner, therefore, this dedication must also be present in the activities of research and knowledge generation. Michael Smithee posits that this dedication is, in essence, a 'mindset' which manifests itself in two ways: (a) the determination to *personally* define, conduct, initiate and complete the research and writing; or (b) the decision to serve in less direct capacities – for example, sponsoring and supporting ISSS research; collaborating with faculty; and monitoring ISSS research as it is published (Smithee, 2015). In essence, the ISSS scholar-practitioner must have (or develop) a will to write that is patient but irrepressible. A corollary of this passionate dedication is commitment to the development of an ISSS comprehensive research agenda. Dedication is the heart of the ISSS scholar-practitioner, and is sine qua non.

Conclusion

Though difficult, the pursuit of scholar-practitioner objectives *must* be embraced in the ISSS professional context despite significant sloughs and pitfalls – for example, the potential for attention being taken away from the boots-on-the-ground daily operations of an ISSS office. Of critical importance: scholar-practitioners *must* be accommodated in their work, and space set aside in their workday for research and writing. This means there must be a commitment from supervisors (at whatever levels these might be) to the activities of the ISSS scholar-practitioner, the ultimate objective being the inclusion of 'scholar-practitioner' in the ISSS professional's job description, and the change of the ISSS professional profile to include the work of the scholar-practitioner. Pertinent to this are Choudaha and Streitwieser's comments on the assessment of campus internationalization and resources necessary to conduct such research:

> – Top-level campus leadership must provide the material and financial resources to substantively support their ... rhetoric. It is these campus leaders who must be engaged to the point where they can clearly designate and support offices and personnel tasked with clearly specified [research] duties.

> – The university's administrative cadre must create and foster real links between researchers and offices that coordinate study abroad and international student services. This level of support must be provided to assist in the substantive collection of data, their rigorous analysis and the reporting of results to upper management and faculty.

> – Designated international offices must, whenever possible, create incentives and support for personnel if they are tasked with collecting data and conducting analysis. If that is not possible, these offices must be given the funds they need to hire at least one person who is knowledgeable in assessment research. And lacking that, these offices need to be linked up with a faculty member trained in assessment and research who can partner with the office to assist in the collection and analysis of data. (Choudaha & Streitwieser, 2014)

It is also essential to understand that the world of the ISSS professional is changing rapidly, and this directly affects the development of a comprehensive ISSS research agenda and the work of the ISSS scholar-practitioner. Aside from the ever-shifting sands of immigration regulations and advances in technology, a sea change in the ISSS sub-field is currently under way which relates to the very nature of what it is to be an ISSS professional. Recent writings in the field (including the recent NAFSA professional competencies) are still rooted in the old-school model of ISSS professionals as generalists, part immigration adviser and part interculturalist. To the dismay of many in the field of international education, this model is frail and dying, a direct result of the increasing demands placed by the USDHS on colleges and universities related to compliance with strict immigration regulations governing the presence of internationals on their campuses. There is no turning back from this.

If the generalist model is sun-setting, what will replace it? A new service model is emerging which not only provides in-bound immigration services to international students, faculty members and research scholars, but also provides comprehensive *outbound* immigration services for all students, faculty members and staff traveling abroad under the auspices of the institution. This change is directly related to growing concerns related both to institutional liability and to the safety and security of persons traveling abroad for study and research. Outbound services are also beginning to include relocation services (potentially high-touch concierge services) for faculty members who have been assigned to academic activities abroad, as well as tax and HR services related to global travel. The new service model is gaining traction in the United States as a direct result of institutional concerns regarding due diligence. Therefore, the ISSS professional must add the emerging reality of sea change to the list of challenges faced by the ISSS scholar-practitioner. These challenges can, and must, be met so that the necessary evolution of ISSS professional to ISSS scholar-practitioner can occur.

References

Althen, Gary (1983) *The Handbook of Foreign Student Advising.* Yarmouth, ME: Intercultural Press.

Berger, Dan, DiStefano, James, Yale-Loehr, Stephen & French, Dahlia, with Dunne, Stephen (2015) Nine Key Concepts College Counsel Must Know About Immigration Law, *Bender's Immigration Bulletin*, 20, 679.

Bista, Krishna (2015) Roles of International Student Advisers: literature and practice in American higher education, *International Education*, April, p. 91.

Choudaha, Rahul & Streitwieser, Bernhard (2014) How Do We Assess the Impact of Internation-alization? In *University World News Global Edition*, 337 (3 October). http://www.universityworldnews.com/article.php?story= 20141002095714747&mode=print (accessed on 10 September 2015).

Colwill, Deborah (2012) *Educating the Scholar Practitioner in Organizational Development*, pp. 16-17. Charlotte: IAP.

Fulbright, J. William (2009) US Department of State. http://eca.state.gov/fulbright/about-fulbright/history/j-william-fulbright/j-william-fulbright-quotes

Jebril, M.Y. (2008) The Evolution and Measurement of Professional Identity. Unpublished doctoral dissertation, Texas Woman's University, Denton.

NAFSA: Association of International Educators (2015) International Education Professional Competencies, pp. 25-30. Washington, DC: NAFSA.

Smithee, Michael (2015) Research and the International Educator, pp. 3-4. https://smitheeassociates.wordpress.com/about (accessed on 10 August 2015).

CHAPTER 8

The Small/One-person Office: the challenge of being both practitioner and scholar

MANDY REINIG

SUMMARY In these ever-changing economic times it becomes challenging for those who manage small/one-person international education offices to keep pace with the increased demands being placed on them and to be both a practitioner and a scholar. Those leading small/one-person international education offices (here, defined as three full-time staff or fewer) may go by many titles; however, all of these individuals carry out a variety of duties that run the gamut of the international education field. One important objective of this chapter is to illustrate the vastness of the duties that are completed by one or a couple of people and how these duties impact their ability to be both a practitioner and a scholar. A recent study revealed that the majority of those managing their office have been given the title of director. However, they are not conducting research as part of their jobs. Instead they must turn their attention to completing the practitioner's tasks required to maintain the office's status quo. This has also resulted in a majority of the directors in small/one-person international education offices believing they are more practitioners than scholars. It is easy to assume that those leading international education offices would be able to be both practitioner and scholar. However, at this level the many challenges presented by working within a smaller environment, but having the same responsibilities as those working for larger organizations, mean that for most directors being a scholar is not easily within reach. However, this chapter ends with potential avenues the field can pursue to increase the role that the scholar plays within their career.

The Small/One-person Office: the challenge of being both practitioner and scholar

Within the field of international education many more professionals now work within a small or one-person office than in previous decades. Offices of this nature have proliferated recently, especially as a result of the expanded focus on increasing US study abroad numbers through initiatives like Generation Study Abroad (Generation Study Abroad, 2015) and the 100,000 Strong Initiatives (100,000 Strong China, 2015; 100,000 Strong Latin America, 2015). The greater focus on study abroad at the institutional level as a result of these initiatives has necessitated the creation of new study abroad and/or international education offices, including at the community college level (Hulstrand, 2011, p. 46). The current economic climate has also contributed to the proliferation of these types of offices for two reasons: (1) institutions have only been able to afford to hire one or a few people to manage the various duties that contribute to the successful administration of internationalization activities; and (2) they have faced budget cuts that result in cutting their staff to the point of being rendered small or one-person offices.

The international education professionals who facilitate and manage the day-to-day operations of these offices usually must do so under the constraints of limited resources, whether that be time, staffing, funding or other support, while at the same time attempting to meet their institutional and office goals. This situation grants them the privilege of being the ultimate practitioner by handling a variety of different aspects of the field, but in many cases gives them little time for scholarly pursuits. In this chapter I share the results of a study that illustrates the many hats that these professionals must wear, how they perceive their role, as well as the challenges they have in attempting to pursue scholarly endeavors while maintaining their regular practitioner duties within a small or one-person office.

Definitions

A 'small office' is defined as being three full-time staff or fewer. This definition comes from the author's experience working with smaller offices and appears to be the cut-off point for when a small office is no longer considered to be a small office but transitions to being a medium-sized office. Additionally, a 'one-person office' is simply that – one full-time person or part-time person. In reality, there are some institutions that have international offices staffed by part-time faculty or staff in which international education is only a percentage of their job. For example, 75% of their time is spent teaching, and 25% of their time is spent advising students on study abroad options. Another example would be a staff person who is 50% program coordinator for a particular major and is also 50% study abroad advisor. None of these situations are ideal, but for many institutions it is the only viable option given limited resources, campus buy-in and administrative support.

What Is in a Name and Who Are These Professionals?

Currently, there are no data available, beyond anecdotal, provided by any of the international education organizations or associations on the number of small/one-person offices in the United States or beyond. The Forum on Education Abroad routinely does a State of the Field Survey; however, this survey does not include information on the size of education abroad or international education offices (Forum on Education Abroad, 2014). The international education field acknowledges that these types of offices exist, and the prevailing impression is that there are quite a number of them, but no one has formally surveyed the field to determine how many actually exist. With this gap of knowledge in mind, a survey was developed, approved by the author's institutional review board, and sent out through all of the main international education organization and association networks, including NAFSA: Association of International Educators, AIEA (Association of International Education Administrators), EAIE (European Association of International Educators), and SECUSS-L (a listserv for education abroad professionals), asking heads of offices with three individuals or fewer, including themselves, for their assistance in collecting this information. The responses were kept anonymous and participation in the survey was voluntary.

Eighty-six individuals responded to the call for participants. There were five individuals who responded that they worked in offices of three or more people, so their responses were excluded from the final results. This left the total number of respondents for this survey at 81. The response rate for this survey is difficult to determine given that the actual number of small/one-person offices is unknown and the subscription to some of these networks and listservs totals in the thousands. However, many of these subscribers were not the target audience for this survey since they work for providers or institutions with four or more staff members. With this in mind, the author estimates that for SECUSS-L the actual target audience of the 7800 subscribers is most likely only about 1%; however, with AIEA's 817 subscribers the target audience estimate is much higher at 10% due to the fact that this group is comprised mostly of directors of international education offices. The NAFSA networks would be targeting exactly the same individuals as the above-named groups since the author targeted the International Education Leadership Network, which overlaps significantly with AIEA. For the EAIE LinkedIn group, this also goes to approximately 7400 members and the target audience for this would mostly likely only be about 1%. When all of this is added together, the response rate would be approximately 37%.

The results of the survey indicated that 51% of the respondents were true one-person offices while 34% were from two-person offices and 15% were from three-person offices. Participants were also asked if they served as the SIO (senior international officer) for their institution.

Sixty-five percent responded yes, 20% responded no, and 15% were not sure. These data demonstrate that the majority of individuals who manage their international education office at the small/one-person level also function as the SIO. Serving as an SIO would automatically add another dimension of responsibility to the international education professional role. It would also create another challenge in the quest to serve as both practitioner and scholar, given the additional duties the SIO role represents. These duties and the challenges they create in the pursuit of being a practitioner-scholar will be discussed later in this chapter.

It is a common notion in the international education field that titles vary across institutions and institutional types, and this situation was also the case among the respondents from this survey. A total of 61.5% held the title of director, 12% were a coordinator of a particular area, 5% were a manager of a particular area, 3.5% were an associate director, 3.5% were an advisor of a particular area, 2.5% were an associate dean, while 12% had another title that was not listed in the survey, such as registrar, assistant provost, executive director, etc. Director of a particular area or of international education seemed to be the preferred title for small/one-person offices, but a deeper analysis would need to be conducted to determine how these titles correlate to the exact office size and institutional type.

There has been a constant discussion within the field of international education as to whether a PhD is needed to advance or whether a master's degree will suffice (NAFSA, 2015c). The answer to this question is still unclear, but 52% of the respondents for this survey held a master's degree while 22% held a PhD or an EdD. Additionally, about 14% only had a bachelor's degree, and 12% either had a professional degree such as a JD, or an associate's degree. The level of education appears to be as varied as the job titles. Among the many tasks associated with a practitioner are student advising, program development, immigration oversight, student recruitment, etc. More advanced tasks may include contract negotiation, curriculum development, budget oversight, staff supervision and crisis management, to just name a few. The majority from the survey held a master's degree, which seems to indicate that a master's is sufficient and appropriate for the work that is done at the practitioner level within these settings (NAFSA, 2015c). Having a master's degree would also be sufficient to complete scholarly-level work since a PhD is not required to conduct research and many scholars in the field, such as the author herself, do not have a PhD and are able to conduct research projects and publish successfully.

One interesting data point from this survey was that 51.3% of the respondents were from private four-year institutions, 16.3% were from master's-level institutions, 11.3% were from associate institutions,

11.3% were from public four-year institutions, 8.8% were from research institutions and 1.3% were from special focus institutions, according to the Carnegie classification of institutions. Figure 1 illustrates this breakdown by institution type. It is particularly noteworthy that over 50% of the small/one-person offices appear to be at private four-year institutions. Unfortunately, the survey did not ask the size of the institution in terms of the number of students that attended, but being a private institution does suggest a different level of institutional structure and priority versus a public institution, which could be reflected back in the size of the international office.

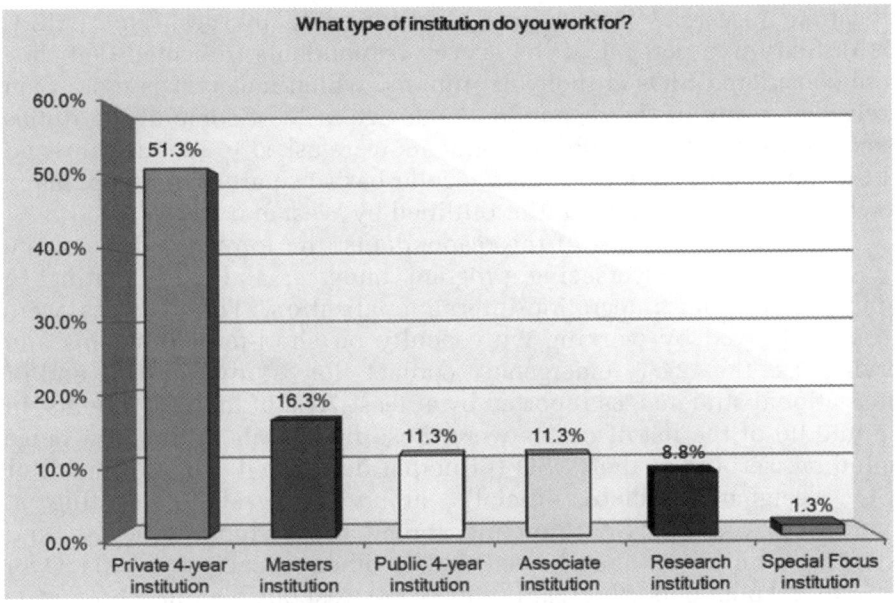

Figure 1. Small/one-person professional institution type.

The reporting structure for these respondents was just as diverse as their titles, with 33.5% reporting to a provost, 12.5% reporting to the dean of students, 14% reporting to a vice president, 10% reporting to the dean of faculty, 5% reporting directly to the president, and 25% reporting to a variety of administrators, including directors, deans and assistant/associate vice presidents.

The Many Hats in the Small/One-person Office and the Challenges to Being a Practitioner-scholar

Those who work in small/one-person offices are often not tied to simply one task such as advising students or writing I-20s. They become expert multitaskers and generally become a jack of all trades and must be knowledgeable of all aspects of international education within the scope of their job and even beyond. In her article in *International Educator* magazine, Charlotte West affectionately calls these positions 'Puzzle Masters' (West, 2014, p. 26). She also discusses the varying responsibilities for SIOs, including leadership of internationalization strategy and oversight of study abroad, international student and scholar services, international enrollment management, partnership relationships, and community programming, to name just a few (West, 2014, p. 30). AIEA also defines SIOs as having multiple areas of responsibility which could include education abroad, faculty exchange, international student admission, intensive English study, international education research, international institutional linkages, etc. (AIEA, 2015). Sixty-five percent of the survey respondents indicated that they were considered SIOs at their institutions, which means it is more than likely that many of the respondents manage at least some of the duties listed above; for this reason, respondents were asked to identify any and all the duties they performed on a regular basis as part of their job, many of which are similar to the duties outlined by West and AIEA.

As reported by 80% of the respondents, the top three duties were advising students, overseeing program budgets, and participating in campus curricular integration/internationalization. These duties were closely followed by working with faculty on short-term programs and serving as the 24/7 emergency contact for study abroad and/or international students, as reported by at least 70% of the respondents. In the middle of the list of duties were those which fall in the 60% range including: serving as the PDSO (principal designated school official) or DSO (designated school official), supervising staff, presenting at conferences like NAFSA, traveling abroad to conduct site visits, and attending admissions open houses and/or other on-campus events. Over 50% of respondents also said they were responsible for negotiating contracts. However, only 17% indicated that they conducted research as part of their regular duties. Figure 2 highlights all the responses received by participants.

A few of these daily duties align with the hats discussed in West's article (2014, p. 30) and with the areas outlined by AIEA's definition of an SIO (AIEA, 2015). However, most of these regular duties are on the practitioner level, whereas West's article and AIEA's definition view an SIO's duties from a more managerial perspective. For example, from this perspective, this person would oversee study abroad or international student services, but they would not probably advise students on a regular basis. However, as is observed in these data, even if the person managing the international office is the SIO, because they are working in a small/one-person office they are more likely to be operating at a micro level than other SIOs in the field. They are still responsible for oversight of their area(s), but are also in the trenches working directly with students and faculty, inputting I-20 information, responding to frantic parent phone calls, etc. In a small/one-person office, there are usually no additional staff members to whom to delegate these responsibilities. This is the biggest difference, and challenge, between small/one-person international education offices and more traditional offices.

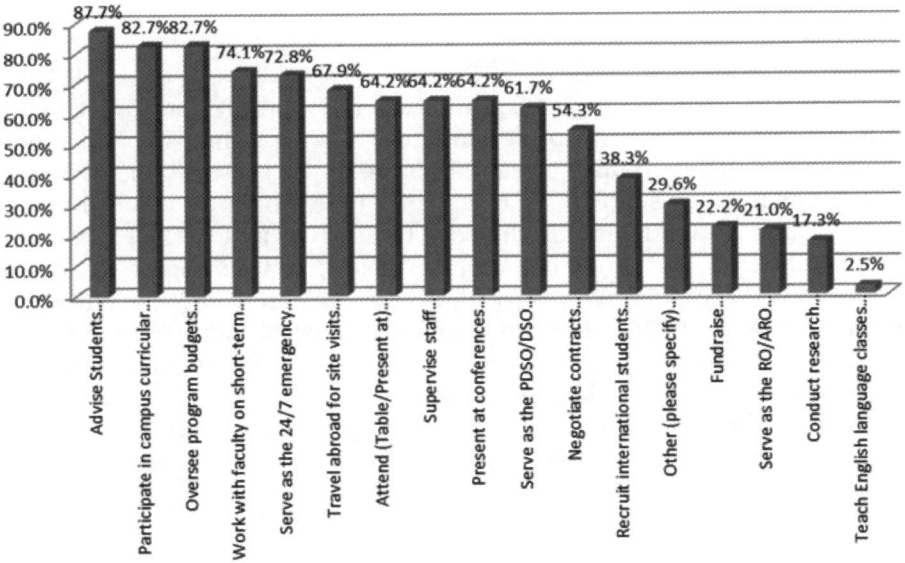

Figure 2. Small/one-person professional duties.

Another challenge faced by smaller offices is maintaining relationships on campus and beyond. As John Heyl reveals in his *IELeaders* article, SIOs must be able to multitask and be able to work with a highly diverse group of constituencies, maybe more so than, or equal to, the provost or even president (2015, para 1). Unfortunately, this survey does not show how many different areas of a campus an international office needs to work with, and for a small or one-person office this situation means that the burden to be the conduit between the different offices is down to just one person or one or two people. For example, not only does the director of the office advise the students on their chosen program, but he/she is also responsible for duties such as making sure the student gets billed properly for the program, being the 24/7 contact for emergencies, assessing each country's risk as situations occur, and acting as a counselor when mental health issues are exacerbated by the study abroad experience. Additionally, the director may have to prepare the faculty for what they may face while taking a group of students abroad or negotiate contracts for their partner programs. Some lesser-known duties include being a chauffeur and picking up international students as they arrive at the airport, taking students to the hospital when they become ill, serving as a travel agent to book group flights or a cell phone salesperson to purchase satellite phones for a short-term program. The list of duties is virtually unlimited in small/one-person offices, and there are additional hats that others do not think about and that are not often worn unless working in a small/one-person office.

Challenges to Doing Research

While this type of experience could be seen as a great opportunity for an international education professional to grow and expand their knowledge quickly, it does present an issue in the pursuit of being both a practitioner and a scholar. The current survey illustrates this point as only 25% of respondents said they did research as part of their job, while 75% indicated that they did not do research (see Figure 3 for an illustration). Of those who have done research, only 62% have either published or presented their research, and most of them have only had the opportunity to present it at international education–related conferences. For those who have done research but have not presented or published, the primary reason for not doing so was lack of time. Several mentioned in their comments that they were too busy with their daily tasks to focus on putting their research together for publication or presentation.

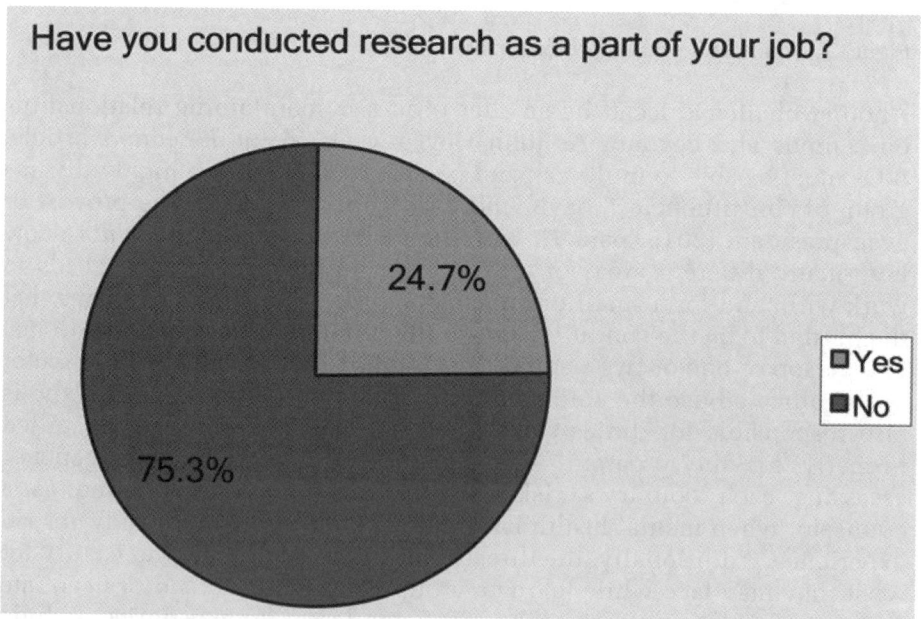

Figure 3. Small/one-person professionals conducting research.

If respondents replied that they were not doing research as part of their jobs, they were asked why they were not actively researching. As with why respondents were not publishing or presenting, the general consensus was that there was no time to do research. Almost all respondents gave this answer and suggested that the demand to keep up with their regular duties was more than they could handle at the moment. Additionally, and somewhat surprisingly, several respondents mentioned that doing research was not part of their job description and they did not feel that their administration would support them in conducting research. Furthermore, a few individuals indicated that they had no background in research methodologies, and thus did not feel comfortable conducting research.

There were a few individuals who were able to conduct research and able to present and/or publish on it, and most were able to do so due to their dual roles as faculty and staff. Most presented scholarly research in their academic area rather than in international education. The same could also be said for their publications. Approximately half of the publications were more in their previous and/ or current academic areas versus international education. In the end, it appears there were more faculty or previous faculty presentations/ publications with international themes than with international education themes.

The survey results suggest that most individuals who direct an international education office at the small or one-person level seem overwhelmed with their regular job duties and that conducting a research study would seem an almost impossible task given the lack of resources that they face. As the survey also illustrates, even if someone were to be able to conduct research, there is little time to complete the final step – publishing or presenting the findings. Only about 60% of those who conducted research had published or presented on it, and most who had chosen to present it had not actually published their research. The major factor behind the lack of research and the lack of publication and presentation is time. For someone who has been able to publish and present, most of that has been completed outside normal business hours and during the author's own time. For those working in small/one-person offices, the daily responsibilities at the practitioner level appear to be insurmountable obstacles to becoming a practitioner-scholar within the field.

What Am I? Practitioner? Scholar? Practitioner-scholar?

The daily tasks for individuals who serve in small or one-person offices may seem to be insurmountable obstacles to conducting their own research, but how do these individuals perceive themselves? Are they solely practitioners? Are they solely scholars? Or are they both practitioners and scholars?

The results of the survey indicated that 74% of respondents saw themselves as practitioners only, while 26% of respondents saw themselves as both a practitioner and a scholar. None of the respondents saw themselves as solely a scholar (see Figure 4). Each individual was then asked why they saw themselves in this way. The answers varied somewhat; however, the overwhelming response was that they had no time to do research and/or it was not part of their regular or required job duties. Other explanations given included the fact that they spent little to no time focused on research or even reading about international education-related issues and have no time to spend on other endeavors. Several individuals also indicated that they felt they were more of a practitioner because they were not faculty and/or they had no ties to the classroom. It is curious to note that some individuals related being a scholar to the requirement of being a faculty member and/or to that of being in the classroom. Being a scholar, in reality, does not really have much to do with being either of those things. It really has more to do with wanting to answer a question and having an inquisitive mind. Outside academia there are quite a few professions where individuals are doing research all day long and they have no ties to the classroom, to being a faculty member or to having a PhD. It is only in academia that we place so much emphasis on this. The nice part about academia is that there are quite a few people around who can assist with developing questions and analyzing the data so that one does not have to be an expert in assessment, which makes being a scholar a bit easier.

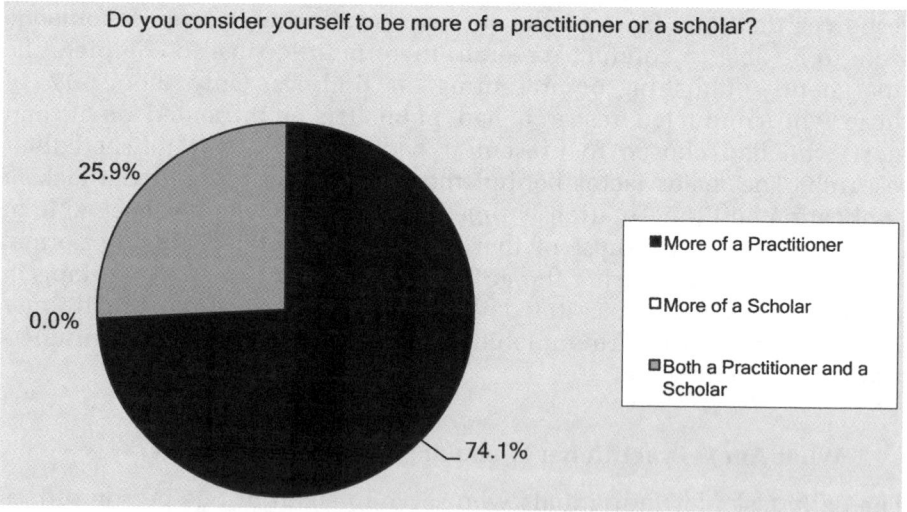

Figure 4. Practitioner or scholar?

For those individuals who felt they that were both practitioner and scholar, they believed so because they had been able to collaborate with faculty on their campus, they taught classes, or they were pursuing an advanced degree that required them to conduct scholarly research. Others stated that they stayed rooted in the scholarly literature, which made them feel like they were both a practitioner and a scholar. However, in the end, due to the demands that everyday tasks placed on the individuals who managed small or one-person offices, most respondents were unable to become practitioner-scholars. Even if they were able to conduct research, it seems as though most individuals in these settings would not have the time to publish or put together a presentation on the information they had gathered.

What Can Be Done?

The research in this chapter has demonstrated that professionals who manage/direct small/one-person international education offices often tend to be SIOs, generally have the title of director, hold at least a master's degree, and oversee several different aspects of international education. The majority of these individuals do not conduct research as part of their job and see themselves more as practitioners than as scholars or as practitioner-scholars. What, then, can the field do to aid these practitioners in their scholarly pursuits, should they so choose?

The solution is not to flood these small/one-person offices with funds or personnel so that they suddenly have time to conduct research, publish it and present it, even if there were such resources available. Instead it is better to create a culture of research first and demonstrate how relative easy it is to conduct, analyze and present/publish it. What can be done by the field is to offer educational opportunities at conferences, and online, to enable those who have never conducted research to learn more about research methodologies. Examples of such opportunities include Contreras, Odgen and Streitwieser's NAFSA webinar 'Education Abroad Research – Identify, Interpret, and Incorporate with Success' (Contreras et al, 2015) and NAFSA's in-person workshop 'Developing Basic Research Skills to Strengthen International Education Practices' (NAFSA, 2015a). Individuals interested in learning more can also reach out to NAFSA's Teaching, Learning, and Scholarship Knowledge Community (NAFSA, 2015b) and/or the Forum on Education Abroad's Data Committee (Forum on Education Abroad, 2015), which both provide sessions at their annual conferences and resources on their respective websites. Additionally, the international education field can provide training for scholars on how to present their research to practitioners in a way that makes the research they have conducted more appealing to practitioners, which would potentially encourage more practitioners to become involved in research activities and partner with international education scholars and practitioner-scholars.

Other means of encouraging scholarly work is to provide training on how to partner with faculty and other departments on their home campus so the idea of research and the task of conducting research do not seem as daunting or as time consuming. As one of the main reasons most do not conduct research is lack of time, practitioners need to be shown that conducting research does not need to be a time-intensive task. Furthermore, they can be shown how to collaborate with already existing resources on campus, such as their institutional research department, to make developing surveys and analyzing data easier. Other institutional ideas can also be found in Choudaha and Streitwieser's 2014 article 'How Do We Assess the Impact of Internationalisation?'

In an ideal world all international educators would be practitioner-scholars. As the field continues to gain additional credibility, hopefully the opportunities for individuals from small/one-person offices to pursue scholarly activities will grow as well. The importance of data and scholarly work in higher education continues to grow, and with the current economic trends at many institutions it will become even more important for international education professionals to be able to demonstrate that their programs are meeting or exceeding the needs of their institution. Small/one-person offices will soon no longer be able to use the 'excuse' that they have no time to conduct research. As anyone who works in on a small/one-person office knows, time is but an arbitrary concept and priorities can shift. It is, therefore, important to be ahead of the changing trends, especially one as important as this. Many have become expert practitioners, but now is the time to become expert practitioner-scholars.

References

100,000 Strong China (2015) http://100kstrong.org/study-in-china/

100,000 Strong Latin America (2015) http://www.state.gov/p/wha/rt/100k/

Association of International Education Administrators (AIEA) (2015) What is an SIO? Association of International Education Administrators. http://www.aieaworld.org/sio

Choudaha, R. & Streitwieser, B. (2014) How Do We Assess the Impact of Internationalisation? *University World News.* http://www.universityworldnews.com/article.php?story=20141002095714747

Contreras, E., Odgen A. & Streitwieser, B. (2015) Education Abroad Research – Identify, Interpret, and Incorporate with Success. *NAFSA: Association of International Educators.* http://www.nafsa.org/Attend_Events/Online/Webinars/Education_Abroad_R

esearch_%E2%80%93_Identify,_Interpret,_and_Incorporate_With_Success//
?impid=hp:may15_webinar:verthi_1_link:jw_2015_04_24

Forum on Education Abroad (2014) State of the Field Survey Report.
http://www.forumea.org/wp-content/uploads/2014/10/ForumEA-State-of-the-Field-Report-2013.pdf

Forum on Education Abroad (2015) Data Committee.
http://www.forumea.org/get-involved/committees-working-groups/data-committee

Generation Study Abroad (2015) http://www.iie.org/Programs/Generation-Study-Abroad

Heyl, J. (2015) When SIOs Multitask – REALLY Multitask! *IELeaders.net.*
http://www.ieleaders.net/archive.html

Hulstrand, J. (2011) Developing Education Abroad at Community Colleges,
International Educator, XX(5), 46-49.

NAFSA (2015a) Developing Basic Research Skills to Strengthen International
Education Practices. http://www.nafsa.org/Attend_Events/In-Person/Workshops/Developing_Basic_Research_Skills_to_Strengthen_International_Education_Practices/

NAFSA (2015b) Teaching, Learning, and Scholarship Knowledge Community.
http://www.nafsa.org/Content.aspx?id=5251

NAFSA (2015c) Transitions, Trends, and Tips: a conversation. *NAFSA's EA
Resources.*
http://www.nafsa.org/Find_Resources/Supporting_Study_Abroad/Transitions,_Trends,_and_Tips__A_Conversation/

West, C. (2014) Puzzle Masters, *International Educator*, XXIII(1), 26-31.

CHAPTER 9

Studying Community Colleges: administrator, practitioner and scholar voices promoting international education

ROSALIND LATINER RABY

SUMMARY International education at community colleges includes reflections on practice, application of theory, and use of assessment to confirm findings. This combination profiles a diversity that challenges a stereotype of community colleges as being solely practitioner oriented. A focus on author lived experiences illustrates a wide range of voices that have, and that continue to, set the tone that advances discourse on community college internationalization efforts. The combination of scholars, practitioners and others who have published on community college internationalization, and who continue to do so, epitomizes a new form of scholarship. The authors of these publications include a combination of senior administrators who are not involved in international program management, practitioners who are involved in international program management, university faculty and graduate students who have former employment with community colleges, and representatives of national and non-profit organizations. Together, this range of voices illustrates how theory is used to inspire practice which anchors advocacy for change as these individuals work together to (a) advocate for internationalization to be seen as an important component of the community college mission; (b) develop strategies for campus support services and professionalization of the field; and (c) assess programs and student outcomes.

Introduction

Research and scholarship have long confirmed the benefits and have identified the unique challenges of community college international education. The authors of these publications include a combination of senior administrators who are not involved in international program management, practitioners who are involved in international program management, university faculty and graduate students who have former employment with community colleges, and representatives of national and non-profit organizations. It is this combination of voices that has always been part of the field and that continues to be an important contributor in guiding change towards a comprehensive internationalization movement.

Raby and Valeau (2007) define historical foundations upon which community college internationalization efforts are based. The four phases are: (a) recognition; (b) expansion and publication; (c) augmentation; and (d) institutionalization. Publications in each phase reflect a maturation process that begins with explanations of why internationalizing is important, continues with how it can be done, and ends with assessment of efforts. While these phases coincide with events in time from 1960 to 2007, Treat and Hagadorn (2013) see these phases in a pre-2001/post-2001 construct in which internationalization is a response to external globalization pressures. Contemporary writings reflect a pattern that spirals these four phases as a continuous process and that delineates the links between advocacy, strategies and assessment.

Understanding the professional role of authors who write about internationalization helps to challenge a stereotype of community colleges as being solely practitioner oriented. Literature in the field depicts authors who share emic perspectives (from those who work(ed) at community colleges), as well as those who share etic perspectives (those who do not work at community colleges). Those who work at community colleges and at community college associations often have a practitioner orientation in which their writings emphasize operational practices. Those with a university affiliation often use a scholarly orientation in which their writings build upon or challenge theories with minimal connection to practice. Both of these contexts highlight the practitioner-scholar dialectic in which an author writes either for practice or for theoretical building. This chapter identifies a third voice, the scholar-practitioner blending, in which community college leaders use traditional scholarly research to enhance practice. In that most community college presidents and many vice-presidents, deans and department chairs hold a doctorate degree (O'Banion, 2015), the scholarly emphasis is not only part of their formal education, but is a definitive characteristic of being a transformative leader.

All of these patterns demonstrate what Kisker (2015) describes as the 'duality about our work as scholars' (p. 308) in which administrators conduct scholarly work that is connected to their practice and scholars conduct analysis that purposefully helps to inform practice. Those who write about community college internationalization exemplify these patterns as many authors float(ed) in between the fields of scholar and practitioner either by changing their professional roles or by simultaneously engaging in both. This chapter explores how the range of different perspectives work together to (a) advocate for internationalization to be seen as an important component of the community college mission; (b) develop strategies for campus support services and professionalization of the field; and (c) assess programs and student outcomes.

Advocacy

A primary purpose of publications on community college international education is to advocate for the advancement of the profession. Some authors advocate by defining the field (Gleazer, 1975), while others use theory to convince a specific generation of senior leaders of the merits of internationalization (Raby & Valeau, 2007). Advocacy is seen in three forms: (a) policy documents, largely written by those working at the American Association of Community and Junior Colleges (AACJC), which later became the American Association of Community College (AACC); (b) mission and vision commentary largely written by community college presidents, AACJC/AACC presidents, vice-presidents and directors and directors at non-profit organizations; and (c) descriptions of specific international programs largely written by community college practitioners in the form of community college faculty or community college international educational coordinators/ directors.

Policy documents. Policy documents advance national dialogue on community college internationalization. The American Association of Community Colleges commissioned several reports, including: 'Building the Global Community: the next step' (Elsner et al, 1994); 'Building Communities' (American Association of Community and Junior Colleges, 1998); 'AACC/ACCT Joint Statement' (American Association of Community Colleges and Association of Community College Trustees, 2006); and 'Reclaiming the American Dream' (American Association of Community Colleges, 2012). These documents reinforce the importance of a globally competent citizenry in an era of global competitiveness. Two of these documents were written by AACJC/AACC staff. The Elsner et al publication represents the voices of two community college presidents and a dean, all of whom served on the board of the American Council on International/Intercultural Education, which was then a sub-committee of AACC. The focus is primarily on the application of internationalization from a practitioner point of view.

Mission and vision commentary. A primary area of advocacy is the alignment of internationalization to community college mission and college vision. A significant number of publications are part of the New Directions in Community College series that creates a forum to chart educational change in community colleges (see King & Breuder, 1979; Greenfield, 1990; Valeau & Raby, 2007; Treat & Hagedorn, 2013; Roggow, 2014). Notable are the number of community college presidents who build theory to share the message about the need to change the direction of community colleges and who define themselves as having the authority and scholarly respect in the field to accomplish those tasks (Breuder, 1972; Adams, 1979; Dobelle & Mullen, 1996; Dellow, 2002; Manns, 2014). Agency to convince readership continues with publications by AACJC/AACC presidents, vice-presidents and directors that are written with the explicit purpose to convince community college leaders to support international education (Gleazer, 1975; Chase & Mahoney, 1996; Boggs & Irwin, 2007). It is interesting to note that despite generations of high-level national leaders who support international education, the field of internationalization is still marginalized. As a result, there continues to be a need for advocacy-based publications for each new generation of leadership.

In addition are voices from university professors and graduate students who advocate with specific theories about community college international education. In the Raby and Valeau (2007) recognition and expansion phase (1967-1990), these scholars built theory for internationalizing curriculum (Grant, 1979), for defining international development efforts (Kintzer, 1979), and for addressing neo-liberal and humanistic applications of globalization (Schugurensky & Higgins, 1996). These theories have withstood time and are influencing a new generation of internationalists. Today, new theories are applying models from business, intercultural learning and educational leadership (Raby, 2012; Zhang & Hagedorn, 2013; Eddy, 2014) to inform campus policy and to enhance program development.

Descriptions of specific international programs. Publications written by community college directors of international education, university professors and community college presidents advocate for internationalization by showcasing specific programs at their colleges. Advocacy results from a demonstration that these programs not only exist, but that by offering details on these programs, they can be easily copied. Each of these publications also includes in its recommendations generalizations designed to inform future practices. Focusing on Lone Star College (Ardalan & Sevanthinathan, 2015), on California community colleges (Raby, 2008) and on Highline Community College (Bermingham & Ryan, 2013), each details its own unique programs and uses its summary for advocacy by encouraging the idea that these programs can serve as the basis of any community college internationalization agenda.

Advocacy also comes from directors of national agencies and from non-profit organizations. As the director of US AID/AASCU, Hochhauser

(1990) wrote about the importance of building campus-community links that involve foreign students. As president of Community Colleges for International Development (CCID), Halder (2002) laid the groundwork for conducting international development projects which a decade later was expanded upon by Treat and Hartenstine (2013) (Treat was a community college international education director and later a community college president, and Hartenstine was a staff member of CCID). Green (2007), Vice-President of International Initiatives at the American Council on Education (ACE), provided advocacy essential for the post-9/11 generation. Finally, as an assistant director of the Peace Corps and former director of international education for ACE, Hayden (1979) set the tone for the need to lobby in Washington which was echoed years later by Cissell and Levin (2002), who represented the US Department of Education and the US Department of State, and by Smith (2013), who represented the US Institute for Peace. These individuals all maintain high-level national, state and organizational positions that provide a stamp of approval for community college internationalization. At the same time, these publications mark a change by which community colleges are recognized by the US government and federal funding agencies.

Noteworthy are advocacy publications that are co-written by those representing different professional focuses. The team of King and Fersh wrote over eight publications in the early years that helped to define the field. King was a community college president and Fersh started as a director at AACJC and later became a community college director of international education. The publications of Raby and Valeau also show the intersection of theory and application, with Valeau being an emeritus community college president and co-founder of a community college leadership consulting firm and Raby holding multiple positions, including university professor, community college practitioner and non-profit organizational director.

Developing Strategies

In the expansion and publication phase (Raby & Valeau, 2007), publications began to document strategies on how to establish, monitor and enhance specific programs. For these authors, commitment to internationalization is deeply rooted in individual experiences. Community college presidents and vice-chancellors wrote about the need to professionalize the field that stemmed from their own vision for educational change. Partly theoretical, partly best practices, the scholar-practitioner blending includes strategies to develop international student programs (Matthewson, 1968), to make contact with leaders as global counterparts (King & Breuder, 1979), and to be aware of consequences resulting from changing public support (Ng, 2007). Each of these executive officers wrote about their own personal experiences in strategy building so that others can build upon knowledge gained.

University professors who were former community college presidents (Martorana, 1978; Dellow, 2007) and former AACJC directors (Diener, 1980) add to the discussion by sharing how research can guide strategic development. Frost et al (2011) use their own professional journeys, as vice-president, university professor and community college president, to define elements needed for transformative leadership training. Finally, Pfaffenroth (1997) describes how fellows in a mid-career fellowship Princeton program collectively defined campus policies for internationalization. In these examples, guidelines to inform practice emerged from scholarly inquiry.

A specific example of scholar-practitioner blending is seen in developing strategies for internationalizing the curriculum. The first publications were written by university professors (Grant, 1979; Tonkin & Edwards, 1980) who defined the parameters of the field as being applicable to community colleges. These ideas were adapted by a community college professor who described how practice can be applied in a range of classrooms (Fersh, 1990). Subsequent research applies these theories for a post-9/11 world (Guerin, 2009). Finally, a community college consortia director, a university professor and a community college professor (Raby et al, 2012) use ethnographic research on how a specific internationalized curriculum program can enhance student learning and faculty engagement. These publications merge theory and practice as they exemplify how scholar-practitioner blending can influence change in the classroom via textbooks, pedagogy and assignments to internationalize a range of disciplines.

Finally, it is not surprising that so many of the how-to publications result from a willingness to share practices written by and for those who work in community college international education. There is a spiraling of information as publications from early practitioners now inform the works of current researchers. The practitioner viewpoint of financial problems of international students (Giammarella, 1986) has relevance for a scholarly study on building strategies to increase international student enrollment (Bohman, 2014). The practitioner description of education abroad procedures (Greene, 1990) is seen in new case studies on conducting service learning opportunities abroad (Kadel, 2002) and adding an intercultural dimension to an education abroad curriculum (Emert & Pearson, 2007). Historical practitioner roots are also found in scholarly discussions on building international partnerships to generate revenue (Violino, 2011) and professionalization of the field (Manns, 2014). Cross-generational links are accentuated as these publications reinforce that strategies found in similar programs can easily be duplicated over time and space.

Program Assessment and Student Learning Outcomes

Program assessment is shared in four different types of publications: (a) benchmark strategies; (b) case-study best practices; (c) comparative studies; and (d) academic studies.

Benchmark studies represent an indirect way to use assessment. The first of these publications were written by community college presidents (Breuder, 1972), state university deans (Robinson, 1990), ACE staff (Green, 2007) and community college international education directors (Hess, 1982), who defined what essential benchmarks work best for community colleges. Here the scholar-practitioner blending is evident as these benchmarks not only define elements of success, but in so doing, form the basis for future theoretical studies.

Current collaborative writing teams continue to redefine these benchmarks with experiences from their multiple perspectives. Malkan and Pisani (2011), a community college professor and a university professor, identify benchmarks for campus comprehensive internationalization. Brennen and Dellow (2013), a former international education director and a former president/current university professor, define benchmarks for using international students as a resource to achieve comprehensive internationalization. Bissonette and Woodin (2013), then EdD candidates and now a university advisor and a non-profit director, use a conceptual framework to track institutionalization efforts. Finally, scholar-practitioner teams (Treat & Hagedorn, 2013; Raby, Culton et al, 2014) use benchmarks to identify a contemporary checklist for optimal internationalization efforts. There is a noted similarity between historical and contemporary benchmarks as they all: (a) implement an educational vision in college documents and mission; (b) commit resources in line-item budgets; (c) create an organizational infrastructure to support reforms; (d) circulate transparency of programs and a designated plan to mentor new faculty, administrators and staff; and (e) encourage coalition building.

Case-study publications illustrate another form of indirect assessment. These publications are practitioner oriented as they describe unique programmatic elements, such as the internationalizing curriculum program at Kapi'olani Community College (Richards & Franco, 2007) and the service-learning program at Madison Community College (Bradshaw, 2013). Some of case studies depict a range of international programs at either a single institution, such as Broward Community College (Greene & Vitale, 2002), or at multiple colleges, such as California community colleges (Raby, 1999). These authors are a mixture of community college presidents, directors of international education programs and university professors. What remains noteworthy is the detailed descriptions of practice that provide a context upon which others can compare their own programs or that act as a guide to build new programs.

Comparative studies across community colleges provide another form of indirect assessment. These publications use survey to compare the extent to which internationalization exists and then highlight commonalities in practice or missing elements as defined by these comparisons. Pre-2007, comparative studies were mostly conducted by staff members of associations that had access to a large number of community colleges. Comparative studies determined the level of internationalization at six eastern community colleges (Fersh, 1990), at 72 California community colleges (Raby, 1999), at 300 AACJC colleges (Shannon, 1976), at 318 community colleges (Green et al, 2008) and at 552 community colleges (Hayward & Siaya, 2001). Post-2007, comparative studies are increasingly part of dissertations or academic studies that represent scholar-practitioner blending. These comparisons often have a specific focus, such as development of consortia (Korbel, 2007), urban-rural differences (Harder, 2010), linking education abroad to career development (Brennan et al, 2005), and defining barriers to education abroad (Raby, 2008). The longitudinal study of the IIE Open Doors reports (Institute for International Education, 2013) exemplifies the scholar-practitioner blending in which those who work at community colleges provide the raw data that are then used in research analysis. In 2014, Open Doors compared 309 community colleges for the international student report and 85 community colleges for the education abroad enrollment report.

Academic studies use various forms of assessment to focus on the role of the individual in effecting educational change. Many of these publications are emphasizing student learning outcomes and are largely written by university professors, graduate students and scholars who have roots as community college practitioners. The blending of both worlds allows a context for these empirical studies to inform practices. Some of these studies link academic and social integration to practices resulting in the persistence of community college international students (Mamiseishvili, 2012), define student retention and completion comparing those who studied abroad and those who did not (Raby, Rhodes et al, 2014), profile who international students are (Hagedorn & Lee 2005), determine student interest in internationalization (Robertson, 2015), examine organization-environment cases (Frost, 2009), and depict the role of administrators in internationalization (Opp & Gosetti, 2014).

A new generation of dissertations use assessment as the foundation for their empirical research design. However, in so doing, these studies also serve as a form of advocacy as community college internationalization is introduced to both the university via the committee members and to a community college audience. As a result of their research findings, these authors are changing practices of community college international student programs (Fitzer, 2007; Anayaha & Kukb, 2015) and community college education abroad programs (Amani, 2011; Willis, 2013). Finally, completing the scholar-practitioner cycle is a practitioner study that uses methodology from an academic study with the explicit purpose of advocating change (Thomas et al, 2015). The foundation for these academic studies is to refine best practices that unite theory and practice.

Conclusion

International education at community colleges, much like other community college research, includes reflections on practice, application of theory, and use of assessment to confirm findings. This focus was highlighted in the Council for the Study of Community Colleges' 2014 theme of supporting policy and practice through research and scholarship. This theme honors the multiple voices that shape educational reform efforts in general and internationalization efforts in particular.

The combination of scholars, practitioners and others who have published on community college internationalization, and who continue to do so, epitomizes a new form of scholarship. Some have little involvement as practitioners and were drawn to the study of community colleges. Through their research, they create partnerships with community colleges for the purpose of testing theories and grounding findings (Zhang & Hagedorn, 2013). Others began their professional careers in the community college and sought an EdD that is practitioner oriented or a PhD that is scholarly oriented as a way to build leadership skills, to bring an academic understanding to areas of their practice, and to gain professional mobility (Frost et al, 2011). Some of these individuals moved to universities and are now partnering with community colleges to apply their research (Dellow, 2007). Others are leading community colleges utilizing the research base that they gained (Raby & Valeau, 2007; Treat & Hagedorn, 2013). Finally, there are those who balance both worlds and who have an opportunity, as Kisker (2015) says, 'to analyze and comment on community colleges but also to help to shape them' (p. 308). Together, these voices illustrate how theory is used to inspire practice which anchors advocacy for change.

References

Adams, Hugh (1979) A Rationale for International Education, *New Directions for Community Colleges. Special Issue: Advancing International Education*, ed. Maxwell C. King & Robert I. Breuder, 26, 1-11. http://dx.doi.org/10.1002/cc.36819792603

Amani, Monija (2011) Study Abroad Decision and Participation at Community Colleges: Influential Factors and Challenges from the Voices of Students and Coordinators. Unpublished dissertation, Graduate School of Education and Human Development, George Washington University.

American Association of Community and Junior Colleges (1998) Building communities: a vision for a new century. A report of the Commission on the Future of Community Colleges. Washington, DC: AACJC Press.

American Association of Community Colleges (2012) Reclaiming the American dream: a report from the 21st-Century Commission on the Future of Community Colleges. Washington, DC: AACC Press.

American Association of Community Colleges and Association of Community College Trustees (2006) AACC/ACCT Joint Statement on the Role of Community Colleges in International Education. http://www.aacc.nche.edu/About/Positions/Pages/ps10012006.aspx

Anayaha, Bernadette & Kukb, Linda (2015) The Growth of International Student Enrollment at Community Colleges and Implications, *Community College Journal of Research and Practice*, 39(12), 1099-1110. http://dx.doi.org/10.1080/10668926.2014.934409

Ardalan, Shah & Sevanthinathan, Nithy (2015) Community Colleges: the perfect enterprise for the 21st century, in Paul Bradley (Ed.) *A Collection of Community College Week's POVs: opinions, issues, solutions*, pp. 28-30. Fairfax, VA: Autumn Publishing Enterprises.

Bermingham, Jack & Ryan, Margaret (2013) Transforming International Education through Institutional Capacity Building, *New Directions for Community Colleges. Special Issue: The Community College in a Global Context,* ed. Tod Treat & Linda Serra Hagedorn, 161, 54-83. http://dx.doi.org/10.1002/cc.20045

Bissonette, Bonnie & Woodin, Sean (2013) Building Support for Internationalization through Institutional Assessment and Leadership Engagement, *New Directions for Community Colleges. Special Issue: The Community College in a Global Context,* ed. Tod Treat & Linda Serra Hagedorn, 161, 11-26. http://dx.doi.org/10.1002/cc.20045

Boggs, George R. & Irwin, Judith (2007) What Every Community College Leader Needs to Know: building leadership for international education, *New Directions for Community Colleges. Special Issue: International Reform Efforts and Challenges in Community Colleges*, ed. Edward J. Valeau & Rosalind Latiner Raby, 138, 25-30. http://dx.doi.org/10.1002/cc.278

Bohman, Eric (2014) Attracting the World: institutional initiatives' effects on international students' decision to enroll, *Community College Journal of Research and Practice. Special Issue: Community Colleges and their Internationalization Efforts*, ed. Pamela Eddy, 38(8), 710-720. http://dx.doi.org/10.1080/10668926.2014.897081

Bradshaw, Geoffrey W. (2013) Internationalization and Faculty-led Service Learning, *New Directions for Community Colleges. Special Issue: The Community College in a Global Context,* ed. Tod Treat & Linda Serra Hagedorn, 161, 40-56. http://dx.doi.org/10.1002/cc.20047

Brennan, Michael & Dellow, Don A. (2013) International Students as a Resource for Achieving Comprehensive Internationalization, *New Directions for Community Colleges. Special Issue: The Community College in a Global Context,* ed. Tod Treat & Linda Serra Hagedorn, 161, 27-37. http://dx.doi.org/10.1002/cc.20046

Brennan, Michael, Frost, Robert, Hagedorn, Linda, Martin, M. & Natali, J. (2005) Education Abroad and the Career Development of Community College Students: four case studies, in Martin Tillman (Ed.) *Impact of Education Abroad on Career Development: four community college case studies II*, pp. 7-16. Stamford, CT: American Institute for Foreign Study Publications.

Breuder, Robert L (1972) A Statewide Study: identified problems of international students enrolled in public community/junior colleges in Florida. Tallahassee: Florida State University. ERIC: ED 062 977

Chase, Audree M. & Mahoney, James R. (Eds) (1996) Global Awareness in Community Colleges: a report of a national survey. Washington, DC: American Association of Community Colleges Press. ERIC Microfiche Collection Number ED 395 610

Cissell, Allen & Levin, David (2002) Federal Funding for Community College International Education Programs and Activities, in Richard M. Romano (Ed.) *Internationalizing the Community College*, pp. 145-159. Washington, DC: Community College Press.

Dellow, Donald A (2002) Why Do Community Colleges Need to Be Involved in International Activities? In Richard M. Romano (Ed.) *Internationalizing the Community College*, pp. 1-13. Washington, DC: Community College Press.

Dellow, Donald A (2007) The Role of Globalization in Technical and Occupational Programs, *Community College Journal of Research and Practice. Special Issue: International Reform Efforts and Challenges in Community Colleges*, ed. Edward J. Valeau & Rosalind Latiner Raby, 138, 39-45. http://dx.doi.org/10.1002/cc.280

Diener, Thomas (1980) Foreign Students and US Community Colleges, *Community College Review*, 7(4), 58-65. http://dx.doi.org/10.1177/009155218000700410

Dobelle, Evan S. & Mullen, James H. (1996) Building Consensus for International and Multicultural Programs: the role of presidential leadership, in Rosalind Latiner Raby & Norma Tarrow (Eds) *Dimensions of the Community College: international, intercultural, and multicultural perspectives*, pp. 175-195. New York: Garland.

Eddy, Pamela (Ed.) (2014) Introduction, *Community College Journal of Research and Practice. Special Issue: Community Colleges and Their Internationalization Efforts*, 38(8), 700-704. http://dx.doi.org/10.1080/10668926.2014.897077

Elsner, Paul A., Tsunoda, Joyce S. & Korbel, Linda A. (1994) Building the Global Community: the next step. Points of Departure for the American Council on International Intercultural Education/Stanley Foundation Leadership Retreat, 28-30 November, Des Moines, IA: Stanley Foundation Press.

Emert, Holly A. & Pearson, Diane L (2007) Expanding the Vision of International Education: collaboration, assessment, and intercultural development, *New Directions for Community Colleges. Special Issue: International Reform Efforts and Challenges in Community Colleges*, ed. Edward J. Valeau & Rosalind Latiner Raby, 138, 67-75. http://dx.doi.org/10.1002/cc.283

Fersh, Seymour (1990) Adding an International Dimension to the Community College: examples and implications, *New Directions for Community Colleges. Special Issue: Developing International Education Programs*, ed. Richard K. Greenfield, 70, 67-75. http://dx.doi.org/10.1002/cc.36819907009

Fitzer, John K (2007) Foreign Students at California Community Colleges: benefits, costs, and institutional responsibility. PhD dissertation. ProQuest Dissertations & Theses: Full Text. Publication No. AAT 3261961.

Frost, Robert A (2009) Globalization Contextualized: an organization-environment case study, *Community College Journal of Research and Practice*, 33(12), 1009-1024. http://dx.doi.org/10.1080/10668920802201369

Frost, Robert, Raspiller, Edward 'Ted' & Sygielski, John J. 'Ski' (2011) The Role of Leadership: leaders' practice in financing transformation, in Stewart E. Sutin, Dan Derrico, Rosalind Latiner Raby & Edward J. Valeau (Eds) *Increasing Effectiveness of the Community College Financial Model: a global perspective for the global economy*, pp. 49-65. New York: Palgrave.

Giammarella, Michael (1986) A Profile of the Foreign Student at a Public Two-year College: the Borough of Manhattan Community College response to the financial problems of foreign students, *Community Review*, 7(1), 6-13.

Gleazer, Jr., Edmund J. (1975) Memorandum to Community College Presidents, 24 March. American Association of Community and Junior Colleges Newsletter.

Grant, Sydney R. (1979) Internationalizing the College Curriculum, New Directions in Community Colleges. *Special Issue: Advancing International Education*, ed. Maxwell C. King & Robert I. Breuder, 26, 19-29.

Green, Madeline F. (2007) Internationalizing Community Colleges: barriers and strategies, *New Directions for Community Colleges. Special Issue: International Reform Efforts and Challenges in Community Colleges*, ed. Edward J. Valeau & Rosalind Latiner Raby, 138, 15-24. http://dx.doi.org/10.1002/cc.277

Green, M.F., Luu, D. & Burris, B (2008) *Mapping Internationalization on US Campuses*. Washington, DC: American Council on Education.

Greene, William E. (1990) Developing American Two-year College Programs Abroad, *New Directions for Community Colleges. Special Issue: Developing International Education Programs*, ed. Richard K. Greenfield, 70, pp. 57-65. http://dx.doi.org/10.1002/cc.36819907008

Greene, William & Robert Vitale (2002) Partnerships Abroad: international affiliates and faculty development, in Richard M. Romano (Ed.) *Internationalizing the Community College*, pp. 81-91. Washington, DC: Community College Press.

Greenfield, Richard K. (Ed.) (1990) Editor's Notes. Developing International Education Programs, *New Directions for Community Colleges*, 70, pp. 1-4. http://dx.doi.org/10.1002/cc.36819907002

Guerin, Stephen H. (2009) Internationalizing the Curriculum: improving learning through international education: preparing students for success in a global society, *Community College Journal of Research and Practice*, 33(4), 611-614. http://dx.doi.org/10.1080/10668920902928945

Hagedorn, Linda S. & Lee, Mi-Chung (2005) International Community College Students: the neglected minority? Online submission to ERIC. http://www.eric.ed.gov/PDFS/ED490516.pdf

Halder, John (2002) Partnerships Abroad: technical assistance and beyond, in Richard M. Romano (Ed.) *Internationalizing the Community College*, pp. 71-81. Washington, DC: Community College Press.

Harder, Natalie J. (2010) Internationalization Efforts in United States Community Colleges: a comparative analysis of urban, suburban, and rural institutions, *Community College Journal of Research and Practice*, 35(1), 152-164. http://dx.doi.org/10.1080/10668926.2011.525186

Hayden, Rose L. (1979) Taking the Word to Washington, in Maxwell C. King & Robert I. Breuder (Eds) *Advancing International Education*. New Directions in Community Colleges series, no. 26, pp. 79-89. http://dx.doi.org/10.1002/cc.36819792611

Hayward, F. & Siaya, Laura (2001) *Report on Two Surveys about Internationalization*. Washington, DC: American Council of Education.

Hess, Gerhard (1982) *Freshmen and Sophomores Abroad: community colleges and overseas academic programs*. New York: Teachers College Press.

Hochhauser, Gail A. (1990) Developing the Campus-Community Link in International Education, *New Directions for Community Colleges. Special Issue: Developing International Education Programs*, ed. Richard K. Greenfield, 70, 99-109. http://dx.doi.org/10.1002/cc.36819907012

Institute for International Education (2013) Open Doors Community Colleges Reports. http://opendoors.iienetwork.org/?p=25122

Kadel, Carolyn J. (2002) Service Learning Abroad, in Richard M. Romano (Ed.) *Internationalizing the Community College*, pp. 59-71. Washington, DC: Community College Press.

King, Maxwell C. & Breuder, Robert L. (Eds) (1979) *Advancing International Education*. New Directions for Community Colleges series, no. 26. San Francisco: Jossey-Bass.

Kintzer, Frederick C. (1979) World Adaptations of the Community College Concept, *New Directions for Community Colleges. Special Issue: Advancing International Education*, ed. Maxwell C. King & Robert I. Breuder, 26, 65-79. http://dx.doi.org/10.1002/cc.36819792610

Kisker, Carrie B. (2015) What We Can Learn from the Sixth Edition of *The American Community College*: CSCC awards luncheon address, *Community College Journal of Research and Practice*, 39(1), 308-313. http://dx.doi.org/10.1080/10668926.2014.981889

Korbel, Linda (2007) In Union there is Strength: the role of state global education consortia in expanding community college involvement in global education, *New Directions for Community Colleges. Special Issue: International Reform Efforts and Challenges in Community Colleges*, ed. Edward J. Valeau & Rosalind Latiner Raby, 138, 47-55. http://dx.doi.org/10.1002/cc.281

Malkan, Rajiv & Pisani, Michael J. (2011) Internationalizing the Community College Experience, *Community College Journal of Research & Practice*, 35(11), 825-841. http://dx.doi.org/10.1080/10668920802201377

Mamiseishvili, Ketevan (2012) Academic and Social Integration and Persistence of International Students at US Two-year Institutions, *Community College Journal of Research and Practice*, 36(1), 15-27. http://dx.doi.org/10.1080/10668926.2012.619093

Manns, Derrick (2014) Redefining the Role, Scope, and Mission of Community Colleges in an International Context, *Community College Journal of Research and Practice. Special Issue: Community Colleges and their Internationalization Efforts*, ed. Pamela Eddy, 38(8), 705-709. http://dx.doi.org/10.1080/10668926.2014.897079

Martorana, S.V. (1978) Constraints and Issues in Planning and Implementing Programs for Foreign Students in Community and Junior Colleges, in Edmund J. Gleazer, Jr. et al (Eds) *The Foreign Student in United States Community and Junior Colleges*. New York: College Board.

Matthewson, Jr., Douglas E. (1968) A National Survey of International Students and Programs in Community Junior Colleges in the United States. April ERIC Microfiche Collection No. ED 024 362.

Ng, Jacob (2007) Campus Politics and the Challenges of International Education in an Urban Community College District, *New Directions for Community Colleges. Special Issue: International Reform Efforts and Challenges in Community Colleges*, ed. Edward J. Valeau & Rosalind Latiner Raby, 138, 83-88. http://dx.doi.org/10.1002/cc.285

O'Banion, Terry (2015) One Hundred New Community College Leaders a Year, *Community College Week*, 17 August, p. 4. www.ccweek.com

Opp, Ronald D. & Gosetti, Penny Poplin (2014) The Role of Key Administrators in Internationalizing the Community College Student Experience, *New Directions for Community Colleges. Special Issue: Strengthening Community Colleges through Institutional Collaborations*, ed. Michael J. Roggow, 165, 67-75. http://dx.doi.org/10.1002/cc.20092

Pfaffenroth, Sara B. (1997) Clarifying Institutional Policy toward International Students: a community college self-study model, *Issues of Education at Community Colleges: essays by Fellows in the Mid-Career Fellowship Program at Princeton University*. Princeton University, June. ERIC Microfiche Collection No. ED 409 945.

Raby, Rosalind Latiner (1999) *Looking to the Future: report on international and global education in California community colleges*. Sacramento: California Community College Chancellor's Office.

Raby, Rosalind Latiner (2008) Expanding Education Abroad at US Community Colleges. IIE Study Abroad White Paper Series 3 (September 2008). New York: Institute for International Education Press.

Raby, Rosalind Latiner (2012) Re-imagining International Education at Community Colleges, *Audem: International Journal of Higher Education and Democracy*, 3, 81-99.

Raby, Rosalind Latiner, Culton, Donald R. & Valeau, Edward J. (2014) Collaboration: use of consortium to promote international education, *New Directions for Community Colleges. Special Issue: Strengthening Community*

Colleges through Institutional Collaborations, ed. Michael J. Roggow, 165, 77-87. http://dx.doi.org/10.1002/cc.20093

Raby, Rosalind Latiner, Kaufman, Joyce P. & Rabb, Greg (2012) The International Negotiation Modules Project: using simulation to enhance teaching and learning strategies in the community college, in Rebecca Clothey, Stacy Austin-Li & Jim Weidman (Eds) *Post-secondary Education and Technology: a global perspective on opportunities and obstacles to development*. New York: Palgrave Macmillan. http://dx.doi.org/10.1057/9781137037770.0016

Raby, Rosalind Latiner, Rhodes, Gary M. & Biscarra, Albert (2014) Community College Study Abroad: implications for student success, *Community College Journal of Research and Practice*, 38(2-3), 174-183.

Raby, Rosalind Latiner & Valeau, Edward J. (2007) Community College International Education: looking back to forecast the future, *New Directions for Community Colleges. Special Issue: International Reform Efforts and Challenges in Community Colleges*, ed. Edward J. Valeau & Rosalind Latiner Raby, 138, 5-14. http://dx.doi.org/10.1002/cc.276

Richards, Leon & Franco, Robert W. (2007) Island Roots, Global Reach: a case study in internationalizing Kapi'olani Community College, *New Directions for Community Colleges. Special Issue: International Reform Efforts and Challenges in Community Colleges*, ed. Edward J. Valeau & Rosalind Latiner Raby, 138, 89-96. http://dx.doi.org/10.1002/cc.286

Robertson, Jennifer J. (2015) Student Interest in International Education at the Community College, *Community College Journal of Research and Practice*, 39(5), 473-484. http://dx.doi.org/10.1080/10668926.2013.879377

Robinson, Brenda S. (1990) Facilitating Faculty Exchange, *New Directions for Community Colleges. Special Issue: Developing International Education Programs*, ed. Richard K. Greenfield, 70, 37-45. http://dx.doi.org/10.1002/cc.36819907006

Roggow, Michael J. (Ed.) (2014) Strengthening Community Colleges through Institutional Collaborations, *New Directions for Community Colleges*, 165.

Schugurensky, Daniel & Higgins, Kathy (1996) From Aid to Trade: new trends in international education in Canada, in Rosalind Latiner Raby & Norma Tarrow (Eds) *Dimensions of the Community College: international, intercultural and multicultural perspectives*, pp. 53-79. New York: Garland.

Shannon, William (1976) *A Survey of International/intercultural Education in Two-year Colleges*. La Plata, MD: Charles County Community College Press.

Smith, David (2013) *Peacebuilding in Community Colleges*. Washington, DC: United States Institute for Peace. https://bookstore.usip.org/books/BookDetail.aspx?productID=358277

Thomas, Janice M., Codding, Amparo & Lynch, Andrea (2015) Moving from a Culture of Anecdote to a Culture of Evidence: assessing the impact of international education programs. Presentation at Community Colleges for International Development (CCID) Annual Conference, Newport Beach, CA.

Tonkin, Humphrey & Edwards, Jane (1980) *The World in the Curriculum*. New Rochelle, NY: Change Magazine Press.

Treat, Tod & Hagedorn, Linda Serra (Eds) (2013) Resituating the Community College in a Global Context, *New Directions for Community Colleges*, 161.

Treat, Tod & Hartenstine, Mary Beth (2013) Strategic Partnerships in International Development, *New Directions for Community Colleges. Special Issue: The Community College in a Global Context,* ed. Tod Treat & Linda Serra Hagedorn, 161, 71-83. http://dx.doi.org/10.1002/cc.20049

Valeau, Edward J. & Raby, Rosalind Latiner (Eds) (2007) International Reform Efforts and Challenges in Community Colleges, *New Directions for Community Colleges*, 138.

Violino, Bob (2011) Community Abroad: international partnerships generate revenue. Opportunity for Colleges in Tough Fiscal Times, *Community College Journal*, 82(1), 14-16.

Willis, Tasha Y (2013) Rare But There: an intersectional exploration of the experiences and outcomes of black women who studied abroad through community college programs. Unpublished doctoral dissertation, California State University, Long Beach.

Zhang, Yi (Leaf) & Hagedorn, Linda Serra (2013) Chinese Education Agent Views of American Community Colleges, *Community College Journal of Research and Practice. Special Issue: Community Colleges and their Internationalization Efforts,* ed. Pamela L. Eddy, 38(8), 721-732. http://dx.doi.org/10.1080/10668926.2014.897082

CHAPTER 10

The Scholar-Practitioner's Role in Advancing Education Abroad Quality Assurance

BRIAN WHALEN

SUMMARY This chapter describes and analyzes an emerging type of scholar-practitioner at the forefront of quality assurance in international education: the education abroad scholar-practitioner (EASP). The EASP engages in scholarly activity thorough researching and becoming grounded in the field's standards, best practices, data and terminology, and research studies on a wide range of education abroad topics. There has emerged a foundational knowledge that is expected to be known and understood among EASPs, and this scholarly activity is not limited to researching information: it includes also improving education abroad based on the research results in order to advance the mission and goals of the EASP's institution or organization. This chapter describes how EASPs are trained through the Forum on Education Abroad's professional certification and quality improvement programs, and how they play a critical role in helping quality assurance at their institution or organization. The chapter concludes by suggesting that the future of education abroad will be shaped by professionals who embrace the scholar-practitioner role in order to meet both the expectations and the challenges for education abroad.

Introduction

Higher education is under increasing scrutiny regarding its value propositions, and whether what it claims to deliver is justified by its price: 'Students, their families, governments and corporations all have high expectations for what higher education should deliver: learning, the hope of employment, and marketable skills' (A. Whalen, 2015). How does the higher education sector best respond to these expectations? 'In this environment, standardized quality assurance mechanisms validate the worthiness of higher education's promises' (A. Whalen, 2015).

Quality assurance in higher education depends on professionals who are able to design and implement effective evaluations and assessments, and analyze and disseminate their results to a wide range of constituents. Such an effort depends on many contributors from across the higher education sector and within and across individual institutions and organizations. Today, working in any area of higher education (advancement, student development, academic affairs, facilities, etc.) requires not only that a person is qualified to complete the tasks associated with his or her position, but also that the person can contribute to evaluating how well that work is being done, and the impact of this work on the institution and its students. A chief challenge for higher education professionals is how to maintain this double consciousness effectively, splitting our attention and energy between 'doing' our jobs and 'evaluating' the effectiveness of what we do.

In education abroad this challenge is perhaps more daunting due to the relative newness of the field as a formal enterprise. It is only over the past ten years, for example, that codified ways of developing, managing, assessing and improving education abroad have been widely agreed upon. The principal way in which this has happened is through the development and publication of an authoritative set of standards of good practice for education abroad by the Forum on Education Abroad (Forum on Education Abroad, 2015). The *Standards of Good Practice for Education Abroad*, now in their fifth edition, form the basis for effective quality assurance practice by providing guidance to institutions about how to oversee education abroad and how to assess it.

While these *Standards* are readily accessible, the means to employ them to advance quality assurance requires, as one would expect, significant effort on the part of institutions. A clear mission for education abroad, adequate staffing and resources, a system for the regular review of programs, and all other principles articulated in the *Standards* are essential for maintaining quality. And the higher education professional who plays the most important role in this effort is the education abroad scholar-practitioner (ESAP).

The Role of the Education Abroad Scholar-Practitioner

The skill set required of an education abroad professional has changed significantly over the past ten years since the launch of the Forum on Education Abroad's *Standards of Good Practice for Education Abroad*. The *Standards* have defined the knowledge and skills that education abroad professionals need to be successful; they serve as the field's core curriculum for education abroad professionals, and provide a shared purpose and shared expectations. In addition to knowledge related to the various content areas of the *Standards*, such as health, safety, security and risk management, positions in education abroad have been shaped by the ways that institutions and organizations value the use of the *Standards* as a quality assurance tool.

The result is that education abroad professionals are no longer merely practitioners. Like other higher education professionals, they are called on to develop the research skills necessary to provide quality oversight of their area of responsibility. To be sure, education abroad scholar-practitioners are not all the same. Some colleagues conduct formal research studies and publish regularly in scholarly journals. However, most education abroad professionals orient their research toward a more practical purpose: to assess and improve education abroad at their institution or organization. These EASPs utilize scholarship to inform practice in order to improve their institutions and organizations.

The link between education abroad research activity and practice is driven by the overall goal of quality assurance. What 'quality' means will understandably vary from institution to institution, depending on the education abroad mission and goals. For example, an organization that focuses on language acquisition as a primary education abroad goal will look at quality differently from an organization that manages only STEM (science, technology, engineering and mathematics) programs in English-speaking countries. The differences between education abroad organizations and programs challenge the EASP to know and understand a diverse range of missions and goals, program models, student learning outcomes, and the practices that support the various forms of education abroad.

The EASP engages in research with a purpose: the improvement of education abroad to benefit students. It is not possible to accomplish this without conducting the research necessary to drive practice. Nor is it effective to conduct research without the intention of utilizing it to improve programming. For the EASP, research and practice are inextricably linked as part of a culture of quality improvement.

One need only examine the articles that appear in the journal *Frontiers: The Interdisciplinary Journal of Study Abroad* in order to realize how research benefits improved practice in education abroad (www.frontiersjournal.org). A critical resource for the EASP, *Frontiers* has been publishing peer-reviewed scholarly articles on education abroad since 1995. Now owned and managed by the Forum on Education Abroad, this journal's content provides a window into understanding the link between education abroad scholarship and practice. A recent analysis of the content of *Frontiers* identified three primary areas of focus to the articles published over its 20-year history: (1) student outcomes; (2) effectiveness of education abroad structures and pedagogies; and (3) the meaning and purpose of education abroad (B. Whalen, 2015).

Articles related to student outcomes seek to identify how students are impacted by education abroad; they include research on intercultural sensitivity, target language acquisition, intercultural development, global awareness, and psychological development such as identity formation and perception. These articles, many written by experts from outside the education abroad field, seek to understand how students are transformed, if at all, by their education abroad experience. Together they provide the EASP with information that informs the development of their organization's mission and goals for education abroad and the ways to assess desired student outcomes.

Frontiers articles related to the effectiveness of education abroad program structures and pedagogies inform the EASP in an additional, useful way. This research explores the potential benefits of education abroad according to program type, location, course content, teaching practices, duration, housing, and a wide range of practices that might be employed to enhance program effectiveness and student outcomes. At the same time, and just as importantly, this research informs the EASP about which student outcomes do not seem to be impacted by education abroad.

Finally, articles in *Frontiers* that examine the meaning and purpose of education abroad offer rich and often provocative theoretical perspectives on the field. For the EASP, these articles provide a larger context for thinking about education abroad and its research and practice.

As the scholarly journal for the education abroad field, *Frontiers* assists the EASP by providing knowledge that improves education abroad practice and enhances its overall quality. As such, EASPs should make it a regular habit to read the articles in *Frontiers* and think about how they inform their work.

How are EASPs Trained?

The skills that are required of the EASP can be identified in the curricula that define the training that the education abroad field offers. There are a variety of graduate programs in the United States in which students may focus on education abroad as part of an MA or PhD degree program; these programs have yielded wide-ranging and useful theses and dissertations. But most EASPs develop their research skills through professional associations that offer a range of professional development and training opportunities that help colleagues to become more effective scholar practitioners. Organizations such as NAFSA: Association of International Education Administrators, the Association of International Education Administrators (AIEA), the European Association for International Education (EAIE) and the International Education Association of Australia (IEAA), among many others, offer training on research and practices related to education abroad. These assist EASPs to advance their skills and contribute to overall quality improvement.

However, only the Forum on Education Abroad has developed intentional, coherent curricula that are based on the field's standards of good practice for education abroad, and which train EASPs for the task of quality assurance. These are offered in two complementary programs that have significantly shaped the EASP's role in advancing quality assurance: Professional Certification in Education Abroad (Certification), a program for individuals; and the Quality Improvement Program (QUIP), a program for institutions and organizations. Together, these two programs are educating a new generation of education abroad professionals, and impacting the education abroad practices of hundreds of institutions and organizations.

Professional Certification and the EASP

The Forum's Professional Certification Program, launched in 2014, offers a comprehensive and rigorous curriculum that requires participants to demonstrate that they can articulate and apply the field's standards of good practice. This program is perhaps the most focused of any on the goal of training people to be scholar-practitioners for the purpose of ensuring quality. The program requires 24 hours of workshop 'seat time' that may be completed in person or online. An additional estimated 20-50 hours (depending on the participant) are required to complete specially designed 'standards assignments' in which participants demonstrate their ability to articulate and apply the standards to real-world education abroad situations. These assignments are assessed by certification assessors, senior-level education abroad experts who are trained to the task. Participants proceed through the program by completing the assignments successfully until all seven assignments, including a capstone exercise, are finished. Once completed, participants are certified education abroad professionals and will then have to maintain their certification by documenting professional development activities and/or how they continue to apply the standards in their everyday work.

These standards assignments are what make the certification program explicitly about training EASPs for quality assurance. The workshop content trains participants how to research information and best practices, while the assignments challenge them to demonstrate their ability to do so. For example, one assignment requires participants to design education abroad training for faculty and staff by utilizing the resources underpinning the standards of good practice, while another challenges them to write a memorandum to their supervisor arguing for enhanced resources in order to adequately meet the standards. Successful completion of these and the other assignments demonstrate that the EASP will be effective in contributing to overall quality of education abroad at his or her organization. In this way, the Forum's Professional Certification Program is shaping a new generation of EASPs and the institutions and organizations that they serve.

Quality Improvement and the EASP

The corollary to individual Professional Certification is the institutional goal of demonstrating education abroad quality. The various accreditation agencies and organizations have established systems in place for the assessment and recognition of overall institutional quality. These exist in different national, regional and disciplinary contexts. What they have in common is that they are based on a set of standards and follow an established protocol. However, they are uneven in the way that they address the education abroad operations of a given institution or organization.

> In her recent publication, *Mapping The Landscape: Accreditation and the International Dimensions of US Higher Education*, Madeleine Green [Green, 2015] outlines how education abroad intersects with U.S. accreditation programs in uneven ways. Some regional accreditation programs have detailed ways in which institutional education abroad programming is judged, while others make little mention of such programs. U.S.-based independent program providers do not fall under these accreditation programs. International institutions hosting U.S. students participate in their country's quality assurance mechanisms. Independent program providers based in other countries may seek accreditation if such options are offered for their type of organization. When U.S. or internationally-based independent program providers work with Schools of Record, accredited U.S. institutions provide quality assurance by overseeing the academic program and faculty. (A. Whalen, 2015)

In 2006, the Forum on Education Abroad inaugurated a program to fill this gap and create a common system to help ensure education abroad quality: the Quality Improvement Program (QUIP). QUIP is based on the US accreditation model and is designed to provide quality assurance, to assist institutions to meet their regional or national accreditation requirements, as well as organizations working outside accepted accreditation structures. In education abroad, it has been common practice that organizations and institutions conduct periodic reviews of their programs using private consultants or members of an advisory committee. While these approaches may serve as useful tools for improving programs, such reviews do not provide the same measure of quality assurance as QUIP reviews.

This is because, like accreditation reviews, QUIP is objective, requires a rigorous self-study and focused site visits, is based on authoritative *Standards of Good Practice for Education Abroad*, and utilizes trained peer reviewers who make judgments about whether the institution's or organization's programs are in conformity with the *Standards*. At the end of the process, a panel of experts reviews the self-study and peer-review report and makes a final determination about whether or not the organization is in overall substantial conformity with the *Standards*. A determination of 'yes' carries the most significant judgment available regarding the quality of education abroad programming.

Since the QUIP program began, over 60 institutions have reviewed their programs. In addition to the role that the program has had in improving the quality of education abroad at these institutions and organizations, QUIP has helped to train the hundreds of people at institutions who participated on the teams that oversaw the institutional self-studies. In addition, over 50 colleagues have served as peer reviewers reviewing the self-study reports and making judgments about whether or not institutions are meeting the standards of good practice. When combined, self-study team members and peer reviewers account for a significant number of people who developed EASP skills through their participation in QUIP.

The mindset of a member of a QUIP institutional self-study team is that of the EASP: he or she researches the practices in place at their institution as well as the documented best practices that form the basis for the *Standards*. For example, institutional data related to student learning outcomes will be compiled and analyzed as part of a self-study, and these will be compared with results and analyses conducted by other institutions by consulting resources such as the Outcomes and Assessment Research Toolbox, which contains assessment tools and strategies that are employed effectively throughout the education abroad community. Other resources offered by the Forum, such as the *Education Abroad Glossary* (2011), surveys and reports on data, and the academic journal *Frontiers: the interdisciplinary journal of study abroad*, also assist the EASP in this process.

The self-study report is the finished product of the QUIP self-study, presenting research related to each of the standards of good practice. The self-study report is the highest level of EASP research in the education abroad field, combining rigorous scholarship and analysis with the focused goal of improving practices in order to ensure overall quality of education abroad.

Brian Whalen

The Future of the EASP and
Education Abroad Quality Assurance

These are interesting and challenging times for institutions and organizations involved in education abroad. There are unprecedented efforts to increase the number of US students who study abroad and expand the capacity of programs. US government-led efforts such as the 100,000 Strong initiatives and the Institute for International Education's Generation Study Abroad program have dramatically increased the attention on expanding education abroad. At the same time, US legislators at the state and federal levels have proposed, and in one case (Minnesota) passed, laws that require institutions to be more transparent about and accountable for education abroad activities. The expressed goal of these efforts is to enhance the health, safety and security of students by improving how education abroad programs function.

The EASP has a critical role to play in an environment in which expansion of education abroad is being promoted along with calls for improvement and greater accountability. Being successful in this environment will require a focus on and commitment to quality assurance, and this should be led by those professionals trained to the task. EASPs understand that the expansion of education abroad must be pursued with a focus on a set of standards that ensure quality. And they know also that if standards are followed, institutions and organizations are accountable to their constituents.

The education abroad field is on the cusp of embracing the EASP as a key driver of quality assurance. While the standards of good practice and their related programs are well known and accepted, many colleagues and institutions have yet to take the step of becoming formally trained in them, and of using them as a means to assess and improve programs. This will change as the Professional Certification Program continues to distinguish itself as the leading credential in the field, and as more institutions recognize the value and benefits of successfully completing QUIP. Public calls for greater accountability and demonstration of quality will continue to motivate institutions and higher education professionals and will make these programs more critically important.

The future of education abroad will be shaped by those professionals who embrace the scholar-practitioner role. Higher education will continue to value data and analysis produced by sound research, and prize those who are able to make decisions and ensure quality through use of these data. The same will be true for the future of education abroad.

References

Forum on Education Abroad (2011) *Education Abroad Glossary*, 2nd edn. Carlisle, PA: Forum on Education Abroad.

Forum on Education Abroad (2015) *Standards of Good Practice for Education Abroad*, 5th edn. Carlisle, PA: Forum on Education Abroad.

Green, Madeleine (2015) *Mapping the Landscape: accreditation and the international dimensions of US higher education*. Washington, DC: NAFSA: Association of International Education.

Whalen, Annmarie (2015) The Value Question: quality assurance in higher education and education abroad, *The Forum Focus*. http://issuu.com/forumoneducationabroad/docs/forum_focus_-_mar2015

Whalen, Brian (2015) How to Publish in International Education: perspectives from editors. Paper presented at NAFSA Annual Conference, Boston, MA, 27 May. https://shelbycearley.files.wordpress.com/2010/06/how-to-publish-in-international-education-perspectives-from-editors-slides.pdf

CHAPTER 11

The Interplay and Co-evolution of Theory and Practice in Preparing Students for International Education Experiences: a retrospective analysis

BRUCE LA BRACK

SUMMARY This chapter will critically analyze the nearly forty-year historical and intellectual evolution of the University of the Pacific's integrated orientation and re-entry courses. It will concentrate on explicating the core elements and pedagogical approaches that are believed to have contributed the most to the success of the program, including a consideration of how those elements might be applied and adapted by educators engaged in similar pursuits. It will provide an account of how these linked, credit-bearing training courses grew and co-evolved with the growing sophistication of both the international education field as well as the theoretical underpinnings of the discipline of intercultural communication. The author briefly discusses how his roles as a scholar-practitioner underwent several transformations beginning with the inception phase of the process through its eventual maturation, with the intention of providing other practitioners with (1) an understanding of what practices and procedures worked best for the orientation and re-entry courses at Pacific; (2) how the program incrementally evolved; (3) how program effectiveness was measured; and (4) how other trainers/teachers might adopt these ideas for their own purposes. The chapter concludes with some reflections and advice about administrative impediments that remain to establishing such programs elsewhere.

The Beginning

Forty years ago, I found myself employed in a university setting where there was a critical need for cross-cultural training to support international education programming. At that time, the literature on education abroad was relatively sparse, and few colleges offered orientation programs or courses that were well developed or particularly sophisticated. In particular, it was a rare institution that dealt with re-entry programming at all.

Of necessity, I became involved in a process of creating training and orientation programs that have continued for decades, undergoing continual alterations over time. In the first period (1975-1986), the work was primarily concentrated on developing theoretically and practically linked pre-departure and re-entry courses that were both required and credit-bearing. In a second phase (1986-2000), these courses underwent significant revisions to reflect growing knowledge in the intercultural communication field, and to incorporate new models and activities into the training, including a shift from a 'culture-specific' to a 'culture-general' approach to culture learning.

After 2000, there emerged a series of concerns about how we were monitoring the educational process and assessing the effectiveness of our international programs. In response to both internal and external pressures at the university, we sought to develop methods to enhance student learning outcomes, and to more accurately gauge how well we (and our students) were meeting our collective goals. This shift included the gradual adoption of more 'interventionist' strategies and revising our qualitative and quantitative measurements, trends that have became increasingly widespread across the field generally. We also decided to share more broadly the models and materials we had developed over decades via the Internet, and created the 'What's Up With Culture?' website, released in October 2003 (La Brack, 2003). Since then, we have continued to fine-tune our orientation and re-entry courses, and to adapt to new challenges and changing circumstances – for example, in such areas as health and safety issues.

The evolution of these courses occurred over time, in tandem with emerging theoretical and applied advances in the fields of international education and intercultural communication. I will provide some background about that co-evolution and relevant linkages, as seen from my perspective as a scholar-practitioner, and also consider how it impacted my academic life, especially in the area of research.

As the focus of this collection is on how the status and roles associated with being a scholar-practitioner have developed and operated in varied contexts, I will address how my work reflected some of these aspects, and how my personal intellectual journey became part of that process. Elsewhere, authors in this book characterize the scholar-practitioner as someone who regularly engages in trans-disciplinary approaches to scholarship (in contrast to inter-disciplinary), often operating in what are called 'liminal' (ambiguous) contexts. To be honest, in retrospect, my entire career in international education seems to fit that definition, constantly straddling the divide between a practitioner and a scholar.

When I began this work, there were few theoretical models to emulate and little data – a situation that I found challenging and frustrating for the first decade (1975-1985). But, ultimately, it turned out to be a period of 'benign neglect' in which I was given the freedom to establish courses, develop policies, hire and train other faculty, and, generally, create, invent and assess what worked for our study abroad students. Being basically left alone administratively was a gift, a situation that, given the realities of contemporary study abroad, is unlikely to be replicated elsewhere. Nevertheless, the autonomy it provided allowed me to experiment with activities that are now recognized as crucial aspects of the scholar-practitioner model.

Early Days as a Scholar-Practitioner

The primary educational context within which I spent the majority of my academic career was the University of the Pacific in Stockton, California, a small comprehensive institution with a long history of international involvement. When I joined the faculty in 1975 as Resident Anthropologist within Callison College, the university had virtually no education abroad orientation programming, which was, unfortunately, rather common at that time.

Subsequently, cross-cultural training at Pacific had a long and complex developmental history that is relatively well known among international education professionals. It marked its fortieth year of operation in 2015, and remains the oldest continuous, conceptually linked credit-bearing program of its type in the United States. Although I will reference events and decisions made at Pacific, I will not provide a detailed outline of its growth or structure, as this information is available elsewhere (La Brack, 1986; VandeBerg & Paige, 2009; La Brack & Bathurst, 2012a, b).[1]

Although the University of the Pacific is a US-based institution and is known for its unique, comprehensive, ongoing orientation programming, the ideas explored here have the potential to be adapted to a much wider range of educational situations. These include international students coming to study for degrees in the United States, as well as shorter-term educational programs, short-term inbound exchange students, preparations for internships and service-learning opportunities, high school exchanges, international business, humanitarian activities, supporting Global Nomad groups, and domestic multi-cultural training contexts.

In this chapter, I will review some decision points and policies that resulted in incremental improvements in the process of preparing people to maximize their experiences, before, during and after an international sojourn. Sometimes these ideas created new platforms and procedures that proved especially helpful to students, and could be made applicable in many educational contexts. At its heart, much of the process we followed over four decades at Pacific was a variation of the practice-theory-practice paradigm, which constantly seeks both to generate theoretical explanations from observed/reported behavior, and to test theoretical constructs by applying them to real-world contexts to see how closely they align.

Although I was originally hired at Pacific as a standard, tenure-track, 'traditional' cultural anthropologist, within one year of my arrival I found myself taking responsibility for creating and teaching cross-cultural pre-departure training for Callison College (a cluster college within the university). None of these activities were initially part of my job description; they evolved because I took seriously the strongly expressed collective concerns by students who were having pervasive re-entry problems after returning from a year-long education abroad program in Japan.

I decided almost immediately that some kind of structured re-entry activity to deal with the students' issues needed to be instituted as soon as possible. It was also equally clear that a substantive pre-departure orientation was desperately needed to help alleviate both initial culture shock and reverse-culture shock. In other words, the original impetus for the training was simply to assist returnees with their readjustment home, but as I considered the larger picture, I was led to the logical conclusion that what was really required was some kind of training at *both ends of the process*. Given the paucity of research at the time on either orientation or re-entry, not to mention the fact that intercultural communication as a field was just beginning to have an impact upon such training, my commitment to providing appropriate instruction to students was as much a gut feeling as a rational decision. While I was highly motivated, the task at hand was to somehow assemble the components, and then develop curriculum for both the pre-departure and re-entry courses that were conceptually linked.

First Crucial Innovations: required courses and linked curriculum

By 1977, every student intending to study abroad with Pacific's Callison College was required to take an orientation seminar prior to departure, as well as a re-entry seminar upon return. When Callison College closed, the home for cross-cultural training became Pacific's School of International Studies (SIS), and, beginning in 1986, every SIS student continued to be required to take both orientation training courses as part of their international education experience.

From the beginning, I was able to convince my colleagues and curriculum committees that if an international education experience was supposed to be an integral and important part of a student's college experience, then preparation related to going abroad and post-sojourn activities should not only be given equal weight academically speaking, but I further argued that students should (1) receive academic credit for such efforts and (2) that such courses should be required for study abroad. The entire program was founded upon the twin requirements of mandated training and course credit, and the fact that they were conceptually linked so there was much less compartmentalization and/or disconnect between what one did in an outbound orientation and what would be required upon return.

It was exactly a decade before I was ready to publicly discuss the Pacific model.[2] I had no idea at the time that it would become a frequently quoted example of what was a singularly complex and unique approach to preparing individuals for an international education experience. At the time of its inception, my decisions to link the courses and require attendance were simply ways to give such training formal academic standing, and ensure that, if it was really as important as we thought it should be, attendance should not be optional.

Further Alterations Based on the Co-evolution of Theory and Practice: culture-specific vs. culture-general frameworks

Initially, the orientation at Pacific was for a single country as the entire sophomore class went abroad for a year (first to India, and then to Japan). Therefore, intensive country-specific materials and readings were appropriate. However, between 1986 and 1996, as the cross-cultural training classes became integrated into the larger university community, the diversity of participants and the growth of variety and locations of international destinations precipitated a gradual shift in emphasis from culture-specific information toward a more culture-general approach derived from intercultural communication theories and models.

Although practical culture-specific information is always useful and necessary, much of it can be readily accessed via the Internet, researched outside of class by the student, or provided by international education offices. The increasing emphasis we placed on the culture-general concepts and theoretical underpinnings of the emerging discipline of intercultural communication explicitly paralleled the simultaneous growth of the intercultural field's sophistication, conceptual tools, and published materials linking cultural competence to the ability to function appropriately and empathetically in any new cultural setting. In a very literal sense, the development of Pacific's programs was intimately linked to emerging developments within the intercultural realm itself. We tried to continually refresh the content and methods we were employing, and to evaluate how well our training was translating into cultural competence abroad.

Personally, the psychological shift for me as an anthropologist – from an emphasis on *culture-specific* knowledge to a more a *culture-general* focus – was somewhat difficult and sometimes a bit disconcerting. On the one hand, I have always appreciated the specificity and breadth of what anthropologists call 'deep cultural' description and understanding. Yet, increasingly, I realized that for my students who were embarking on an international education experience a broader perspective based upon culture-general principles might be more productive in both the short and the long term. Pacific's program has emphasized a largely culture-general approach for over two decades now.[3]

Essentially, I was forced to rethink my own preconceptions of what might work best. I became convinced of the advantages of employing such intercultural communication frameworks in my own training, and sought to regularly integrate and update such perspectives into Pacific's existing orientation courses.

The Shift from Prior 'Laissez-faire' Attitudes to 'Interventionist' Strategies

Gradually, beginning around 2000, I became convinced from a mounting body of research evidence that the primary intercultural learning from an international education experience did not necessarily accrue solely from being abroad (or while being *in situ*). Nor was it likely to occur automatically. When such learning was demonstrably enhanced, it was primarily the result of particular kinds of reflection on the experience abroad – and the frequency and depth of those reflections could be increased by structured interventions before, during and after the education abroad experience.

Like many of my colleagues, I came to realize that simply putting people 'in the vicinity of events' was woefully insufficient as pedagogy. All the current research literature I am aware of supports the efficacy of direct interventionist training as a part of the overseas sojourn. The edited collection by VandeBerg, Paige, and Lou (2012) makes clear that the overwhelming preponderance of evidence indicates that students provided with regular challenge and support gain the greatest benefit from their educational experience. A typical interventionist program they would recommend would ideally include a thorough pre-departure training reinforced by an initial in-country orientation, regular contact with some type of mentor/monitor while abroad, followed by preparatory pre-re-entry training, and a re-entry seminar post-arrival. Students who get this kind of ongoing orientation support almost always perform better overseas, especially when augmented with timely advice and frequent feedback while abroad. They also experience more post-return satisfaction. Although we had been using 'interventionist' activities at

Pacific from the very beginning, since 2001 it has been more deliberate, overt, direct and consistent. More importantly, we can demonstrate that our programming works.

Assessment: moving from self-reportage to qualitative and quantitative measures

Academics are always looking for ways to appropriately measure the progress and the knowledge base of students in their courses. How to do so when the experience is happening far away is a more complicated situation. Further, one may not always have access to correlating reports from homestay families, program directors and course instructors. For almost three decades at Pacific we relied primarily upon post-sojourn, self-reported student surveys. Such satisfaction surveys are not a particularly accurate way to gauge how well students perform while abroad. Other than their academic course grades there were few ways to objectively triangulate their level of cultural competency.

I was intrigued when I first encountered Milton Bennett's Developmental Model of Intercultural Sensitivity (DMIS) in the mid-1980s, and followed the subsequent development of the Intercultural Development Inventory (IDI) as an assessment instrument a decade later (1998). The original version was created by Mitchell R. Hammer in collaboration with Milton Bennett; Hammer has been responsible for all subsequent revisions. It currently is the most widely used assessment instrument in the intercultural assessment field (Hammer et al, 2003).

We began employing the IDI as part of our Pacific assessment program in 2004, and gradually increased the number of times and groups we administered it to between 2005 and 2008. Beginning in 2009, we administered it at least three times over the career of an SIS student: within a few weeks of arriving on campus as an incoming first-year student, just prior to going abroad, and during the senior year following their overseas program, just prior to graduation. The results were gratifying, showing an average gain of 17.46 points between the initial and final IDI administrations, one of the largest gains recorded so far for such programs.[4]

Recently, I have also been intrigued by the research of Lilli Engle, at the American University of Provence, on ways to construct more reflective qualitative assessment/questionnaire instruments. A recent article (Engle, 2013) outlines her approach, discusses how to make instruments more reflective of the reality of students' experience, and suggests how to construct questions that reveal the extent to which the goals of the program were behaviorally and attitudinally met. The complexity and specificity of her arguments preclude summary here, but I highly recommend her approach.

Other Pieces of the Puzzle: additions, subtractions and the Internet

If one were to review forty years of syllabi related to our cross-cultural training, it would be obvious that the curriculum has undergone (and continues to undergo) tinkering, some of it by individual trainers trying out new ideas or models, some from including pieces we decided needed to be added to the core topics/activities that every training syllabus must contain. Two examples of additions to the curriculum made shortly after they appeared in the literature include critical incident frameworks (Brislin et al, 1986), which were used sporadically before becoming formalized in 1999, when we began to assign and collect them in every re-entry seminar, and adding Hammer's conflict styles inventory in 2002.

Keeping such courses dynamic, up to date and engaging is a serious obligation, but, above all, the information needs to be accurate and reliable. An example of an important deletion from the courses is the downplaying of the much-venerated and widely used 'curves of adjustment' (U- and W-versions), particularly when linked to the 'iceberg' and related models. Once I became aware that Kate Berardo's MA thesis amply illustrated that these models are neither predictive nor descriptive, we no longer wanted to highlight them for those reasons (Berardo, 2006).

Further Inventions: what's up with culture?

At the turn of the century, as I was contemplating retirement, I realized that although the materials generated and compiled for the Pacific training courses would continue to exist under the care of other faculty members, little would be available to anyone outside the university. While I had considered writing a book on training that would contain the 'best of' our advice and models in a format useful to college-age participants, the work involved seemed daunting. In 2000, Dr Gary Rhodes, then at the University of Southern California (USC), serendipitously suggested that I join him on a grant application for a large FIPSE (Foundation for the Improvement of Post-Secondary Education) project. We proposed to FIPSE that I create modules as part of a web-based cross-cultural training resource targeted at traditional-aged (18-24 years old) US-American undergraduate students intending to study abroad. It was intended to be free, interactive, and allow unrestricted access to users. It was also designed to be self-contained, self-paced, self-graded/assessed, and be reasonably encyclopedic in scope. Our project was funded for three years, and with the invaluable assistance of the Payson Center for International Development and Technology Transfer at Tulane who guided the adaption of content to the Internet, the finished product went online in October 2003.

'What's Up With Culture?' contains 10 modules: six on pre-departure, one on in-country issues, and three combining pre-entry and re-entry. To date, over four million users from at least 35 countries have utilized the site, and portions of these modules are currently used in orientation and re-entry activities at over 100 institutions worldwide. Some international organizations use the site as a 'mirror image' to explore the values of their international students who plan on coming to the United States, especially how their cultural patterns might compare, contrast or conflict with the American values identified.

The University of the Pacific remains the host of the 'What's Up With Culture?' website (http://www2.pacific.edu/sis/culture/). Of all of my academic projects, I find this one to have had the greatest impact beyond the university; not only is it a free resource, but large numbers of people are using it regularly.

Final Lessons and Reflections

So what lessons did I learn from all this concentration on preparing people to confront cultural differences? First, that intercultural communication is encountered everywhere, everyday ... domestically and in foreign contexts. However, it is seldom recognized as such because people lack the conceptual frameworks to process what is happening. Second, that culture-learning requires new perspectives and new ways to process interactions if the resulting behaviors are to be appropriate and acceptable. This absolutely necessitates some kind of pre-encounter orientation; otherwise, it will not happen. Moreover, I have come to believe that a great deal of what one 'learns' from an international education experience happens in the process of trying to integrate one's education abroad learning into one's ongoing academic and personal spheres. That is why re-entry is such a crucial 'capstone', and why returnees' readjustment home may benefit significantly from 'interventionist' post-sojourn debriefings. While re-entry training has become much more common on campuses, it is far from universally available. I consider this a significantly missed educational opportunity because a great deal of additional learning and insight can occur in the process of reflecting on an experience. As proponents of experiential learning note, it is possible that one can only truly make sense of an experience in retrospect. In other words, what an experience 'means' is likely constructed following the experiential event itself.

Besides education abroad participants, who might benefit from such intercultural training and orientations on the average college campus? Just about everyone. International students coming for degrees or shorter periods of study could certainly be helped by receiving this type of cultural information, in addition to the logistical, academic and administrative advice they already receive. Anyone working with international students might benefit from some understanding of the values and attitudes of their clients, at least from a culture-general

177

framework. In my opinion, it is possible that so-called short-term programs, which now comprise the majority of overseas programs, might actually require not only a 'normal' orientation but may also require a different, and possibly longer, re-entry debriefing precisely because the time available to make sense of their experience while abroad is structurally limited.

I am frequently asked why the Pacific program is not more widely emulated. The answer is not simply that it is a complex and integrated set of courses that evolved over a long time frame (although all of that is true). I think the greatest impediment might be who is responsible for what constituencies on a campus, and how their roles and duties are apportioned. Although combined offices have always existed, one of the oldest divisions within US academia is the separation on campus of international student services and education abroad. This is something the original NAFSA (National Association of Foreign Student Advisors) wrestled with for years, and, finally, appended 'Association of International Educators' to its name to emphasize the teaching potential of all its members. The formation of the Teaching, Learning and Scholarship Knowledge Community (TLS) in 2005 re-focused organization-wide attention on curriculum internationalization, research that informs practice, and intercultural communication. TLS was created to serve the entire membership, including faculty, administrators, graduate students/post-docs, researchers, intercultural trainers, cross-cultural counselors, and other professionals in international education. This emphasis on teaching and research is a major step in the right direction; however, the physical locations in which the members do their daily work are often isolated from one another due to the decoupling of education abroad and international student offices – they are seen to serve different constituents, even when their teaching activities, in terms of training, might be more similar than is supposed.

Another issue that remains contentious is the relative status of people who are on the academic side as opposed to those who occupy staff positions. I do not believe that one needs a PhD to be a good intercultural trainer, as practical exposure and a sensitive approach gained by other means (Peace Corps, foreign employment, education, living abroad, etc.) can be an invaluable resource. Certainly anyone with the interest and aptitude can be sufficiently trained in intercultural theory and practice to effectively deliver training. The problem is not a lack of people interested in helping others gain intercultural competence, but the existence of administrative structures and policies that preclude certain people being eligible to initiate or offer such training, or that reserve input on curricular committees, where courses are proposed and vetted, exclusively to those of faculty status. I do not want to suggest that there is some kind of unbridgeable divide, but there certainly exist significant bureaucratic impediments for individuals who wish to propose creating such courses but do not hold faculty designation.

I recognized very early on the problem of how my orientation courses were going to be integrated into the entire curriculum of both the School of International Studies and the university, including how such 'practitioner' activity was going to be evaluated in terms of faculty participation and workload. Like the original issue of whether to require attendance and grant credit for the orientation courses, if our students were to take our orientations seriously, the university was going to need to support our recommendations. Similarly, if we thought that such teaching/training was valuable, then the instructors providing those courses should be treated no differently from those teaching any other academic subject. I decided to take my proposals directly to the senior administration. As a result, all cross-cultural training courses are taught by tenured or tenure-track professors who have completed their doctorates (in a variety of disciplines, including political science, history, anthropology) and who hold at least partial appointments in SIS. Further, all anthropologists hired by Pacific are expected to teach the cross-cultural training courses, and this requirement is discussed during job interviews, although it is recognized that the field of intercultural communication is distinct from anthropology in its methods, assumptions and core body of knowledge.

I confronted some aspects of this within my own discipline of cultural anthropology when I would attend national conferences of the American Anthropological Association and offer sessions on how anthropologists could get involved in study abroad training and why their skills might be helpful. Such sessions were sparsely attended and mostly met with a basic indifference because: (1) this kind of anthropology would be considered 'applied' rather than theoretical, and carry less professional weight; and (2) the 'home' of such training was usually outside the departmental structure and, admittedly, interdisciplinary. Although this attitude has changed somewhat these days, the fact remains that anthropologists, in spite of their cross-cultural training and fieldwork expertise, are found in the study abroad field less than one might expect.

Because of the recognition that some immediate faculty development is needed to teach cross-cultural training courses, all faculty members who are going to do orientation training are required to undergo a minimum of one week of formal instruction in intercultural training design at the Intercultural Communication Institute's Summer Institute for Intercultural Communication in Portland, Oregon, USA. They are also required to audit each training course at Pacific prior to teaching it. More experienced colleagues provide further support, as needed, in the form of mentoring while the course is being taught, especially during the first semester. In terms of faculty promotion, tenure and merit raises, teaching orientation and re-entry courses are considered an integral and normal part of their regular teaching assignment and workload. In this way we signal to students, faculty and administration that such courses are the equivalent of any curricular offerings within the university.

In closing, I must admit that I never had to prepare more than 150 Pacific students to go abroad in any single semester, so when faced with numbers in the thousands (as at a Penn State or a Wisconsin), clearly the Pacific model would not work. But the basic operating principles involved are much simpler: (1) if at all possible, require ongoing orientations that have pre-departure, while abroad, and re-entry components – even if it has to be done via the Internet; (2) offer orientation programming for academic credit; (3) stress a culture-general approach; and (4) cover at least the core intercultural communication concepts as part of any orientation.

On a final and very personal note, the work I did preparing students to have a successful and fulfilling experience abroad and upon return turned out to be the most rewarding aspect of my career, even if it had exceedingly humble beginnings. Nothing else provided such intrinsic and immediate positive impacts for my students. For me, no other kind of teaching was nearly as personally engaging and consistently interesting and rewarding as preparing students for an international educational experience, and guiding their readjustment once they returned home. All of this was a result of the institution both allowing me for decades to freely pursue being an active scholar-practitioner without restrictive administrative obstacles, and also supporting study abroad training long before I was able to quantify its benefits. For this rare act of academic faith I remain personally and professionally grateful.

Notes

[1] See also online articles originally published by the author in *SAFETI (Safety Abroad* 1999-Winter 2000), as part of a project of the Center for Global Education: (1) 'The Missing Linkage: The Process of Integrating Orientation and ReEntry', a reprint of a 1993 article; and (2) 'The Evolution Continues: the UOP cross-cultural training courses.' Materials currently available online through the Center for Global Education include: http://globaled.us/safeti/v1n12000ed_missing_linkage.asp; http://globaled.us/safeti/v1n12000ed_evolution_continues.asp; http://globaled.us/safeti/v1n22000ed_how_do_we_really_know_what_ha ppens.asp; http://globaled.us/safeti/safety_reentry_survey.asp

[2] Originally published as R. Michael Paige (Ed.) Orientation as Process: the integration of pre- and post-experience learning, in *Cross-Cultural Orientation: new conceptualizations and applications* (Lanham, MD: University Press of America).

[3] An anthropology colleague and I co-wrote an article outlining the most salient theoretical differences between anthropological approaches to cross-cultural training and that of intercultural communication. This is a research topic that would have been unlikely to arise if we had not both had similar experiences making the shift from one disciplinary perspective to another (La Brack & Bathurst, 2012a).

[4] A summary of the baseline data is available in Sample, 2010, 2013.

References

Berardo, K. (2006) *The U-curve of Adjustment: a study in the evolution and evaluation of a 50-year-old model.* Luton: Luton Business School, University of Bedfordshire.

Brislin, R.W., Cushner, K., Cherrie, C. & Yong, M. (Eds) (1986) *Intercultural Interactions: a practical guide.* Beverly Hills: SAGE.

Engle, L. (2013) The Rewards of Designing Qualitative Assessment Questionnaires Appropriate to Study Abroad, in *Frontiers: The Interdisciplinary Journal of Study Abroad* 22, Winter 2012-Spring 2013.

Hammer, M.R., Bennett, M.J. & Wiseman, R. (2003) Measuring Intercultural Sensitivity: the intercultural development inventory, in *International Journal of Intercultural Relations*, 27, 421-443. http://dx.doi.org/10.1016/s0147-1767(03)00032-4

La Brack, B. (1986) Orientation as Process: the integration of pre- and post-experience learning, in R.M. Paige (Ed.) *Cross-cultural Orientation: new conceptualizations and applications.* Lanham, MD: University Press of America. Reprinted in 1993 as 'The Missing Linkage: the process of integrating orientation and reentry', in R.M. Paige (Ed.) *Education for the Intercultural Experience.* Yarmouth, ME: Intercultural Press.

La Brack, B. (Ed. and primary author) (2003) What's Up With Culture?' Online cultural training resource for study abroad website. http://www2.pacific.edu/sis/culture/

La Brack, B. & Bathurst, L. (2012a) Anthropology, Intercultural Communication, and Study Abroad, in M. VandeBerg, R.M. Paige & K. Lou (Eds) *Student Learning Abroad: what your students are learning, what they're not, and what you can do about it.* Sterling, VA: Stylus.

La Brack, B. & Bathurst, L. (2012b) Shifting the Locus of Intercultural Learning: intervening prior to and after student experiences abroad, in M. VandeBerg, R.M. Paige & K. Lou (Eds) *Student Learning Abroad: what your students are learning, what they're not, and what you can do about it.* Sterling, VA: Stylus.

Sample, S.G. (2010) Study Abroad and the International Curriculum: assessing changes in intercultural competence. Conference Proceedings, Intercultural Development Inventory Conference, Minneapolis, 28-30 October.

Sample, S.G. (2013) Developing Intercultural Learners through the International Curriculum, *Journal of Studies in International Education*, 17(5), 554-572. http://dx.doi.org/10.1177/1028315312469986

VandeBerg, M. & Paige, R.M. (2009) The Evolution of Intercultural Competence in US Study Abroad, in D.K. Deardorff (Ed.) *The SAGE Handbook of Intercultural Competence*. Newbury Park, CA: SAGE.

VandeBerg, M., Paige, R.M. & Lou, K. (Eds) (2012) *Student Learning Abroad: what your students are learning, what they're not, and what you can do about it.* Sterling, VA: Stylus.

CHAPTER 12

Lessons from a Late-blooming International Education Scholar-Practitioner for Combining Practice with Scholarship

ELIZABETH BREWER

SUMMARY In the United States, any number of graduate programs teach theory and provide opportunities to apply it outside the classroom, with the aim of preparing graduates to combine scholarship with practice in careers as international educators. Such training is relatively new. In fact, only recently did a discipline of international education emerge. Those who came before often had PhDs in other disciplines, and became international educators more by chance than by design. Some transitioned into international education in response to calls from their institutions to help them internationalize. Against this background, this chapter is informed by the experiences of a practitioner who received her graduate training in one field but later moved into international education without the grounding of many of today's newcomers. At first primarily focused on practice, she began engaging in scholarship when institutional needs demanded that she acquire greater historical and theoretical perspectives on internationalization, student development, and assessment. Her trajectory was aided by the emergence of a more robust literature on international education and of educational associations devoted to the field. The chapter offers advice for newcomers entering the profession, and suggestions for negotiating one's place within a particular institution and the discipline itself.

Introduction

This chapter is directed primarily at those preparing for careers in international education, whether they are graduate students training to become international educators, college and university faculty and administrators seeking to enter the field sideways, as did the author, or professionals outside of higher education. The discussion seeks to provide guidance for future international education scholar-practitioners deciding between tracks that may be more practitioner oriented or more scholar oriented, or ideally combinations of both, and offers advice based on one scholar-practitioner's career pathway in a time in which the field and profession have seen significant developments.

Graduate programs in international education often combine the study of quantitative and qualitative research methods, the history of higher education and internationalization, ethical issues associated with research, institutional partnerships, and student mobility with learning principles of program design and outcomes assessment. (For a compendium of programs, see Altbach & Engberg, 2001. See also chapter 18 [Woodman & Punteney] in this volume for a lengthier discussion of program types).

Doctoral programs may have different tracks to train students for different sectors, including higher education (e.g. the doctoral program in international education within New York University's Steinhardt School [New York University, n.d.]). Others aim to bridge 'educational theory, research, and practice' and offer 'both international education policy- and practice-oriented studies' (Lehigh University, n.d.), or to offer professionals working full time in intercultural or international education membership in a 'learning community in which members support and learn from each other' (University of Minnesota, n.d.).

At the master's level, a program might focus on 'personal interaction and reflective experience' to develop 'culturally aware, collaborative leaders' with coursework offered in intercultural theory as well as professional skills such as grant writing and international student admissions and recruitment (Lesley University, n.d.). Or a program may be rooted in a commitment to social justice and intercultural communication, with course work in these areas, but include as much experiential education, in the form of internships, as coursework. Thus, students may study financial management and other practical subjects of potential use to host organizations and future employers (School for International Training, n.d.)

Graduate training in international education offers advantages. Coursework provides a common grounding in international education theory, history and practice, and there are opportunities for specialization as well as application of knowledge and skills in real-world settings. Students learn from each other and from faculty, and develop the 'identity and commitment' that will enable them to become members of a disciplinary community (Becher & Trowler, 2001, p. 47).

Many working in international education today, however, did not have such specialized training. Some pursued graduate studies and/or careers in other fields. They may not identify as practitioners (see Bartunek & Rynes, 2014, for an insightful discussion of the tension between academics and practitioners) or pursue scholarship in international education. My own training in international education occurred on the job in various university positions and as a volunteer abroad. Out of habit and conscious of job classifications, I am more likely to call myself an administrator than an educator or practitioner. I only began seriously reading and writing about international education after working in higher education for fifteen years. Scholarship is not in my job description, earns me no extra pay, and is not a consideration in performance reviews. I largely undertake it on evenings and weekends. Despite this, I would not want to abandon it: it enriches my intellectual life, gives me knowledge and tools that make me a better educator, and enables me to enter into dialogue with others engaged in examining, complicating and advancing international education.

In this chapter I aim to offer some lessons from my career path as to the limits and benefits of on-the-job training, why combining practice with scholarship matters, and how professional associations can serve as a source for both alternative and continuing education for practice and scholarship in international education. I conclude with some thoughts on negotiating one's place within one's particular institution as well as the discipline of international education.

Practice: on-the-job training and its lessons

My PhD is in German languages and literatures, but did not become a Germanist, that is, a specialist in German language, literature, and culture. I have taught German language but never published in the field. Jobs in Germanistics were scarce when I finished, and personal circumstances kept me close to the university where I earned my doctorate when it came time to look for work. I thus found myself taking a job in the university's international programs office. International education was not yet widely considered a discipline, but my boss was a leader in the field, and in collaboration with other pioneers, was doing the research, writing, organizational work and advocacy that ultimately would lead to international education being taken seriously. The office had a strong emphasis on international exchanges at faculty, student and institutional levels, something that continues to influence my work.

I was working on a different level, however, in the trenches, as a clerical worker translating study abroad transcripts, informing students about study abroad options, and performing entry-level office work. When the office administrator left during a hiring freeze, I volunteered to take on her duties and eventually was appointed to the position. Reading transcripts had taught me quite a bit about different educational systems, and now as the administrative officer, I tracked and reported on the numerous separate budgets kept for study abroad programs, and managed the office's finances. I also served as the point person for

185

several exchange and summer study abroad programs. A student of literature, I learned that numbers also tell stories – about program design, higher education funding in the United States and abroad, and decision-making. Fresh to the work, I asked for help. Staff in the accounting office responded with kindness and generosity, teaching me what I needed to know. I was learning to read an institution of higher education and to be collegial, and I better understood the work of an international programs office.

If I had now completed the equivalent of classes in budgeting and financial management, study abroad principles and program management, my next on-the job training would focus on program development and design. I took a position in the college of arts and sciences, half of it devoted to managing area studies programs. There were five with a collective budget of $2,000. Enlisting area studies faculty members, I looked for opportunities to supplement the budget and strengthen the programs. Over a period of two years, activity expanded in each program; support came from humanities councils, the Fulbright program, the US Department of Education and smaller entities. My job was to help generate ideas for programming, approach departments and deans for support that included matching funding, and pull grant proposals together. With funding in place, we ran conferences, hired faculty and hosted visiting scholars, and the library acquired new books.

I was often out of my depth. What did I know about Muslims in America, Latin American area studies, dissident Soviet artists, or Southeast Asian refugee needs? I learned to rely on faculty members' expertise, to listen well enough to develop a narrative and craft a budget, and to be entrepreneurial in identifying opportunities and approaching potential partners.

In *How College Works* (2014), Chambliss and Takacs discuss the role of membership in groups – formal and informal – in helping students feel they belong, and how that in turn leads to success in college. The same applied to my work. Planning and implementing projects and events built common purpose and energy. As a clerical worker and an administrative officer, I had learned to reach out to staff in other offices. I now learned to collaborate with faculty and to report up to gain the support and guidance of the deans I worked for. I had now completed the equivalent of coursework in higher education management, area studies, program design and proposal writing.

I worked at two more universities. At one, I focused on study abroad. Membership in an informal network and involvement in NAFSA at the regional level helped me keep up to date. At the next, I joined a graduate school, leaving study abroad behind for student affairs. I monitored progress toward degrees, developed an advising program, and oversaw financial aid, scholarships and admissions. Although international education was tangential to my main duties, I oversaw international student advising, managed a Title VI area studies program and revitalized three exchange programs. I also supported graduate students applying for fellowships, among them the Fulbright program and the then new and controversial National Security Education Program. This new, on-the-job 'coursework' had covered international student advising, graduate student advising and fellowship advising, and I had completed advanced work in proposal writing, program management and educational exchange.

My next step was to leave academia. After seven years in graduate student affairs, I wanted to re-enter international education full time, and to do that, felt I needed to first spend time at the 'sharp end of the stick' (Theroux, 2002a), on the ground in a country I did not know and in an unfamiliar environment. I needed to see if I could still learn another language and if I was capable of the experiential education I understood to be a new focus in higher education in general and in study abroad in particular. I joined the Peace Corps.

As a volunteer, ignorance – my own – was a steady companion for longer than I liked, something I try to help the students and faculty I send abroad prepare for. Learning to read an unfamiliar country and the organizations that hosted me proved harder than learning to read an institution of higher education. The task was made harder by the fact I only began learning the language of my host country upon arrival. I apply lessons I learned from participant/observation and language learning during Peace Corps service daily.

My work focused on staff and organizational capacity building. Again I helped design projects and wrote proposals, and I acquired new skills by creating training manuals, designing workshops and training staff, and with the staff, trained trainers. Community engagement and community development, the focus of my host organizations, had been new to me, as had asset-based approaches to problem-solving, and I became better versed in challenges and ethical dilemmas of volunteering. To record observations and process experiences, I wrote, something I encourage study abroad students to do. My graduate 'coursework' completed, it was time to apply what I had learned and to begin pursuing scholarship.

Reasons for Scholarship: responding to institutional needs with help from collaborations and professional associations

Initial Foray into Scholarship: institutional history

I joined Beloit College as Director of International Education in 2002. I had applied for other jobs after my return to the United States, but this was the one I wanted. The college wanted to build its capacity to extend international education to all students, not just those who studied abroad or came from abroad, and faculty and staff needed to be enlisted to do this. The college also wanted to understand the lessons of mobility, which, as Josef Mestenhauser and others had pointed out, were not being applied to the curriculum (Pickert & Turlington, 1992; Mestenhauser & Ellingboe, 1998). My work with area studies and as a volunteer had made me a believer in capacity building, and I sensed that the position would help me build capacity at multiple levels. Further, the position had been recast to facilitate internationalization, as opposed to administering discrete components of international education, and the director was expected to be both an administrator, getting things done, and an educator. Fortunately, scholarship about international education had grown, and there was interest in Europe and the United States in internationalization as a means to institutional transformation (see e.g. Nilsson & Otten, 2003; Kehm & Teichler, 2007, on the developments of internationalization at home). The American Council on Education had also recently established an internationalization collaborative, which Beloit College had joined.

Invited to serve on a three-person panel on international education at the faculty conference opening the 2002 academic year, I enlisted the help of the college archivist and the registrar to construct a paper on 'International Education at Beloit College' (Brewer, 2002) that examined the history of international education at the college with reference to national developments, provided a current profile of it, and raised questions for its future. (An updated version was later published; see Brewer, 2015.) Doing the research for the paper gave me insight into my institution's past and present international work, and the conference taught me about the aspirations of faculty and staff for its future. It also engaged me with researching and writing about international education. Additionally, the paper and conference provided the college dean and staff in the development office with information that could help them secure resources for internationalization, and faculty were better positioned to collaborate with my office. Above all, I learned that if I were to pursue scholarship related to international education, it had to be rooted in the history of international education and current developments in the field, and in the mission and priorities of the institution for which I was working.

First Book: curriculum integration

In the context of education abroad, curriculum integration 'refers to a variety of institutional approaches designed to fully integrate study abroad options into the college experience and academic curricula for students in all majors' (NAFSA: Association of International Educators, 2013). Arguments for such integration in US undergraduate studies have been made since at least 1990 (see e.g. Carlson et al, 1990), and the

University of Minnesota's curriculum integration initiative has served as a model for other institutions.

Beloit College had made substantial progress toward making study abroad available to students across the institution by 2002. However, there was concern about another question – namely, how to use integration to take 'academic experience to new levels' (Macey, 2005, p. 57). Anecdotal evidence suggested that students were not learning as much when abroad as they and their faculty advisors might like. In plenary sessions and small group discussions at meetings of the American Council on Educations' Internationalization Collaborative, we began to generate ideas. A series of curriculum development activities then led to the introduction of Cities in Transition courses, taught from Beloit to students at selected exchange program sites. Simply putting students on the ground did not result in learning; they needed to be taught to engage critically with their host environments. To this end, Cities in Transition assignments were constructed using participant observation and reflective writing, and students were asked to undertake extended, site-based projects of their choosing. By coincidence, the study abroad organization IES Abroad offered to send us a faculty member to give a lecture and meet with faculty; his interests coincided with ours and we brought him back as a Fulbright Scholar-in-Residence to help us refine the project. Darren Kelly shared invaluable theoretical perspectives from cultural and urban geography and literary studies, as well as pedagogy he was using with American study abroad students in Ireland. Funding from the Andrew W. Mellon Foundation helped us grow the project, and a small grant from the Internationalization Collaborative enabled us to discuss theory and pedagogy with Kalamazoo College faculty, who were similarly concerned with study abroad integration.

Together, Beloit and Kalamazoo faculty shared our discussions at a collaborative meeting, and the resulting curriculum development at an annual conference of the Association of American Colleges and Universities. Asked by Stylus Press to translate the work into a book, we accepted. Kiran Cunningham, a Kalamazoo College anthropologist, and I spent the summer doing a literature review and worked with our respective faculty teams to produce, refine and edit chapters. *Integrating Study Abroad into the Curriculum: theory and practice across the disciplines* was published in 2009 (Brewer & Cunningham, 2009). My first extended writing on international education, it was the result of the continuing education I and my colleagues were receiving through the American Council on Education's Internationalization Collaborative, and teamwork to address institutional needs. I then approached *Frontiers: The Interdisciplinary Journal of Study Abroad* about doing a volume on study abroad and the city; Beloit College was not the only institution thinking about the relationship. The editorial board approved the proposal, Michael Monahan was asked to join me as co-editor, and in 2011, *Study Abroad and the City* was published as a special issue (Brewer & Monahan, 2011). Twenty-two authors contributed twelve articles.

Second Book: assessment

In 2011, I was asked to join the Forum on Education Abroad's Outcomes and Research Committee. Like me, some committee members had little experience with assessment, but our institutions needed us to do this work, and Forum members wanted more guidance on assessment. The committee identified several tasks, with some of us assembling a bibliography of research on education abroad outcomes assessment, others developing a glossary, and others creating a workshop for newcomers to assessment. Today, much of the committee's work is included in a toolbox for assessment on the Forum website.

The timing was propitious. Beloit College was taking assessment more seriously and developing a strategy of embedding assessment in existing students' work, such as course assignments and reflective writing used in advising. Kelly McLaughlin of Yale University and I chaired an Institute on Outcomes Assessment at the 2012 annual Forum conference, gaining more insight into current rationales and practices. The Associated Colleges of the Midwest (ACM), to which Beloit College belonged, organized two very helpful sessions on assessment, first with Mark Salisbury, now the institutional researcher at Augustana College in Rock Island, IL, and later with Charlie Blaich and Kathy Wise of the Center for Inquiry in the Liberal Arts at Wabash College. The sessions reinforced the validity of using post-study abroad reflective essays as one basis for assessment, an approach my office was taking in keeping with the institutional approach. We wanted a method that would facilitate both assessment and learning; student reflection on learning accomplishes that (Earl, 2003). Influenced by an occasional paper by Blaich and Wise (2011), we began recruiting teams of faculty, students and staff to help with assessment, an approach that has widened the circle of those thinking about study abroad and its role in teaching and learning.

At a Forum conference, Vic Savicki, Professor of Psychology Emeritus at Western Oregon University, mentioned interest in editing a book on study abroad outcomes assessment. I asked if I could join him. I knew that working on the book would challenge me to continue to study outcomes assessment. Vic and I felt there was need to examine the small-scale approaches education abroad practitioners were using to understand what and how students learn and act on the findings. Commercially available pre- and post-experience instruments tended to dominate discussions of assessment in education abroad, as did calls for large-scale studies. Yet the former had limitations, and both would be out of reach for many education abroad offices. By now Vic and I could identify a pool of potential authors as well as a possible structure for the book and Stylus Press was interested in publishing it. The book was published in November 2015 (Savicki & Brewer, 2015).

Concluding Thoughts

This book explores the tension between scholarship and practice in international education. My own pathway into life as an international education scholar-practitioner has been marked, on the one hand, by questions as to the degree to which I, as an administrator in higher education, practiced a discipline or was an educator, and on the other, by whether, as someone lacking the formal training needed for 'rigorous' scholarship, I should attempt scholarship at all.

To address the first point: in a 2013 blog posting related to the *SAGE Handbook of International Higher Education* (Deardorff et al, 2012), John Heyl discussed the degree to which international education has become a discipline, and concluded that its status is uncertain (Heyl, 2013). Becher and Trowler's work (2001) on disciplines as academic tribes is also useful on this question. With 'identities' and 'patches of intellectual ground', academic tribes are characterized by 'traditions, customs and practices, transmitted knowledge, beliefs, morals and rules of conduct' and 'linguistic and symbolic forms of communication' (p. 47). Further, becoming a member of an academic tribe requires both proficiency in the discipline of the tribe, and 'loyalty' to its members and 'adherence to its norms' (p. 47). Tribes have hidden curricula; interactions between students and instructors teach as much about professional attitudes and values as the formal curriculum (p. 48). Pathways into tribes are also diversifying, with many tribal members earning PhDs late in life (p. 47).

Those receiving graduate training in international education are gaining the theoretical and intellectual tools via a formal curriculum that will help qualify them to join the international education tribe. Organizations such as the Forum on Education Abroad, with its standards of practice, or the Association of International Education Administrators, which is developing standards for the senior international officers who lead internationalization, support opportunities for both continuing education and the hidden curriculum for their members. However, those coming to their positions through graduate training will also have to pay considerable attention to understanding the mission, priorities, resources and culture of the institutions and organizations they join. A difficult challenge for recent graduates of international education programs can be operationalizing the theories and principles they have learned in light of the constraints under which institutions and organizations operate. Referring to the standards in the field rarely receives a warm welcome, nor do calls for comprehensive plans. Rather, institutions, and the people who constitute them, want to feel paid attention to using a familiar language, and most likely, progress will be incremental.

To address the second point (whether, as someone lacking the formal training needed for 'rigorous' scholarship, I should attempt scholarship at all): tensions between calls for rigor in research and scholarship on the one hand, and preference for relevance on the other, are not likely to disappear, nor are they limited to international education. (See e.g. the informative discussion by Bartunek & Rynes, 2014, and the chapters by Hudzik and Light in this book.) Luckily, the language used in most writing about international education, as is true in fields such as history, is 'couched in familiar, everyday language and ... [is] – on the surface at least – readily accessible' (Gerholm, 1985, quoted in Becher & Trowler, 2001, p. 116). This makes it easier for those not trained in international education to nonetheless both access and contribute to the literature on international education, and for those trained in international education to transmit their ideas and knowledge to those who are not. However, disciplinary tribes also exclude (Becher & Trowler, 2001, p. 47) and privilege. Large, replicable studies carry more weight than small-scale studies, and theoretical work is more valuable than applied work. The danger for international education practice is that emphasis on rigor can be paralyzing; many international education practitioners hesitate to engage in critical areas such as assessment because of lack of qualification and limited resources.

Similarly, disciplinary tribes tend to privilege writing by fellow tribal members, overlooking the potential contributions to be made from individuals who do not belong to the tribe. Rebecca Solnit's work (2005) on getting lost in order to discover can be helpful to devise ways for students to navigate and take ownership of study abroad experiences. Geographer Ian Cook's discussion (Cook et al, 2005) of positionality, hardly a conventionally written piece of scholarship, can inform questions asked of study abroad applicants or returnees. Short essays by Theroux (2002b) can help students learn to derive meaning from seemingly mundane experiences abroad. We will be better practitioners and scholars if we turn to sources both in and outside international education.

Finally, institutions and organizations engaged with international education would be stronger if arbitrary boundaries between different kinds of positions were relaxed. Does it really make sense to restrict engagement with intellectual inquiry to certain kinds of positions? An argument can be made that such inquiry benefits practice and, through more informed practice, the ability of institutions and organizations to achieve their missions.

References

Altbach, P.G. & Engberg, D. (2001) *Higher Education: a worldwide inventory of centers and programs.* Phoenix, AZ: Oryx Press.

Bartunek, J.M. & Rynes, S.L. (2014) Academics and Practitioners are Alike and Unlike: the paradoxes of academic-practitioner relationships, *Journal of Management*, 40(5), 1181-1201. http://dx.doi.org/10.1177/0149206314529160

Becher, T. & Trowler, P.R. (2001) *Academic Tribes and Territories*, 2nd edn. Buckingham: Society for Research into Higher Education and Open University Press.

Blaich, C.F. & Wise, K.S. (2011) From Gathering to Using Assessment Results: lessons from the Wabash National Study. NILOA Occasional Paper No. 8. January. Urbana, IL: University of Illinois and Indiana University, National Institute for Learning Outcomes Assessment.

Brewer, E. (2002) International Education at Beloit College. Unpublished paper.

Brewer, E. (2015) Beloit College: internationalization in the American Midwest, in J. Hudzik (Ed.) *Comprehensive Internationalization: institutional pathways to success*, pp. 135-143. Abingdon: Routledge.

Brewer, E. & Cunningham, K. (2009) *Integrating Study Abroad into the Curriculum: theory and practice across the disciplines.* Sterling, VA: Stylus Press.

Brewer, E. & Monahan, M. (Eds) (2011) Study Abroad and the City, *Frontiers: the interdisciplinary journal of study abroad*, XX, i-213.

Carlson, J.S., Burn, B.B., Useem, J. & Yachimowicz, D. (1990) *Study Abroad: the experience of American undergraduates.* Westport, CT: Greenwood Press.

Chambliss, D.F. & Takacs, C.G. (2014) *How College Works.* Cambridge, MA: Harvard University Press. http://dx.doi.org/10.4159/harvard.9780674726093

Cook, I. et al (2005) Positionality/Situated Knowledge, in D. Sibley, P. Jackson, D. Atkinson & N. Washbourne (Eds) *Cultural Geography: a critical dictionary of key concepts*, pp. 16-26. London: I.B. Tauris.

Deardorff, D., de Wit, H., Heyl, J. & Adams, T. (Eds) (2012) *The SAGE Handbook of International Higher Education.* Thousand Oaks, CA: SAGE.

Earl, L.M. (2003) *Assessment as Learning: using classroom assessment to maximize student learning.* Thousand Oaks, CA: Corwin Press.

Gerholm, T. (1985) On Tacit Knowledge in Academia, in L. Gustavson (Ed.) *On Communication: no. 3.* Linköping: University of Linköping Department of Communication Studies.

Heyl, J. (2013) Is International Education a Discipline? AIEA blog post, 23 May. https://aieablog.wordpress.com/

Kehm, B.M. & Teichler, U. (2007) Research on Internationalisation in Higher Education, *Journal of Studies in International Education*, 11(3/4), 260-273. http://dx.doi.org/10.1177/1028315307303534

Lehigh University (n.d.) PhD Comparative and International Education. http://coe.lehigh.edu/academics/degrees/phdcie

Lesley University (n.d.) Master of Arts (MA) in International Higher Education and Intercultural Relations. http://www.lesley.edu/master-of-arts/international-higher-education-and-intercultural-relations/

Macey, D. (2005) Intellectual Growth and the Integration of Study Abroad Experience, *Frontiers: The Interdisciplinary Journal of Study Abroad*, 12 (November), 56-58.

Mestenhauser, J.A. & Ellingboe, B.S. (Eds) (1998) *Reforming the Higher Education Curriculum: internationalizing the campus.* Phoenix, AZ: American Council on Education and Oryx Press.

NAFSA: Association of International Educators (2013) Curriculum Integration: best practices. http://www.nafsa.org/findresources/Default.aspx?id=8352

New York University (n.d.) PhD in International Education. Program Overview. http://steinhardt.nyu.edu/humsocsci/international/phd

Nilsson, B. & Otten, M. (Eds) (2003) Special Issue: internationalisation at home, *Journal of Studies in International Education*, 7(1).

Pickert, S. & Turlington, B. (1992*) Internationalizing the Undergraduate Curriculum: a handbook for campus leaders.* Washington, DC: American Council on Education.

Savicki, V. & Brewer, E. (Eds) (2015) *Assessing Study Abroad: theory, tools, and practice.* Sterling, VA: Stylus Press.

School for International Training (n.d.) Master of Arts in International Education (on Campus). http://graduate.sit.edu/sit-graduate-institute/sn/degree-and-certificate-programs/masters-degree-programs/master-of-arts-in-international-education-on-campus/

Solnit, R. (2005) *A Field Guide to Getting Lost.* New York: Viking Penguin.

Theroux, P. (2002a) At the Sharp End: being in the Peace Corps, in *Fresh Air Fiend*, pp. 40-45. Wilmington, MA: Mariner.

Theroux, p. (2002b) Five Travel Epiphanies, in *Fresh Air Fiend*, pp. 46-48. Wilmington, MA: Mariner.

University of Minnesota (n.d.) OLPD PhD: comparative and international development (CIDE) track. http://www.cehd.umn.edu/OLPD/grad-programs/CIDE/LIIE/default.html

CHAPTER 13

Deschooling International Education: toward an alternative paradigm of practice

RICHARD SLIMBACH

SUMMARY Despite its aspiration to leaven the world with 'global souls' formed through transformative intercultural experiences, the field of global education has thus far failed to escape the runaway costs, the marginal learning, and the absence of an ultimate *why* that bedevils American higher education. Indeed, hundreds of consumerist organizations and commoditized educational products only reinforce the instrumental value of foreign peoples and places, and that for a tiny global elite. 'Market realities' rule, pressuring students and institutions alike to narrow their commitments from the broader social good to the 'needs of industry'. What does the role of 'scholar-practitioner' look like in the light of these realities? This chapter puts a spotlight on three factors – educative experience, conceptual mentoring and active experimentation – to help us imagine an alternative ('deschooled') paradigm of international education: one that is radically affordable and accessible, more personalized and self-directed, more community-driven, and ultimately more relevant to the challenges faced by the majority of people on the planet.

In 1971, following many years spent grappling with the structure and myths driving modernity, Ivan Illich published *Deschooling Society*. Although he had much to say about mandatory schooling, the book was more fundamentally about modern civilization, especially the world of all-encompassing 'instrumentalization'. Illich faced this world as an Austria-born son of a Croatian father and a German-Jewish mother, an ordained Jesuit priest, a PhD in history, and one of the most original social commentators of our time. He spoke nine languages with almost no accent. Radicalized through years of service among largely Irish and

Puerto Rican immigrants in New York City, and then in Puerto Rico, he eventually founded the Centre for Intercultural Formation in Cuernavaca, Mexico to further the spread of what he called 'intercultural sensibility'.

During the 1970s Illich became widely known for his brilliant, polemical books that revealed the disabling effects of major institutions most of us uncritically embrace as marvels – education, medicine, transport, technology, social services and communications, among others. His personal travel style epitomized his quest for a more 'convivial' – that is to say, spontaneous, equitable and participatory – society. He toured Latin America by bus, from one carnival and festival to another. To get a feel for Africa, he undertook a walking tour through the southern Sahara. During his repeated visits to Benares, he sought lodging in Hindu temples.

Upon reading Illich for the first time, my initial impulse was to dismiss his forceful critique of modernity's shadow side as the musings of a mad reactionary. But then I recalled E.F. Schumacher's reply to the accusation that he was a 'crank'. 'A crank is a very elegant device,' he quipped. 'It's small, it's strong, it's lightweight, energy efficient, and it makes revolutions.' That was Illich.

In this chapter I will advocate for greater 'crankiness' among international education professionals. Instead of contenting ourselves with being free-spirited cultural diplomats inhabiting the fringes of higher education, I will argue that we, as scholar-practitioners, are uniquely positioned and qualified to re-imagine global learning outside the box of mainstream higher educational practice, and to develop alternative models more responsive to twenty-first-century realities.

Cracks in the Ivory Tower

Re-envisioning international education begins with re-focusing attention on those questions we tend to suppress or ignore – questions like: What are colleges and universities for? Who do they serve? How and what should they teach? And how should learners use what they know? Illich, for one, was not convinced that schools were 'the most practical arrangement for imparting education'. To the contrary, he agonized over young people who were '"schooled" to confuse teaching with learning, grade advancement with education, a diploma with competence, and fluency with the ability to say something new' (Illich, 1971, p. 1). But the failure of schooling was a mere symptom of a far larger problem: the commercialization of knowledge fueled by the professionalization of human goods like learning.

Over the last few years a wide range of educational commenters have warned of a looming 'crisis' in higher education. Their disturbing exposés describe a kind of educational apocalypse of runaway costs, crushing student loan debt, declining graduation rates, administrative bloat, grade inflation and marginal learning. But perhaps the most consequential 'crack' in the ivory tower is the acute loss of an ultimate *why*. Forget 'love of learning' or 'becoming global citizens'. Students regularly tell me they are in college 'just to get through'. In their minds, college is an investment in a single entity: oneself. Economic insecurity within a modern world built on specialization drives them to convert credits and credentials into cash as quickly as possible. The intense instrumentalism that defines their choices and character is but a by-product of an age dominated by utility and productivity.

Faculty members and campus administrators also appear to be adrift. Complaining of heavy teaching loads and service requirements, faculty hunker down in narrow subject specializations divorced from community applications. Campus administrators, preoccupied with the bottom line, adopt narrow business models centered on boosting reputational status and expanding profit margins. Both groups were once absorbed with pedagogical concerns – like how to foster practical wisdom and form lives of consequence. Now, energies are devoted to guarding professional interests. No wonder the individual and institutional attitude toward promoting the broader public good is largely indifference.

The results bear a troubling resemblance to conditions Illich described in the early 1970s: knowledge reduced to a saleable commodity; students reduced to clients or customers; minds isolated from bodies; solitary bodies sequestered from wider relationships in human and natural communities; and a highly personalized process between master and apprentice turned into an impersonal set of 'hoops' to qualify graduates for the job market. Even global service learning and education abroad find themselves subject to marketplace demands. No doubt both have extraordinary potential to arouse student concern for why certain realities exist, how their lives may be implicated in those realities, and what their basic obligations are. Too often, however, they deteriorate into mere résumé builders and fantasy adventures for the upwardly mobile.

Whither Scholar-Practitioner?

As a professional body, international educators have offered few alternatives to the predicament profiled above. Despite our aspiration to leaven the world with global souls formed through transformative intercultural experiences, our field has thus far failed to escape the issues that bedevil the wider academy. Perhaps we feel largely impotent before global forces we can barely understand, much less control. Or maybe we simply recognize that we are now 'as gods', as Stewart Brand (2009), publisher of the *Whole Earth Catalog*, puts it, and accept our responsibility to manage the planet through rational, expert-directed, technical systems.

From a 'techno-global' perspective, global educators best serve students by helping them comprehend a world unbounded by the old divisions of territory and history and tradition. Student identities no longer need to involve neighborly bonds and local allegiances. Indeed, the role of international education is to develop persons to think and act *beyond* the boundaries of place. They are thus relieved of any burdensome obligations to others. And what about the social, economic and ecological breakdown spreading across the planet? Not to worry. Some combination of trade, aid, entrepreneurial zeal and scientific ingenuity will steadily improve livelihoods. Led by a new generation of digital cosmopolitans, we will 'build the world we want rather than the world we fear' (Zuckerman, 2013, p. 272).

Deschooled international education is rooted in an alternative, expressly non-managerial rendering of scholar-practitioner. These persons think and act independently, defying easy classification as conservative, liberal or progressive. Their non-partisan 'worldliness' grants them a wide horizon, a keen awareness and a critical outlook. Cognitive complexity enables them to constantly 'think on their feet' and to generate new patterns of practice. Illich effectively challenged the status quo because he was not beholden to it. In an era when prestige and money both form and distort higher education, deschooled scholar-practitioners must learn to navigate institutional cultures without being compromised by the stimulants of status and affluence. Although physically inhabiting educational space, their ultimate loyalty lies elsewhere, in a vision of 'the good' that transcends institutional interests and bounded conventions. They make a unique contribution to cultural renewal by staying intellectually and spiritually fluid, constantly combining elements from alternative cultural perspectives and value sets. This semi-nomadic condition wears various monikers: sojourner (apostle Paul), exile (Edward Said), marginal man (Robert Park), stranger (Georg Simmel), intellectual iconoclast (Thorstein Veblen), double consciousness (W.E.B. DuBois), liminality (Victor Turner), and constructive marginal (Jane Bennett).

When it comes to an archetype of an institutionally embedded yet never fully adjusted scholar-practitioner, I immediately think of Ernest Boyer. As president of the Carnegie Foundation for the Advancement of Teaching, Boyer articulated a synthesis of the roles of scholar and practitioner under the rubric of a 'scholarship of engagement'. He boldly challenged traditional standards of scholarship in favor of disciplinary knowledge serving the common weal. 'The academy,' wrote Boyer, 'must become a more vigorous partner in the search for answers to our most pressing social, civic, economic, and moral problems.' By doing so, higher education could recover its sense of moral purpose and reverse the drift toward being 'a place where professors get tenured and students get credentialed ... a private benefit, not a public good' (Boyer, 1996, pp. 19-20).

Reading Boyer today almost feels like some bizarre hallucination. Although lip service is given to 'civic engagement' and 'global citizenship', college and university leaders rarely make even the pretense of preparing students to embrace their moral obligations to community or polity, much less planet. Their dominant outlook is decidedly economic and political: how to control overhead and costs while increasing market share through enhanced institutional prestige. The general public has followed suit. There is little expectation that scholar-practitioners will deploy their considerable talents in service to community needs and opportunities.

Boyer was a strong advocate of student success and satisfying, socially contributive work. But, like Illich before him, he could not accept the technological determinism, the 'bottom line' economic logic, or the narrow careerism that effectively sidelines questions of the common good. For Boyer, 'success' had little to do with upward social mobility, and everything to do with developing students to find that place where their personal passions and the world's needs intersect. Boyer's hopeful vision of a coherent and 'engaged' university reflected, to a large extent, the imprint of his devoutly Quaker grandparents. In mid-life they moved their family from the farmlands of Ohio into the slums of Dayton. For the next 40 years, recounts Boyer, 'grandpa' ran the city mission, 'working for the poor, teaching me more by deed than by word that to be truly human one must serve' (Boyer, 1997, p. 112).

So, how are we to understand scholar-practitioner amid competing readings of the university-society relationship? How do we inculcate world-mindedness at a time when experience and knowledge have been reduced to tradable commodities, things to be bought in order to make money? I do not have any easy answers, only a dogged faith in the distinctive mission of a global education. That mission, in my view, is to facilitate the creative inquiry into peoples, places, institutions and ecologies – participating in them, learning from them, and in the process and as a result, serving them.

The reflections that follow suggest how scholar-practitioners might support this mission through a fundamentally deschooled approach to international education. The prefix 'de' in 'deschooled' is deliberately not un-, much less anti-. 'Un' signifies the removing of something – in this case the entire institutional framework of global learning as it currently operates within higher education. Deschooling, by contrast, signifies the devolution of highly bureaucratic learning systems. In their place, I propose a paradigm of practice that both 'roots' in educative experience and conceptual mentoring, and 'routes' in active experimentation with global learning models that are more affordable and accessible, more personalized and self-directed, more community-driven, and ultimately more relevant to the challenges faced by the majority of people on earth.

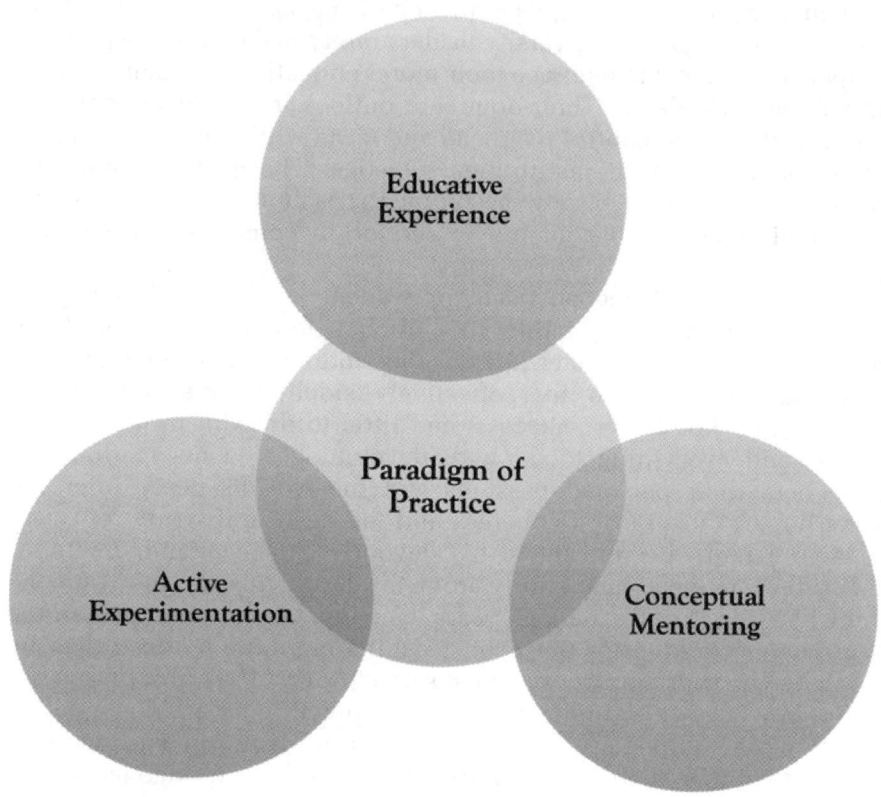

Figure 1. Key processes in scholarly practice.

Educative Experience: foreign worlds

Eduard Lindeman, a colleague of John Dewey, famously stated, 'The resource of highest value in adult education is the learner's experience' (1926/1961, p. 6). Agreed, I would hasten to add: a particular type or quality of experience. Most of what happens in our lives is non-educative for the simple reason that most of us, most of the time, live on autopilot. Not being consciously aware of what is taking place around us and within us, we fail to benefit from our life experience.

As this is a book profiling international educators, permit me to get personal. Without question, the greatest source of knowledge in my life has been 'educative' experiences that extend back to adolescence. Graduation from high school signaled emancipation from the monotonous sprawl of Los Angeles and an entrance to the lush, unspoiled wildness of the Kalalau valley on the north coast of the Hawaiian island of Kaua'i. There I joined a restless group of exiles from the mainland (mostly from California) who had formed a makeshift, clothing-optional community. We built multilevel tree houses on bamboo stilts, and subsisted on wild fruit, fish and garden-grown vegetables. There were no cars, no electricity, no bills to pay, no written rules and no official rulers. Some, like me, were anti-war protestors fleeing from the shadow of the draft. Others had simply concluded that 'dropping out' and 'tuning in' was the rational response to modern, mechanized life. Withdrawal from civilization gave everyone the chance to re-examine the dominant paradigm of living, and to re-imagine a more peaceful, self-reliant, convivial and low-carbon mode of existence.

But even in a tropical paradise, I couldn't escape the troubled self that I carried along with me. It didn't take long to realize that my inward quest to find deep personal meaning merely through new geography was doomed to failure. If new experience were to have transformative potential, I would need to live from something and exist for something that reached far beyond me.

Within a matter of months I was back on the mainland, struggling to connect fresh self-understandings with a growing awareness of my need to grow beyond the largely affluent and racially homogeneous society that I called 'home'. I had no guidance from global educators or a text like this. All I knew is that I needed to venture out into a wider world – the 'other America' – where I could put my homespun self to the test of radically different social and cultural spaces. In the process I could hope to better understand what it was that effectively separated 'me' from 'them'.

For the next two years, off and on, two buddies and I followed the national migrant circuit. We harvested melons in south Texas, apples in southern Illinois and grapes in California's San Joaquin Valley. Camps and fields became our classrooms, and farmworkers and growers our most compelling teachers. Together, they revealed political economy in ways that books, lectures and films could not. No academic supervision was provided, and no credit earned, but rigorous questions related to global interdependence and moral responsibility assumed center stage: Where and how is my food grown? Who harvests it and under what conditions? How is my life, as a consumer, connected to the lives of producers? Immersion in this separate universe underscored a central truth in global learning best expressed by world systems analyst Immanuel Wallerstein: 'What is needed educationally is not to learn that we are citizens of the world, but that we occupy particular niches in an unequal world' (1998, p. 63).

What was my responsibility in such a world? Senegalese poet and environmentalist Baba Dioum helped me to chart a path toward answering that question through a declaration that connected care, cognition and context. 'In the end,' says Dioum, 'we will conserve only what we love; we will love only what we understand; and we will understand only what we [directly experience].'[1] And so, for the next decade, direct (deschooled) experience became my primary teacher. Residence was taken up in several intentional communities where learning and living were a single piece. Journeys from Mexico to Ladakh led me into enchanted landscapes and serendipitous encounters. A string of self-initiated learning projects, both international and domestic, progressively refined a framework for global learning that confirmed the necessity of subjecting the whole self to an unfamiliar and unsettling set of real-life contingencies.

Principles of Practice

Five convictions laid the foundation for a paradigm of deschooled practice:

1. Human beings have a natural capacity for learning.
2. Deep learning that significantly influences behavior is usually not the result of teaching (programmed instruction); it is self-discovered and self-appropriated.
3. We learn best not by taking in abstract ideas through our minds, but by first doing new things with our bodies – things that require risk-taking and carry emotional force.
4. Learning the new involves unlearning the old, which entails an optimal level of uncertainty, uncomfortable questioning, and contained adversity.
5. Thinking cannot change while behavior remains largely unaffected. We don't think our way into right acting; we act our way into new thinking (Palmer, 2008).

Conceptual Mentoring: framing ideas

Although the most significant life educator up to this point had been a special type of 'travel schooling', I also picked up academic degrees along the way. My primary motivation was to engage in serious conversations with thoughtful people on issues that mattered. I also hoped for a type of cognitive apprenticeship where I, the protégé, could further develop under more experienced and knowledgeable 'masters'. John Dewey, perhaps the most influential educational philosopher of the twentieth century, wrote about the value of bringing one's life experiences into dialogue with the world of ideas. 'There is no discipline in the world so severe as the discipline of experience subjected to the tests of intelligent development and direction' (Dewey, 1938, p. 90). I wanted and needed that discipline. So, throughout my college years, I looked for an elder-mentor, someone who cared deeply about their subject, saw my potential, and was willing to have me 'shadow' their intellect and practice.

I'd like to say that my professional life was marked by a succession of such mentorships within academic settings, but that was not the case. To be sure, incidental conversations with classmates (and later colleagues) provided important moral and conceptual support. But the source of my truest intellectual companioning was to be with mentors never met – that is, in the pages of books. Extensive reading, rather than in-person apprenticing, inducted me into an enlarging vision for how global education might serve the common good.

Book mentors were culled to address issues that I found impossibly perplexing: human nature, happiness, love, social inequality, urbanism, ecology, economy, religious faith, power, propaganda, ideology, social change, technology, moral obligation, and community development, among others. I imagined myself sitting across from a really insightful, ethically animated person with my head full of questions: What does it mean to be human? Does life offer an ultimate order that transcends the world's chaos? How might we imagine the 'good society'? What does such a world require of me? How might world learning clarify these obligations? Because such questions deal with the (re-) structuring of human relations with the world, I found them of direct relevance to international educational practice.

Gradually a vision of global learning emerged that looked more like a free-range farmyard than a battery-hen farm (Abbott, 2014). Conceptual contributors included the usual suspects and their signature ideas: John Dewey (learning by doing), Ernest Boyer (scholarship of engagement), David Kolb (the experiential learning cycle), Paulo Freire (critical consciousness) and Jack Mezirow (transformative learning). But many other wise voices filled my being with meanings consistent with a deschooled pedagogical process. These included Dorothy Day (revolution of heart), Martin Buber (the 'I-Thou' encounter), Margaret Mead (ethnographic fieldwork), Jane Jacobs (urban design), Wendell Berry (restorative economy), Gustavo Gutiérrez (liberatory theology), Jacques Ellul (rule of technique), Martin Luther King, Jr. (triple evils), Sheldon Wolin (managed democracy), Nicholas Wolterstorff (natural human rights), William Stringfellow (institutional power), Ivan Illich (learning networks), Erich Fromm (automaton conformity), Thomas Merton (quest for true self as quest for God), Parker Palmer (undivided living and learning), Kwame Appiah (rooted cosmopolitanism), Manuel Castells (network society), Robert Chambers (sustainable livelihoods), Noam Chomsky (power and ideology), Reinhold Niebuhr (American mythology) and Thích Nhất Hạnh (compassion through suffering).

Each of these theorists penetrated the certitudes and systems of modern life with great precision. In particular, they discerned the pathological dependence of citizens on institutionalized and professionalized services – in education, religion, government, media and medicine – as a threat to what it is to be human. When functioning well, social institutions have the potential to organize human activity around the commonwealth ideal. But they also possess a life that operates independently of the functions of those individuals (like scholar-practitioners) who are housed by them. (The existence of schools does not mean we have education, and the existence of media does not mean that we have objective reporting.) In fact, virtuous and truly creative bureaucracies have become increasingly rare in modern life. The one moral principle that governs virtually all institutions is its own survival.

Surprisingly enough, many of the thinkers who offered the most trenchant social analyses did so with a deeply religious voice. Not as a creedal commitment, mind you, but as a means of probing places of human experience that politics, economics and science cannot explain or address. Today, most global educators and development workers are justly suspicious of religious conviction, especially when it is laced with 'health-wealth' promises, patriarchal authority, blind loyalty to the state, and rapture-esque indifference to nature. But long before a fanatical religious conservatism gave 'the faith factor' a bad name, there were those – like Freire, Day, Fromm, Gutiérrez, Illich, Stringfellow, Buber, Merton, Boyer and Berry – who recognized its liberating potential. Religious communities are often incubators of vital virtues like honesty, goodwill, self-restraint, forgiveness, compassion and courage. These virtues not only drive and sustain healthy human cultures, they also distinguish the best global learners. Conceptual mentors seemed to intuitively know that to marginalize the religious impulse was to move against the grain of human flourishing and transformative learning.

Principles of Practice

Sitting with the experiences and ideas of great souls contributed six more principles to a paradigm of deschooled practice:

1. *Common good.* For public benefit to follow personal experience, our mind and volition must first be gripped by a vision of what is good for the world. Global learning then enables us to embody and engender that vision as we place our goods (time, talent and treasure) at the service of others.
2. *Preferential respect.* Global learning begins with, among and for the most vulnerable and at-risk human and other-than-human communities. A progressive simplification of lifestyle enables us to see reality 'from below', and to incorporate those views into our understandings of, and responses to, the world.

3. *Solidarity/accompaniment.* Global learning puts us alongside those in the places of marginalization and pain to share their resources and their risks. Genuine mutuality and friendship replace 'touristic', 'professional' and even purely 'educational' relations. Power is used, not to 'power over', but to 'power with' and 'power on behalf of'.

4. *Spirituality.* The inner landscape of our lives is central to socially relevant global learning. Noah Webster recognized this back in 1790: 'The virtues of men are of more consequence to society than their abilities; and for this reason, the heart should be cultivated with more assiduity than the head.' Spirituality underscores 'spirit' (the passions that motivate us), moral sense (the values and ideals that guide us) and being (the kind of person we are, or wish to be, in and for the world).

5. *Social analysis.* Knowing that complex social institutions are sometimes oppressive and other times productive, global learning engages us in historically deep analysis of structural forces and systems to discern how and why some individuals and groups are especially vulnerable to misfortune and injustice.

6. *Subsidiarity.* Nothing should be done by a larger and more complex organization that can be done as well by a smaller and simpler organization. We expect the common good to be driven not by technological 'solutions' or expansive government programs, but by the active self-organization of people within local settings.

Active Experimentation: 'crafty compromises'

Educative experience and conceptual mentoring encouraged a way of being in the world where living and learning, immersion and reflection became all of a piece. The personal impacts were so profound that I determined to devote professional energies to creating similar opportunities for the next generation. Based in a private, faith-based university in southern California, I was given the opportunity to actively experiment with global learning designs that aimed to foster passion, autonomy, discovery and responsibility. The result, over a period of two decades, was three dozen courses in three urban field programs. What follows highlights two of these programs: the Los Angeles Term and the Global Learning Term.

During the semester-long LA Term, students live with culturally contrastive host families in South Los Angeles, intern with advocacy-oriented community organizations, rely exclusively on public transportation (no cars are allowed), and complete fifteen units of interdisciplinary coursework. The curriculum seeks to bridge the local/regional-international divide by introducing students to 'global' challenges related to land conversion, biodiversity loss, water depletion, labor migration, informal economy, sweatshop labor and social polarization. By starting at their 'doorstep', students learn to value the near over the far, and tangible duties toward the stranger next door over an abstract love of the world.

Successful completion of the LA Term is a prerequisite for the second off-campus term of the global studies major: the Global Learning Term (GLT). The educational ideal borrows from philosopher Kwame Appiah's (1997) call for rooted cosmopolitans – persons who are 'attached to a home of one's own, with its own cultural particularities, but taking pleasure from the presence of other, different places who are home to other, different people' (p. 618). The GLT shares certain elements in common with conventional study abroad programs, but there are noteworthy differences. Students travel exclusively to sites in the Majority World. The average term extends to 6 or 7 months in order to facilitate intensive language learning and cultural adaptation. In common with the LA Term, students live with local families in marginal communities, serve with community-based organizations, and complete contracted coursework in a self-directed manner.

During the GLT, power shifts from professional educators and cloistered campuses to a field-based learning network comprised of host parents, language coaches, agency staff and supervisors, and local research guides. Each lends their energy and expertise to a community-driven global learning process that is essentially 'deschooled'. Students travel to their destination sites in pairs and establish, over time, a social-emotional support system composed mainly of host nationals. While no in-field resident directors orchestrate (or chaperone) student activities, each student is assigned an academic advisor who encourages, guides, resources and evaluates them. Students, however, retain virtually all decision-making responsibility within their field settings. Of course, this lends certain intensity to the whole experience, requiring participating students to be self-motivated, self-organized and self-regulating, not to mention a bit intrepid.

The values that the Los Angeles Term and Global Learning Term actively emphasize are largely at right angles to conventional structures:

- at the *program* level: decentralized management, non-hierarchical relationships, community voice, student selectivity, flexible curricular form, structural analysis;
- at the *individual* level: curiosity, embodiment, visceral experience, self-direction, contemplation, delight, critical thinking, compassion, moral courage, personal responsibility;
- at the *community* level: rootedness, participation ('doing with'), local wisdom, solidarity, appropriate scale, mentoring, mutual benefit, collaborative action.

Programs defined by divergent values necessarily take the form of 'crafty compromises' within established systems of higher learning. It follows that scholar-practitioners who 'think different' must learn to successfully operate 'in but not of' these systems. Being 'in' the institutional structure means that one recognizes that colleges and universities provide precisely what DIY learning does not: an integrated educational structure that combines broad learning across multiple disciplines with opportunities to interact with a community of scholars. Not being 'of' the institution, however, means that one's ultimate commitment is to a set of alternative values that shapes global learning for the common good. Fidelity to those values requires that one resist the many myths and illusions trapped within academic institutions.

The task of the global education scholar-practitioner is to build upon the unique assets of the modern university, while challenging the fraudulent values and consumerist messaging that confirm students as faithful servants of the status quo. In a profit-driven economy where one is less 'educated' than 'trained', do we dare to imagine a no-frills, non-bureaucratic, highly personalized, socially responsible and profoundly formative model of global learning? If so, can it be built within the shell of the old order? Or will growing concerns over prestige, liability, profitability, managerial control and student satisfaction ultimately suffocate real innovation and relevance, forcing us to look for experimental spaces outside the academy?

Try to imagine a four-year, multi-civilizational, entirely field-based global education. Vernacular communities become multi-functional 'campuses' and an open, cross-disciplinary curriculum addresses the 'grand challenges' of the twenty-first century.[2] The school is freed from its obsession with branding, prestige rankings and real estate. Its performance is measured solely by its ability to intelligently and passionately engage the world's most pressing problems.

The model's pedagogical orientation combines the best of liberal learning and practical experience. Self-paced online learning is 'blended' with face-to-face discussion, language tutoring and subject area mentoring. Specially designed research projects and apprenticeships allow for the exchange of knowledge, expertise and innovation. Within a general curricular structure, learning is driven by what students feel naturally curious about. Not only do they decide what to learn, they also decide where, when and with whom. Although students exercise considerable autonomy, the process is far from an educational free-for-all. A network of community educators 'intervenes' with local knowledge and practical wisdom to develop students' ability to think-in-context and generate comparative perspectives on consequential issues. Learning assessments measure acquired capability – what students can actually *do,* and *how* they do it – while competency transcripts communicate the graduate's value to prospective employers.

What about the business model? A deschooled design aims to maximize global learning while minimizing frills. There are no campus compounds and no owned buildings. No resort-style dorms or lavish cafeterias. No fitness centers or NCAA sports teams. No physical libraries or 'smart' classrooms. No superfluous administration or student services. Expensive infrastructure that does not directly relate to learning is 'unbundled' from the cost model. Estimates come in at about one-quarter of a conventional private university (Carey, 2015; Craig, 2015).

As you're reading this, hundreds of educational innovators are hatching plans for new, radically affordable and globally relevant learning systems. Minerva Project, the entrepreneurial start-up based in San Francisco, already uses a sophisticated interactive online learning platform to offer seminar-style college courses to high-performing students residing in cities around the world (Wood, 2014). Others, like UniversityNow's Patten University, Peer2Peer University and University of the People, offer low-cost alternatives to the traditional bricks-and-mortar residential campus. Still others are using the capabilities of new technology to 'hack' the college experience apart from traditional classrooms (Kamenetz, 2010).

Conclusion

All of this may smack of wishful thinking, at least in the short term. But a range of indicators suggests that college as we know it is on the cusp of a complete re-set: books freed from the printed page; courses freed from geographical classrooms; individual faculty and students freed from enrolling in a single institution; and diplomas freed from academic institutions. Global education 2.0 will similarly undergo radical change. Rising scholar-practitioners will be pressed to find ways to design international learning experiences that are radically affordable, near-universally accessible, and endlessly customizable to student interests. A new generation will be afforded creative opportunities to develop the intellectual, moral and intercultural capacities needed to take reconstructive action in the world. Colleges and universities best support this movement by providing new space for the new beginning to take root and develop.

Notes

[1] Baba Dioum's quote is derived from a 1968 speech made in New Delhi to the general assembly of the International Union of Conservation of Nature. In the original, his statement ended with: 'we will understand only what we are *taught*'. The revision reflects my own journey towards recognizing the central role of experience in understanding and action.

[2] See http://grandchallenges.org/

References

Abbott, J. (2014) Battling for the Soul of Education. The 21st Century Learning Initiative. http://www.battlingforthesoulofeducation.org

Appiah, K.A. (1997) Cosmopolitan Patriots, *Critical Inquiry*, 23(3), 617-639. http://dx.doi.org/10.1086/448846

Boyer, E. (1996) The Scholarship of Engagement, *Journal of Public Outreach*, 1(1), 11-20. http://dx.doi.org/10.2307/3824459

Boyer, E. (1997) *Selected Speeches: 1979-1995*. Princeton, NJ: Carnegie Foundation for the Advancement of Teaching.

Brand, S. (2009) *Whole Earth Catalog: an ecopragmatist manifesto*. New York: Viking.

Carey, K. (2015) *The End of College*. New York: Riverhead Books.

Craig, R. (2015) *College Disrupted: the great unbundling of higher education*. New York: St. Martin's Press.

Dewey, J. (1938) *Experience and Education*. New York: Macmillan.

Illich, I. (1971) *Deschooling Society*. New York: Harper & Row.

Kamenetz, A. (2010) DIY U: *edupunks, edupreneurs, and the coming transformation of higher education*. White River Junction, VT: Chelsea Green.

Lindeman, E. (1926/1961) *The Meaning of Adult Education in the United States*. New York: Harvest House.

Palmer, P.J. (2008) *A Hidden Wholeness: the journey toward an undivided life*. San Francisco: Jossey-Bass.

Wallerstein, I. (1998) *Utopistics: or historical choices of the twenty-first century*. New York: New Press.

Webster, Noah (1790) On the Education of Youth in America, in Andrew Milson et al (Eds). *Readings in American Educational Thought: from Puritanism to Progressivism*, p. 107. Scottsdale, AZ: Information Age Publishing.

Wood, G. (2014) The Future of College? *The Atlantic*, September. http://www.theatlantic.com/features/archive/2014/08/the-future-of-college/375071/

Zuckerman, E. (2013) *Rewire: digital cosmopolitans in the age of connection*. New York: W.W. Norton & Company.

CHAPTER 14

An Unholy Trinity: conservative dynamics and the scholar-practitioner

MICHAEL WOOLF

SUMMARY Education abroad is a curious profession. The contrasting roles of administrator and educator, and practitioner and scholar create tensions that are sometimes paradoxical and ambiguous. The holy trinity of curriculum integration, cross-cultural learning and benchmarking creates a conservative ethos which subverts creativity and innovation. Curriculum integration is the principle by which universities create, select and endorse courses abroad that most resemble those that they teach at home. That objective restricts radical revision through the imperative of alignment with what already exists. Another conservative dynamic derives from the fact that the perceived benefit of study abroad resides, in part, in the assumption that other countries are different from the USA. Almost by unspoken consensus, that difference has been defined in terms of 'culture': an idea that derives from a core misconception – the belief that political and cultural borders are in some kind of alignment. The notion of benchmarking is a further conservative restraint in that future development is measured against pre-existing standards. Collectively, these factors enforce an innate conservatism that the educator and the scholar ought to find profoundly unsatisfactory.

Introduction: who is the scholar-practitioner?

In the curious profession of education abroad, a primary responsibility is to make opportunities happen and to make them happen safely. The imperative is to manage the tasks associated with taking young people from one country to another, housing them, teaching them, counselling them, and bringing them back in one piece – ideally with an enhanced understanding of both the subjects they studied and, critically, the location in which they studied them.

All learning is, of course, situated within a geographical, political and historical context. In education abroad, however, the location is an explicit part of the learning agenda (whereas in the domestic context it is predominantly an unacknowledged, even unrecognized, factor). In most education abroad models, 'abroad' is integral to learning objectives; interactions between the subject studied and the host environment are embedded within the pedagogy. This involves, in one way or another, multi-disciplinary perspectives and teaching strategies that are unlikely to be the norm domestically. Best practice customarily includes some form of experiential engagement: action research, basic ethnography, site visits, internships, service learning or other forms of teaching that make specialist demands on faculty. Experiential education is not uncommon in domestic higher education; in education abroad it is an essential and integral part of the academic environment. The idea that there is benefit in leaving the home environment to study elsewhere is, of itself, implicitly at least, an endorsement of the potential for educational enrichment through experiential education.

It is evident that the tasks that make up the education abroad endeavor involve both administrative practice and scholastic responsibilities. By way of an over-simplistic summary, the job of the practitioner is to make things happen effectively and efficiently. The job of the scholar is to ask whether or not those things are the right things to make happen. The practitioner asks how. The scholar asks why. Those functions are not uncommonly combined within one role and the individual is required to balance conflicting, not always easily reconcilable, demands. In practice, in international education administrative obligations have taken priority and that is not an unreasonable emphasis given that, above all, the health and welfare of students is paramount.

It is also important to recognize that international education is a broad concept encompassing a diverse range of practices and objectives from centralized, politically motivated European models to the more fragmented, laissez-faire approach in the USA. Objectives may, for example, address trans-national institutional relations, graduate mobility, faculty research, and a host of other variables. In this context, the focus is on the manner in which international education is interpreted within US higher education as a mechanism to enhance undergraduate teaching and learning; this is commonly known as education (or study) abroad.

Education abroad creates significant potential for innovation in terms of teaching techniques and course construction. That potential exists, however, in tension with the need to conform with the largely conservative requirements and expectations of US higher education.

Those conflicting dynamics define the somewhat paradoxical environment in which education abroad functions.

A frequent requirement is that courses selected or created should broadly align with US institutional priorities. This is sometimes called curriculum integration. Health and safety standards are required to be appropriate and effective. This commonly means developing procedures that cohere with standards of good practice: benchmarks broadly accepted as meeting field requirements. In addition, some kind of engagement with the host location needs to be integrated into the overall program. This is often described as inter-cultural learning.

Education abroad operates commonly by reference to this trinity of principles: curriculum integration, inter-cultural learning, and benchmarking. These reference points define the constructed space within which the scholar-practitioner has academic and intellectual responsibilities: to maintain valid learning objectives; to review and develop those appropriately; to create an ethos in which creative and innovative teaching is the norm; to challenge students to explore and analyze learning environments with commitment and curiosity; to disrupt and disturb students' assumptions through interaction with new ideas in new places. Students are temporary residents in a world elsewhere that is both geographical and intellectual space: separated from the parochial comforts of home literally and metaphorically, and dislocated from the security of the familiar. The unfamiliar is a fertile learning environment.

There are, of course, limitations to the degree of freedom within which to shape and define these spaces. There are personal constraints of expertise, experience and ideas. Students may avoid some (or all) physical and academic challenges embedded in engagement (or confrontation) with the unfamiliar. Faculty may struggle with the teaching skills needed to expand the learning environment beyond the formal classroom. The greatest limitation, however, may well be the conventions, requirements and expectations of US institutions that send their students abroad.

A Conservative Ethos

Higher education in general is not renowned for innovation or radical reform. It is a conservative environment which values continuity and tradition. US higher education is no exception. At the undergraduate level, academic rigor continues to be measured through the mechanistic, if convenient, measure of the number of hours a student spends in the classroom. Other, more sophisticated, systems exist and are periodically debated: workload, student outputs and competencies are common enough variants in other parts of the world. In the USA, contact hours are, for the time being, sacrosanct.

The legitimacy of education abroad depends substantially on the extent to which it meets the standards of US higher education. US institutions may accept, with some reluctance, the perceived eccentricities of foreign universities, though they will almost always create mechanisms to mitigate the impact of deviance from their norms. When they operate their own programs or work with international educational organizations abroad (sometimes oddly called 'providers'), the standards they anticipate and demand are those that align with domestic practice: benchmarks against which 'quality' is measured. Proven but conservative standards are, as far as possible, exported.

Benchmarking is certainly more complex than indicated here. However, a common factor is that activity is measured against standards defined elsewhere. Hans de Wit describes the practice as follows: 'Benchmarking is ... a way of finding and adopting good practices which go beyond the mere comparison of data, since it focuses on processes by which results are achieved' (de Wit, 2009, p. 124). Occasional Paper 22 of the European Association for International Education (EAIE), 'Measuring Success in the Internationalisation of Higher Education', grapples with the notions of benchmarking and quality from a number of diverse perspectives. Typically, 'benchmarking adds an external focus to internal activities' (van Gaalen, 2009, p. 78).

A benchmark is, then, a standard set by precedent: a conservative strategy in that excellence is measured against practice validated by usage. This is probably a wise policy as long as there is some confidence in what constitutes quality. That this is not always unproblematic is demonstrated by Robert Coelen. In a 1995 survey of student opinion, a law school at one of America's most prestigious universities was heartily endorsed:

> Princeton University has a lot of prestige associated with it
> and would be able to attract talented law students to its law
> school, save for the fact that it does not have one. This did not
> stop students ranking its law school as among the top ten in
> the nation. (Coelen, 2009, p. 43)

However skeptical we may be about quality and benchmarking, a concern with standards has profoundly improved provision in education abroad. That has been the primary purpose in the definition of 'Standards of Good Practice' by the Forum on Education Abroad:

> The Forum's commitment to developing and promoting
> standards of good practice for the field of education abroad
> lies at the core of The Forum's mission. The ultimate goal of
> the Standards is to improve practices in education abroad, so
> that our students' international educational experiences are as
> rich and meaningful as possible.[1]

Benchmarking reveals bad practice and inefficient administration and, thus, offers a relatively simple mechanism for internal review and improvement. It exposes deviance which is, after all, the godfather of ineptitude. However, deviance from convention is simultaneously, and paradoxically, the godfather of innovation. If benchmarks are inflexible, or if they are based upon problematic assumptions, innovation and reform are likely to be stifled. Such an environment does not have much fertile soil in which new ideas might bloom.

Curriculum integration and a focus on cultural learning create benchmarks that make the practitioner happy. They enforce the norm and offer easily comprehended and unchallenging ways of acting and thinking. The scholar ought to view that scenario with some unease.

Curriculum Integration and the Problem of Knowledge

Curriculum integration is the mechanism by which universities create or select courses abroad that most resemble those that they already teach. This is an entirely reasonable policy for US universities. It is a form of benchmarking that ensures the seamless transfer of credit and, therefore, that progress toward graduation is not delayed. The University of Minnesota pioneered important work in this area and a key intention is 'to match major coursework, internships, or research requirements to appropriate education abroad programs. Education abroad is not time away from degree progress – an "extra" or an "enhancement." It is integral.'[2]

In short, while education abroad is not exactly the same as study at home, it is not all that different either. It is, explicitly, not an 'enhancement' or an 'extra', but a mode of learning that integrates with domestic norms. Curriculum integration undoubtedly makes a valuable contribution towards moving education abroad from the periphery to the center of the mainstream academic agenda. However, it achieves that admirable aspiration, at least implicitly, by domesticating the disturbing disruptions and dislocations that may lurk in foreign lands and on alien shores. The unfamiliar is contained and reconstructed within the comforting boundaries of hearth and home.

Whatever anodyne implications are embedded in the concept, the benefits are very clear and, in most cases, the principles of curriculum integration are applied with intelligent and nuanced discrimination. The initiative also engages academic departments in the education abroad process and this too is a clear, demonstrable improvement.

Nevertheless, curriculum integration may raise additional reservations that modify wholehearted endorsement. Courses taught abroad are conducive to inter- and multi-disciplinary approaches. Core disciplines and situational modifiers coexist to enrich learning potential in ways not commonly associated with study at home. Engagement with the host environment creates an expanded learning space requiring a distinctive pedagogy. While education abroad encourages creative innovation, curriculum integration might, if crudely applied, restrict radical curriculum development. Traditional disciplines and conventional ways of defining areas of knowledge are, also, potentially subverted in education abroad. However, a realignment of learning boundaries may conflict with the interests of academic departments that have an investment in protecting the discrete nature of their disciplines. The need 'to match' the foreign with the domestic limits the parameters within which innovation is possible.

This is not an inevitable scenario but it is a possible source of conflicting priorities unless scholars in education abroad can initiate dialogue with their practitioner colleagues in universities and with 'provider' organizations on the basis of equal credibility. To achieve this, education abroad needs to be perceived as an independent, academically viable endeavor rather than as a set of mechanisms that reproduce the conventions of mainstream higher education.

If education abroad is not an 'enhancement', it is logically contained within a tradition of academic conservatism: unfamiliar, but not so unfamiliar as to be a source of unease. In contrast, it could be argued that education abroad ought to unpack the baggage of convention, disturb and disrupt not only the students, but also their teachers.

In short, the scholar needs to initiate developmental conversations among practitioners and fellow academics in which domestic conventions are seen critically, through foreign lenses. There is, after all, no monopoly on wisdom.

If They Prick Me Do I Not Bleed?

A shared assumption in education abroad is that students should cross frontiers and boundaries to engage with the unfamiliar. The benefit of education abroad resides in part, therefore, from the assumption that other countries and their inhabitants are different from the USA. If they were more or less the same, it could be (erroneously) argued that there is little point in encouraging students to travel in pursuit of the new. The environment of education abroad creates a perceived obligation to embed, somehow or another, an idea of something somewhat unfamiliar in the learning experience (even if that difference can be safely contained within the norms of domestic education).

Almost by consensus, that difference has been defined in terms of 'culture': the idea that, in one way or another, culture offers a grand narrative or global explanation of difference. This is not an ethically neutral emphasis, nor is it inevitable. It is a conscious choice to focus on what separates us. There are many common aspirations, hopes and fears that transcend national or cultural boundaries. Parents want a better life for their children. We all need shelter, food and water. We all seek care and comfort when we are sick. We all hope for security, and seek love. Shared needs, fears, hopes and aspirations are part of what it means to be human.

In contrast and problematically, the focus on inter-cultural or cross-cultural communication constructs culture as a set of barriers that students need to be taught to overcome. That is arguably implicitly reactionary and parochial in so far as it prioritizes that which divides humanity over that which we have in common. In that respect, it contrasts with ethical implications embedded in cosmopolitanism and internationalism: the notion that beneath our ostensible differences there is a common human core, expressed eloquently and painfully by Shylock, the Jew:

> Hath not a Jew eyes? hath not a Jew hands, organs,
> dimensions, senses, affections, passions? fed with
> the same food, hurt with the same weapons, subject
> to the same diseases, healed by the same means,
> warmed and cooled by the same winter and summer, as
> a Christian is? If you prick us, do we not bleed?
> (William Shakespeare, *The Merchant of Venice*, Act III,
> Scene I)

The principle of human rights encompasses the idealistic aspiration that certain values are universal and, consequently, take precedence over national or cultural practices. Thus, the execution of an 18-year-old in Somalia by stoning for the 'crime' of homosexuality in March 2013 is indefensible and unforgivable by any criteria. The fact that something may be described as 'cultural' does not make it less inhuman or barbaric. There are cultural norms that include torture, abuse of women, persecution of minorities, bribery, public execution, female circumcision, the amputation of limbs for criminal acts, the imprisonment and execution of homosexuals, stoning, honor killing, and slavery.

An emphasis on inter-cultural communication has inadvertently embedded respect, tolerance and appreciation of cultural diversity in the agenda of education abroad, sometimes at the expense of morality and common sense. In most circumstances, respect for diversity is a well-meant, liberal value that few would dispute. However, at what point does endorsement of difference become a position in which acts of inhumanity are excused or tolerated on the grounds that they are 'cultural'? The question exposes a moral and ethical vacuum at the heart of cultural relativism. The practices of the Taliban or ISIS are entirely consistent with some regional and cultural behaviors that include vicious gender discrimination, medieval concepts of justice, ignorance and intolerance. We should aspire to teach students not to tolerate, but to make informed and intelligent choices between things: the smart and the stupid, the crass and the clever, the moral, amoral and immoral, the real and the unreal, the humane and the inhumane, the barbaric and the civilized. The lenses of cultural discourse in this context encourage moral myopia.

It is, of course, possible to argue that this represents a form of ethical imperialism. If it does, so be it. Education is not ethically neutral. It prioritizes knowledge over ignorance; encourages debate and welcomes disagreement; values reading books rather than burning them. We need to have the courage and moral intelligence to say that certain values and practices are beyond the boundaries of tolerance. However complex and ambiguous the context may be, that is the responsibility of educators; that is the responsibility of a humane sensibility.

This is not an unproblematic position because, as we are all aware, boundaries between the acceptable and unacceptable are porous and contested. The debate over capital punishment or gun control in the USA demonstrates precisely these complexities. Nevertheless, we have a responsibility to commit to principles that define what it means to be part of a 'human family' as expressed, for example, in the Universal Declaration of Human Rights (1948): 'All human beings are born free and equal in dignity and rights. They are endowed with reason and conscience and should act towards one another in a spirit of brotherhood.'

The alternative is moral chaos. The slaughter in Rwanda had a cultural context, as did Hitler's Final Solution. No practitioner in education abroad would consider that these, and other inhumane outrages, ought to be tolerated or respected. However, it is a logical and ultimate (though unintended) consequence of prioritizing unqualified respect for cultural diversity.

That is the most profound, problematic consequence, but there are other reasons to approach this area critically. It can be argued, for example, that the things that students have in common transcend national or cultural differences. They wear the same clothes, listen to the same music, and have modes of communication that are curiously ignored in the prevailing discourse: revolutions in technology have disappeared in a kind of analytical amnesia. Jude Mikal recognizes what probably ought to be obvious: 'The theories of intercultural adjustment that have dominated research on acculturation stress and culture shock are based on notions of transition that have failed to keep pace with changing media technology' (Mikel, 2011, p. 17). In short, trans-national social media have eroded the notion that national or cultural characteristics are necessarily barriers. The complexities of communication between the young are, where and if they exist, linguistic, not cultural. Similar trans-national communities created by shared faith, language, class, sexual preference, professions and so on challenge the emphases on culture as a divisive dynamic in our reality. Simultaneously, the preoccupation with cross-cultural or inter-cultural studies is based upon a misunderstanding of what education abroad actually does.

Intercultural versus Inter-country

A critical misconception is the belief that taking students from one country to another necessarily involves crossing cultural boundaries, as if political and cultural borders were in some kind of alignment. To believe that countries are synonymous with cultures is to misunderstand the history and politics of national development. Nations are invented political constructs, not cultural entities; their borders reflect the consequence of war, colonialism, expediency, stupidity, greed and so on. Countries are not natural or permanent structures but have been formed and unformed throughout history. Where is Yugoslavia? Montenegro came, went and came back again. Students cannot understand the worlds they inhabit without understanding that basic reality.

The statement 'I am an American', for example, is less about cultural identity than it is about political citizenship and association with some prevailing myths. The 'cultures' of New York, rural Georgia, southern California and Appalachia do not suggest a cohesive identity. Similarly, the United Kingdom is a fragile political association made up of significantly diverse identities.

The example of Africa in particular demonstrates the fact that cultures and countries do not align. African countries were invented by European colonial powers as part of a sequence of post-conflict treaties without any reference whatsoever to indigenous associations or identities, as the subsequent history of this troubled continent indicates. In 1890, the British Prime Minister Lord Salisbury described the process of nation construction in what is often known as 'the scramble for Africa':

> We have been engaged in drawing lines upon maps where no white man's foot has ever trod; we have been giving away mountains and rivers and lakes to each other, only hindered by the small impediment that we never knew where the mountains and rivers and lakes were. (McCorquodale & Pangalangan, 2001, p. 867)

What we do in education abroad is to take students from one country to another for educational purposes. We may or may not take students from one culture to another; what we certainly do is take them from one political and historical construct to another. When cultural issues are placed at the center of education abroad we are demonstrating a failure to understand the realities of history; we create learning priorities that are anodyne and that lead us to focus on matters of, at most, secondary significance.

The degree to which the language of education abroad is rooted, myopically, in questions of 'culture' has not enhanced our credibility as educators. Critical questions of history, politics, religious difference, inequality, social injustice, nationalism, racism, tribalism, conflict are muted because culture is a less disturbing and challenging subject than, for example, the politics of global injustice. This represents a failure of historical analysis.

Culture in the History of Education Abroad

The comprehensive and consuming focus on (often imprecise) notions of culture raises some obvious questions: What are we not talking about? Why are we not talking about those things? Why are questions of politics, inequality, social injustice, history so muted in education abroad? At least one explanation derives from the history of education abroad in the twentieth century.

This field limped towards maturity in the 1950s at precisely the point when it became suspect and foolhardy to say too much about internationalism, cosmopolitanism, or the politics of trans-national relations (unless you were against all of them). In the USA in the 1950s, on university campuses (and elsewhere) it was, simply, a risky business within the parochial and paranoid ethos generated by McCarthyite distrust of foreign ideas. William Allaway (the founder of the University of California's Education Abroad Program in 1962) argued, in conversation with the author, that those historical conditions constrained discussions; it was easier and safer to talk about the relatively unchallenging and less troubling question of culture. A politic adjustment to the parochialism and hysteria of McCarthyism became a habit of mind that replaced critical thought.

The scholar has an obligation to ask questions that challenge that orthodoxy both in theory and in practice. If we demonstrably grapple with the larger questions that have defined and shaped our reality we may move from the periphery towards the center of academic relevance.

Making the Case

The argument for the importance of education abroad has not, in many cases, yet gone beyond the level of rhetoric. Growth in participants does not support the notion that education abroad is perceived as a vital element in US higher education. What growth there has been is, at least in part, a reflection of general expansion in the numbers of US students (at all tertiary levels), from around 15.3 million in 2000 to 20.2 million in

2015 (National Center for Education Statistics).[3] This scenario should not, however, be regarded as an indication of a uniformly bleak situation.

There is hardly a strategic plan in any US higher education institution that does not claim to prioritize the 'global' and/or embrace the 'international'. It is easy to be dismissive of endorsements that remain largely at the level of rhetoric but it would be foolish not to recognize that an ethos of approval is an enviable basis for development. Compared with US higher education in general, education abroad has been subject to relatively few critical crises (and none that have permanently undermined generalised endorsement): familiarisation trips, school of record arrangements, home-fee tuition, occasional worries about the dangers of 'abroad' – these have been relatively minor showers compared with the storms that have engulfed higher education in general (related to inflated fees, presidential excesses, athletes and those who train them, and so on). The climate that education abroad enjoys is relatively mild. The problem is how best to take advantage of those fair winds.

The case for education abroad needs to be made on the basis that it offers learning environments that are potentially creative, innovative and particularly relevant to student experience in a world where 'all fixed, fast-frozen relations, with their train of ancient and venerable prejudices and opinions, are swept away, all new-formed ones become antiquated before they can ossify. All that is solid melts into air' (Marx &, Engels, 1848/1888, p. 16). Embedded in the structure of education abroad is a responsiveness to the dynamics of change: non-traditional approaches to curriculum and teaching strategies are the norm.

The case for education abroad should not, therefore, be made on the basis of the degree to which it replicates domestic higher education. In any case, US higher education, for all its strengths, does not offer an untroubled model of creative excellence. Instead, a review of the implications of cultural relativism and benchmarking would be a positive step towards the development of credible, flexible, distinctive theoretical foundations for education abroad. A convincing case for the centrality of this mode of education cannot be made by benchmarking contemporary realities against inert conservatism of uneven and contested validity.

The search for an ideal, an academic holy grail, at home or abroad, is almost certainly futile. A commitment to revision and innovation is, in this imperfect universe, likely to lead towards richer educational spaces, not Nirvana, but messy, complex, divergent worlds that are more fertile than the arid landscapes of unthinking conformity.

Conclusion: what is to be done?

It is clear from the preceding arguments that there is a crucial and necessary function for the scholar and the practitioner in education abroad: to interrogate critically the unholy trinity. Traditional ways of defining knowledge are becoming increasingly static and artificial. Reliance on notions of culture distorts learning objectives and derives from an error of analysis. Benchmarking is an inappropriately conservative strategy when applied to an intrinsically innovative educational model.

The critical task is to demonstrate to colleagues in mainstream academia that education abroad is different but complementary. Above all, it is an educational endeavor with serious aspirations aimed, precisely, at enhancing the domestic academic agenda, broadening and deepening the manner in which students are empowered to analyze and explore their worlds. Without the endorsement and encouragement of those colleagues, growth will remain limited and education abroad will be seen in some circles as a peripheral luxury. This is a complex task that requires significant intellectual leadership.

The question arises, however, of from where that leadership is likely to come. The professionalization of education abroad may have complicated the situation. A proliferation of postgraduate degrees in international education over the last 10 years or so has had significant benefits in terms of good administrative practice. A potential disadvantage is that the emerging leadership may come into the field with shared assumptions based on common postgraduate experience. Previous leadership tended to emerge from a very wide variety of disciplines and perspectives: language and area studies, natural sciences, humanities, social sciences and so on. This may have created a tendency towards haphazard improvisation but it also encouraged diverse strategic initiatives, an ethos of risk-taking, and a kind of discordant creativity. There is potential danger in the comfort of consensus.

This should lead us also to consider recruitment policies. Participants in education abroad are not representative of the US undergraduate population. Nevertheless, when vacancies are advertised, a very frequent requirement is that candidates should have studied abroad. In that manner, the unrepresentative nature of the student population is replicated in the profile of personnel recruited to work in the field. A fanciful, and probably illegal, job advertisement might carry the following caveats if diversification was a priority: 'A man with postgraduate qualifications in one of the STEM disciplines is preferred. Applicants who have studied abroad need not apply.' This may be fantasy but it signals the kind of thinking we will need if there is a serious intention to broaden the professional base of those from whom new leadership will emerge.

In short, a radical challenge to traditional assumptions would be timely. Mostly, we are very good at how we do things; we are much less consistent when it comes to asking why we do them. The voice of the scholar-practitioner, skeptical and querulous, needs to be heard more loudly, more frequently, and more consistently, probing and disrupting comfortable conformity.

Note

[1] http://www.forumea.org/resources/standards-of-good-practice (accessed 6 September 2015).

[2] http://umabroad.umn.edu/professionals/curriculumintegration/general/m innesotamodel- (accessed on 6 September 2015).

[3] http://nces.ed.gov/fastfacts/display.asp?id=372 (accessed 6 September 2015).

References

Coelen, R.J. (2009) Ranking and the Measurement of Success in Internationalisation: are they related? In H. de Wit (Ed.) 'Measuring Success in the Internationalisation of Higher Education', pp. 39-47. Occasional Paper 22. Amsterdam: European Association for International Education (EAIE).

de Wit, H. (2009) Benchmarking the Internationalisation Strategies of European and Latin American Institutions of Higher Education, in H. de Wit (Ed.) 'Measuring Success in the Internationalisation of Higher Education', pp. 123-129. Occasional Paper 22. Amsterdam: European Association for International Education (EAIE).

Marx, K. & Engels, F. (1848/1888) *Manifesto of the Communist Party*, trans. Samuel Moores. London, William Reeves.

McCorquodale, R. & Pangalangan, R. (2001) Pushing Back the Limitations of Territorial Boundaries, *European Journal of International Law*, 12(5), 867-888.

Mikel, J.P. (2011) When Social Support Fits into Your Luggage: online support seeking and its effects on the traditional education abroad experience, *Frontiers: the interdisciplinary journal of education abroad*, 21 (Fall), 17-40.

Universal Declaration of Human Rights (1948) http://www.un.org/en/documents/udhr/ (accessed on 9 September 2015).

van Gaalen, A (2009) Developing a Tool for Mapping Internationalisation: a case study, in H. de Wit (Ed.) 'Measuring Success in the Internationalisation of Higher Education', pp. 77-91. Occasional Paper 22. Amsterdam: European Association for International Education (EAIE).

CHAPTER 15

Blind Spots, Troublesome Narratives and Arrested Fields: towards the scholar-practitioner

GREGORY LIGHT

SUMMARY This chapter is a critical reflection looking at the practice of international education (commonly promoted through study abroad offices) from the perspective of a parallel academic practice focused on promoting innovative learning and teaching in the university (typically promoted in teaching centers). It takes as its point of departure the fluctuating relationship between these two academic practices at a Midwest research-intensive university. On the face of it they are very close – in location, personal relationships and university structure – but in reality they are deeply separate practices. The chapter argues that this separation is grounded in a lack of a culture of scholarship between the two practices. The author then draws on his long experience in the practice of learning and teaching to explore the individual and institutional conditions and barriers preventing the robust development of the research and inquiry culture and narratives essential for the practitioner-scholar to thrive. He argues that practices that fail to engage in scholarly work but remain primarily arrested at the basic practitioner level of their field undermine their own ability to make important theoretical and practical connections to other practices or even to innovations within their own field. The chapter then argues that current national initiatives provide the opportunity to develop scholarship in these fields more forcefully. It concludes by describing one such research project which bridged the gulf between learning and teaching and international education practices.

Separated by our Practices

While I have spent much of my academic career studying and promoting learning and teaching practices in multiple international locations – including Europe, North America, Latin America and the Middle East –

the practice of international education was always a rather faraway field. I knew of it of course, I supported the idea of it, I encouraged my children to engage in it – indeed, for a dozen years the study abroad office at our university was just across the street. They often used our conference and meeting spaces. I knew the director(s) of the office well. We frequently had lunch together and regularly discussed the challenges and activities of our respective centers. Nevertheless, for many years international education was essentially in my academic blind spot. It had its practices and, as the director of the learning and teaching center, I had mine. The practices were essentially separate and distinct. The two sets of practices drew on different practitioner literature, had different roles, fulfilled different functions and accomplished different goals. Until scholarship in the field with Bernhard Streitwieser – the editor of this book and a close colleague – engaged a deeper interest in the practice.

This chapter is both a personal reflection and critical analysis of some of the broader ideas about practitioner scholarship raised by this separation and eventual collaboration. And while the specific relationship between these two practices – providing international experiences and promoting new teaching pedagogies – is not in and of itself of special importance, the issues it reveals are symptomatic of much more serious challenges to scholarly endeavor at the core of the fields which these practices epitomize. I will argue that these practices have been under-recognized, under-theorized and under-researched, due in part to the development of their role outside the main scholarship and research locations of the university, but also due in major part to the failure of both the university and the field to address major 'blind spots' in the dominant perspectives and narratives that characterize their relationship. It is worth noting that these blind spots are not necessarily unique to these two practices – the scholarly work of many parallel academic 'service' practices in the modern university is similarly discounted.

The Conditions of Scholarship

I will primarily illustrate my argument with the example of my own practice – learning and teaching in higher education – and then circle back to how the experience of becoming a scholar practitioner in this field led towards a bridging of the blind spot between my work and international education.

My practice and scholarship in the field of learning and teaching and faculty development spans almost 30 years, about half of that time in the United Kingdom and the other half in the United States. In both cases I was at large research-intensive universities. In the United Kingdom, however, both the position and the practice were situated within a robust academic department. In the United States, on the other hand, the position was situated in a center outside the traditional academic departments of the university. This meant that the development of the research and scholarship dimension of the practice was very different in the two locations. In the former, practice was situated in an active research context. In the latter, the context was essentially divorced from research and scholarship. Practice was informed by scholarship but did not contribute to it.

At the same time, during this 30-year period the key aspects of that practice – and the academic field which began to emerge around it – substantially changed in both countries. And in both countries these changes were driven by a broad range of factors, including increasing numbers of students, increasing diversity among students, emerging curriculum stressing a focus on global competencies, rapid changes in technology and a major shift in the culture, moving away from an almost limited focus on teaching excellence towards a broader focus on improving learning (Light et al, 2009). Indeed, thanks to the impact of globalization on higher education, these factors have rapidly become drivers of change more widely. They are now rooted in the growing and expanding university systems of most developing countries. Much of my own work in this field during the last five years has been in the Middle East, mainly in the West Bank, but also in Tunisia and Morocco, and in Brazil and Chile in South America. The impetus for change in these regions is vigorous and frequently engages their universities in classroom innovations more broadly and rapidly than is the case in many American and European institutions (Daragmeha et al, 2012).

This comprehensive response to national and international changes – still very much in the works – has been accompanied by the development of an expanded body of research and knowledge, both generic and discipline based. Empirical evidence concerning the many questions about learning, learners, teaching, teachers, and the plethora of relationships between them has begun to accumulate within existing disciplinary journals and academic meetings as well across a whole array of new academic conferences and journals on the practice. Nevertheless, the field, and the body of research informing it, is still young and emergent.

There is no doubt, however, that this general transformation of the field has brought about substantial change in the practice. When I first began in the field in London 30 years ago, teaching was deeply embedded in what I have referred to as the ad hoc paradigm of faculty development (Light, 2000). This paradigm described the situation that evolved and predominated in higher education until late into the last century and that is still ubiquitous today. It essentially assumes that a teacher's teaching expertise lies in their mastery of the content. Pedagogical skills are picked up informally in an ad hoc manner: through watching teachers and/or colleagues, because of an innate interest in the practice or out of sheer desperation. A second paradigm began to develop with the expansion of student numbers in the last century and the development of new technologies. This *skills* paradigm highlights 'the accumulation and reproduction of performance and communication skills, competencies, and tips' (Light, 2000, p. 12). The focus is on the application of best practices furnished by faculty developers and, more recently, as new technologies, social media and online applications have expanded, by instructional designers. More recently a third paradigm – the *professional* paradigm – has begun to develop in the field, in which the instructors become the designers. This paradigm emphasizes reflective practice and to some extent the development of communities of practice. It draws upon professional knowledge and higher-level application of design principles (Light et al, 2009; Light & Micari, 2013).

These momentous changes in practice are still very uneven across the field and particularly within the practitioner base that promotes and sustains it. Nevertheless, research in the field over the last 30 years has brought about the conditions for a broader engagement of practitioners in scholarship, from informed literature reviews, to the development of more original and interesting research questions, the use of innovative methodologies and methods, new analytic techniques and so on. Unfortunately, these conditions have not (especially in the United States) inaugurated a major practitioner-scholar movement. Practitioners may have become more scholarly – that is, informed by the research – but they are still not moving substantially towards the scholar end of the practitioner spectrum. The majority of practitioners do not themselves actually engage in the research that is moving the field forward, or in the active kinds of scholarship that have the potential for revitalizing the practices and transforming student learning in higher education. While there is some research being conducted by scholar-practitioners in teaching and learning centers (mainly in Europe and Australasia), the preponderance of the research has been conducted by researchers and scholars in academic departments – primarily in education schools, but also in psychology and sociology, as well as science-related fields such as medicine and engineering.

This is a serious problem facing the field of learning and teaching because, in addition to reflecting the questions and challenges confronting the field, most of the really important and urgent research questions arise in the context of actual practice. Indeed, even the broader questions with institutional and national implications originate in those very specific practitioner contexts. The practitioner knowledge resulting from such research and scholarship is referred to as type 2 knowledge. Gibbons et al (1994) contrast this knowledge with type 1 disciplinary-based knowledge in which disciplinary experts discover/construct knowledge which typically does not have immediate application. Type 2 knowledge, on the other hand, is transdisciplinary, is located in the context of practice, and arises from application. The scholarship and research which result in type 2 knowledge are best conducted by practitioners, assisted where necessary and appropriate by experts from other fields with, for example, particular methodological and analytical skills which the practitioner may not have.

The Arrested Nature of the Field

So, given the expansion of research and knowledge informing the field and the urgency for research on new types of practitioner scholarship, why has the scholarly development of the field been arrested? Why have so many of the practitioners in the field not capitalized on national and international research developments to carve out a more robust cadre of practitioner scholars? And why, despite drawing on an increasingly rich theoretical and empirical research base – including theoretical frameworks that advocate for faculty and the graduate student instructors they work with to take scholarly approaches to teaching and learning practices – has there been so little progress in this direction? Two troublesome perspectives or narratives have prevailed which define the field as essentially a practitioner field, and appear to have stalled the development of more widespread scholarship. They are the self-narrative that dominates practitioner perspectives of the field and the institutional narrative which governs the university's academic perspective of the field.

Ironically, the first perspective is characterized by a non-scholarly – in many cases, an anti-scholarly – narrative of the field. Despite most of the senior practitioners in the field having substantive research training from their graduate and doctoral education – indeed, they are usually required to have a PhD for a senior position – neither the academic culture of the field nor the practitioner's understanding of the field includes them actually doing research in the field. Possible explanations for this include the following.

Practitioner academic background. Practitioners often bring with them to the field research and scholarship backgrounds which they do not see as applicable to the field. They assume their own research and thinking skills are not as appropriate as, for example, those from an educational or social science field. Their own self-narrative discounts the years of training in research and scholarly ways of thinking, including their own potential for constructing robust and innovative interdisciplinary approaches to the problems and challenges in the new field. This failure to see one's own academic skills outside the confines of their own specific background is a major failing of graduate training more broadly.

Training future practitioners. There is no formal program for training practitioners. Graduate work is normally a requirement, and for senior positions in the field this includes a PhD. But there are no particular graduate programs or trajectories specifically for this field. There are graduate-level courses – usually at the master's level – which touch on the issues central to the practice, but they rarely include any substantive research training. While many younger practitioners first engage in the work through programs and centers when they are in graduate school, they, nevertheless, tend to see these two aspects of their academic lives as separate, even diametrically opposed from the standpoint of scholarship. This is in part, as we shall see below, due to the prevailing tension between the education and research missions of the modern university.

The flight from scholarship. In many cases the field, such as it is, has attracted practitioners precisely because it is not regarded as scholarly, at least not scholarly in the active sense of conducting scholarship and research. Many practitioners see the field and the centers that populate it as a haven from the negative experiences of research they endured in graduate schools. While they enjoy working in a university environment and like the intellectual (albeit passive) experience of scholarship informing the field, they are loath to engage in it themselves and appreciate the apparent 'practitioner only appointments' that define the field. This issue is particularly insidious as eventually this can lead to an unreflective field dominated by complacency and ignorance.

In addition to the adverse practitioner perspective, the dominant narrative of the field as not scholarly is bolstered by an equally unsympathetic institutional perspective.

The location and appointment of the practice. Because the central educational nature of the work on learning and teaching is regarded as cutting across the wide range and variety of the university's disciplines and schools, it has meant that most of the field's programs and centers have been located outside traditional academic schools and colleges where faculty with research positions are traditionally situated. For the most part they have been located in the provost's office or similar offices with other 'service' units which have broad, pan-university foci. This location and the service depiction of practices within the location have contributed to a general view of the learning and teaching center's practices and its practitioners as non-scholars, even non-academic. As such, practitioner appointments tend to be categorized as staff positions, with some having secondary faculty appointments. It is a rare appointment that is solely faculty, although in some cases a non-practitioner faculty member may be given a supervisory director position as practitioners are not deemed academically appropriate for such a position.

Origin of the field. As noted above, faculty development around teaching as an organized project developed from a skills paradigm (Light et al, 2009) in which practitioners were not viewed as having or needing any advanced content knowledge. Their teaching expertise lay in a set of skills (primarily in communication and technology) and the practitioner was focused on helping faculty develop this set of skills or competencies. This was born out of a particular competency model of faculty development that held that faculty development was a service much like that provided by human resources (HR) or information technology (IT) units. Indeed, many programs developed from HR departments (Light, 1998) and more recently from instructional designers in IT departments.

The educational mission. Perhaps the major issue constraining the field in terms of it developing a scholarly culture and practitioners is the very educational nature of its mission. The promotion of learning and teaching is seen, understandably enough, as being part of the university's broad teaching mission. Historically, however, the teaching practices of this mission have been regarded as incongruous with the practices of its research mission (Colbeck, 1998). Barnett and Hallam (1999) refer to this as the 'incompatibility thesis', and recent studies of the relationship between the two – in terms of time expended, academic contribution, institutional reputation and personal status – suggest that there is an intrinsic opposition or 'rivalry' between these two broad practices (Light et al, 2009). Ironically, given that research and scholarship on professions and practices outside the university are considered academic fair game, embedded in this understanding of the educational mission is the view that research and study on its own institutional practices is neither fitting nor academic.

In both perspectives the underlying troublesome narrative is a consequence of historical development rather than the result of any well-thought-out specific policy decisions. Indeed, in the United Kingdom a different historical trajectory has led to the practitioners in the field being regarded as faculty (Light et al, 2009). This, of course, makes the current understanding in the United States all the more culturally entrenched and – with the accompanying lack of time and resources for engaging scholarship – the viability of developing and sustaining scholarly practice more challenging.

Reaching Beyond: building a culture of scholarship

That being said, there is no formal policy against the idea of the scholar-practitioner in the field, and certainly no intellectual reason for the field and its scholarship to remain in an arrested state. But the stimulus for change must come from the field and its practitioners. And the conditions for change are somewhat encouraging. Indeed, in the United States a number of national developments provide the foundations for a renaissance of scholarship in the field. Two recent initiatives driving potential change are: new requirements in the process of accreditation of universities to assess the student learning outcomes of educational programs; and the increasing requirement by large research funders, both public (e.g. National Science Foundation [NSF]) and private (e.g. Howard Hughes Medical Institute [HHMI], Mellon Foundation, Teagle Foundation), to fund the development and evaluation of educational innovations. It is a rare university that can resist efforts that support its accreditation and bring in funding. It is the stuff that change is made of, the key to transforming prevailing self and institutional narratives of the field. It provides scholar-practitioners who are able to connect their scholarship to these and other developments with increased access to funding, time, resources and status within the academy.

My experience provides a useful illustrative example. When I joined the Searle Center at Northwestern University in 2000, it was a strong practitioner-based teaching center with a range of admirable programs and activities informed by the latest literature. The seeds of research were in the air but not in a concerted fashion. It was not part of the mission. Today the center has established itself as one of the key scholar-practitioner centers in the nation with dozens of institutional, national and international funded grants and projects in any given year. It has established itself as a key partner and collaborator with related faculty projects and grants across all schools and colleges of the university. Its scholar-practitioners have given many hundreds of conference and meeting presentations about their work and published over 150 books, chapters, peer-reviewed journal articles and conference proceedings (Searle Center, 2015). And this is just one case. Similar endeavors are happening in other centers in the field. Together, these centers and their practitioners have established a meaningful culture of scholarship and research with senior practitioners having academic appointments and research expectations.

Importantly, these developments have begun to rejuvenate the field with a host of new theoretical issues and frameworks, which have (as new ideas and findings do) created new paths of scholarship which bridge previous gaps in our knowledge and understanding. In my own case, as noted at the outset of this chapter, it exposed me to a previous blind spot in my scholarship. It led to a robust research collaboration within the field of international education – scholarship that would not have happened without the development of a new culture and narrative of scholarship, or, of course, without a colleague with expertise in the field, and an abiding curiosity about the question.

This particular research and scholarship grew out of work we were doing on student learning, employing a relatively new methodological approach – phenomenography (Marton & Booth, 1997) – to identify different ways in which students understand specific phenomena and experiences. Work in this area had been done from widely different contexts, from creative writing (Light, 2002) to nano-technology (Swarat et al, 2011). So why not from experience of international education? Seed funding in the university was obtained and a collaboration rapidly formed with colleagues with practitioner experience in international education. The research is still in progress but has so far identified four robust student understandings of international education and five student conceptions of global citizenship with significant implications for practice (Streitwieser & Light, 2011, 2015). In one fell swoop this blind spot had dissolved.

There are of course other blind spots of which by their very nature I am not aware, just as there are multiple troublesome narratives – both self and institutional – waiting to be challenged and transformed. As well, there are practitioners and fields in various states of arrest which need to be ignited. At the same time, we must also be careful about the kind of narratives and identities to which we aspire. There is something refreshing about doing our scholarship beneath the academic radar, so to speak. It can be liberating. By entering the dominant academic community, we run the risk of constraining ourselves within existing and traditional descriptions and rules of what is academic, rather than using our unique positions and situations to challenge those descriptions. Ironically, the major challenges we face to establishing ourselves as scholar-practitioners within the university may also turn out to be the source of the vitality and originality of our work.

References

Barnett, R. & Hallam, S. (1999) Teaching for Supercomplexity: a pedagogy for higher education, in P. Mortimore (Ed.) *Understanding Pedagogy and its Impact on Learning*. London: Paul Chapman.
http://dx.doi.org/10.4135/9781446219454.n7

Colbeck, C.L. (1998) Merging in a Seamless Blend: how faculty integrate teaching and research, *Journal of Higher Education*, 69(6), 647-671.
http://dx.doi.org/10.2307/2649212

Daragmeha, A.-K., Drane, D. & Light, G. (2012) Needs Assessment and Beyond in the Setup of Centers for Teaching and Learning Excellence: An-Najah University center as a case study, *Procedia – Social and Behavioral Sciences*, 47, 841-847. http://dx.doi.org/10.1016/j.sbspro.2012.06.745

Gibbons, M., Limoges, C., Nowotny, H., Scott, P. & Trow, M. (1994) *The New Production of Knowledge: the dynamics of science and research in contemporary societies*. London: SAGE.

Light, G. (1998) The Professionalization of Teaching in Higher Education, *Learning Matters* 2, 1-4. Institute of Education, University of London.

Light, G. (2000) Lifelong Learning: challenging learning and teaching in higher education, in A. Hodgson (Ed.) *Policies, Politics and the Future of Lifelong Learning*. London: Kogan Page.

Light, G. (2002) From the Personal to the Public: student conceptions of creative writing in higher education, *International Journal of Higher Education and Educational Planning*, 43(2) (March), 257-276.

Light, G., Cox, R. & Calkins, S. (2009) *Learning and Teaching in Higher Education: the reflective professional*, 2nd edn. London: SAGE.

Light, G. & Micari, M. (2013) *Making Scientists: six principles for effective college teaching*. Cambridge, MA: Harvard University Press.

Marton, F. & Booth, S. (1997) *Learning and Awareness*. Mahwah, NJ: Lawrence Erlbaum Associates.

Searle Center (2015) http://www.northwestern.edu/searle/research/index.html

Streitwieser. B. & Light, G. (2011) University Students and Conceptions of Global Citizenship: a case study. Working Paper No. 10-001. Available at Northwestern University's Buffett Center for International and Comparative Studies website: http://buffett.northwestern.edu/publications-projects/working-papers/cge/university-students-and-conceptions-of-global-citizenship.html

Streitwieser, B. & Light, G. (2015) The Grand Promise of Global Citizenship through Study Abroad: the student view, in Jos Beelen, Robert Coelen, Elspeth Jones and Hans de Wit (Eds) *Local and Global Internationalization* (series editor: Philip Altbach). Rotterdam. Sense.

Swarat, S., Light G., Park, E.-J. & Drane, D. (2011) A Typology of Undergraduate Students' Conceptions of Size and Scale: identifying and characterizing conceptual variation, *Journal of Research in Science Teaching* 48(5), 512-533. http://dx.doi.org/10.1002/tea.20403

CHAPTER 16

The Scholar-Practitioner and Translating Research into Working Practice

JANE EDWARDS

SUMMARY The frantic pace and many agendas of campus internationalization can push us to react rather than plan. Utilizing research to guide our work can help us to be both more analytical and more applied to topics of significance to international educators, to illustrate the essential connections between scholarship and practice in international education.

The pace of change in American higher education over the past twenty years has been extraordinary, and the uncertainty surrounding the work of higher education has become a central topic of discussion. Daniel Weiss (2014) summarizes the factors driving the current uncertainty of the enterprise:

> A distressed and (presumably) unsustainable economic model; the proliferation of dazzling and potentially transformative technologies; a seismic demographic shift in college-eligible students; and increased public skepticism about the purpose and value of a college education. (p. 25)

Twenty years ago, the impact of globalization and the need to manage collaboration, recruitment and mobility internationally would probably have made the list of destabilizing factors. But internationalization was a challenge, or a set of challenges, that was amenable to planning and prioritizing on an individual institutional basis. Many institutions built 'international' or 'global' into their mission statement in one way or another, and this work is now built into planning processes. But the current major challenges Weiss lists are systemic, and for the most part external to the life of the institution. They create a more complicated institutional climate for international educators as we pursue our agenda. We recognize that we must bring a new intentionality to our work, and that we must accept new and sometimes competing priorities, new standards of accountability, and new expectations for innovation.

In this chapter I argue that if managers of international education in higher education institutions can remain alert to the pressures implied by these new external dynamics, we can structure our work in ways that will make our institutions better able to respond to these challenges. While some of us choose to conduct and publish our own research, others may use the work of scholars as the foundation for practice. In this chapter I suggest that utilizing the intellectual habits of scholarship, and the fruits of research in international education and in other fields, can make this intentionality rewarding as well as effective, for ourselves and for those who work with us. I will offer three examples: recalibrating the daily implementation work of international education through mining the literature on the impact of commodification in higher education; informing program design for students and faculty working abroad with research associated with service learning; and using the literature of anthropological analysis to shape the ways in which we advise students about international experience.

Let me begin with the question of commodification. It may seem quixotic to begin a working day in an American university administrative office with a discussion of the work of French philosopher Jean-François Lyotard. But our work will be more useful and better regarded within our institutions if we can understand how the externalities listed by Weiss impact us, and something about why they have emerged. This knowledge will help us in our – often mandated, clearly necessary – quest concerning how to work towards cost-effectiveness, use the new technologies in the best ways, think about access as we design our systems, and make coherent and evidence-informed arguments for the value of what we do. If we are serious about doing this as well as possible, we might, as practitioners who are also scholars, systematically explore with our staff the larger issues which govern institutional life, as part of our management strategy.

One way to do this would be to begin with the study of a foundational text (I here propose Lyotard), move on to the secondary literature which ties that text to specific cases and analyses, and then look at the national debate in the professional, mainstream and popular fora in all media. I am proposing a process for management of the intellectual life of an office. We can substitute for the deadly boredom of most staff meetings a space where strategic goals and daily implementation are tied together by a shared vision of what is driving our work at every level, based in the rewarding activity of doing what universities do best: laying out, discussing and working through all aspects of the subject at hand. Scholar practitioners can drive this work – essentially that of the classroom – and bring new urgency and engagement through what I think of as the translational activity of bringing theory squarely into the world of practice.

As I have indicated, preliminary examination of the factors enumerated by Weiss suggests that a significant element in the shift in expectations of and attitudes towards higher education in the United States is the phenomenon shorthanded by the term 'commodification' crisply summarized by Peter Roberts in his essay on New Zealand higher education (1998):

> The market has been seen as the ideal model on which to base educational arrangements. Competition between students, staff and institutions has been encouraged. Students have been redefined as 'consumers', and tertiary education institutions have become 'providers'. Bureaucrats now talk of 'inputs', 'outputs' and 'throughputs' in the education system. Any notion of educational processes serving a form of collective public good has all but disappeared; instead, participation in tertiary education is now regarded as a form of private investment ... a long tradition of university education is simply one more factor for students to take into account in attempting to maximize utility through their tertiary purchasing decisions. (p. 4)

This pattern is the end product Lyotard predicted in his classic essay 'The Postmodern Condition' (1984), with the outcomes that Roberts suggests: 'Knowledge is and will be produced in order to be sold, and will be consumed in order to be valorized in a new production: in both cases, the goal is exchange' (Lyotard, 1984, pp. 4-5). This proposition has become familiar in one way or another to us all, and has become part of the national discourse, for example in contributions to the *Chronicle of Higher Education*. Carlos Alonso comments on the impact of the 'culture of accountability' and the 'crisis of social legitimation', which devalue in the public debate the very essence of humanistic study (Alonso, 2010). Philosopher Gary Gutting (2015) engages the basic conflict between capitalism and liberal education, and concludes that we must defend what universities do by defining broadly the learning which can transform the intellectual, emotional and aesthetic engagement of the student. There is a great deal of hand-wringing here about the distortion of the relationship between student and university brought about by the relocation of knowledge in diverse sources outside of the mind of the professor, and the lack of clarity in the relationship between university education and a life of productive employment this implies. But a closer examination of Lyotard's arguments and an exercise in asking concrete questions about what this means for the students and faculty with whom we work can prompt reflection rather than despair.

Lyotard's essay discusses the impact of the technologies on the perceived location of knowledge. He observed and imagined the miniaturization and commercialization of machines, and would certainly have greeted the iPhone with no surprise. As he predicted, students now see knowledge not as stored in the head of an individual, but as present in a variety of sources accessible in many different ways. All kinds of issues of legitimation thus arise in respect of institutional premises and practices, since students bring multiple sources of information into the classroom and to their decision-making about international experience. If students do not automatically accept the notion that we know better than they do, then we have to make better arguments and marshal these arguments more effectively. The questions that this new reality raises are of pragmatic significance. An understanding of Lyotard's thinking, and a use of the secondary studies that draw on his model (e.g. Giberson & Giberson, 2009) – or a similar process using a different foundational text – can help us modify our practices to take into account the changes that we see but often do not pause to analyze. The work usually associated with the classroom – the translation of ideas for others – can be used to use theory to craft with our staff premises and strategies to manage good pragmatic responses to these new realities.

The utility of this process is to ask how we can change our work to improve the nuts-and-bolts work of advising and program design. The next step might be to ask what we know about student expectations and behaviors in this changed landscape. The body of research into generational characteristics has the advantage of bridging the academic and the popular agenda. At the far popular end is the email invitation (received at the time of writing) to purchase a report from Mindswarms.com on 'The Ideal Millennial Shopping Experience'. At the other end of the spectrum is the set of reports produced on the millennial generation by the Pew Research Center (2010). Generational research has become a significant element in mass-media discussion of the behaviors of young people over the past two decades, in part no doubt because of the anxiety of parents, and the increased consumer power of teens and young adults. Howe and Strauss, using a framework refined over the past decade, suggest that dominant trends in the attitudes and behaviors of these students can be characterized as: special, sheltered, confident, team-oriented, achieving, pressured and conventional (2003).

Putting this framework together with an understanding of the dynamics of commodification allows for the development of plans and tactics for working with these students. This can result in changed models of advising and program design which will better meet their needs and help them achieve their goals. So, for example, an understanding that on some level students individually feel special, expect to receive information designed for them individually and coming from many sources, and also see their education as something that they have purchased leads to a redesign of information and of advising. This is an exercise for the staff who work with students daily, and has the merit of allowing us to abandon practices that no longer attract or effectively engage students (education abroad fairs, broad impersonal information sessions) and invent new and more useful formats. For example, the combination of searchable and concrete online information, which students are expected to use in preparation for individual sessions, does not have to address basics but can become serious advising discussions derived, in our Center at Yale, from just such a process of analysis.

To take a more specific example, let us think about advising students for education abroad. This is often, with this generation of students, a transactional process – opportunities are identified online or by word of mouth from friends, and decisions are made on the basis of the attractiveness of the education abroad 'product' as a kind of combined résumé-builder and photo opportunity. Advising then becomes a matter of deadlines and credit transfer and visas. But advising is very different if grounded in a serious consideration, based in knowledge gained from the research in the field, of the specific outcomes of experience abroad for a student's integrated undergraduate experience. The conversation can begin with a challenge to students, who, in our experience, ordinarily aspire to do the right thing but lack experience in dealing with the complex sets of variables that come into play with cross-cultural interaction. Students may need guidance to think about how they plan to achieve the goals they identify These goals are themselves varied and complex, and might include language acquisition, engagement in the developing world, making friendships with young people from a society the student has studied, learning about the practice of business or healthcare delivery abroad. Developing the habit of thoughtful decision-making can be systematically encouraged in this way.

This mode of advising recognizes how reflection can be tailored, often using online blogging or chat-room tools, to allow students to understand and grow from what they experience rather than simply checking off a box for something accomplished. Advisers will also suggest strategies for learning honed in the field. There are many accessible resources. For example, we have used *Maximizing Study Abroad* (Paige et al, 2002) to generate exercises and foster reflection. For well-intentioned but tethered Millennials, whose perceptions of a globalized world and their place in it may be at odds with the worldviews they will encounter abroad, guidance is helpful on ways in which students can negotiate, in ethical and respectful ways, their relationship with the community they enter. For the adviser, the goal becomes to educate students to think about experience abroad not as a product that they buy, but as a part of their human development. To be effective, this must be done using the tools demanded by an understanding of how this generation of students sees the world. If we get it right, then the concerns identified by Weiss – that parents worry about the value of an education and expect tangible returns on their investments, and that the technologies will be used in new and interesting ways – can be answered. And this can make our work better aligned with the institutional need for accountability and for relevance, as well as far more rewarding for advisers and useful for students.

This is obviously no more than a cursory summary of what is an investigative, discursive and iterative process for management practice. But experience shows that it is an excellent way in which to use the resources of scholarship to create processes, which range from staff development and interactive workshops to the revision of entire curricula. This is, after all, the core work of education, and the practice can then feed back into the scholarship, which will provide new avenues and analyses that can make the work that we do more effective. A summary of how this works might be:

- Notice an issue of significance, in the national debate about higher education, or in institutional planning, or in making the work effective on a divisional basis.
- Identify a foundational text which can help challenge assumptions or change thinking about this issue, share it with colleagues, and lead a discussion of the text and its implications.
- Identify additional readings from a range of text and Internet sources which broaden the discussion and which if possible propose alternatives in the way work is organized or initiatives are developed.
- Create with the group case-based exercises which lead to proposals for innovation.
- Implement a new, intentional and integrated process.

This might be described as the work of translation: just as bench research is translated into implementation strategies in the medical fields (Woolf, 2008), so scholarship can guide practice in international education.

If looking at the pressures on higher education can lead to meetings about texts on commodification, and exercises in generation analysis, there are other ways in which scholarship within the field of international education can inform practice directly. In higher educational institutions for at least the past two decades the expectation that students will engage in some kind of service activity has (for complex reasons beyond the present scope) become baked into both our admissions and our student development agendas. Students learn in high school that such work can be both rewarding and an essential addition to a résumé, and – with considerable encouragement from institutions, parents, communities and the media – seek to structure their experience in college to include significant service activity. Institutional missions align with student goals (McBride & Mlyn, 2013), and as education abroad program designers have embraced concepts and practices in experiential learning, student service activity has become part of the expectation for the development of international initiatives. We are asked to develop and support such initiatives, for and with faculty and students. But there are many ethical and practical considerations in implementing such programs, and this is an area in which scholarship is fundamental to the development of good practice.

Fortunately, international service learning (defined as the integration of service activities into an academic framework) is an area of international education which has for many years been rooted in the curriculum, and it parallels domestic community engagement programs. There is excellent research to drive practice. The Indiana University-Purdue University of Indiana (IUPUI) has a history of leadership in the development and management of service programs fostering a rich series on service learning and engaged scholarship research, which has in recent years included the development of conceptual frameworks for international service learning (Bringle & Hatcher, 2011; Jones & Steinberg, 2011). There are evidence-based analyses of the outcomes for students and for host communities of these programs (Tonkin, 2004). This research has to a great extent run in parallel with the research agendas of the education abroad community, and has been driven by the integration of the experience of service into a course structure which is designed and implemented by faculty members. In recent years, however, as we increasingly describe international education as a broad range of activities including not only study and research but also service and work abroad, the research on service learning has begun to inform understanding of service abroad (Eyler, 2011). No one needs to design an opportunity for service abroad without a strong theoretical basis, and the same process of interrogation described above can guide better practice in this area.

When we meet with our staff to talk about why students pursue service opportunities, and about how we should meet this desire and manage it to good effect, we do not have to grapple alone with the key challenge for program design: the integration of student learning goals in service abroad. The landscape has been laid out for us if we choose to mine the work of researcher-practitioners such as Richard Kiely, whose companion essay in the same volume as Eyler's, on the utility of research about education abroad (2011), lays the groundwork for any such work. For the practitioner this research can provide the foundation for the questions we need to ask about the goals and anticipated outcomes of all our programming initiatives. And institutional pressure to support student activity because it is 'service', and therefore automatically a good thing, can be combatted most effectively by drawing on the work of those whose research tells us how complicated the dynamics of cross-cultural exchange can be in any such activity (Ogden, 2007).

In this domain of program development and assessment, the translation process laid out above works best if modified: a set of case studies and essays can be assigned among staff, with the mandate to bring to the table issues raised, solutions proposed, theoretical matrices offered, and lessons learned from the field. This exercise informs program design, providing ammunition against ethically risky projects driven – usually inadvertently – by impulse, opportunism or self-interest. Ideally, the corpus of research in the area of service learning can be used as part of a pedagogy which includes those who design international service activities, students who seek to lead these initiatives, and the communities which host them. Using an iterative process involves drawing on the research, inviting participants to identify specific cases for analysis, and developing a series of exercises to be used as material for responsible planning. Such a process can honor the ideal of service and guard against the dangers of 'voluntourism', currently much discussed in Internet posts and blogs (such as a series on the *Huffington Post* site [1]) that can help students understand dynamics that may be initially hidden by the general celebration of good intentions. In this area, the process of the translation of scholarly research informs a process where theory, case study and practical exercises contribute to constructively rethinking the premises of the educational experiences we foster.

A third example of the value of the daily use of research in informing good practice is the use of the strategies of cultural anthropology to propose a methodology for international cultural learning for students abroad. The translation process for this is an easy one, because ethnography – analytical description of human social behavior – is accessible and attractive for international educators, and indeed for students. The work of drawing on research in this area amounts to identifying excellent resources and working with staff and then with the faculty and students who engage in learning abroad. A foundational text by one of the great ethnographer-critics, perhaps James Clifford (1997) or Clifford Geertz (1973), can inspire lively and often inspiring discussion. If each member of the reading group (or office staff) pairs this reading with an ethnography chosen because the author interrogates in an accessible way the whole process of participant observation (there are dozens – e.g. Belmonte, 1979; Wafer, 1991; Taylor, 1998), the discussion can be linked with reflection on the best ways to advise and assist students in their experience in very different kinds of communities abroad. Ideally an anthropologist on the faculty will facilitate and engage with this work, and extend this to discussion with faculty in other disciplines who lead groups of students abroad. This is where the classroom meets the office, and where an engagement with research can translate into a model for advising and indeed for re-conceptualizing the activities of international education.

As a field, international education has radically underutilized this literature. As an international educator trained in the field of cultural anthropology, I fault myself for having often neglected to identify and use anthropological studies to help students develop an understanding of cultural difference that goes beyond the superficial. While anthropologists talk among ourselves about the ways in which *Tristes tropiques* (Lévi-Strauss, 1972) or Geertz's essay on Balinese cockfighting (Geertz, 1973, pp. 412-453) changed the way in which we thought about our place in that complex world. But that is often as far as it goes. But we could think of our community as a sort of book club of readers of ethnography. And we could use this research literature to supplement the work within the field of international education on cross-cultural communication and learning that derives from psychology and education and to a lesser extent from cultural studies. We might pair *Reading National Geographic* (Lutz & Collins, 1993) with *Student Learning Abroad* (Vande Berg et al, 2012). If this is done in the context of planning and constantly reviewing advising practices, then both staff and advisees work with better intellectual tools.

Advising changes when students understand the dynamic of participant observation; program design changes when we engage students in systematic observation and analysis of the different, rather than letting them respond emotionally to it; and our recognition of the significance for hosting communities of the arrival of outsiders can change the way in which we support and assess activities undertaken for the benefit of young Americans. The literature of anthropological analysis can serve, if we choose, as a set of case studies in what actually happens when we focus on learning about other cultures as the goal, not the by-product, of experience abroad.

My argument is that all the work that we do as international educators is better done with systematic and purposeful use of research from a range of fields. A key role of the scholar who works as a practitioner in this field is to translate and mobilize this research to create better practice. The rewards for this effort include an engaged and thoughtful staff; the ability to align activities with institutional agendas; and a highly developed and informed interest in the turbulent national and global debates that affect the impact of the work we do.

Note

[1] http://www.huffingtonpost.com/news/voluntourism/

References

Alonso, C.J. (2010) Paradise Lost: the academy becomes a commodity, *Chronicle of Higher Education*. http://chronicle.com/article/Paradise-Lost-the-Academy-as/125669/

Belmonte, T. (1979) *The Broken Fountain*. New York: Columbia University Press.

Bringle, R.G. & Hatcher, J.A. (2011) International Service Learning, in. R. Bringle, J.A. Hatcher & S. Jones (Eds) *International Service Learning: conceptual frameworks and learning*, pp. 2-28. Sterling, VA: Stylus.

Clifford, J. (1997) *Routes: travel and translation in the late twentieth century*. Cambridge, MA: Harvard University Press.

Eyler, J. (2011) What International Service Learning Can Learn from Research on Service Learning, in R. Bringle, J.A. Hatcher & S. Jones (Eds) *International Service Learning: conceptual frameworks and learning*, pp. 225-242. Sterling, VA: Stylus.

Geertz, C. (1973) *The Interpretation of Cultures*. New York: Basic Books.

Giberson, T. & Giberson, G. (Eds) (2009) *The Knowledge Economy Academic and the Commodification of Higher Education*. Cresskill NJ: Hampton.

Gutting, G. (2015) Why College is Not a Commodity, *Chronicle of Higher Education*. http://chronicle.com/article/Why-College-Is-Not-a-Commodity/233011

Howe, N. & Strauss, W. (2003) *Millennials Go to College*. Great Falls, VA: American Association of Collegiate Registrars and Admissions Offices (AACRAO) and Life Course Associates.

Jones, S.G. & Steinberg, K.S. (2011) An Analysis of International Service Learning Programs, in. R. Bringle, J.A. Hatcher & S. Jones (Eds) *International Service Learning: conceptual frameworks and learning*, pp. 89-112. Sterling, VA: Stylus.

Kiely, R. (2011) What International Service Learning Research Can Learn from Research on International Learning, in R. Bringle, J.A. Hatcher & S. Jones (Eds) *International Service Learning: conceptual frameworks and learning*, pp. 243-273. Sterling, VA: Stylus.

Lévi-Strauss, C. (1972) *Tristes tropiques*, trans. J. Russell. New York: Athenaeum.

Lutz, C.A. & Collins, J.L. (1993) *Reading National Geographic*. Chicago: University of Chicago Press.

Lyotard, J.-F. (1984) *The Postmodern Condition: a report on knowledge*, trans. G. Bennington & B. Assumi. Minneapolis: University of Minnesota Press.

McBride, A.M. & Mlyn, E. (2013) Civic Engagement and Higher Education at a Crossroads, *Huffington Post*. http://www.huffingtonpost.com/amanda-moore-mcbride/civic- (accessed on 26 September 2015).

Ogden, A. (2007) The View from the Veranda: understanding today's colonial student, *Frontiers: the interdisciplinary journal of study abroad*, 15 (Winter), 35-56.

Paige, R.M., Cohen, A.D., Kappler, B., Chi, J. & Lassegaard, J.P. (2002) *Maximizing Study Abroad: a students' guide to strategies for language and culture learning and use*. Minneapolis: Center for Advanced Research on Language Acquisition, University of Minnesota.

Pew Research Center (2010) Millennials: confident. Connected. Open to Change. http://www.pewsocialtrends.org/2010/02/24/millennials-confident-connected-open-to-change/

Roberts, P. (1998) Rereading Lyotard: knowledge, commodification and higher education, *Electronic Journal of Sociology*, 3, April, Special Issue. http://www.sociology.org/content/vol003.003/roberts.html

Taylor, J. (1998) *Paper Tangos*. Durham, NC: Duke University Press.

Tonkin, H. (Ed.) (2004) *Service-learning across Cultures: promise and achievement*. New York: IPSL.

Vande Berg, M., Paige, R.M. & Lou, K.H. (2012) *Student Learning Abroad: what our students are learning, and what they're not, and what we can do about it*. Sterling, VA: Stylus.

Wafer, J.W. (1991) *The Taste of Blood: spirit possession in Brazilian Candomblé*. Philadelphia, PA: University of Pennsylvania Press.

Weiss, D.H. (2014) Challenge and Opportunities in the Changing Landscape, in R. Chopp, S. Frost & D.H. Weiss (Eds) *Remaking College: innovation and the liberal arts*, pp. 25-40. Baltimore, MD: Johns Hopkins University Press.

Woolf, S.H. (2008) The Meaning of Translational Research and Why It Matters, *Journal of the American Medical Association*, 299(2), 211-213. http://dx.doi.org/10.1001/jama.2007.26

CHAPTER 17

Key Theoretical Frameworks Guiding the Scholar-Practitioner in International Education

DARLA K. DEARDORFF

SUMMARY This chapter synthesizes several integral theoretical frameworks for intercultural development and learning which are essential for scholar-practitioners in international education. This chapter highlights several theories that are vital for more fully understanding intercultural practice, including a discussion of the first researched-based framework of intercultural competence by Deardorff with updated research on this framework. Other relevant theories, such as Bennett's developmental model of intercultural sensitivity, Sanford's challenge-support, Allport's contact hypothesis and Maslow's hierarchy of needs, are synthesized in relation to intercultural development. In addition, some non-western concepts around intercultural competence are discussed, in more fully understanding this key concept and its application in international education. Theories from other disciplines are also highlighted as they pertain to practice and research in international education.

Josef Mestenhauser, a prime example of the scholar-practitioner, whose scholarship in international education provides a strong foundation for current scholar-practitioners, often stated the importance of employing a holistic systems perspective to the scholarship and practice within the field of international higher education. According to Mestenhauser (2011), a systems perspective is 'a conceptual framework and body of knowledge and tools that help us understand the whole' (p. 71). He continues by observing that 'the systems perspective is not only a multiplier of learning, but it also provides a new cognitive structure for dealing with complexity' (p. 161). This chapter attempts to address Mestenhauser's call for a systems perspective by providing an overview of some key theoretical frameworks that scholar-practitioners can put in their 'toolbox' as they make connections between those frameworks to practice within international education.

In a recent survey conducted among university leaders, knowledge of intercultural theories was rated as one of the key knowledge areas needed by leaders who are charged with internationalizing their institutions (AIEA, 2014). Further, the International Association of University's 4th Global Survey on Internationalization, completed by over 1300 higher education institutions from over 130 countries, emphasized the centrality of intercultural, global and international learning outcomes to internationalization efforts (Egron-Polak & Hudson, 2014). Given this increased focus on intercultural learning and theory, the scholar-practitioner needs to be knowledgeable about some of the integral theoretical frameworks which are key in providing a foundation upon which to build research and practical efforts to further intercultural learning within international higher education. Such frameworks are crucial in understanding learners – their needs, development and encountered challenges. While much can be learned through practical experience, theory provides a framework in which to place experiences, moving deeper into understanding the 'how' and 'why' which underlie the learning. Knowledge of such theories is not enough though; rather, scholar-practitioners know that it is important to consider the practical application of theory to help improve the effectiveness of those working with students. Through this deeper understanding of learners based on theory and research, scholar-practitioners can design more effective interventions and experiences.

This chapter, then, synthesizes several integral theoretical frameworks for intercultural development and learning which are essential for scholar-practitioners in international education, as well as students, who can also be scholar-practitioners in their own right. Often practitioners base their work primarily on experience. Scholars may spend a lifetime studying phenomena but lack the experience in bridging theory to practice. Increasingly, scholar-practitioners, defined here as international educators who are able to navigate between academic scholarship and practice, are able to contextualize theory within practice – in this case, within international higher education. The key for scholar-practitioners is in the *application* of scholarly knowledge and theory. So, what are some of the foundational intercultural and educational theories for scholar-practitioners? This chapter highlights several theories that are vital for more fully understanding intercultural practice, including a discussion of the first researched-based framework of intercultural competence (Deardorff, 2006, 2009), with updated research on this framework. Other relevant theories, such as Bennett's developmental model of intercultural sensitivity, Sanford's challenge-support, Allport's contact hypothesis, and Maslow's hierarchy of needs, are synthesized in relation to intercultural development. In addition, some non-western concepts around intercultural competence will be discussed, in more fully understanding this key concept and its application in international education. Theories from other disciplines will also be highlighted as they pertain to practice and research in international education. And while it is not possible for this chapter to cover all the relevant theories needed by scholar-practitioners in international education, highlighting at least a variety of theories from different disciplines provides a more holistic systems view that can be applied to international education, as espoused by Mestenhauser (2011), one of the first major scholar practitioners in international education.

Exploring Intercultural Competence

At the core of comprehensive internationalization efforts, and specifically intercultural learning outcomes, is intercultural competence. Intercultural competence, like other concepts in international education, is frequently used even by scholar-practitioners without defining it. There are over thirty different terms used for this concept, depending on the discipline and context, such as global competence, cultural intelligence, global learning, twenty-first-century skills, and so on (see Fantini, 2009 for more on terminology). So what is intercultural competence? Though intercultural competence has been addressed in scholarly literature for over fifty years, the first research-based framework of intercultural competence (Deardorff, 2006, 2015) emerged in the early part of this century. The consensus definition of intercultural competence that emerged from this research can be categorized into the basic dimensions of competence which are commonly defined as knowledge, skills and attitudes (Pottinger, 1979). These can then be further synthesized into internal and external outcomes. Below are brief descriptions of this research-based definition of intercultural competence, starting with attitudes.

Attitudes. Three key attitudes emerged as part of the consensus documented in the Deardorff study: respect, openness and curiosity/discovery. Respect for others involves demonstrating that they are valued, including through showing interest in them and listening attentively to them. Openness and curiosity both imply a willingness to risk and to move beyond one's comfort zone. These attitudes are foundational to the further development of the knowledge and skills needed for intercultural competence. One way to move individuals toward these requisite attitudes is by challenging their assumptions about their own views of the world and the ways in which they perceive others.

Knowledge. Intercultural scholars in this study concurred on the following broad categories of knowledge: cultural self-awareness (meaning the ways in which one's culture has influenced one's identity and worldview), culture-specific knowledge, deep cultural knowledge (including understanding other worldviews), and sociolinguistic awareness. It is important to note that for the purposes of this discussion, 'culture' is defined as values, beliefs and norms held by a group of people which shape how individuals communicate and behave – that is, how they interact with others. The one element agreed upon by all the intercultural scholars was the importance of understanding the world from others' perspectives. This last piece has significant implications for international education: how do intercultural experiences help participants see from others' perspectives?

Skills. The skills documented in this study as part of the consensus understanding of intercultural competence address the *processing* of knowledge: observing, listening, evaluating, analyzing, interpreting and relating. This concurs with an observation by the former president of Harvard University regarding the importance of 'thinking interculturally' (Bok, 2006). Given these skills, self-reflection is essential to the development and assessment of intercultural competence.

Internal outcomes. These attitudes, knowledge and skills ideally lead to internal outcomes that consist of flexibility, adaptability, an ethnorelative perspective and empathy. These are outcomes that emerge within the individual as a result of the acquired attitudes, knowledge and skills necessary for intercultural competence. If these internal outcomes are achieved, individuals are able to see from others' perspectives and to respond to them according to the way in which the other person desires to be treated. Individuals may reach this outcome with varying degrees of success.

External outcomes. The summation of the attitudes, knowledge and skills, as well as the internal outcomes, is demonstrated through the visible behavior and communication of the individual. How effective and appropriate is the individual in intercultural interactions? This then becomes the agreed-upon definition of intercultural scholars – that intercultural competence is the *effective* and *appropriate* behavior and communication in intercultural situations, with the *effectiveness* being determined by the individual and the *appropriateness* being determined by the other person(s) in the interaction. It is important to understand that this definition is predicated on particular requisite elements of knowledge, skills and attitudes as agreed upon by experts in this study as outlined here. These elements are combined into the framework shown in Figure 1.

Some key points of this framework include the importance of the developmental process within intercultural competence, the lifelong nature of the process, the specific contexts of the interactions with others who are from different backgrounds (whether cultural, ethnic, religious, age, gender, socioeconomic, etc.), and the requisite starting point of attitudes, especially that of respect – of truly valuing the other. Further, this framework refers not only to interactions between those from different national cultures, but also to interactions between individuals from different backgrounds (which can include a range of differences, including socioeconomic, religious, gender, age, etc.). This model can and should be used not in isolation but in conjunction with other theoretical concepts, some of which are described in this chapter. (For more on this particular framework, see Deardorff, 2006, 2009, 2015.)

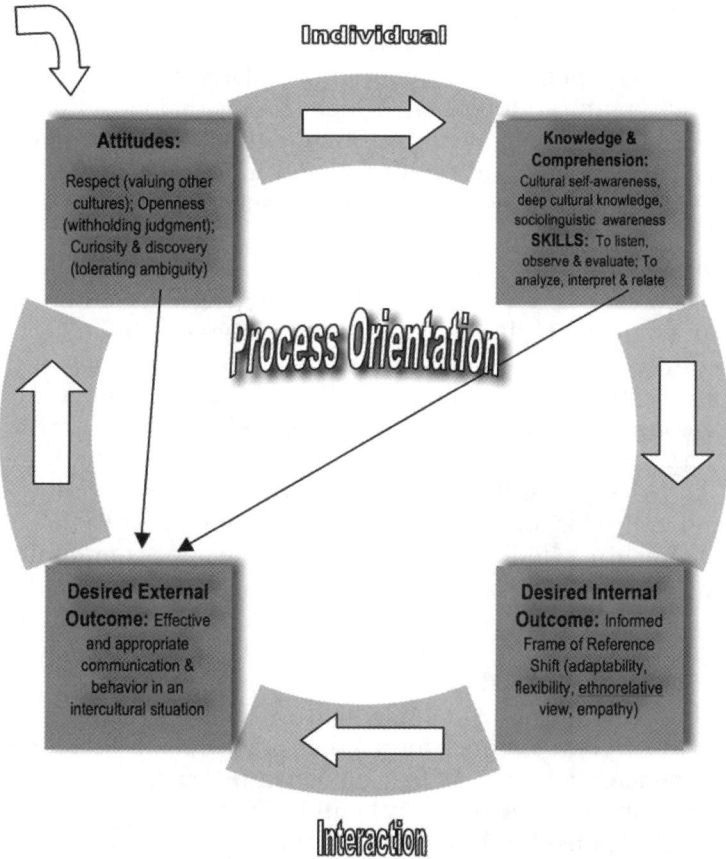

Notes: Begin with attitudes; move from individual level (attitudes) to interaction level (outcomes); degree of intercultural competence depends on acquired degree of attitudes, knowledge/comprehension, and skills.

Figure 1. Process model of intercultural competence (Deardorff, 2006, 2009).

A common question that scholar-practitioners should ask is: What are the implications of this framework for practice? In this particular intercultural competence framework, the first implication for practice is that the focus should be more on the process, and not as much on the results of achieving intercultural competence, since developing such competence is a lifelong process. Further, each person is at a different place in their development process, so a one-size-fits-all approach or program will not meet learners where they are. Given this framework, it is important that programs and experience go beyond the acquisition of knowledge, since intercultural competence is so much more than that. Thus, experiential learning that allows for real-life interactions, and skill development becomes very important, beyond contrived and isolated courses or programs. A final implication is that it may not be so much about intercultural competence as about how others are approached initially – through cultural humility, which means being self-aware about how little is really known about the other (cultural self-awareness), how much more there is to learn (curiosity), and how important it is to value others (respect), regardless of differences (including differences in thinking, beliefs, and so on).

One other frequently cited definition and framework of intercultural competence, especially within language teaching and within European contexts, is that of Byram (1997). Byram's intercultural competence definition was also one of the most highly rated ones in the Deardorff study (2006). Byram outlines five areas of intercultural communicative competence of intercultural speakers as follows: critical cultural awareness, which is at the heart of the model, along with four other areas: knowledge, skills of discovery/interaction, skills of interpreting, and attitudes of curiosity/openness. Byram links this to intercultural citizenship, which stresses the importance of communities of action within civil society, beyond local, national or global politics, although political education is inherent in notions of intercultural citizenship. Given that Byram's model comes from the language field, the role of language is also addressed in intercultural competence.

So, what does this mean to practice (and to scholar-practitioners)? The implications of Byram's model for scholar-practitioners include an expanded way conceptualizing global citizenship (such as through communities of action), the role of critical cultural awareness (which can impact learners' reflections, for example), and the implications to foreign language teaching of going beyond acquisition of language skills to the inclusion of intercultural competence as vital to language learning.

There are many other definitions of intercultural competence in the literature, many of them not based on actual research and most coming from scholars in the Global North. (For more on these different definitions, see Spitzberg & Changnon, 2009.) Scholar-practitioners, however, may want to explore other intercultural competence frameworks in informing their own research and practice in this increasingly crucial area of international education.

Other Cultural Perspectives on Intercultural Competence

Many of the theories and frameworks in general emerge from a predominantly western context. This is particularly true for theories and definitions around intercultural competence. So, what are some other definitions of intercultural competence? From the South African context, the philosophical concept of *Ubuntu* emerges. There is much literature that has been written about Ubuntu (Makgoba, 1999; Nwosu, 2009; Khoza, 2011), as found in a Zulu proverb *Ubuntu Ngumuntu Ngabantu* – meaning that a person is a person because of others. This concept of Ubuntu, also referred to as African humanism, can be used within intercultural competence as well as within global citizenship to illustrate the importance of identity, relationship and impact. In fact, it could be argued that global citizenship is in effect another way of expressing Ubuntu – with its emphasis on connectedness, compassion, empathy, humility and action. However, unlike western conceptions of global citizenship, Ubuntu stresses the importance of collective action – and de-emphasizes the individual.

In looking at concepts related to intercultural competence in other cultures around the world, several align quite closely with intercultural learning. For example, a related philosophical concept to Ubuntu comes from the Andes: *Alli kawsay*, loosely translated as good living, which emphasizes 'reciprocal, complementary, and cooperative relations' (Medina-López-Portillo & Sinnigen 2009, p. 251), is a philosophical concept that can contribute to western notions of global citizenship in shifting from an individualistic paradigm to one that collectively looks at addressing ecological, social and economic crises. Similarly, another Andean concept, *nandereko*, stresses harmonious living, which one could argue is core to intercultural competence. From a Chinese perspective, there is a focus on *zhong dao*, 'the way of being appropriate, fitting one's communication to the situation', with *cheng*, which is sincerity and internal consistency, as the axis of *zhong dao* (Chen & An, 2009). And from an Indian perspective comes the Hindu concept of *Vishwaroopa Darshan*, or oneness, also termed unity within diversity (Manian & Naidu, 2009), upon which intercultural competence is built. These are but a few examples of other perspectives that can contribute to and inform practice within international higher education. (For more on other cultural perspectives on intercultural competence, see Deardorff, 2009 and UNESCO, 2013.)

What are the implications of some of these concepts? First, it is especially important for scholar-practitioners to go beyond a reliance on theories and models coming from solely western and Global North contexts. More specifically, scholar-practitioners need to consider how they are addressing issues such as identity, worldview and context, and how theories and frameworks from the Global South can help inform their understanding of these concepts. In regard to intercultural competence, the locus may not be so much with the individual but rather within the larger context of relationships and interactions, as well as in the social, economic, political and historical realities. Thus, it may be best for the scholar-practitioner to address intercultural competence within a more holistic context.

Other Essential Theories Impacting Intercultural Development and Learning

Essential intercultural theories include those found in the interdisciplinary field of cross-cultural communication, including those on communication styles and value orientations. (The theories of Hofstede, Hall, Kluckhohn & Strodtbeck, Geertz, Triandis, among others, are the 'classics' which have been heavily cited.) It behoves scholar-practitioners to be familiar with these cross-cultural theories given their relevance to intercultural development. With the wealth of materials already written about those theories, along with the limited scope of this chapter, the focus here will be on briefly highlighting other theories that impact intercultural development.

Sanford and challenge and support. Nevitt Sanford (1967) posited that for maximum growth and learning to occur, there needs to be a balance between challenge and support in the learner's experience. This means that if there is too much challenge, the learner will disengage; likewise, if there is too much support, learning will not occur to the extent it needs to. This theory has clear implications for scholar-practitioners in that within intercultural experiences (especially in education abroad settings), it is incumbent to balance the degree of challenge with the amount of support, thus optimizing learning. (See also Paige's intensity factors, below, which serve to create greater challenge in many cases.)

Allport and the contact hypothesis. Coming from social psychology, contact theory helps explain and evaluate conditions for promoting understanding in human interaction. According to Gordon Allport (1954/1979), contact alone is not sufficient; rather, in order to maximize contact between those from different cultural backgrounds, the following four criteria need to be observed in an experience in order for meaningful learning and contact to occur: equal status; intergroup cooperation; common goals; and support by social and institutional authorities. The contact hypothesis theory has significant relevance to international education programs in helping to understand why it is not sufficient to bring students together and expect understanding to occur. Rather, Allport's criteria need to be in addressed in order to achieve deeper goals of understanding and relationship-building.

Bennett and the developmental model of intercultural sensitivity (DMIS). Developed by Milton Bennett (1993) and used widely in international education, this model helps explain individuals' response to cultural difference. The key to this model is its developmental nature, emphasizing that the acquisition of intercultural sensitivity is a developmental process – six stages in this case. The first three stages of this model – denial, defense/polarization, and minimization of difference – are considered to be ethnocentric stages, focused on the individual's cultural lens, while the latter three stages – acceptance, adaptation, and integration of difference – are considered to be ethnorelative, moving beyond one way of seeing the world. It is crucial that scholar-practitioners understand these stages and design appropriate learning interventions to move students to the next stage of their intercultural development. Further, given that students are generally not at the same stage, a 'one-size-fits-all' learning intervention would not be as effective.

King and Baxter Magolda's model of intercultural maturity. Another developmental model, used often in student affairs, is King and Baxter Magolda's (2005) developmental model of intercultural maturity. They place their model within the context of a holistic approach based on the work of Kegan (1994), noting that such an approach 'allows one to identify underlying capabilities that may guide a learner's ability to integrate knowledge, skills, and awareness, and to act in interculturally mature ways' (p. 572). In their multidimensional framework, King and Baxter Magolda propose three domains of development: cognitive, intrapersonal, and interpersonal. For scholar-practitioners, this model emphasizes a holistic approach which may often be missing in international education programming.

Mezirow and transformative learning theory. Jack Mezirow (1978, 1991) focused on meaning-making through 'disorienting dilemmas', or situations that are either surprising or disturbing in that they contradict what is known. This causes individuals to incorporate new understandings, perspectives and assumptions about how the world works, which in turn leads to transformation, defined as a deep shift in one's interpretation of the world. Transformative learning occurs through critical reflection on previously held assumptions (others' assumptions as well as one's own), based on objective (others') and subjective (one's own) reframing. In international education, disorientating dilemmas often occur through education abroad experiences, although intercultural service learning and community engagement can also serve as a catalyst for such dilemmas, as can experiential learning within a classroom. Regardless of where they occur, the key to transformative learning, according to Mezirow, lies in the critical reflection on such dilemmas, which involves not just content reflection (what was learned) but also process reflection (how the learning occurred) and premise reflection (evaluation of the learning). Reframing, which is the process of rewriting personal narratives in making sense of the experience, becomes key in the transformational process. For scholar-practitioners who want to understand more about transformational learning processes, Mezirow becomes a foundational theorist.

Paige's intensity factors. According to R. Michael Paige (1993), the following ten intensity factors impact one's intercultural development and adjustment: cultural differences (the degree of cultural difference encountered); ethnocentrism (the degree to which one believes one's own culture is best); language (the role language plays in one's adjustment to an intercultural setting) [1]; the degree to which one is immersed in another culture); cultural isolation (the degree to which one is connected with others in the local context); prior intercultural experience (the amount and quality of one's previous intercultural experiences); expectations (the extent to which realistic expectations are managed in an intercultural setting); visibility and invisibility (the degree to which one is either visible [not like the others] or invisible ['blends in'] in a different cultural setting); status (the degree to which one is viewed as having status [or loss of status] in a different cultural setting); and power and control (the degree to which one feels in control [or not] of a situation). Scholar-practitioners need to be aware of the degree to which these factors can exacerbate or enhance the learner's intercultural experience, and address these through expectation management, which is key in mitigating these factors.

Kim's stress-adaptation-growth model. Young Yun Kim developed a stress-adaptation-growth spiral model to demonstrate the adaptation process in adjusting to new cultural situations (such as in study abroad contexts). While various other cultural adaptation models (such as the U- or W-curve) are often used in international education, those are not based on research (Berardo, 2006). Instead, Kim's model, which is based on research, focuses more on the process one goes through when confronted with a situation outside one's comfort zone. For scholar-practitioners, this model provides a different way to frame adaptation as a growth process, and one that can occur in both domestic and cross-border contexts.

Schlossberg's transitions theory. Nancy Schlossberg (1981) developed a theory that looked at four major factors which influence a person's ability to cope in transition, defined as an event or non-event that involves a change (in relationships, routines, etc.). The 'S' factors are: situation (and the degree of change); self (i.e. demographic characteristics); support (i.e. relationships, social networks, etc.); and strategies (in modifying the situation, managing stress, etc.). For scholar-practitioners, this transitions theory, when coupled with Kim's stress-adaptation-growth model (Kim, 2001), can aid in designing programs that help students through intercultural adjustment and adaptation.

Goleman and emotional intelligence. Psychologist Daniel Goleman (1995) posited the theory of emotional intelligence, which involves one's ability to monitor one's own and others' emotional responses and to use emotional information to guide thinking and behavior. Goleman's model outlines five elements of emotional intelligence: self-awareness (of one's emotions); self-regulation (of one's emotions); social skill in managing relationships; empathy (considering others' feelings); and motivation. Given that intercultural development does not occur in isolation, but rather, is influenced and connected to one's emotions and emotional intelligence, it is important for scholar-practitioners to remain aware of how emotional intelligence is being addressed within international educational programming so as to address the more holistic nature of international education contexts, including the role of emotion.

Exploring Other Relevant Theories for Scholar-practitioners

Other relevant scholars and theories which impact international higher education scholarship and practice, with practical implications for addressing intercultural development, include the following:

Dewey and learning through experience. John Dewey, a twentieth-century American philosopher, with his emphasis on pragmatism, developed an educational philosophy that focused on principles and levels of learning, found in his well-known work called *The Child and the Curriculum* (Dewey, 1902). In particular, he wrote about three levels of activity, the first through sensory experiences, the second through the use of authentic materials found in the environment, and the third level of discovery through investigation of a genuine problem and subsequent searching and testing for solutions. This meant that the school environment became a learning laboratory. For scholar-practitioners, Dewey's work points to the importance of learning by experience (which does not necessarily mean studying abroad, but also viewing the local environment as a learning laboratory) and the exploration of relevant problems and solutions, which fits quite well within the larger context of global citizenship.

Piaget and developmental psychology. Even though Jean Piaget focused much of his work on early childhood and children through the age of fifteen, his work in developmental psychology laid a foundation for future scholarship on stages of human development (which built on the work of previous scholars, such as Comenius in the 1600s and Rousseau in the 1700s, both of whom stressed stages of human development). Interestingly, Piaget looked at adaptation within the context of the environment and defined adaptation as a process in which the person 'assimilates the factors of the environment' and 'adjusts to the requirements of the environment' (Ornstein & Levine, 1984, p. 138). Piaget stressed individualized instruction/interventions that align with developmental stages, ensuring that activities were appropriate for the person's developmental stage. The implications of Piaget are still quite relevant for scholar-practitioners today in moving beyond a 'one-size-fits-all' approach.

Bloom's learning taxonomy. Bloom (Bloom et al, 1956) developed a taxonomy of thinking skills that has long served as a basis for instructional design in education. According to Bloom, learning starts with knowledge acquisition and comprehension, the first two levels in his taxonomy. Higher-order thinking skills follow: application, analysis, synthesis, and evaluation. Later iterations by other scholars added creativity. For scholar-practitioners, this taxonomy can be used in writing specific learning goals and objectives for programs and courses, and it encourages learning beyond (cultural/global) knowledge to application, which is crucial in developing global citizens.

Maslow's hierarchy of needs. This classic theory, developed by Maslow (1943), categorizes human need into five different levels, starting with the most basic level of (1) physiological needs – which consist of food, water and shelter. This level is followed by (2) safety needs, including both psychological and physical, (3) social needs, related to the social nature of human interaction and relationships, (4) esteem needs, or the desire to be valued by others and (5) self-actualization needs, related to a sense of self-fulfillment and achievement of one's own self-understanding and achievement of one's own destiny. This particular model is relevant in international education in terms of structuring content in orientation programs (both for study abroad students as well as for international students), as well as for understanding the vital role physiological and safety needs play in the success – or failure – of international education programming.

Chickering's seven vectors of identity development. Arthur Chickering (1969) developed seven tasks that are instrumental in one's identity development (particularly at the undergraduate level, although this is not age-specific): (1) developing competence – intellectually, physically and interpersonally; (2) managing emotions; (3) developing autonomy – emotionally and practically; (4) establishing identity – responding to the quintessential life question of 'Who am I?'; (5) freeing interpersonal relationships – moving from dependence to interdependence; (6) developing purpose (i.e. life goals); and (7) establishing integrity, which involves living meaningfully within society. There are many other identity development models (Helms, Sue & Sue, Josselson, Phinney, Cass, etc.) related to stages of one's identity; what is important to recognize for scholar-practitioners is that students may be at different stages in developing their racial/ethnic/sexual identities and programming needs to be aligned appropriately with those different stages.

Knowles and self-directed learning. Malcolm Knowles (1975), known as the 'father of andragogy', championed the concept of self-directed learning as a way of empowering learners by making learning more relevant to their needs. A key tool in self-directed learning is the learner contract, which is negotiated with the teacher. Central to self-directed learning is the importance of experience, of immediate relevancy of the learning, and of the more problem-focused approach vs. the content-focused approach (similar to Freire, below). Knowles' work has direct relevance to scholar-practitioners in its focus on experiences and on empowering the learner through learning contracts. For example, how might scholar-practitioners incorporate learning contracts into education abroad programs or into the classroom?

Freire and problem posing. Paulo Freire's revolutionary *Pedagogy of the Oppressed* (1970) was the foundational work for critical pedagogy, which viewed education as a political act. Viewing education as connected to power, Freire emphasized 'conscientization', or realizing one's consciousness, as the first step in taking action against oppression. One of the key teaching methods put forth by Freire is that of problem posing, which involves dialogue between teacher and student (as opposed to the more traditional approach of teacher imparting knowledge to students, called the 'banking concept' by Freire). Freire's work has numerous implications for intercultural and global citizenship development; in particular, scholar-practitioners are challenged to think about how to partner with students through problem posing, helping students connect to their own realities and empowering them to take action.

Kolb's learning cycle. David Kolb (1984), building on the work of Dewey (see above), has developed a widely used learning styles theory, which is often presented in the form of a learning cycle. In this theory, Kolb emphasizes four styles of learning: concrete experience (do); reflective observation (observe); abstract conceptualization (think); and active experimentation (plan). According to Kolb, these styles need to follow in sequential order, although the starting point can be at any one of the four. Scholar-practitioners can use Kolb's learning cycle in designing programs and experiences for students, ensuring that different learning styles will be met.

Schön's reflective practice. Donald Schön (1983), building on the work of Dewey and others, developed the practice of reflection into two concepts of 'learning in action' and 'learning on action'. These concepts highlighted the importance of integrating reflection and practice and, in particular, of thinking about 'lessons learned' from experience which results in action. There are many other theories around reflective practice, including that of Rolfe (2001), who developed the reflection questions of 'what', 'so what' and 'now what' to use in reflective practice. Scholar-practitioners may find the work of Schön, Dewey, Rolfe and others useful in integrating reflection into international education experiences, thus becoming a tool for furthering learning.

Beyond the theories highlighted here, there are many other theories which can help inform the work of scholar-practitioners. Readers are encouraged to delve into materials in different disciplines to explore theories such as those related to human ecology, systems theory, organizational development and culture (e.g. Schein), mind brain education, linguistics theories, mindfulness, multiple identities, cognitive development, connected leadership, personal leadership, and human consciousness. Newer theories include self-authorship, Fink's taxonomy in class design, good learning environments, and those in mind brain education. These and other theoretical perspectives can add much to framing international education and are more than what can be discussed within the constraints of this chapter.

Conclusion

What does all of this mean for international education scholarship and practice? Scholar-practitioners are in a unique role to utilize these theories as tools to strengthen the work of international educators and facilitate the application of theory to practice. From these various theoretical concepts, several questions emerge that can be used as a checklist to inform the continued work of scholar-practitioners, as they bridge scholarship, theory and practice:

- Do programs have clearly articulated learning objectives (based on Bloom) and do they involve learners in this process (i.e. Knowles' learning contracts)?
- Are programs and experiences grounded in relevant theories, including non-western theories?
- Have terms been defined adequately and based on the literature (such as intercultural competence – i.e. Deardorff, Byram, Bennett and others)?
- How do the theories inform program design (to ensure that programs are more effective in meeting learners' needs – i.e. per Maslow, Piaget)?
- Do programs address aspects of intercultural competence development (per Deardorff, Byram, Bennett and others)?
- Do programs move beyond a 'one-size-fits-all' approach and, instead, are they tailored to meet students where they are *developmentally* (per Dewey, King & Baxter Magolda, Bennett)?
- Do programs go beyond content and knowledge, to actual skill development and active engagement in civil society (Freire, Chickering)?
- Do programs involve experiential learning (Dewey), following Kolb's learning cycle?
- And are there opportunities for critical reflection (per Mezirow) and reflective practice (per Schön)?

- Do programs meet learners where they are and empower learners (per Freire, Knowles)?
- Do programs address learners' holistic development (i.e. intercultural, emotional, identity, etc. as informed by Goleman, Chickering and others)?
- Do programs include the appropriate balance of challenge and support to maximize learning (per Sanford)?
- Do programs include conditions necessary for meaningful contact and relationship development (per Allport)?
- Have intensity factors been considered, as well as the factors for successful transition and adjustment (per Paige, Schlossberg, and Kim)?

This chapter has provided an overview of some of the key theoretical frameworks and scholars whose work can inform the work of scholar-practitioners in international education. Undoubtedly, there are many other theoretical tools and concepts that can be added, some of which may have been inadvertently not included in this chapter. Regardless, the challenge is to search continually for theories and tools, especially in other disciplines, that can be used to help inform international education research and practice, thus enhancing student learning and development. In an ever-more complex world, theory provides scholar-practitioners with tools with which to understand that world and to help learners make meaning of their realities. Grounding programs, practice and scholarship in theory ensures that the work of scholar-practitioners is coherent and rigorous and, more importantly, that it becomes more relevant in meeting the needs of learners as they continue to develop into interculturally competent citizens contributing meaningfully to society.

Note

[1] http://www2.pacific.edu/sis/culture/File/sec1-5-4h4.htm

References

Allport, G. (1954/1979) *The Nature of Prejudice*. Reading, MA: Addison-Wesley.

Association of International Education Administrators (AIEA) (2014) SIO Profile Executive Summary. http://www.aieaworld.org

Bennett, M. (1993) Toward Ethnorelativism: a developmental model of intercultural sensitivity, in R.M. Paige (Ed.) *Education for the Intercultural Experience*. Yarmouth, ME: Intercultural Press

Berardo, K. (2006) The U-curve of Adjustment: a study in the evolution and evaluation of a 50-year old model. MA thesis, Luton Business School, University of Bedfordshire.

Bloom, B.S., Engelhart, M.D., Furst, E.J., Hill, W.H. & Krathwohl, D.R. (1956) Taxonomy of Educational Objectives: the classification of educational goals, in *Handbook 1: cognitive domain.* New York: David McKay.

Bok, D. (2006) *Our Underachieving Colleges: a candid look at how much students learn and why they should be learning more.* Princeton, NJ: Princeton University Press.

Byram, M. (1997) *Teaching and Assessing Intercultural Communicative Competence.* Clevedon: Multilingual Matters.

Chen, G. & An, R. (2009) A Chinese model of Intercultural Leadership Competence, in D.K. Deardorff (Ed.) *The SAGE Handbook of Intercultural Competence.* Thousand Oaks, CA: SAGE.

Chickering, A. (1969) *Education and Identity.* San Francisco: Jossey-Bass.

Deardorff, D.K. (2006) The Identification and Assessment of Intercultural Competence as a Student Outcome of Internationalization at Institutions of Higher Education in the United States, *Journal of Studies in International Education*, 10, 241-266. http://dx.doi.org/10.1177/1028315306287002

Deardorff, D.K. (2009) *The SAGE Handbook of Intercultural Competence.* Thousand Oaks, CA: SAGE.

Deardorff, D.K. (2015) *Demystifying Outcomes Assessment for International Educators: a practical approach.* Sterling, VA: Stylus.

Dewey, J. (1902) *The Child and the Curriculum.* Chicago: University of Chicago Press.

Egron-Polak, E. & Hudson, R. (2014) *Internationalization of Higher Education: growing expectations, fundamental values.* Paris: International Association of Universities.

Fantini, A. (2009) Assessing Intercultural Competence: issues and tools, in D.K. Deardorff (Ed.) *The SAGE Handbook of Intercultural Competence.* Thousand Oaks, CA: SAGE.

Freire, P. (1970) *Pedagogy of the Oppressed.* New York: Continuum.

Goleman, D. (1995) *Emotional Intelligence.* New York: Bantam Books.

Kegan, Robert (1994) *In Over Our Heads: the mental demands of modern life.* Cambridge, MA: Harvard University Press.

Khoza, R. (2011) *Attuned Leadership: African humanism as compass.* New York: Penguin.

Kim, Y. (2001) *Becoming Intercultural: an integrative theory of communication and cross-cultural adaptation.* Thousand Oaks, CA: SAGE.

King, P.M. & Baxter Magolda, M.B. (2005) A Developmental Model of Intercultural Maturity, *Journal of College Student Development*, 46(6), 571-592. http://dx.doi.org/10.1353/csd.2005.0060

Knowles, M.S. (1975) *Self-directed Learning: a guide for learners and teachers.* Englewood Cliffs, NJ: Prentice Hall/Cambridge.

Kolb, D. (1984) *Experiential Learning: experience as the source of learning and development.* Englewood Cliffs, NJ: Prentice Hall.

Makgoba, M. (1999) *African Renaissance: the new struggle*. Cape Town: Mafube & Tafelberg.

Manian, R. & Naidu, S. (2009) India: a cross-cultural overview of intercultural competence, in D.K. Deardorff (Ed.) *The SAGE Handbook of Intercultural Competence*. Thousand Oaks, CA: SAGE.

Maslow, A. (1943) A Theory of Human Motivation, *Psychological Review*, 50, 370-396. http://dx.doi.org/10.1037/h0054346

Medina- López-Portillo, A. & Sinnigen, J. (2009) Interculturality versus Intercultural Competencies in Latin America, in D.K. Deardorff (Ed.) *The SAGE Handbook of Intercultural Competence*. Thousand Oaks, CA: SAGE.

Mestenhauser, J. (2011) *Reflections on the Past, Present, and Future of Internationalizing Higher Education: discovering opportunities to meet the challenges*. Minneapolis: Global Programs and Strategy Alliance at the University of Minnesota.

Mezirow, J. (1978) Perspective Transformation, *Adult Education*, 28, 100-110. http://dx.doi.org/10.1177/074171367802800202

Mezirow, J. (1991) *Transformative Dimensions of Adult Learning*. San Francisco: Jossey-Bass.

Nwosu, P. (2009) Understanding Africans' Conceptualizations of Intercultural Competence, in D.K. Deardorff (Ed.) *The SAGE Handbook of Intercultural Competence*. Thousand Oaks, CA: SAGE.

Ornstein, A. & Levine, D. (1984) *An Introduction to the Foundations of Education*. Cengage Learning.

Paige, R. Michael (1993) *Experience for the Intercultural Experience*. Yarmouth, ME: Intercultural Press.

Pottinger, P.S. (1979) Competence Assessment: comments on current practices, in P.S. Pottinger & J. Goldsmith (Eds) *Defining and Measuring Competence*. San Francisco: Jossey-Bass.

Rolfe, G., Freshwater, D. & Jasper, M. (2001) *Critical Reflection in Nursing and the Helping Professions: a user's guide*. Basingstoke: Palgrave Macmillan.

Sanford, N. (1967) *When Colleges Fail: the study of the student as a person*. San Francisco: Jossey-Bass.

Schlossberg, N. (1981) A Model for Analyzing Human Adaptation to Transition, *The Counseling Psychologist*, 9(2), 2-18. http://dx.doi.org/10.1177/001100008100900202

Schön, D.A. (1983) *The Reflective Practitioner: how professionals think in action*. New York: Basic Books.

Spitzberg, B. & Changnon, G. (2009) Conceptualizing Intercultural Competence, in D.K. Deardorff (Ed.) *The SAGE Handbook of Intercultural Competence*. Thousand Oaks, CA: SAGE.

UNESCO (2013) *Intercultural Competences*. Paris: UNESCO.

CHAPTER 18

Graduate Education in Context: preparing scholar-practitioners as future international education leaders

TAYLOR C. WOODMAN & KATHERINE N. PUNTENEY

SUMMARY This chapter examines international higher education graduate programs in the United States. Using this analysis as a foundation, the authors explore characteristics unique to each of six types of graduate programs in international higher education. The chapter introduces the tensions between the theoretical foundations that guide the work of international education practitioners and the increasing pressure from students and stakeholders to provide relevant, practical experience. In their exploration of these program types and current tensions facing these programs, the authors identify possible ways to shape international education curricula to prepare students to be scholar-practitioners. Through cases studies of their respective graduate programs, the authors examine two programs that combine the application of theory with applied programming in order to develop scholar-practitioners. One of the programs features client-based courses and practica, while the other program incorporates an experiential international program within an education abroad course. From these examples, the authors share their recommendations for how graduate programs can prepare scholar-practitioners to be the future leaders in international education.

Challenged to meet the growing demand for leaders in international higher education, graduate degree programs are proliferating. Graduate educators shaping these programs struggle to adapt to national and global trends in higher education and to reassure students burdened with anxiety about the need to quickly develop job skills for employability.

Increasingly, professionals are asked to be scholar-practitioners, experienced in the operational management of international education programs, knowledgeable about the theoretical foundations of the field, and skilled in research and assessment.

This chapter examines US international higher education graduate programs and delineates these programs into six types. The authors offer their perspectives to describe the unique characteristics of each program type while addressing the challenges and opportunities faced by graduate degree programs. Two graduate programs in which the authors teach are offered as cases illustrating curricular approaches that utilize the programs' strengths and missions to develop scholar-practitioners. Recommendations are offered for prospective students and graduate educators in order to help develop the knowledge and skills needed for future international education leaders.

Growth in International Higher Education Graduate Programs

In contrast to decades past when people with international interests often fell into the profession through happenstance, now more and more people are choosing international education as a career path, seeking out specialized graduate training. Employers hiring international education professionals are increasingly requiring a graduate degree (Dessoff, 2006; Urias et al, 2007; Mueller & Overmann, 2014). In a survey of international education employers, 67% agreed that there is an increasing demand for international education professionals to have master's degrees, while only 13% disagreed (Bentsen et al, 2010). The Forum on Education Abroad surveyed its membership and found that 87% hold a master's degree or higher (Forum on Education Abroad, 2013). Analysis of international education job postings conducted at the Middlebury Institute of International Studies at Monterey in 2010 found that for positions below the director level, a master's degree was either preferred or required (Bentsen et al, 2010). The same study found that for director-level positions, a master's degree was always required, while a doctorate was often preferred. The Association of International Education Administrators (AIEA) conducted a survey of senior international officers and found that 81% hold a doctoral or professional degree (AIEA, 2012). The Forum on Education Abroad (2013), in its member survey, further found that doctoral degrees were held by 37% of directors, 60% of deans, 87.5% of provosts, and 62.5% of vice-presidents.

Analysts in the field of international higher education project continued growth in the number of internationally engaged institutions, programs and participants (Knight, 2008; Macready & Tucker, 2011). The increasing quantity and scope of international higher education programs has created a need for more talented professionals to design and facilitate programs. This expansion of the international education job market, combined with the expectation that international education professionals will hold graduate degrees, has created a demand for new graduate programs. Graduate programs in international higher education are being established to meet the need for well-educated and well-trained professionals. A 2006 article in *International Educator* magazine listed graduate programs at 27 institutions (Dessoff, 2006). The authors have compiled a list of 87 current graduate-level master's, doctoral and certificate programs in international higher education, available at 57 US institutions. Programs included reference international higher education in their mission, curriculum or alumni positions after graduation. This list was developed through online search, literature review, and with the assistance of staff at NAFSA: Association of International Educators, who shared their extensive list of programs.

Challenges Facing Graduates and Graduate Programs

The unprecedented growth and variety of international education graduate programming and the demand for leaders to facilitate international activity places pressures on the university curriculum that call for adaptations in a vast and ever-changing landscape. Many of these demands put pressure directly on the university to build a curriculum that handles the unique challenges facing international educators. Pressures on the university curriculum arise from a great variety of organizational settings outside of the space where faculty and students meet (Slaughter, 1997). While Slaughter and others discuss in detail the various stakeholders influencing curriculum, this chapter focuses on four main stakeholders: students, graduate educators, researchers, and practitioners, with the students at the center. These stakeholders' demands, while sometimes complementary, can also conflict.

The most significant pressures come directly from the students attending these graduate programs and the economic pressures they face within the current financial context. Many students have anxiety over receiving the necessary skills to enter their chosen professions, which we refer to as jobs skills anxiety. Job skills anxiety can result in the scholarly underpinnings of the field being cast aside by the student in order to achieve short-term knowledge of practice. Students may see themselves solely as customers who pay for skills that relate directly to their employability in the labor market. The increasing demand on higher education institutions to justify their tuition expense combined with the political shift in treating higher education as a private, rather than public, good exacerbates the curriculum pressures. In the face of reduced funding for their programs, graduate educators are pressured to focus on the marketability and efficiency of their programs. To compete in these markets, institutions may make curriculum decisions based on what will attract students and not necessarily on the needs of the profession (Slaughter & Rhoades, 2009). In international higher education programs, this may mean an emphasis on professional skills at the expense of theoretical grounding. The authors believe there is an urgent need for graduate programs to inculcate the value and skills of both scholarship and practice to further understanding of the field and ground the practice of international higher education.

Scholarship and Practice in Graduate Education

International higher education graduate programs may teach research and scholarship skills by assigning students to read research or analyze existing research in relation to the strengths and weaknesses of the research design. Most graduate programs incorporate research methods courses and have students conduct research in research methods courses and in thesis/dissertation projects. The variance arises in the amount of emphasis in the curriculum on research skills, the depth of research training, and whether greater emphasis is placed on graduates as consumers of research or as producers of research.

Likewise, there is a range in the way practice is taught to students across degree programs. Courses may be taught by practitioners, students may conduct informational interviews and job shadowing with working professionals, and there may be guest speakers and field trips. Students may do applied projects or have an internship component to their degree. In addition, some programs are online or hybrid programs geared towards working international education professionals, building into the degree program the application of learning to the students' workplace context. The extent to which the curriculum is applied and allows students to actively practice the skills of the profession varies greatly between degree programs.

A 2007 study examined 34 master's programs in international higher education and established standards for quality graduate programs, articulating the need for both scholarship and practice (Urias et al, 2007). Through a multi-round consensus-building process the study solicited the opinions of international education administrators, graduate educators and internationalization specialists. Key among the resulting standards is the expectation that faculty of graduate programs are actively involved in original international education research and that students in the programs are presenting research at conferences and submitting research for publication. Also identified as essential is that graduates need to be able to develop and manage international education programs, working with colleagues and constituents across the institution in the practice of international education. By presenting a typology of graduate programs and two case studies for analysis, this chapter examines the ways in which the development of both research and professional skills can be integrated within graduate programs.

Typology of Graduate Programs in International Higher Education

The authors examined the descriptions and course offerings of the 87 current graduate-level master's, doctoral and certificate programs identified by them. This analysis led to the conclusion that, with some overlap, international higher education graduate programs fall into six broad categories. While most of the program websites describe a range of career options for graduates, here the authors describe their opinions of the career paths that each category of program best prepares alumni to undertake. In addition, the curricular foci and andragogical approaches of each program type are described in the section below and summarized in Table I.

Comparative and International Education

Comparative and international education is a social science research field focused on understanding education systems and policy around the world through comparative research. There is an emphasis on understanding education systems in cultural and historical context, and on using that understanding to develop recommendations for education policy makers. Graduate programs in this field emphasize research skills and often offer students a direct pathway from a master's to a PhD within the same institution. With an emphasis on both library and field research, and on scholarship and publication, graduates are well prepared for careers in academia, in either teaching or research.

International Development and Education

Programs focused on development and education prepare international development practitioners for employment in the education sector. The mission of these programs is to prepare graduates to work towards economic development and the eradication of poverty. The emphasis is typically on access and outcomes of public K-12 or higher education in developing nations. Coursework emphasizes educational policies aimed at development such as the Education for All initiative and the Millennium Development Goals. Students learn about advocacy for social change and principles of community engagement, and often do applied fieldwork. Educational planning, programming and assessment are typical focus areas for graduates. Graduates often go on to work in non-profit or intergovernmental organizations focused on development.

International Education Policy

International education policy programs focus on policy analysis and making recommendations for policy makers. Courses examine education policy at the global, regional, national and local levels. Policy topics might include access to education, educational outcomes, funding, centralization of education systems, teacher training, equity issues, and innovation in education. The approach to learning is typified by library research and policy research and writing. There is an emphasis on scholarship and publication. Graduates may consider careers in policy analysis with think tanks or in government agencies.

International Education Administration and Management

Programs in international education administration and management typically focus on the design and operations of programs such as education abroad that move students and scholars across borders for the purpose of increasing intercultural understanding. Course topics likely include finance, marketing, management, curriculum design, assessment of learning, internationalization, and other applied topics. While most emphasize higher education, a few of these programs focus on the administration of youth programs and international schools. Applied projects and internships are common educational components of these programs. Graduates are well prepared for careers in education abroad, international student and scholar services, or recruitment and admissions.

Intercultural or Multicultural Studies

Degree programs in intercultural studies focus on interpersonal interactions, self-awareness and intercultural communication. Students study sociological and psychological theories of identity development and interpersonal and intergroup interactions. Study of the multicultural affairs literature on power, privilege and oppression may also be included. Not only do students in these programs reflect on their own cultural values and biases, they focus on how to develop intercultural competence in others while minimizing societal inequities. There is typically an emphasis on training or teaching careers. There may be an emphasis on working with minority students within the home country as well as on working with international populations. Graduates work to effect organizational change and to offer services to individuals for the betterment of society as a whole.

Higher Education and Student Affairs

Master's and doctoral programs in higher education or student affairs may offer the opportunity to specialize in international education. In these programs, understanding of international education programs will often be framed within student development theory, leadership theory, or the broader functioning and purposes of higher education. The curriculum typically includes courses on educational curriculum design and assessment, student advising, and administrative knowledge sets such as education finance, law, and policy. Applied coursework and internships provide students with the ability to apply theory in context. Graduates are well prepared for careers in academic administration or student services, including the possibility of specializing in international education.

Scholarship and Practice among the Program Types

The curricular foci and teaching approaches of the six types of programs lend themselves to particular career trajectories where students can best make use of their graduate training. Each program type offers graduates a particular strength in terms of having a specialized knowledge and skill set to take into their professional work. While we have suggested ideal career trajectories for each type of graduate program, the reality is that all of the programs have alumni who work in the profession of international education as well as alumni who are actively contributing to scholarship in the field.

All six types of graduate programs in international higher education include some emphasis on both scholarship and practice. The difference is often one of degree – the percentage of the curriculum that is focused on the development of research skills versus the percentage spent learning about the profession of managing international education programs. In order to effectively develop scholar-practitioners, those programs with a stronger research emphasis need to be deliberate in adding applied practice opportunities, while those programs that have an emphasis on practice must be intentional about ensuring that research and theory is the foundation of the applied coursework. Through thoughtful and intentional curriculum development, capitalizing on the strengths of the type, each program type has the capacity to prepare international higher education scholar-practitioners. To place these curricular approaches in context, the authors share examples from their representative institutions.

Program Type	Curricular Foci	Andragogical Hallmarks	Career Trajectories	Representative Institutions
Comparative and International Education	- Social science research methods - Education policy and systems around the world - Informing policy through comparative research	- Library research - Field research - Scholarship and publication - Presentation at academic conferences	- Combined MA and PhD programs common - Academic careers	- Pennsylvania State University - Stanford University
International Development and Education	- Grounded in international/ sustainable development field - Emphasis on education for purposes of economic development and the eradication of poverty	- Applied fieldwork with non-govern-mental organizations and intergovern-mental organizations - Analyzing policies such as EFA and the MDGs - Advocacy for social change	- UN agencies - USAID or other national development initiatives - Non-govern-mental organizations	T- he George Washington University - University of Minnesota
International Education Policy	- Examination of educational policy at the global, regional, national, and local levels. - Access to education, educational outcomes, equity issues - Funding models - Teacher training	- Library research - Policy research and writing - Scholarship and publication	- Policy analyst - UN or government agencies - Think tanks	- Harvard University - University of Maryland

	- Innovation in education			
International Education Administration and Management	- Emphasis on the profession of international education - Management skills such as budgeting, marketing, staff management, etc. - Curriculum design and assessment of learning	- Applied coursework - Client-based projects - Internships	- Education abroad - International student services - Recruitment and admissions - Program coordination	- Middlebury Institute of International Studies at Monterey - SIT Graduate Institute
Intercultural or Multicultural Studies	- Intercultural theory and research - Social inequities	- Emphasis on self-reflection and self-knowledge - Training design	- Intercultural trainer or teacher - Diversity officer	- Lesley University - University of San Francisco
Higher Education and Student Affairs	- Student development theory - Student affairs - Leadership theory - History and role of higher education - International higher education	- Applied coursework focused on administration - Practicum experience	- Educational administration - Student services	- University of Wisconsin-Madison - Vanderbilt University

Table I. Typology of international higher education graduate programs.

Case Studies

Both authors teach in international higher education graduate programs, and they introduce the two cases to highlight the variance between types of program and their approach to preparing scholar-practitioners through deliberate curriculum design and intervention.

University of Maryland

The University of Maryland (UMD) offers an international education policy (IEP) program at both the MA and the PhD level that is an example of the international education policy program type. UMD's graduate program examines educational policy at the global, regional, national and local levels and focuses on issues of access and equity in education policy. The program lends itself to a more scholarly approach to international education. The program consists of three core courses each taught by one of the tenured IEP faculty in their specialty areas. Each of the three core courses (Political Economy of Education, Culture and Education in a Global Context, and Comparative Education) align with one of the four specializations within the UMD program. The fourth specialization focuses on Intercultural Education & International Student Exchange. In addition to the IEP core courses, specialization courses and research methodology courses, students choose electives which may be theoretically or professionally oriented. Students complete a research-based seminar paper (MA) or dissertation (PhD). Recent examples of graduate student research within the Intercultural Education and International Student Exchange specialization include an examination of the effects of mandating education abroad and another study looking at aligning growth and quality in an education abroad office. Many of the MA graduates go on to complete doctoral programs.

The Intercultural Education & International Student Exchange specialization offers students interested in the profession an opportunity to undertake applied coursework. In an effort to create scholar-practitioners and help students gain intercultural experience, the program offers internships for credit and recently added an education abroad course in Cuba to its curriculum. The Cuba education abroad course is modeled on experiential learning theory, which emphasizes knowledge created through transformative experience (Kolb, 1984). Students are exposed to information through course texts, lectures and discussions on Cuban culture, the Cuban education system and best practices in education abroad. Throughout the course, students start to see themselves in dual roles as both a student participant and a knowledgeable international educator. Synthesis occurs as students connect their international experience to the work of their future research practice and their future professional practice. Students are asked to reflect in writing on the course design, the research process and their participation in the course. Students compare this insight to best practices in education abroad and use their own behaviors as examples of how students challenge our attempts to structure international experiences. With experiential learning theory as its foundation, the education abroad course aims to bridge the divide between theory and practice.

The increased variety in course offering within the IEP program at UMD responds to the desires of students to apply theoretical knowledge gained in the classroom to international education practice. Adding experiential courses to a degree program focused primarily on international education policy scholarship strengthens the program's emphasis on practice and reduces some of students' job skills anxiety, without undermining the theoretical emphasis of the degree program or restructuring the full curriculum. UMD's curriculum expansion serves as an example of how a theoretically oriented program can combine practice and theory to enhance graduate education and create future scholar-practitioners.

Middlebury Institute of International Studies at Monterey

One of the authors founded and chairs a three-semester Master of Arts program in International Education Management at the Middlebury Institute of International Studies (MIIS) in Monterey, California. The MIIS program is an example of the international education management and administration program type, characterized by an emphasis on preparing practitioners for the profession. Graduates are prepared to work in education abroad, international student services, language program administration, citizen diplomacy, and non-profit organizations. The practitioner-oriented approach is epitomized by the applied coursework, the experiential client-based projects students complete in collaboration with international education organizations during each semester of the degree, and the required internship component of the program.

During the first semester, students develop a marketing and recruitment plan for an international education organization. Projects have included marketing a new education abroad destination for an education abroad provider organization, recruiting corporate clients for an intercultural executive education program, and recruiting international students from Latin America for a US university. A highlight of the second semester is developing a program design and assessment project for an international education organization. Sample projects include design and assessment of education abroad re-entry programs, intercultural courses, and international student orientations.

During the third and final semester, students complete a full-time professional practicum with an international education organization, completing extensive advanced project-based work. Samples of projects include development of a global health ethics reader, a civic engagement workshop series, an education abroad ambassadors program, social media strategy, and partner outreach plans. Other students have conducted social network analysis, assessed student support services for an English as a Second Language (ESL) program, piloted a communications audit, written grant proposals, conducted curriculum evaluation, and surveyed international students.

Each of the client-based projects and the practicum engages students in reading and applying relevant theory, including the theory of change, logic model, marketing theory, recruitment ethics, and standards of best practice (e.g. Kallur & Reeves, 2006; Sinclair, 2010; Deardorff, 2015; Forum on Education Abroad, 2015). Theory and research are introduced in the three courses associated with the client-based coursework, as well as in other courses taken concurrently by the students. Complementary bodies of scholarship introduced across courses include comparative and international education, academic mobility, international higher education, student development/student affairs, intercultural communication, service-learning and volunteerism, language education, international development, and business management.

The graduate students not only read scholarship but actively engage in conducting research in these applied courses. Previous student research projects include conducting market research, performing competitor analysis, developing instruments to measure student learning outcomes, directing needs assessments, and assessing programs. Through the projects, students focus on the practice of management as they work with real-life organizational budgets, timelines, and competing objectives and shifting priorities from the organization's managers. Students write structured reflections on their work, ensuring that they are able to understand the connections between theory and practice, scholarship and management. They present their work at conferences, in presentations to clients, and in written reports. Through the three semesters, the graduate students transition from student to professional, taking on increasingly complicated and independent projects. While the program strength is in preparing students for the profession of international education, deliberate care is taken to ensure that graduates have the ability to consume, produce and share applied research as scholar-practitioners.

Discussion

Within the context of the expansion of international higher education programs, increased job skills anxiety among students, and a push within higher education to create increasingly short and marketable graduate programs, it is essential that graduate programs do not lose sight of their missions. Programs must develop curricula that represent the best of the scholarly field, as well as training graduates for the profession of international higher education.

The authors argue that a combination of research and practice are essential to graduate curricula in international education. Essential research competencies include developing the student's ability to consume and conduct research; interpreting conceptual and theoretical frameworks; understanding critiques and limitations of research; and utilizing appropriate evidence to make arguments and advocate for international education. Graduate programs must also help the students face the challenges of future practice. To do this, students need to be able to affect and assess student learning outcomes; disseminate their research; develop research-grounded approaches to curriculum design, orientation and advising; justify budget requests; and communicate the value of international education.

The case studies demonstrate two specifically designed curricular approaches to the development of the next generation of international educators as scholar-practitioners. The programs each build on their strengths and are deliberate about developing both practice and research skills in their graduates. Programs of all six types must combine both research and practice elements in their curriculum design, in a way that maintains the integrity of their program type.

Recommendations

Earlier chapters in this volume offer insight into international education career paths that offer varying degrees of focus on scholarship and on the day-to-day administration of programs. Students considering graduate coursework as a way into the international education profession need to carefully examine the programs they are considering to identify the type of program and the relative emphasis on research versus management in the curriculum. Students must consider their preferred learning style and their career goals in order to determine which program is the best fit for them personally, while ensuring that the program of their choice offers a synthesis of scholarship and practice. Commitment to engaging concurrently in program management and research as a scholar-practitioner will facilitate a graduate's career advancement and position as a future leader in the international education field.

Educators teaching in graduate programs must recognize and teach global trends affecting the current higher education environment, including rapid internationalization and changes in the economic climate. At the same time, students possess job skills anxiety, which creates a demand for skills-based programs with an emphasis on the practice of the profession. Educators need to create courses and programs which offer a theoretical and research-based foundation upon which students can practice applied skills. Identifying the strengths of their program type and looking for ways to complement those strengths is an important first step. For example, a more heavily research-based program might consider developing experiential learning opportunities that allow students to engage in the field. Fieldwork that allow students to apply theory, conduct research and synthesize through reflection will better prepare students to be both scholars and practitioners. Offering courses abroad may further strengthen the experiential and intercultural learning opportunities. By contrast, a program whose strength is its applied coursework must be deliberate in making explicit the theoretical and research foundations of the profession. Opportunities for applied research can help students to develop their skills as scholar-practitioners while maintaining the program's strength in application.

Conclusion

Graduate programs serve as conduits for future leaders who understand and utilize best practices in both research and practice in international higher education. Six types of graduate programs have been identified, each of which has a distinct curricular emphasis and andragogical approach. While all of the programs have alumni working in the profession of international higher education, there are varying degrees to which each graduate program type incorporates scholarship and practice. Each graduate program must be deliberate in its curricular approach to putting research in context and utilizing experiential education to connect theory to job skills. Opportunities for achieving this balance include adding international or experiential courses to the curriculum, incorporating client-based projects, establishing an internship program, and ensuring the inclusion of theory and research as the foundation of all applied work. Sole focus on scholarship or practice will only limit the future of the international education field and students' career advancement. Graduate programs focused on expertly developing a talented group of scholar-practitioners are vital to ensure the future impact of international higher education.

References

Association of International Education Administrators (AIEA) (2012) A Survey on Senior International Officers: individual and institutional profiles. http://www.aieaworld.org/assets/docs/Surveys/2011siosurveyexecutivesum maryfinaldraft5b15djune2012.pdf

Bentsen, A.F., Benum, C., Morgan, E., Raess, K. & Mehringer, S. (2010) International Education Management: a feasibility study of a new program at the Monterey Institute of International Studies. Available from Middlebury Institute of International Studies at Monterey.

Deardorff, D. (2015) *Demystifying Outcomes Assessment for International Educators: a practical approach.* Sterling, VA: Stylus.

Dessoff, A. (2006) Master's Degrees: a key to your career?, *International Educator*, January/February, 36-43.

Forum on Education Abroad (2013) Preliminary Report. 2013 Institutional and Program Resources Survey: individual member response data. Carlisle, PA: Forum on Education Abroad.

Forum on Education Abroad (2015) *Standards of Good Practice for Education Abroad*, 5th edn. Carlisle, PA: Forum on Education Abroad.

Kallur, R. & Reeves, M. (2006) *Guidelines for Ethical Practice in International Student Recruitment.* NAFSA: Association of International Educators.

Knight, J. (2008) *Higher Education in Turmoil: the changing world of internationalization*, pp. 97-122. Taipei: Sense.

Kolb, D.A. (1984) *Experiential Learning: experience as the source of learning and development.* Englewood Cliffs, NJ: Prentice Hall.

Macready, C. & Tucker, C. (2011) *Who Goes Where and Why: an overview and analysis of global educational mobility.* New York: Institute of International Education.

Mueller, S.L. & Overmann, M. (2014) *Working World: careers in international education, exchange, and development.* Washington, DC: George Washington University Press.

Sinclair, J. (2010) *International Enrollment Management: framing the conversation.* Washington, DC: NAFSA: Association of International Educators.

Slaughter, S. (1997) Class, Race and Gender and the Construction of Postsecondary Curricula in the United States: social movement, professionalization and political economic theories of curricular change, *Journal of Curriculum Studies*, 29(1), 1-30. http://dx.doi.org/10.1080/002202797184170

Slaughter, S. & Rhoades, G. (2009) *Academic Capitalism and the New Economy: markets, state and higher education.* Baltimore, MD: Johns Hopkins University Press.

Urias, D., Deardorff, D. & Heyl, J.D. (2007) Standards of Quality for Master's Degree Level Programs in International Education: ensuring quality and effectiveness, in *Atlas of International Student Mobility*. Washington, DC: Institute of International Education.

CHAPTER 19

A Librarian's Lens:
thoughts for scholar-practitioners

TAMAR BRESLAUER

SUMMARY Even before conducting their own research, scholar-practitioners inform their practice by locating existing work. But what is the landscape of international higher education? In a field that includes topics as diverse as higher education policy, comparative education, student learning assessment and organizational change, as well as research approaches as varied as ethnographic studies, discourse analysis and surveys, how does a scholar-practitioner identify all relevant research? What tools are available to help simplify this process? This chapter addresses such questions by considering the nature of the field of international education through specific types of resources available to scholar-practitioners, primarily in academic libraries. In addition, it suggests ways of evaluating and organizing these resources. The chapter concludes with a proposal for a newly imagined definition of a scholar-practitioner.

Introduction

Librarians support scholar-practitioners in all disciplines by sharing their expertise in the practice of scholarship. They identify tools and organizational systems to support the practice of research. Scholar-practitioners apply a critical lens to interpreting scholarship; librarians apply a critical lens to the finding, evaluating and organizing of scholarship. Librarians serve particular clientele in a particular context. Yet, the strategies of finding, organizing and evaluating research can, in some ways, be generalized.

This chapter shares some of these generalizable strategies. While in no way a substitute for consultation with the librarians at individual institutions who have expertise in the resources specific to their collections, the hope is that these strategies will open up some pathways for those unfamiliar with conducting research in international higher education.

International higher education offers some challenges for librarians. The field boasts scholars with very different disciplinary backgrounds who apply different research methods. Scholars approach the field from many angles: some might research ways to improve international recruitment; others consider student learning; others evaluate the effectiveness and the ethics of internationalization; others take a comparative approach; others are focused on policy. The list could go on.

To address this variety, the chapter considers five different types of library resources through five different 'lenses': first, the professional lens examines resources that collect materials specifically tagged as international higher education; second, the multidisciplinary lens discusses resources that group materials from many topic areas together so they can be searched as a single unit; third, the disciplinary lens examines ways to take advantage of the organization of resources within particular disciplines; fourth, the specialized lens considers ways of finding research by research need rather than by topic; and, fifth, the scanning lens suggests places to look to get an overview of scholarship and trends in the field. A comparison of these lenses can be found in Table I. The last three sections of the chapter consider how to evaluate resources using the framework of information literacy, how to organize resources using citation management tools, and what can be learned from the librarian's lens that informs an understanding of the scholar-practitioner.

The Professional Lens: a database for international higher education

The most comprehensive bibliographic citation database specifically focused on international education is the IDP Database of Research on International Education. Providing bibliographic citations to resources in international education since 1990, the database includes individual articles, reports, dissertations, conference proceedings, books, government documents and other materials. It is supported and managed by the Australian Council for Educational Research (ACER).[1] Currently, it includes over 13,000 books, journals, dissertations, association reports, websites and other types of documents (IDP Education, 2015). The IDP database does not restrict its contents to a particular type of resource. It includes citations of dissertations, peer-reviewed articles, non-peer-reviewed articles, conference proceedings and reports by associations and think tanks. Editors of the database scan literature from multiple sources, including tweets by international educators, print and online journal releases, publishers and library catalogs, and from individuals who submit items. Individuals may request items to be added to the database (Proctor, 2015, p. 3). Each record is indexed and can be searched by keyword, date, organization, title of journal, country of origin, author and subject country.

Lens	Selected resources[a]	Examples of topics[b]
Professional	IDP Database	International student recruitment Internationalized curricula Education abroad Branch campuses International student services Internationalization strategies
Multidisciplinary	Proquest Research Library; EBSCO Academic Search Complete	Pedagogy Student Learning Assessment Curricular design Technology
Disciplinary	ERIC; Business Source Complete; HEDBIB; PAIS; ABI Inform; Medline; etc.	Company or industry background Studies from particular fields, like nursing Documents from NGOs Public policy issues
Specialized	Annual reviews; subject encyclopedias; *PolicyFile; Tests in Print;* Library of Congress country Studies; etc.	Concept overview Directory information Statistics Country report Tests for intercultural competence
Scanning	NAFSA Research Connections; conference programs; *Chronicle of Higher Education; New York Times;* BBC; etc.	Trends Policy ramifications Public response to policy Identify new scholars

[a]This list is not comprehensive. In addition, the databases within the same category are not necessarily equivalent in scope or content. It is advised to always check with the librarian at one's institution for guidance.
[b]I will remind the reader that this table oversimplifies. There is clearly overlap in the different lenses, and some of the decision of what to search comes from user preference.

Table I. Summary of research lenses.

In addition, the IDP database provides a Twitter [2] feed that allows a first glance at new publications before they appear within the database. By viewing the Twitter feed, readers can see a range of new publications on international higher education, including new blog posts, news items, reports, new dissertations and calls for papers.

This range of sources evident in the Twitter feed and in the IDP database reflects the interdisciplinary nature of the field. In fact, the report released in 2015 offered a statistical review of the contents of the database from 2011 to 2013 which, among other things, revealed that most of the journals in the database appear five or fewer times (Proctor, 2015, p. 11). Scholarship in areas associated with internationalization appears in many places – and the IDP database attempts to capture all of these places. An article on global citizens and study abroad in the journal *Compare: A Journal of Comparative and International Education* (Doerr, 2013), an article on international accreditation in the journal *Higher Education* (Blanco Ramírez, 2015), an exploratory essay on what internationalization in higher education should learn from internationalization in secondary schools in the journal *Perspectives: Policy and Practice in Higher Education* (Yemini, 2014) and the edited book by Bernhard Streitwieser, *Internationalisation of Higher Education and Global Mobility* (Streitwieser, 2014), all appear in the database. The database captures topics from many frameworks.

The Multidisciplinary Lens:
databases that search across disciplines

The topics that are covered in the IDP database tend to have a clear relationship to the international function of a campus. But not all scholarship relevant for international educators has such a clear relationship. For example, topics such as student engagement, assessment, pedagogy and student outcomes may appear in disciplines such as nursing, business, education, political science, anthropology and others. While some articles on 'global learning' appear in the IDP database, topics such as critical thinking, reflective learning, active engagement, problem-based learning and backward design appear in many fields that are outside the scope of the IDP database.

Thus, for some topics, such as those concerning learning, pedagogy and critical thinking across disciplines, it often helps to search in multidisciplinary databases. For example, the ProQuest Research Library allows users to search over 6000 journals and 150 subject areas published since 1971 (ProQuest, 2015d). EBSCO Host's Academic Search Complete database indexes over 13,000 journals, starting from 1887 (EBSCO Host, 2015a). Multidisciplinary databases search multiple disciplines at once. A keyword search on 'reflection and pedagogy', for example, reveals items from journals, dissertations, magazines and conferences in fields as varied as engineering, geography, teacher education and nursing. The breadth – in terms of the time period, disciplines and document type – encourages consideration of the topic from diverse angles. Searching within these multidisciplinary databases can reveal disciplines that a researcher may have not previously considered and suggest different frameworks with which to approach a topic.

For example, a scholar-practitioner who is interested primarily in the role of power in an experiential learning course may find it interesting to locate an article on how to teach about power in the classroom from a political science journal (Mott, 2015). Another who is considering ways of assessing intercultural competence may find it informative to read an article discussing assessment in terms of ability, aptitude and achievement from a journal in educational psychology (Stemler, 2012). A scholar-practitioner interested in the way diverse students in the classroom can inform discussions about perceptions of their reality in media may gain insight from an article on the way the goal of multiculturalism manifests itself in a version of *Sesame Street* in Nigeria from a comparative education journal (Moland, 2015). While in and of themselves these publications may not refer either to 'global learning' or 'internationalization', their content serves as a platform to explore in a different way the goals and objectives of these areas. The authors themselves may not apply their work in this way, but that does not detract from their relevance to the conversation. Using multidisciplinary databases to locate these kinds of articles can enhance, and help reimagine, both scholarship and practice.

To help guide a search in these large multidisciplinary databases, users can limit searches to specific databases within the collection. In addition, users can specify the kinds of publications they wish to search (for example, peer-reviewed publications, particular languages, and particular document types such as book reviews, videos, dissertations or primary sources). In addition, unlike free databases like the IDP database, commercial databases permit more sophisticated searching. The commercial multidisciplinary databases also often offer the full text of the resources in addition to the abstract and citation.

The Disciplinary Lens: databases by academic field

Of course, it is not always the case that scholar-practitioners wish to search across multiple disciplines. Some research questions require a search within a particular discipline. For example, scholar-practitioners may be interested in an industry or a company with which they want to partner; others might be interested in educational research that has undergone extensive peer review by experts who examine research to practice issues; others might want information about a topic relevant for a particular education context.

For these kinds of questions, using databases from particular disciplines can help as they allow scholar-practitioners to specify their search by these unique characteristics. For example, the business database Business Source Complete allows searching by the NAICS (North American Industry Classification System) code and by company name; the education database, ERIC (Educational Resource Information Center), allows limiting a search to research that has been reviewed by the What Works Clearinghouse [3] (ERIC, 2015). The EBSCO version of ERIC allows further refinement by educational level (e.g. one can conduct a search on 'intercultural competence' and specify educational level as higher education) (EBSCOhost, 2015b). These kinds of sophisticated searching options are often available in discipline-specific databases.

In addition, disciplinary databases can be used to find articles and reports that explore the 'context' of higher education in which international higher education exists. These discipline-specific databases provide ways of finding materials about the role of international and non-governmental organizations, politics, communications studies, higher education policy, migration, social issues, ethics, economics and more.

For example, the field of higher education brims with fascinating scholarship on issues such as organizational change, immigration, competency-based education, public policy, learning outcomes and funding of education. Researching these topics in databases specific to higher education or educational research can help identify related work that informs the specific scholarship within higher education. Free databases such as HEDBIB, a database maintained by the International Association of Universities (IAU) and supported by many other IAU member organizations, indexes and abstracts books, documents and articles on higher education policy around the world (International Association of Universities, 2015). For research on international public policy issues that includes publications in multiple languages, from many different source countries, one might search a database like PAIS (Public Affairs Information Service), which includes not only journal articles and book chapters, but also indexes government document and pamphlets from publications in French, German, Italian, Spanish and Portuguese (ProQuest, 2015b). The resource has been in existence in print since 1915. For research on business, marketing, industries or companies involved in international higher education, the ABI/Inform database, for example, includes industry surveys and working papers and allows searching by a company name (ProQuest, 2015a). Looking through a disciplinary database can help users explore particular contexts relevant to their research topic.

The Specialized Lens: databases that address a particular information need

Both disciplinary and multidisciplinary databases presume that the user has a topic in mind. But sometimes the user has a very specific need. In addition to the bibliographic databases already described, other resources in the library can help users address these needs. While it is impossible to discuss all of these specialized resources, discussing a few examples illuminates the possibilities.

Sometimes scholar-practitioners desire an overview about a subject area. Annual reviews are a specific type of journal that have a specific purpose: to provide a critical analysis of a topic looking from the roots of the issue to the newest discussions about the issue. Each article has a comprehensive, multipage bibliography that leads readers to foundational, as well as current, scholarship. For example, international educators may be curious about the research regarding language and identity, yet they may not have any previous knowledge of the research on the topic. They might turn to Patricia Duff's 'Transnationalism, Multilingualism, and Identity' in the *Annual Review of Applied Linguistics* (Duff, 2015) for bibliography, historical background of the research as well as current trends. Looking specifically for annual reviews can provide the needed information without having to search in a larger database. Annual reviews exist in many fields, including anthropology, political science, psychology, sociology and many others.

Other publications similarly provide access to reviews of research, or discussions of new research. In education, the *Review of Educational Research* has similar objectives to the series of annual reviews as it also publishes critical reviews of research (Dolby & Rahman, 2008). The Association for Study in Higher Education (ASHE) publishes research monographs in its *ASHE Higher Education Report* series, which can serve as invaluable reviews of research in a specific topic area. Recent topics covered include critical race theory (McCoy & Rodricks, 2015), the relationship between research and higher education policy (Hillman et al, 2015) and, in 2012, a special issue on study abroad (Twombly et al, 2012).

If a long essay is not what is required, subject encyclopedias are useful resources. In subject encyclopedias, brief entries of one to four pages provide an overview of a topic or a term. For example, a subject encyclopedia like *The SAGE Encyclopedia of Qualitative Research Methods* offers a convenient way to understand specific research methods that may appear within the literature (Given, 2008). For the scholar-practitioner, the subject encyclopedias can be a useful guide both to finding and to understanding scholarship.

Other reference tools that can be useful include *Tests in Print* and the *Mental Measurements Yearbook*, which allow users to search for tests for particular purposes (such as tests for intercultural competence)

(EBSCOhost, 2015c). For those conducting comparative research, free resources such as the Library of Congress Country Studies provide extensive guides to particular countries (Library of Congress). For researchers who are searching for reports from think tanks, it can help to know that a database such as PolicyFile indexes documents from think tanks, research organizations and other such associations (ProQuest, 2015c). Other specialized databases include citation indexes, such as the Web of Science, which allow users to trace who is citing a particular person or a particular article (Thomson Reuters, 2015). This can help identify new research gleaned from studying citations rather than topics. While it may seem that the best place to start research is in a bibliographic database, understanding the strengths of specialized resources may lead scholar-practitioners to select a different option instead.

The Scanning Lens: how to keep abreast of the field

Sometimes a scholar-practitioner desires not to conduct research in a topic area, but rather wants to scan the various topics about which others are writing. Scanning the higher education context by reading the *University World News* [4], *Times Higher Education* [5], the *Chronicle of Higher Education* [6], *Inside Higher Ed* [7], the *PIE News* [8], as well as mainstream press such as the *New York Times* [9], the *Guardian* [10], NPR [11] and the BBC [12], informs the work of scholar-practitioners by keeping them aware of trends. Examples include a report on NPR on the difficulty in measuring non-cognitive skills (Kamenetz, 2015) and an article on a Harvard study about what education is really teaching children about compassion (Lahey, 2014). The mainstream press helps give an overview of issues that are in the minds of parents, students and colleagues, and circulating in the environment in which international educators work. From a press source, one can easily read the full studies that are being reported. This step is particularly important as sometimes the reporting of research may bear only a small resemblance to the research itself!

In addition to reading the news, associations such as NAFSA: Association of International Educators and IIE (the Institute of International Education) direct interested practitioners and scholars to particular research and news stories through weekly newsletters. NAFSA's *Trends and Insights* (NAFSA: Association of International Educators) and the *Research Digests* of the IEAA (the International Education Association of Australia) (IERN & IEAA) are two examples of publications by associations that help scholar-practitioners view the scholarship. NAFSA's Research Connections Community [13] similarly provides a useful guide to new publications and conversation about provocative issues. Receiving alerts for new publications from the

Observatory on Borderless Higher Education (OBHE) [14], the Organisation for Economic Co-operation and Development (OECD) [15], the World Bank [16], the Federal Reserve Board [17] and other such organizations can help a scholar-practitioner scan the field. Looking at recent conference programs from organizations such as the American Educational Research Association (AERA) [18], the Association for Studies in Higher Education (ASHE) [19] or the Comparative and International Education Society (CIES) [20] also provides a way of scanning what is of interest in the world of scholarship. For example, the Bologna Process Research Conference: Future of Higher Education released all of the conference papers on its website.[21] Attending talks, workshops and webinars offers additional ways of scanning the field. Even looking at conference themes can help those scanning the field identify the way research is being framed.

Evaluating Resources

In addition to finding information, however, it is also crucial to think critically about how to use and interpret that information. Not all resources are created equal. Some articles and reports represent the goals of a funder; others may have problematic control groups; others may misrepresent research. Unfortunately, the tool one uses to find a resource does not guarantee the validity of that resource.

For example, the IDP database includes peer-reviewed publications alongside master's theses and reports from think tanks. The scholar-practitioner must be alert for biases in reports due to the source of funding or the ideology of the organization producing research. Commercial multidisciplinary databases often allow for limiting searches to peer-reviewed resources, yet even some peer-reviewed sources can be suspect for quality.[22] Disciplinary databases include a range of types of resources all of which have different standards of quality control. Within a study, different definitions of a concept might exist.

How can a reflective scholar-practitioner feel assured about the quality of the sources that have been discovered?

Librarians teach courses for students and faculty in a field of study known as information literacy. While impossible to discuss in great depth here, the goals of an information literacy course may be helpful to consider. The American Colleges and Research Library (ACRL) board proposed a framework for considering information literacy that includes six components: 'authority is constructed and contextual; information creation as a process; information has value; research as inquiry; scholarship as conversation; searching as strategic exploration' (Association of College and Research Libraries Board, 2015). While the framework is a guide to help students learn to think about information in critical ways and connect the instruction that occurs in academic libraries to the instruction on a university campus, reading through the framework can also help the scholar-practitioner think critically about the resources they use and how to evaluate those resources. The following are some selected questions that a scholar-practitioner might wish to ask when evaluating resources:

- Who sponsored the research?
- What is the background of the author?
- How recent is the piece?
- Whom does the author cite?
- Whom does the author fail to cite?
- Who is the intended audience of the research?

Organizing Resources

In addition to helping with finding and evaluating resources, librarians can also help with organizing them. Many universities offer free access to citation management tools such as RefWorks [23], Zotero [24] and NoodleBib.[25] Free citation management tools, such as Mendeley [26], also offer a way to store, sort and take notes on resources, as well as share documents with colleagues. A citation management tool that is flexible but also user-friendly can make it even easier to reflect on scholarship. Searching within one's citation management database for a funding organization may illuminate trends in research that previously had been unnoticed. Conducting a search on an author's name within one's citation management database may uncover a family of articles that take a similar approach to a research question. Organizing hundreds, if not thousands, of articles from one's own collection can help reveal ideas and avenues for future study. The following are some suggestions for selecting and using these tools.

- Use a citation management tool that makes intuitive sense and has the features most important for the project.
- Tag items using vocabulary that will help sort the resources into usable groupings.
- Think of ways to mark items that will help the retrieval process.

Limitations

The goal of this chapter, to introduce both new and experienced scholar-practitioners to selected resources found in an academic library in the US context, has some limitations. First, in an attempt to distinguish between types of sources, some of the contrasts may be stronger than necessary. Resources in one type of database can be found in another. Second, some research does not involve searching databases at all. Following citations from an article or book, looking at the CV of a scholar, or asking colleagues for reading material are all excellent research strategies. Third, individual libraries offer unique tools to help researchers, such as the ability to search across multiple databases simultaneously. This chapter does not address these kinds of tools. Finally, individual scholar-practitioners have access to their own libraries, and they also have access to their own reference librarians. It is highly advised that scholar-practitioners consult these librarians, who are experts in the resources offered at their particular institutions.

Conclusion

Librarians understand the relationship between scholarship and practice using a distinct lens. They specialize in supporting scholar-practitioners navigate the research process. Yet, in many ways, this navigation is itself a kind of scholarship. As this chapter has illustrated, the process of research involves thinking broadly, and narrowly, about a topic; creatively considering multiple sources of information; evaluating specific resources; as well as thinking deeply about how to organize these resources. Is this not the nature of scholarship, too? Scholarship, like the process of research, demands critical, creative and evaluative thinking.

Perhaps the lens of the librarian offers another model of a scholar-practitioner. The scholar-practitioner may be one who creates research, but the scholar-practitioner may also be one who critically navigates the research world. The scholar-practitioner may be one who, like the librarian, thinks critically, creatively and deeply about the process of research. Seen in this way, some scholar-practitioners may never write a paper, conduct a research project or present at a conference. Instead, their efforts can be seen in the way they think about their job, and the kinds of questions they ask about their work.

And where does this kind of scholarship appear? In what kind of database? In what kind of publication? It may be harder to locate this scholarship in a library, but it is possible to capture. Talk with colleagues; comment in online outlets such as NAFSA's Research Connections Community; ask questions at presentations. The critical, creative and deep thoughts of scholar-practitioners should be shared and valued. By including their insights, scholar-practitioners can help shape the future of international higher education for scholars, practitioners and librarians alike.

Acknowledgements

I consider myself incredibly fortunate to have received insightful feedback on earlier drafts of this chapter from many gifted scholar-practitioners. I am indebted to my colleagues Chad Goeden, Heather

MacCleoud and Soren Peterson; my supervisor, Kevin Hovland; and international higher education researchers, Dr Anita Gopal and Dr Anthony Ogden. Finally, I thank my father, S. Daniel Breslauer, who, while a scholar, always encouraged me to keep on practicing.

Notes

[1] To access the IDP database, visit its website at http://opac.acer.edu.au/IDP_drie/index.html

[2] The Twitter handle is @IDPRIE.

[3] For more information on the What Works Clearinghouse, visit its website at http://ies.ed.gov/ncee/wwc/. The What Works Clearinghouse, sponsored by the Institute of Education Sciences, reviews research papers and reports and rates them.

[4] Visit the *University World News* at http://www.universityworldnews.com/

[5] Visit the *Times Higher Education* at https://www.timeshighereducation.co.uk/

[6] This subscription newspaper can be found at most libraries either in print or online. Visit its homepage at http://chronicle.com/section/Home/5

[7] Visit this free e-newspaper at https://www.insidehighered.com/

[8] Visit the *PIE News* at http://thepienews.com/

[9] This subscription-based newspaper is available in print and online through many libraries or on its homepage at http://www.nytimes.com/

[10] The *Guardian*, a UK-based newspaper, is available online at http://www.theguardian.com/us

[11] NPR stations around the United States offer various local, state, national and international news and programming. Visit their main homepage at http://www.npr.org/

[12] The BBC, or British Broadcasting Corporation, offers news from around the world online, on television and on the radio. Visit its homepage at http://www.bbc.com/

[13] Learn about NAFSA Research Connections at http://www.nafsa.org/researchconnection. Join the community by creating a free login and entering http://www.nafsa.org/researchcommunity

[14] For more about the OBHE, visit its website at http://www.obhe.ac.uk/

[15] For more about the OECD's higher education research, visit its website at http://www.oecd.org/edu/imhe/

[16] For more about the World Bank, visit its website at http://www.worldbank.org/

[17] See, for example, the Federal Reserve Bank of Boston's New England Public Policy Center, which frequently shares reports on immigration and higher education: https://www.bostonfed.org/economic/neppc/index.htm

[18] For more about AERA, visit its website at http://www.aera.net/

[19] For more about ASHE, visit its website at http://www.ashe.ws/

[20] For more about CIES, visit its website at http://www.cies.us/

[21] Visit http://fohe-bprc.forhe.ro/papers/ to read the extensive conference papers.

[22] See this list of predatory publishers, for example: http://scholarlyoa.com/2014/01/02/list-of-predatory-publishers-2014/

[23] For more about RefWorks, visit its website at https://www.refworks.com/

[24] For more about Zotero, visit its website at https://www.zotero.org/

[25] For more about NoodleBib, visit its website at http://www.noodletools.com/

[26] For more about Mendeley, visit its website at https://www.mendeley.com/

References

Association of College and Research Libraries Board (2015) Framework for Information Literacy for Higher Education. http://www.ala.org/acrl/standards/ilframework

Blanco Ramírez, G. (2015) International Accreditation as Global Position Taking: an empirical exploration of US accreditation in Mexico, *Higher Education*, 69(3), 361-374. http://dx.doi.org/10.1007/s10734-014-9780-7

Doerr, N. (2013) Do 'Global Citizens' Need the Parochial Cultural Other? Discourse of Immersion in Study Abroad and Learning-by-doing, *Compare*, 43(2), 224-243. http://dx.doi.org/10.1080/03057925.2012.701852

Dolby, N. & Rahman, A. (2008) Research in International Education, *Review of Educational Research*, 78(3), 676-726. http://dx.doi.org/10.3102/0034654308320291

Duff, P.A. (2015) Transnationalism, Multilingualism, and Identity, *Annual Review of Applied Linguistics*, 35, 57-80. http://dx.doi.org/10.1017/S026719051400018X

EBSCO Host (2015a) Academic Search Complete. https://www.ebscohost.com/academic/academic-search-complete

EBSCOhost (2015b) ERIC. http://support.ebsco.com/help/?int=ehost&lang=en&feature_id=Databases&TOC_ID=Always&SI=0&BU=0&GU=1&PS=0&ver=live&dbs=,eric

EBSCOhost (2015c) *Mental Measurements Yearbook with Tests in Print*. https://www.ebscohost.com/academic/mental-measurements-yearbook-with-tests-in-print

ERIC (2015) How Does the ERIC Search Work? http://eric.ed.gov/?advanced

Given, L.M. (2008) *The SAGE Encyclopedia of Qualitative Research Methods.* Los Angeles: SAGE. http://dx.doi.org/10.4135/9781412963909

Hillman, N.W., Tandberg, D.A. & Sponsler, B.A. (2015) Public Policy and Higher Education: strategies for framing a research agenda, *ASHE Higher Education Report*, 41(2), 1-98. http://dx.doi.org/10.1002/aehe.20020

IDP Education (2015) *IDP Database of Research on International Education.* 23 August. http://opac.acer.edu.au/IDP_drie/index.html

IERN & IEAA (n.d.) IEAA Research Digest. http://www.ieaa.org.au/international-education-research-network/ieaa-research

International Association of Universities (2015) HEDBIB: international bibliographic database on higher education. http://hedbib.iau-aiu.net/

Kamenetz, A. (2015) A Key Researcher Says 'Grit' isn't Ready for High-stakes Measures. 13 May. http://www.npr.org/sections/ed/2015/05/13/405891613/a-key-researcher-says-grit-isnt-ready-for-high-stakes-measures

Lahey, J. (2014) Parent-teacher Conference: teaching children empathy, *New York Times*, 4 September, Motherlode. http://parenting.blogs.nytimes.com/2014/09/04/teaching-children-empathy/

Library of Congress (n.d.) Library of Congress Country Studies. Library of Congress: http://www.loc.gov/collections/country-studies/about-this-collection/

McCoy, D.L. & Rodricks, D.J. (2015) Critical Race Theory in Higher Education: 20 years of theoretical and research innovations, *ASHE Higher Education Report*, 41(3), 1-117. http://dx.doi.org/10.1002/aehe.20021

Moland, N. (2015) Can Multiculturalism be Exported? Dilemmas of Diversity on Nigeria's Sesame Square, *Comparative Education Review*, 59(1), 1-23. http://dx.doi.org/10.1086/679014

Mott, M. (2015) Want to Study the Nature of Power? Start by Moving the Chairs!, *PS: Political Science & Politics*, 48(3), 488-491. http://dx.doi.org/10.1017/S104909651500030X

NAFSA: Association of International Educators (n.d.) *Trends and Insights.* http://www.nafsa.org/Explore_International_Education/Trends/TI/Trends___Insights/

Proctor, D. (2015) What's Hot in International Education Research? February. http://www.ieaa.org.au/documents/item/415

ProQuest (2015a) ABI/Inform. http://www.proquest.com/products-services/abi_inform_complete.html

ProQuest (2015b) PAIS International. http://www.proquest.com/products-services/pais-set-c.html

ProQuest (2015c) PolicyFile. http://www.proquest.com/products-services/policyfile.html

ProQuest (2015d) ProQuest Research Library. 16 August. http://www.proquest.com/products-services/ProQuest-Research-Library.html

Stemler, S.E. (2012) What Should Admissions Tests Predict?, *Educational Psychologist*, 47(1), 5-17. http://dx.doi.org/10.1080/00461520.2011.611444

Streitwieser, B. (Ed.) (2014) *Internationalisation of Higher Education and Global Mobility*. Oxford: Symposium Books.

Thomson Reuters (2015) Web of Science. http://wokinfo.com/

Twombly, S.B., Salisbury, M.H. & Tumanut, S.D. (2012) Study Abroad in a New Global Century, *ASHE Higher Education Report*, 38(4), 1-152. http://dx.doi.org/10.1002/aehe.20004

Yemini, M. (2014) Internationalisation Discourse: what remains to be said?, *Perspectives: policy and practice in higher education*, 18(2), 1-2. http://dx.doi.org/10.1080/13603108.2014.888019

CHAPTER 20

Exploring a Possible Future for the Scholar-Practitioner[1]

FIONA HUNTER & LAURA E. RUMBLEY

SUMMARY This chapter provides a perspective on the possible future evolution of the roles and experiences of scholar-practitioners (or 'practitioner-researchers'). Practitioners work increasingly in an 'expanding knowledge environment', exerting ever-stronger pressures on practitioners to 'know' more about their own work, to account for their actions rigorously and accurately, and to understand and articulate how their professional activities fit into a broader context. However, practitioner-researchers are often left with the sense that they must develop this deeper knowledge in isolation, among other reasons because the research community focused on higher education is concerned with questions that do not have clear implications for (or resonance with) practitioner concerns. Moved to undertake research focused on their own, scholar-practitioners must confront the very real challenges of researching one's own field. Ultimately, a robust future for the scholar-practitioner will turn on effective capacity building in research methods for these individuals, as well as concerted collaboration between less experienced practitioner-scholars and colleagues with more refined research skills and more extensive experience with rigorous academic inquiry. Fundamentally, a commitment by key stakeholders to the notion of 'intelligent internationalization' is needed, which implies more effective and systematic engagement across policy, practice, and academic communities concerned with international higher education.

Professionals in the early 21st century are required to practise more effectively amid the increasing challenge of uncertainty and complexity. The widespread call for evidence-based practice is a major response to this. Yet contemporary approaches to research often fail to produce adequate evidence

or knowledge about practice for use in variable situations. How is professional practice to be researched better, to provide a basis for improved practice? This question affects us all, and is answered in both similar and different ways across a range of countries and professions.
(Salisbury Forum Group, 2011, p. 4)

Introduction

It goes without saying that information generation, application and dissemination are defining activities of our time. From books to blogs, briefs to tweets, information is ubiquitous, and our need and desire to acquire it and leverage it seem to be insatiable. The fast-moving, highly interconnected world in which we find ourselves in the second decade of the twenty-first century is unquestionably a place of 'uncertainty and complexity' (as expressed above by the quote from the Salisbury Forum Group that introduces this chapter). It is also clearly a context that puts a premium on professionals who are as well informed as possible about the world around them and their place in it. In this vein, we note that professionals working in the field of international higher education are challenged to make sense of the highly localized concerns of their specific institutions and surrounding communities, while also needing to understand much broader trends and developments at regional and even global levels. There is a further necessity for the acquisition of knowledge that is both intellectually sophisticated and highly applicable to the 'real world' of daily practice and quotidian realities. In an era of intense competition, limited resources and heightened interest in accountability, international higher education professionals are increasingly obliged to generate much clearer indications of their substantive contributions to the academic and administrative enterprises with which they are affiliated.

Knowledge generation has long been the purview of academics or researchers, strictly speaking, but in international higher education today (as well as in a variety of other highly applied fields) we see an emerging nexus between theory and practice, researcher and practitioner. Indeed, the Salisbury Forum Group's 'Salisbury Statement' (2011) notes:

A major problem is a mainstream assumption that research leads practice. But research also needs to be practice-minded in order to better study and develop knowledge which emerges directly from the complex practices themselves. Practice research, involving equal dialogue between the worlds of practice and research is an important concept, since it seeks to develop our understanding of the best ways to research this complexity. It is important at this time in history given that concerns with new accountabilities now converge with doubts about the adequacy of scientific knowledge as a sole basis for improving practice. (pp. 4-5)

Into this breach, a growing class of scholar-practitioners (often also referred to as practitioner-researchers) has begun to take tentative steps. This chapter endeavors to provide a perspective on the ways that the roles and experiences of scholar-practitioners may evolve in the future, in light of current realities as well as in the face of ongoing challenges and opportunities to expand and strengthen this unique function in international higher education. We first set the scene through an examination of what we term the 'expanding knowledge environment'. We then consider carefully the challenges and opportunities of researching one's own field. And, finally, we present our take on the prospects for a strengthened practitioner-researcher paradigm, with a call to commit to the notion of 'intelligent internationalization'.

Our Current and Future Context: the expanding knowledge environment

Higher education, in general, is an expanding field, in terms of research as well as training at the graduate level. Rumbley et al (2014) found that, globally, there are some 279 journals and other relevant publications focused on higher education, along with 217 research centers around the world focused primarily on higher education, as well as 277 academic programs granting graduate-level degrees or other credentials in the field of higher education studies. Roughly half of the identified research centers were found to have been established since the year 2000. For the academic programs, year of establishment information was only available for 56% of the programs (or 169 of the total of 277). However, for the 169 with identifiable years of establishment, 35.5% of the academic programs were launched as of the year 2000. Clearly, there is a growing interest around the world in researching the higher education enterprise and in producing professionals to lead and manage it.

Furthermore, a significant proportion of both the research centers and the academic programs in higher education list 'comparative or international studies', as well as 'globalization and internationalization', among their primary areas of specialized focus or expertise (Rumbley & Altbach, 2015), as evidenced in Table I.

Again, an examination of the ages (i.e. years of establishment) of the centers and programs included in the inventory reinforces the pervasive sense that globalization and internationalization are areas of growing interest. Among research centers focusing to some extent on these topics, more than half (56%) were established from the year 2000 onwards; also in the last 15 years, 60% of the academic programs indicating some specialization in globalization and internationalization were established (Rumbley & Altbach, 2015).

299

Particularly in relation to the growth in numbers of academic programs offering degrees in the study of higher education, we see practitioners bringing their practical experiences to the study of higher education, and pursuing lines of inquiry related directly to their practice. Their motivations may be personal and/or professional in nature. On a personal level, many practitioners simply need and want to understand what is happening around them in their institutions and in their specific roles. On the professional front, practitioners are being asked to operate increasingly on the basis of 'data' – that is, they must craft decisions and account for their impact in ways that go beyond matters of intuition, self-satisfaction or anecdote. As the dynamics of internationalization and international higher education become more complex and high-stakes, the expanding knowledge environment represents a powerful self-perpetuating phenomenon that exerts stronger and stronger pressures on practitioners to 'know' more about their own work, to account for their actions rigorously and accurately, and to understand (and be able to articulate) how their professional activities fit into a broader context. Researching the environment with which the practitioner is directly engaged, most familiar with, and most concerned about understanding and affecting is a natural response to these developments. However, this decision (admittedly, often a 'necessity') brings with it a set of particular opportunities and challenges that require careful navigation.

Centers	
Focus Areas	Percentage
Comparative or international studies	42.9
Administration, management, or leadership	41.9
Economics, financing, or funding of higher education	33.6
Globalization or internationalization	31.8
Quality assurance, assessment, or accreditation	25.8
Programs	
Focus Areas	Percentage
Administration, management, or leadership	75.0
Comparative or international studies	44.7
Curriculum and instruction or teaching and learning	40.8
Economics, financing, or funding of higher education	31.6
Globalization or internationalization	30.3
Academic Profession	30.3

Table I. Most frequently selected 'primary areas of specialized focus or expertise' for higher education research centers and programs worldwide, by percentage. *Source*: Rumbley & Altbach (2015).

The Burdens and Blessings of Being an Insider Researcher

Occupying the New Space

Becoming a practitioner-researcher is often driven by the desire to investigate specific challenges or concerns in everyday practice and to generate research findings that can make a difference. Scholar-practitioners are people genuinely motivated by their work, who believe that greater internationalization can serve to enhance the quality of higher education in general. As these practitioners engage in research and become creators of knowledge, they undergo personal and professional changes, as well. They find themselves 'occupying a new space': through their contribution to research based on their specific expertise, they are able to develop and implement new professional practice. They become more reflective and research-minded in the way they operate and interact with others. So, engaging in practitioner research is good for the individual as well as for the field.

However, it must be said that much of the research being done currently in internationalization of higher education is being carried out by relatively inexperienced researchers who are carrying out small-scale inquiries, often within their own institution, and frequently as part of study undertaken for master's or PhD programs. This is a natural starting point for many, but it does mean that practitioner research is often perceived as being less relevant, or of lower quality, than 'real' research. This is an important challenge that needs to be overcome, because there is real value in the practitioner-research enterprise.

As Fox et al (2007) state, practitioner research is not any different from other forms of research. It uses the same research techniques and has the same purpose of generating new knowledge. It is the practitioner-researchers who create the difference, as a result of their unique position in the research process and the issues they identify as being worthy of research. Their research questions emerge from their professional experience and practice, and this gives them 'the opportunity to promote research that is joined up and break the academic fragmented approach to knowledge' (Fox et al, 2007, p. 3).

Carrying out research in one's own field raises another issue that is not as widely recognized as it should be. Typically, higher education researchers are the same people who are directly involved in (i.e. working in) higher education. This sets them apart from other higher education colleagues who might be researching other kinds of institutional settings, such as offices, households, prisons, etc. Internationalization of higher education is an even more restricted field, researched mainly by practitioners, or by researchers who began their careers as practitioners. Consequently, scholar-practitioners are frequently left with a sense of isolation, a feeling that it's 'just us' – and that few others from the research community – inside or outside of higher education – seem much interested in researching the questions of interest to practitioners focused on the internationalization of higher education.

While it is most encouraging that many practitioners are now undertaking research in this field, it does create a problem of credibility – or at least it should. First, practitioners have a direct interest in the outcomes of their research. Meanwhile, they can have particular difficulties in taking a more impartial approach to their inquiry, in terms of being able to shift the institution or organization they are researching from 'familiar' to 'strange'. These two aspects tend to overlap in the form of implicit, taken-for-granted assumptions about the 'ideal' university or the 'ideal' model or approach for internationalization, and act as benchmarks against which current practices are evaluated.

It is important that practitioner-researchers become aware of what is distinctive about doing research on internationalization of higher education from the practitioner perspective, and what the implications of that distinctiveness are for how the research should be undertaken. If practitioner-researchers become more aware of the risks of self-examination, they will become better equipped to take action that will improve the quality and relevance of the research they undertake.

Assets and Liabilities of Distinctiveness

Practitioners who take the bold decision to undertake research alongside their heavy work schedules do have the advantage of being able to draw on a number of assets that can facilitate their inquiry. Since many initiate their research venture via a program of study, they will undertake small-scale investigations as single researchers, and since they are frequently seeking to explore aspects of professional practice, they will often choose a qualitative approach to carry out their investigation.

Case studies with interviews as key data collection tools are often selected, since they are recognized as a powerful means to enter other people's worlds and reveal the particularities of institutional settings. The aim of the research is often to explore uniqueness or complexity of specific institutional settings rather than seeking to make claims to generalizability or representability. However, it is also true that it may be the intention to draw conclusions from those cases that contain information of value for a wider sector, and from which lessons can be learned. Validity of the research is then paramount.

Practitioner-researchers are often able to exploit their practical knowledge of the context in which they operate when it comes to identifying suitable cases for their inquiry. The advantage of familiarity within the field, coupled with an extensive network of professional contacts and good relations, can provide easier access to gatekeepers for authorization to use the institution as a case study. The 'cultural literacy' of practitioner-researchers, through their shared understanding and knowledge of the environment at different levels, can produce more candid responses from the interviewees, if the interviewer is trusted and perceived as more credible than an outside researcher.

Many choose to undertake research at their own institution, as it is more practical (and less expensive) to do this as opposed to initiating research elsewhere, especially when part of a master's or doctoral dissertation. It can often make data collection easier and there can be greater flexibility in setting up interviews. There is also the expectation that the hard work will pay off and there will be an opportunity to create impact once the research has been completed and disseminated.

However, the research process can also be fraught with considerable challenges, many of which derive precisely from practitioner researchers' status as 'insiders' both within their institution and in the field itself. This can raise a number of hidden methodological and ethical dilemmas that are often not adequately taken into consideration or sufficiently researched (Labaree, 2002).

It is important that practitioner-researchers take into consideration that researching as an 'insider' will lead to an inevitable combination of their own interpretation alongside the often highly subjective nature of respondents' comments within their own institution. This will play itself out differently in different institutional settings. While practitioners researching in their own institution may be able to see beyond the portrayed reality, there is inevitably much in the narratives of other institutions that they will not be able to see. This can make objectivity difficult when seeking to compare outcomes across institutions.

Shared experience and implicit knowledge of the institution and/or the field between researcher and respondents can lead in many different ways to a degree of bounded rationality that can potentially skew the analysis. Greater familiarity can lead to blind spots or myopia, and without appropriate critical distance, the study and its conclusions can lose credibility. However, there are ways to compensate and counterbalance these liabilities. The first step in the process is becoming aware of the potential pitfalls.

Shifting to a More Impartial Stance

How might practitioners compensate for the constraints of being an insider and adopt a different approach? Evered and Louis (1981) provide good insight into several different dimensions in modes of inquiry from the inside and the outside. Crucially, though, it is important to point out that the practitioner-researcher is not seeking to become a total outsider, but rather to blend inquiry as an insider who has the shared experiential knowledge of the institution or phenomenon under examination with the detachment and neutrality of an outsider. The purpose of seeking this new position is to create greater distance in order to rediscover the organization in a way that will enable the researcher to become more self-critical and see the institution differently.

Total objectivity as an insider is impossible, and even undesirable. It is helpful to think of the notions of 'insider' and 'outsider' on a continuum (Labaree, 2002) rather than as a dichotomy (Mercer, 2007) since 'insiderness' is not a fixed value (Trowler, 2011). Even within the same institution, researchers may have varying degrees of 'insiderness', based on their place of work, the role they fulfill, the knowledge they possess and the people with whom they habitually engage.

What is important in seeking to take on some of the characteristics of the outsider is to create a level of self-detachment that will enable the insider researcher to rediscover the organization, to test the findings that have emerged, to explore the topic through a different lens and gain new perspectives – in other words, to make the organization 'strange'. This process of 'making the organization strange' is vital, because the goal of 'good' practitioner research – any solid research, for that matter – is to generate *new* knowledge, the value of which can be appreciated by *anyone*, even those lacking the privileged knowledge of 'insider'. Regardless of the strategies undertaken or the research methodology employed, navigating the complexities of being close to the subject of one's research is both one of the most fundamental strengths of, and one of the most serious challenges for, the practitioner-researcher seeking to produce rigorous findings. Indeed, practitioner-researchers face the daunting task of needing to step back from the quotidian, stop talking about what they already know, and think critically about what is going on around them, including their own contributions to that work.

Thinking differently – and most importantly, *critically* – about a familiar context is no easy feat. This may be particularly so in a field such as international higher education, where the prevailing narrative is one of unbridled optimism and unquestioned certainty that internationalization is a positive force in the world. Uncritical 'group think' within the field perpetuates the implementation of untested policies and practices. This dynamic prevents our own deeper understanding of the work we do, including its impacts, and potentially undermines us in our own best efforts to improve that practice. From the perspective of those outside the field, poorly executed research about our work can reinforce unhelpful stereotypes about the lightweight nature of international higher education as a field of study and undercut important efforts to advocate for support.

There are, therefore, real stakes involved in the discussion of practitioner-researcher activities and the outcomes of that work.

Rigorous Training and Concerted Collaboration: a stronger future for scholar-practitioners in international higher education

Ultimately, we believe there is an important place for scholar-practitioners in the field of international higher education. As a field of practice, the practitioner perspective is crucial, and welcome, in the ongoing effort to make better intellectual meaning of what is happening in this field. At the same time, as in all areas of scholarly inquiry, research requires rigor if its full potential to contribute to the creation of new knowledge is to be achieved.

To enhance the ways in which practitioners participate effectively in the scholarship arena moving forward, attention must be paid to the role of the practitioner-researcher in two main areas: capacity building and network strengthening. As a means to bridge the gap between the two worlds of research and practice, practitioners setting out to undertake research must be willing (and provided with opportunities) to engage in research methodology training. Key areas that should be emphasized in such training include rooting one's research in the body of knowledge that already exists with respect to the focus of the research. Many aspiring practitioner-researchers may have limited experience conducting literature reviews, and may unwittingly find themselves attempting to recreate the wheel, in the absence of knowledge about related or complementary research that may already have been conducted. Closely connected to this notion is the fact that aspiring scholar-practitioners should be encouraged, and guided, to identify and leverage more experienced colleagues as they undertake new research. Experienced practitioner-researchers can be well positioned to offer expert guidance and/or opportunities to collaborate with more junior/ less experienced researcher-practitioners. This dynamic provides an important avenue for knowledge sharing among scholar-practitioners and ideally provides newcomers with both examples of good practice and access to dissemination channels, which are crucial for the field.

Although we know that programs offering graduate-level study in higher education have grown around the world over the last two decades, we also know that particular regions of the world are much less well-served by these opportunities. For example, Rumbley et al's (2014) global inventory of higher education programs found 'just six programs in Africa ... (four of these in South Africa ...); three across the whole of Latin America ...; and just one in the MENA [Middle East and North Africa] region' (Rumbley et al, 2014, p. 7). Many scholar-practitioners in international higher education who aspire to formal study, and related research activities, lack access to programs, adequate supervisors, and communities of colleagues with a similar affinity for practitioner research. As a result, there are severe obstacles when it comes to receiving good-quality training, connecting with peers undertaking practitioner research, or accessing information on relevant resources.

These challenges require urgent attention. At a very fundamental level, a commitment by key stakeholders to the notion of 'intelligent internationalization' is needed. This implies more effective and systematic engagement across policy, practice and academic communities concerned with international higher education (Rumbley, 2015). The Salisbury Forum Group (2011) has issued a similar plea for 'systemic and collaborative action' among 'educationalists, practitioners, researchers, managers and employers', along with support by research-funding bodies and a 'culture which supports the engagement of practitioners and researchers' (p. 7).

To achieve this, much work needs to be done, on several fronts. Fundamentally, practitioner-researchers around the world must be better recognized as the resources they are. This recognition must first and foremost take place at the 'local' level – that is, in the institutions where these individuals work and conduct most of their research activities. Indeed, the greatest impact of practitioner-researcher activity is overwhelming realized at the institutional level, and there is much that could be done by institutions to leverage the enthusiasm of their own practitioner-researchers, while carefully cultivating their research skills to maximum effect. This investment by institutions, in terms of support and training for practitioner-researchers, has the potential to create powerful mutual benefits – among them, generating better in-house information and analysis, and cultivating higher levels of confidence, commitment and skill among the individual practitioner-researchers involved.

At the same time, the recognition of what practitioner-researchers have to offer can, and must, extend to the broader professional, scholarly and policy communities that intersect within the field of international higher education. These communities should commit to identifying and connecting with promising practitioner-researchers, improving the channels of communication with these individuals, and offering opportunities for practitioner-researchers to develop stronger skills in relation to research and analysis, policy implementation and evaluation, and peer training. Again, the potential for mutual benefit is salient. There are highly relevant insights about internationalization to be gained all along the continuum of stakeholder engagement. Facilitating communication among all interested parties strengthens the work of each, and presents opportunities for important synergies to play out between the world of ideas and the world of lived experience.

Practitioner-researchers represent a very special group within the field of international higher education, increasingly eager and willing to position themselves across the lines of scholarship and practice and to draw meaningful connections between these dimensions. Willingness, however, is not enough. The complex world in which we currently live, the breathless pace of change we experience in the field of international higher education today, and the persistent, high-stakes matters of quality assurance and resource allocation that frame so much of the higher education experience in the contemporary context demand that we rely on ever more, and ever-higher-quality, information and analysis to guide our work. We think that practitioner-researchers can and will contribute substantively to this call for more and better research on international higher education. But that will require new kinds of commitments – by individual practitioner-researchers to enhance and refine their research activities by seeking out training and guidance; by institutions providing the space and opportunity for practitioner-researchers to undertake research activities; and by the gatekeepers of research knowledge and policy expertise to welcome and engage with aspiring practitioner-researchers.

Internationalization of higher education is a relatively young but increasingly strategic imperative for institutions and entire systems of higher education around the world. Practitioner-researchers represent an enormous pool of untapped potential that could be leveraged to advance our understanding of the complex dynamics inherent in internationalization, and cultivating this pool of talent could yield crucially important results of mutual benefit to both researchers and practitioners. The field of international higher education has everything to gain from ensuring that 'those participating in the elaboration of internationalization activities and agendas have access to the information, ideas, and professional skill-building opportunities that will enhance their ability to navigate the complex and volatile higher education environment of the next 20 years' (Rumbley, 2015, p. 17). This includes the opportunity for practitioner-researchers to develop the highest-quality research skills to explore and enhance their own practice and to advance the greater good.

Note

[1] Please note that this chapter employs the terms 'scholar-practitioner' and 'practitioner-researcher', as well as 'internationalization' (of higher education) and 'international higher education', interchangeably.

References

Evered, R. & Louis, M.R. (1981) Alternative Perspectives in the Organizational Sciences: 'inquiry from the inside' and 'inquiry from the outside', *Academy of Management Review*, 6(3), 385-395.
http://dx.doi.org/10.5465/AMR.1981.4285776

Fox, M., Martin, P. & Green, G. (2007) *Doing Practitioner Research*. London: SAGE.

Labaree, R.V. (2002) The Risk of 'Going Observationalist': negotiating the hidden dilemmas of being an insider participant observer, *Qualitative Research*, 2(1), 97-122. http://dx.doi.org/10.1177/1468794102002001641

Mercer, J. (2007) The Challenges of Insider Research in Educational Institutions: wielding a double-edged sword and resolving delicate dilemmas, *Oxford Review of Education*, 33(1) (February), 1-17.

Rumbley, L.E. (2015) 'Intelligent Internationalization': a 21st century imperative, *International Higher Education*, 80 (Spring), 16-17.

Rumbley, L.E. & Altbach, P.G. (2015) The Local and the Global in Higher Education Internationalization: a crucial nexus, in E. Jones, R. Coelen, J. Beelen & H. de Wit (Eds) *Global and Local Internationalization*. Rotterdam: Sense.

Rumbley, L.E., Stanfield, D.A. & de Gayardon, A. (2014) From Inventory to Insight: making sense of the global landscape of higher education research, training, and publication, *Studies in Higher Education*, 39(8), 1293-1305. http://dx.doi.org/10.1080/03075079.2014.949546

Salisbury Forum Group (2011) The Salisbury Statement, *Social Work and Society: international online journal,* 9(1).

Trowler, P. (2011) Researching Your Own Institution. British Educational Research Association online resource. https://www.bera.ac.uk/researchers-resources/publications/researching-your-own-institution-higher-education (accessed on 10 August 2015).

Pathways of the Scholar-Practitioner

To support our belief that the biographies behind the authors of each chapter matter almost as much as the arguments they are making, we have included a final chapter with brief personal narratives of all authors in an effort to highlight the many pathways they have taken to becoming scholar-practitioners of international education today.

David Austell, PhD, Columbia University

I was born and raised in North Carolina, in a small southern town very much in the vein of Andy Griffith's *Mayberry*. In the 1960s, the 'culture' of my home town was essentially that of 'black folks and white folks' embracing the turmoil of civil rights, and I had no international experience at all growing up. This changed when I left for Chapel Hill and the University of North Carolina. My roommate freshman year was from Iran, and only a few weeks into the fall semester, friendship intervened, especially in our perceptions of each other's cultural strangeness; we realized that the likenesses we shared as humans far outweighed our cultural differences. Suddenly my experience of Planet Earth began to change and to expand very much larger than the world of *Mayberry*.

After completing degrees in English literature, I had the opportunity to travel abroad with my wife for the first time to England and Scotland. I was at this time a young English instructor at St. Augustine's College in Raleigh, where I had my first experiences with international students in my classes (primarily from the Caribbean and from Central and Southern Africa). After four years in the classroom, I returned to UNC for doctoral studies in higher education, and soon after I was advanced to candidacy for the PhD, I was hired as the 'Foreign Student Adviser' in the UNC International Center. This was the job that changed the trajectory of my career. I was training to be an academic, but I loved the profession of international education, and by the time I left Chapel Hill for Tampa and my first directing role at the University of South Florida, I was a newly minted PhD and the Associate Director of the UNC International Center.

The year before I left for Tampa, I was granted a Fulbright award for study in Japan and Korea. It was during my tenure at USF that I began to engage in fairly regular international travel for the university (China,

Belize, Venezuela). I also had my first academic appointment as Assistant Professor in the USF School of Education, where I began to develop the course that would evolve into 'The Practice of International Education', a course which I taught for five years at NYU and which is now a permanent part of the NYU Steinhardt School's International Education program (but I'm getting ahead of myself).

After Tampa, I was the Executive Director of the Office of International Programs at Wayne State University in Detroit for two years before being called to New York University as Assistant Vice President and Director of the Office of Global Services. After seven years in this role, I was called to Columbia University as Associate Provost and Director of the International Students and Scholars Office. I've been very fortunate in being able to direct the largest international student services program in the United States (at NYU), and the fourth largest program (at Columbia), and to lead service expansion projects at both institutions.

A very important factor in my various leadership roles in international education has been my connection to the faculty via academic appointments. One of my great loves is teaching, and I'm able teach at least one graduate course every year, typically in the evenings (since I have a day job). Even after almost 30 years on the front lines, I continue to be fascinated and challenged by leadership in this wonderful field, and despite the job's demands, I have been able to continue publishing and teaching. It can be done. When I'm not at work, I dabble in poetry.

Louis Berends, PhD, School for International Training

Like so many international educators, my path into the field was interesting, but not exactly linear. I studied sociology and criminology as an undergraduate, thinking I would enter law school upon graduation. But then I studied abroad and everything changed – my worldview, my appreciation for baseball, and perhaps most interesting, it changed the way I thought about teaching and learning. To be sure, education abroad transformed me personally, yet it also altered my professional path considerably. So I decided not to pursue law school and instead enrolled in a master's program in comparative and international education at Loyola University Chicago.

Having studied abroad at the University of Oxford (St Catherine's College), I was introduced to a completely different pedagogy: the tutorial system. No longer did I have the option of hiding in the back of class and avoiding class participation whenever possible. Instead, I was front and center one on one with my professors and expected to 'talk' for at least 45 minutes about the chosen topic of the week (I studied comparative government and moral philosophy). The next 10-15 minutes was full on intellectual boot camp that made me question what I was doing in such an academically rigorous setting while my prof 'broke me down' and explained the major considerations that I 'forgot' to mention during my discussion of the readings. Each week I was required to write a 10-page paper that synthesized the most salient arguments (and counterarguments) and was encouraged to attend numerous lectures and debates offered across the university.

My interest in comparative government peaked during my time working as a research assistant at the British Houses of Parliament, where I worked for a Member of Parliament, Frank Roy, representing two Scottish constituencies. Incredibly, I was able to write a question in advance of the weekly 'Prime Minister's Questions', and on one fateful Wednesday, the then Prime Minister of the United Kingdom, Tony Blair, answered a question that I wrote on Mr Roy's behalf (I still have the Post-it note that reads, 'Frank, thanks for the question. –Tony').

Since my time working and studying abroad, I have embraced the scholar-practitioner approach in international education and have conducted several field-based research projects abroad, and in the United States I directed education abroad and cultural programs at the Illinois Institute of Technology in Chicago, and have presented many papers in various settings, including Harvard's Graduate School of Education, the Comparative and International Education Society (CIES), the Forum on Education Abroad, and NAFSA: Association of International Educators, among others. Most recently, I joined Walden University in 2014 as Contributing Faculty for the Global and Comparative Education doctoral program in the Richard W. Riley College of Education and Leadership.

Giselda Beaudin, Rollins College

I travelled abroad for the first time at the age of eleven, missing four weeks of sixth grade for the opportunity to explore parts of Europe with my family. We had already moved four times within the United States, so the continued expanse of the world beyond the Atlantic, the differences and similarities, were both familiar and unfamiliar. When I was fourteen, we travelled again to Europe, this time to spend two semesters abroad, in France and Italy. This was my first education abroad experience, struggling through classes at French public school, running around Rome with friends from all over the world. Before this year, I was in danger of succumbing to the stifling normativity of Connecticut suburbia. Suddenly the horizon lifted and there were other ways to be, other ways to see myself. I studied abroad again in college, a six-week language intensive program in Beijing. The summer made me reframe again – I was not the sophisticated traveler I thought I was. I struggled with my Mandarin. I struggled to put my feelings about my time in China into words.

I graduated from college, sifted through several career options, and then decided to return to school to work on my writing. I wrote and read and taught for two years (and finally wrote my story about China). But I wasn't sure I wanted to teach and so passed on the opportunity to pursue a PhD. A position opened up in the Office of International Programs at Binghamton University – I fell into this field.

At first it was fine to focus on practice, to put aside my writing and my scholarship, but over the years this came to feel like an important loss. I began to seek out opportunities to step back towards the academic. I spent three weeks in Quebec brushing up on my French. I came to Rollins College and kept finding spaces to be more than a practitioner. I began presenting at conferences and writing essays and articles about international education. And I began to teach again, courses that mixed genres and fields, in the same way that I resist now, in my own scholarship and practice, academic classification. I feel uniquely positioned as a scholar-practitioner. My practice feeds my scholarship and my scholarship feeds my practice. I hope through my work to resist categories and model a different way to think about education.

Tamar Breslauer, NAFSA: Association of International Educators

At age five, research meant trailing my father in the library stacks at the University of Kansas as he raced from floor to half-floor. I remember feeling petrified because it seemed not quite legal to be on a floor numbered 4.5. My dad taught me that research must be something extraordinary to be worth the risk of traveling to half-floors.

My trepidation contrasted markedly with my father's excitement at being in the library. From observing him, I associated research with extremes: success or failure, frustration or delight, exasperation or bliss. As a student doing my own research, I realized that not only *practicing* research led to these extremes, but so did trying to *understand* that research. Research led to questions that demanded to be explored, only to lead to further questions, to more unsatisfactory answers, and then to more questions. To be a researcher meant to be forever complicating one's life. As a student, I felt very much like I did as a child on the half-floors: terrified.

And then, I met a librarian. After weeks of searching through countless indexes for a secondary source on the Jacaltec language, a fellow student suggested that I go to the reference desk for help. There the librarian, with tremendous enthusiasm, showed me a marvelous resource – an annotated bibliography of scholarship on Mayan languages. It solved my immediate need, and instilled in me an idea for a future career.

Yes, practicing and thinking about research were complex and complicated; but, from this interaction, I discovered that there were those who knew how to make researchers' lives easier. There were those who understood the passion, frustrations and goals of researchers – and, despite that knowledge, wanted to help. I was enthralled. I decided at that moment that I, too, wanted to be one of those people. I, too, wanted to be a reference librarian.

Now, many years, many institutions and many time zones later, I still strive to model what I learned from the reference librarian I met in college. I strive to mitigate the anxiety produced when doing research. I strive to share my enthusiasm for research. I strive to provide guidance and encouragement both to current scholars as well as to those wishing to become scholars. And I strive, in my own way, to help make the practice of scholarship what it should be: something extraordinary.

Elizabeth Brewer, PhD, Beloit College

I was five when my family moved to San Antonio, Texas. A girl in my fourth-grade class was from Waco and had a trampoline in her yard, and told us Waco was very different from San Antonio. Two high school girls down the street, one a tomboy, one a prom queen, became nuns when they graduated, as did my older sister's boyfriend. We were not Catholic. Weekends, we sometimes took excursions to Spanish mission churches, but my mother instructed me to lock the car door when we drove through Mexican neighborhoods at night. My brother went to a high school where a brahma bull was the mascot and was followed around the track by bagpipe players before every football game. Some of my teachers had twangs when they spoke; I was instructed to avoid that.

After fifth grade, we moved to Germany, where marks were used instead of dollars and cents. Before arriving, I imagined people making marks on paper to make purchases, and skiing to school in the winter. Instead we bought groceries from the PX on our NATO Air Force base, and I went to one of the two elementary schools for base families. The Fourth of July fireworks display, assembled by airmen on assignment, seemed to last hours. Germany was in the woods on the base where I rode my bike, tobagganed when there was snow, and picked blueberries in the summer. It was in the women who walked through the woods to work for families as cleaners, reversing the trip at the end of the day to return to their villages. It was in the people who waved when we rode past on excursions off-base.

When I finished sixth grade, my family went camping in northern Italy. Upon return, I was enrolled in a Catholic girls' school off-base. I knew no German. I was not Catholic. I had not been asked if I wanted this. But it was a relief. I did not want to go to seventh grade, where girls generally conformed to roles based on looks and personality that frightened me. In my new school, I was a fish out of water, but I fished my classmates and wanted to know, whereas I imagined that in the

American junior high, I'd be an ostracized fish. I began to live a dual life: German in school, American at home.

Awareness of difference. Puzzling out position. Wondering about culture and language. Code switching.

My career trajectory will not be unfamiliar to international educators. PhD in German literature. Studies in Germany toward that degree. Segue into administration work when a career with German proves unlikely. Varied positions in international education (education abroad, area studies, graduate fellowships and international student services) at different universities (the University of Massachusetts at Amherst, Boston University, the New School for Social Research). Less predictable, a three-year sabbatical as a Peace Corps volunteer in Slovakia. Return to the United States. Six-month job search. Bingo: offer from Beloit College to help it extend its internationalization beyond education abroad and international student enrollments. That was also my call to shift from administering international education programs to studying and practicing international education.

David Comp, PhD, University of Chicago

During my second year of high school I learned of an opportunity to go to Rosenheim, Germany for four weeks during the summer as an exchange student as part of a school-to-school exchange my high school had with Finsterwalder Gymnasium. While I didn't speak German, nor was I studying the language, I was more than eager to take advantage of this opportunity as a 15-year-old. It should go without saying that that experience had an incredible impact on me, and my family hosted a student from Finsterwalder the following year and I again participated on the program the summer after I graduated from high school.

During my search for colleges to apply to I was drawn to the University of Wisconsin-Eau Claire as it was the only school to highlight its education abroad programs during my campus tours. As a Spanish and Latin American studies major, I was drawn to and participated on a semester-long education abroad program in Valladolid, Spain during my junior year.

While I searched for a job in international education after graduating from college, I was unsuccessful and spent seven years working in the field of Human Services with juvenile delinquents, troubled and disadvantaged youth and individuals with developmental disabilities. This led me to pursue a Master of Science in Family Science from the University of Nebraska-Lincoln which I describe as a Master of Social Work degree without the clinical portion. My thesis, however, focused on outcomes of education abroad as the international education bug never left me.

314

Weeks after graduating with my master's degree I moved to Chicago and dedicated myself to finding a professional position in international education, and I was fortunate to quickly secure a position at the University of Chicago, where I have worked for the past 15 years. As a result of the work on my thesis, I developed a strong interest in and appreciation of the scholarly literature in the field. This led me to become active in the field and in particular with NAFSA and the Forum on Education Abroad, with early contributions on compiling annotated research bibliographies on both US students abroad and international students in the United States, and later transitioning to writing. After four years I started a doctoral program in cultural and educational studies with a concentration in comparative and international education at Loyola University Chicago, where I received my PhD in 2013.

Darla Deardorff, EdD, Duke University

We must learn to live together as brothers,
or perish together as fools.

This quote by Martin Luther King, Jr. sums up what drives my work as a scholar-practitioner in the field of international higher education. This deep motivation stems from my own personal faith beliefs around being a peacemaker. From an early age, I was taught about the importance of being a peacemaker in this world. Then, as a high school student, I had the opportunity to participate in my first exchange – to Germany. During that exchange, I remember hearing an adult remark: 'If only the world could come together like this.' Later, as an undergraduate student, I had an internship at the United Nations in Geneva, Switzerland. My rationale for such an internship was thinking that the international level would be one of the best ways to work toward peace. However, after that experience, I came away with the belief that working towards peace needed to happen at the grassroots level. Thus, the internship experience was pivotal in pushing me into the field of international education, where I have worked ever since – first as a volunteer and then later in a study abroad office, in an international student office, as an English as a Second Language teacher, as a teacher trainer, as a cross-cultural trainer, as a researcher, as a consultant, as an author, as a faculty member, and as a leader in a national professional organization in the field.

During this time, I also pursued my graduate degrees – a master's in adult education, focusing on English as a Second Language teaching – and later a doctorate in higher education administration, focusing on international education. My doctoral dissertation on intercultural competence was ultimately about what is necessary for humans to get along together, again stemming from my deeply held beliefs. And ironically, this has all come full circle for me now through the opportunity to work at the international level (through my work with the

315

Association of International Education Administrators, as well as a number of international organizations, including the United Nations and the Council of Europe) as well as at the grassroots level, through teaching, consulting and mentoring.

What stands out to me in this journey is the importance of underlying beliefs and motivations. To me, this is much more than a profession or career – being a scholar-practitioner in internationalization for me is about aligning one's life work with core values and beliefs. It's about keeping the bigger picture in mind, which for me is the idealistic pursuit of helping to make this world a better place, a world in which we can all live together peacefully. Learning to live together is a lifelong process, one that we must pursue relentlessly and intentionally – through research and praxis – a process that doesn't see a utopia, but rather a process that calls us to understand the essence of our humanity – which is as Desmond Tutu describes it: 'My humanity is bound up in yours, for we can only be human together.' Our future, therefore, is one inextricably connected with each other in a holistic, collective existence.

Jane Edwards, PhD, Yale University

I got my first job in international education as a result of what I suppose might be described as 'experiential learning' – I was hired at the University of Pennsylvania, where I had completed my doctorate (in folklore and folklife, now once more a sub-field of cultural anthropology) to serve as a foreign student adviser. This was no doubt on the basis of my experience there as a foreign student from the UK, since my skills as a folklorist were not immediately relevant to immigration law. My second job, in the early 1980s, was at the Harvard Institute for International Development, and it was my experience in Argentina – where I had done my dissertation field research – that convinced economists to hire me. Moving around the world came easily – I took a gap year as an au pair in Paris before Cambridge, I liked learning languages and as a '60s Londoner I was independent and risk-tolerant to a fault. Like so many international educators, the intentionality and stimulation of travel in this profession has been one of the main reasons I have settled cheerfully into the hybrid role of academic-turned-administrator.

At UPenn in that first job I ended up co-authoring a book called *The World in the Curriculum* with my (faculty) boss – whose time constraints resulted in my doing more of the work than either of us had initially anticipated, thus the credit. One of the reasons I had not pursued a conventional academic research and teaching career was that I did not want to continue the kind of research I had been doing in graduate school. But I discovered through this work that research based in the daily pragmatics of the field of international education can guide good professional decision-making and add interest to the quotidian. The research agendas promoted through organizations like EAIE and NAFSA, and the evolving narratives of cultural anthropology, have kept me interested because they provide context and resonance for what might otherwise be no more than the housekeeping of administration.

My professional life managing international education offices and programs has followed this pattern. Moving around the United States in the classic improvised career meanderings of a woman of my generation (I have worked at six US universities, one of them twice), I found that my work became a nice tangle of thinking and planning and teaching my colleagues as well as my students. There is significant intellectual pleasure in encountering, in all those conversations during conferences and site visits, interesting dilemmas and propositions which then translate into plans for action, or research papers, when we are back home in the office.

John D. Heyl, PhD, IELeaders.net

My professional pathway as scholar-practitioner has evolved in ways that sometimes made sense and sometimes surprised me. Working to earn tenure at Illinois Wesleyan University (Bloomington, IL) (1969-1988) meant continuing my scholarly work in modern German history, even at an institution emphasizing its commitment to teaching. Thus, at IWU, my scholar and practitioner identities ran along parallel lines with my scholarship addressing an external specialist audience among historians and my practice meeting institutional needs at home, including helping to found an interdisciplinary international studies major and leading several short-term education abroad programs to Europe.

My stints as senior international officer (SIO) at the University of Missouri-Columbia (1988-2000) and at Old Dominion University (Norfolk, VA) (2000-2006) reflected a decisive tilt toward a practitioner role. I gave up tenure – including giving away much of my research library. My role was now that of a Provost Office administrator – a full-time practitioner – leading comprehensive international offices, seeking grant funding for international projects, helping create a global faculty development program (Missouri) and a master's program in international education leadership (ODU) and trying to both stimulate and coordinate campus-wide international initiatives. I retired from ODU in 2006.

At least I thought I had retired. But having relocated with my wife to Tucson, Arizona, I was alerted to a an academic leadership position at a for-profit education abroad company I had never heard of – CEA Study Abroad – located up Interstate I-10 in Phoenix. My practitioner role at CEA was dominated by the challenge to raise a provider organization's academic profile to both prospective students and university partners –

all in the context of a rigorous business model of operations. A former campus colleague once remarked (jokingly, I'm sure) that I had finally gone to the 'dark side'!

But as it turned out, during my 'retirement' years, I became increasingly interested in writing about leadership issues in the field. This led to the publication of *The Senior International Officer (SIO) as Change Agent* (2007). The widespread use of this little guide – built on the growing scholarship on international education as well as on leadership in academia, business and public affairs – has been particularly gratifying. While consulting with CEA, I joined Darla Deardorff, Hans de Wit and Tony Adams in co-editing *The SAGE Handbook of International Higher Education* (SAGE, 2012). Still later, with Danny Damron (University of Utah), I explored a particularly difficult topic in 'Should I Stay or Should I Go? Career Dilemmas for International Educators' for *International Educator* (September–October 2014). Unlike my earlier scholarship – highly focused, solitary work, distinct from my institutional practitioner roles – this scholarship was *about* my IE practice – more collaborative, more interdisciplinary and based on actual leadership experience.

My current venture in international education was launched in 2014 when IELeaders.net went 'live'. My recent writing, all collaborative in one way or the other, convinced me that there was room for collaborative reflections on leadership issues with and for senior IE practitioners. We shall see.

John Hudzik, PhD, Michigan State University

While I came to the work of internationalization later than many, the seeds were planted early – but took long to bloom into a career. Perhaps it began with my grandparents, immigrants from Poland, whom a two-year-old thought 'talked funny' and was curious why. Maybe it was because my little town was very Dutch in culture and immigration, but paradoxically it was pretty inward looking, and for most kids a trip to an adjacent state was adventurous and foreign enough.

The intellectual seed was planted in the fifth grade with a world geography course that used a textbook ostensibly written by a kid my age who travelled the world with his father. I was hooked by the world of diverse places, maps, photos and events, and I wondered constantly what it must be like in all of those other places. But I could only wonder.

In high school, two foreign languages constituted our 'international curriculum': Latin (to understand English better), and Spanish because of a growing migrant population. A freshman-year college roommate from Thailand began my 'internationalization at home'. I discovered how similar we thought but from different perspectives. I majored in political science and comparative politics. A mesmerizing Russian history professor turned me toward a 'minor' in Soviet and Eastern European studies, and these were later part of my master's and PhD work on political science.

I took a job at Michigan State University which was partly an administrative appointment and partly a faculty appointment. Both focused me domestically. I gravitated toward justice and judicial systems areas of scholarship – which I maintain today, and which led me to a tenured full professorship in the mid-1980s. But the international beckoned.

I taught an overseas political science program in London. I then took over the comparative justice system program in London, and later developed a similar one in Australia, as well as helping create parliamentary internships there. The international beat kept on – a bit on the eclectic side. A Fulbright Senior Fellowship took me to Australia in the late 1980s. In the '90s, I participated in judicial system development projects in Tomsk, Siberia, Indonesia, Kosovo and Mongolia.

Without predicting it, a transition to a *career* in internationalization began in 1994 when the president of MSU asked me to chair a university-wide taskforce on education abroad which recommended more than tripling education abroad participation to nearly 3000 annually. I was later appointed dean of international studies and programs at MSU with the very clear charge of expanding the university's already significant levels of international engagement in teaching, research and development throughout the world. Intellectually and administratively, this became all consuming.

For the last two decades my growing and now principal area of scholarly work is around the internationalization of higher education institutions. I bring to this my academic background in public policy, public administration and organizational theory. Equally, I bring experiences as an education abroad leader, as dean and vice-president for international programs and strategy, a stint as acting provost and also as president of AIEA and then of NAFSA. My 2015 book *Comprehensive Internationalization: institutional pathways to success* (Routledge) is a reflection of the last two decades of my career and scholarship.

I guess you could characterize my journey through internationalization as going from curiosity, to hiatus, to sampling an eclectic mix of experiences, to redirecting my career and scholarship.

Fiona Hunter, DBA, Universita Cattolica el Sacro Cuore

International higher education has always been part of my adult life through the places in which I have worked, studied and lived, and I have always been curious to explore and engage in events beyond my own institutional setting. Among others, I was involved in the Bologna Process in Italy as a member of the National Experts Team and have been an active member in the European Association for International Education since 1998. These external involvements have always offered me many opportunities to expand my understanding and update my professional skills, but a number of years ago I was searching for an academic experience that would provide a framework for more formal learning and enable me to move forward. When I discovered the DBA in Higher Education Management at the University of Bath I knew instinctively that I had found the right educational program, although I confess I did not fully comprehend the journey I was about to embark upon and to what extent it would impact on my professional development.

Undertaking doctoral studies enabled me to broaden my understanding of higher education away from the focus of internationalization and enabled me to see higher education institutions in a more holistic and global context. I gained insight into how universities operate and how they interact with national legislations, external environments and drivers for change. It enriched me with stronger critical and analytic skills, enabling me to reflect more on practice and possible pathways for change.

It has also transformed my professional life. In 2012, I left my job as international director and set myself up as an independent higher education consultant, trainer and researcher, so that I could bring my professional and academic knowledge together on a daily basis. This new professional identity would not have been possible without a formal learning experience that provided me with a different way of thinking and acting and enabled me to occupy a new space.

Bruce La Brack, PhD, University of the Pacific

My childhood was highly unusual, highly mobile, and probably strongly influenced my eventually becoming an anthropologist. Born in New York, I subsequently lived in thirteen cities in nine US states by my eighteenth birthday because my father's profession was renovating hotel properties and managing them. So 'normal' was living in fancy downtown city hotels while attending a long succession of local public inner-city schools. Being the eternal 'new kid' at school and the 'boss's kid' in the hotel provided ample opportunity early in life to experience and witness all kinds of diversity, practice intercultural adaptive skills (although I had no concept that was what I was doing), and become adept at 'participant-observation' techniques as part of survival strategies needed to fit into wildly disparate social environments. Norma McCaig claimed I was a domestic version of the folks she called Global Nomads.

Initially an indifferent student, it took almost my entire undergraduate education to find something that kindled my curiosity; it was comparative literature, mostly because it offered insights into other cultures and mental worlds that fascinated me. I finished my BA and worked for five years in various capacities in advertising until I realized that neither my liver nor my soul was going to survive that profession. I returned to study for an MA, concentrating on South Asian cultures and languages. My first serious overseas experience was as an American Institute of Indian Studies Hindi Language Fellow in New Delhi, India, where I met many Sikhs and developed an interest in the history of migration outside of the sub-continent. This topic was to become a major research topic of mine for my entire career, and my PhD dissertation was an ethnographic study of the Sikhs of California centered in the Yuba City area. The University of the Pacific, where I joined the faculty in 1975, is only 100 miles from Yuba City, which facilitated multi-generation longitudinal research that continues.

Upon joining the Pacific faculty, I immediately become involved in the international education process and the creation of orientation and re-entry programs, which is the subject of my chapter in this volume. It also led to a specialization in re-entry theory and practice, which became my other lifelong research passion.

I made up for a late start in personal overseas experience by conducting research in India (three years), Japan (three years), England (one year), and Uganda (six months), while traveling to over 85 countries. In retirement, I continue to work on my global 'bucket list'.

Gregory Light, PhD, Northwestern University

Born in Canada, my international experience began when I was four years old and moved to eastern France with my family for four years. From there I was fortunate to have travelled to almost 20 countries by the time I was eight. Later, during my undergraduate studies in math, physics and philosophy at the University of Toronto I took a year off and travelled Europe for a year, exploring a growing interest in other cultures, people and places, primarily through the lens of theater. After completing my first two degrees I returned to Paris, where I lived for 4 years and practiced, taught and investigated different forms of performance through the American Center for the Arts. This eventually led me to London where I lived, married, raised children, researched academic forms of performance and began my academic career.

After London, I extended my international experience through my work in the United States. During my time at Northwestern University, I worked on educational projects focused on student learning with academic colleagues across the world, most recently in Europe, the Middle East (where I am an international consultant to the new Association of Palestinian Academic Developers) and South America, primarily through work with the LASPAU center at Harvard. For more than five years I have – when time and resources permitted – been investigating key questions of student learning and student understanding of international experience. Indeed, I continue to work on all these international projects – despite having arrived back full circle to Canada after 40 years.

In all this time away, my teaching and research primarily focused on the theory and practice of learning, teaching and assessment in higher and professional education in multiple international contexts. It is a relatively new field, to which I have made a modest contribution. I have published over 50 papers and chapters in national and international peer-reviewed publications and given over 100 invited talks, workshops and conference presentations in North and South America, Europe, Africa and Asia. I am also the author, with Susanna Calkins, of *Learning and Teaching in Higher Education: the reflective professional* (SAGE, 2001, 2009); and, with Marina Micari, of *Making Scientists: six principles for effective college teaching* (Harvard University Press, 2013).

Anthony C. Ogden, PhD, University of Kentucky

A Kentucky native, I had hardly been outside of Kentucky before my first job after graduating from Berea College took me across the world to Japan, where I taught English in rural Kumamoto Prefecture for three years. The only non-Japanese resident in the region, I quickly began to understand the importance of language proficiency, intercultural competency and international understanding. After several subsequent years traveling throughout Southeast Asia and Australia, I decided to move to Cameroon to support the ongoing development of Jomatt College of Technology, a secondary institution supporting youth education in rural Cameroon.

These early professional experiences taught me much about the value of international education and intercultural learning and led me straight to the School for International Training (SIT), where I earned a master's degree in international and intercultural management, specializing in international education and training. As part of my studies with SIT, I returned to Japan to work for an organization committed to supporting Japanese students in studying abroad.

My career in international education, however, really took off when I was invited to serve as the director of the Tokyo Center of the Institute for the International Education of Students (IES). At IES, I was able to build a successful program for US university and college students and take my first steps as a scholar-practitioner. I regularly offered anthropology courses on the social organization of Japan and submitted my first publications on international education programming and delivery. Over the years, it became increasingly obvious to me that I needed and wanted to pursue my doctoral studies, and so I was delighted when the Pennsylvania State University offered me the opportunity to serve as its first associate director for education abroad with the flexibility to pursue a doctorate in educational theory and policy with a dual title in comparative and international education.

Years later, I am back home in the Commonwealth of Kentucky, where I am gladly serving as the executive director of education abroad and exchanges at the University of Kentucky and maintain an active teaching and research agenda on international higher education policy. This is an exciting time for me to be in Kentucky, where I am working shoulder to shoulder with collegues throughout the state to enhance international education and intercultural learning opportunities for all our students. Although I came up in the profession as a practitioner, I welcome my role as a scholar-practitioner today and accept the responsibilities and expectations it brings. It is an honor to harness my academic training to inform our practice and to leverage my professional standing to guide scholarship and research.

Katherine Punteney, EdD, Middlebury Institute of International Studies at Monterey

I got my start in international education through Girl Scouting. As a high school student, I had the opportunity to spend two weeks in Japan and later two weeks in Singapore at international Girl Scout encampments. Once I got a taste of international education, I couldn't get enough.

Through the University of Puget Sound, I participated in the Pacific Rim Asia Study-Travel program, spending a year travelling through Asia with a professor, two staff and 24 students. When that education abroad program took me to South Korea, Vietnam, Japan, China, India and Nepal, I encountered for the first time the vast disparity of wealth in our world and the conditions in which the poorest of the poor are living. I had to come to terms with my own feelings of guilt, pity, shame and helplessness at being born to such privilege.

Out of university, I began to work with Japanese students in the United States and then went to Japan to teach English to junior high and high school students for three years. These experiences taught me about indirect communication and the role of silence, that sometimes nothing said means something important. I saw the significance of harmony and consensus in decision-making, and the importance of saving face.

After completing a master's in international education, I was hired to manage international exchange programs for the World Association of Girl Guides and Girl Scouts in Pune, India. Along with an international staff team, I designed and ran events for teenage and adult participants from around the world. While at the center, I established an international service-learning program that engaged participants with local non-governmental organizations (NGOs) as well as offering a language and culture curriculum.

I joined California State University, Chico's international student services team and was able to get involved in recruitment, admissions, orientation and alumni outreach in addition to advising. Believing deeply that developing globally competent graduates is integral to the mission of higher education, I became a leader in California State University, Chico's campus internationalization effort working on curriculum, communications, intercultural training, and more. Through a doctorate in educational leadership, my dissertation research examined the increasing need for today's college graduates to develop global competencies and receive advice on international career opportunities.

Now at the Middlebury Institute of International Studies at Monterey, I am the founding faculty member of an MA in international education management program that prepares future leaders in the field. My research interests are in campus internationalization and intercultural communication, and I teach both intercultural communication and international education courses.

Rosalind Raby, PhD, California Colleges for International Education

My personal path mirrors those who held multiple roles as a scholar and as a practitioner. My academic and professional experiences allow me to understand context from multiple perspectives and enable me to more fully appreciate the opportunity to shape policies and practice as a result of sharing my research. As a practitioner, I worked for the Institute for International Education at the Los Angeles Community College District from 1985 to 1993. Part of my duties included synthesizing and applying the how-to publications of the 1980s. Using these constructs, I created programs in the fields of internationalizing curriculum and education abroad. Annual assessment of all international educational programs at the Los Angeles Community College District then led to opportunities for advocacy, that led to changes in practice, and ultimately to revising program agendas.

As a director of the non-profit consortium California Colleges for International Education (CCIE) in 1985, I began to advocate for community colleges to include internationalization in their missions and policies, and through ongoing research, provided context to support this advocacy. One example of this occurred in the late 1990s when I was given the opportunity to work with the State Chancellor's office and be part of a task force to develop the Board of Governor's policy on internationalization that continues to support the field today. Another example is the use of the annual CCIE State-of-the-Field surveys (1985-2015) that illustrate how research can not only share best practices, but be used to promote new activities by showcasing what has been done and what can be done.

Throughout the decades, research remains at the foundation of all my work. I consistently try to unite theory and practice to illustrate how things are being done and how they can be improved. I was not part of the pioneering generation highlighted in this chapter. However, I was their student. While not a leader in the field, many of my books (with amazing co-authors) have taken the field into new directions. The Raby and Tarrow (1996) book asked authors to not only depict best practices but to utilize research and theory to help ground their ideas. The Valeau and Raby book (2007) asked individuals who were known for their national leadership capabilities to specifically emphasize advocacy. The Raby and Valeau book (Palgrave, forthcoming 2016) unites research in the field with case studies to build new theories and enhance assessment.

My generation was one about creating a voice and a presence for community college internationalization. Today, there are numerous EdD programs in community college leadership that promote research and practitioner training programs offered by a range of associations that promote scholarship. Using the information from these sources, I continue to learn, re-learn and un-learn through reflection and assessment.

Mandy Reinig, St. Mary's College of Maryland

As a first-generation college student from Michigan I had never been away from home for an extended period of time until I went abroad for a semester to England and attended Edge Hill College University. Little did I know when I set foot on the plane to England how much that semester would change my life. I left for England as an athletic training major who was already working with teams at my university, and I returned home and changed my major at the beginning of my junior year to international studies with a double minor in Spanish and international business. This change took place because I felt that if I could study abroad given my circumstances, then everyone could and should and I wanted to help facilitate that.

After undergrad, I immediately started graduate school at Ohio University and also kept working on my plan to assist others in studying abroad by working in its education abroad office until I graduated. Post-graduation, and in the usual panic in searching for a job, I landed at Penn State Altoona as the sole education abroad advisor. In this position, I built the office, as there was no other international educators before me. We successfully went from 5 to 100 students abroad in my first five years there. I also assisted them in developing short-term, faculty-led programs, among other things. It was there that I first developed my interest in scholarly research. I began working with a few faculty members on research projects looking at students' perceptions of education abroad barriers.

After six years in Altoona I moved to my current position at St. Mary's, where I now work within an office of three, including myself; plus I have the added duties of working with international students, being the SIO, and overseeing a myriad of other aspects of international education for our college. I have an active travel schedule in this position and, combined with my daily responsibilities, this makes scholarly pursuits difficult. However, recently a colleague and I have begun conducting focus groups to determine whether our education abroad learning outcomes are being met. I thoroughly enjoy being a practitioner and having direct contact with students. I also like the fact that I can conduct research and have been able to make use of the resources available to me to become more of a practitioner-scholar. I will always think of myself as a practitioner first and a scholar second but am happy to share my knowledge with others as well as continue to learn more from my colleagues and my own scholarly pursuits.

Laura E. Rumbley, PhD, Boston College

A childhood involving nearly five formative years of living outside of my home country, the United States, followed by two years abroad as a university student, led me easily and naturally to an internationally oriented career. My first professional experience had me working in a refugee resettlement organization, coordinating community volunteers (many of them returned US education abroad students) to assist refugee families beginning new lives in the United States. From there, I found my way to a master's program combining international education with a heavy focus on matters of social justice, at the School for International Training (now the SIT Graduate Institute) in Brattleboro, Vermont.

I went on to hold positions in international student admissions/marketing and immigration counseling at Boston University. It was there that my love affair with higher education began. Not only did this early professional experience allow me to become more aware of the field of international education (or internationalization, as it is now more widely known), but I began to gain a sense of the idea of the 'university in the world', or higher education as a global phenomenon, with a fascinating array of trends and developments unfolding across the planet.

Moved to dig more deeply into what higher education really means, I undertook doctoral study in higher education administration at the Boston College Center for International Higher Education, under the tutelage of renowned international and comparative higher education scholar Philip G. Altbach. My preliminary goal with respect to acquiring the PhD was to be better equipped to return to an administrative position of leadership at a college or university. Slowly but surely, however, I realized that I took immense satisfaction from the work of developing new ideas and insights related to policy and practice in the field of international higher education, not necessarily serving the exclusive interests of one specific institution.

After completing my PhD, I was given a remarkable opportunity to further develop my research, writing and analysis skills for two years at a Brussels-based organization, the Academic Cooperation Association, focused heavily on internationalization policy and practice in the European context.

Now back at the Boston College Center for International Higher Education, I find myself engaged in a range of stimulating pursuits that provide me with constant opportunities to learn and explore, create and collaborate. I help to conceive and execute international research projects, write on topics of interest in the field, edit a wide array of materials for publication, lead a publications committee for a major international education practitioner association, co-edit an academic journal, and teach and advise graduate students interested in international and comparative higher education. I consider myself exceedingly lucky to be able to be so actively involved in such a meaningful cross-section of activities that relate to the unique, and yet closely related, worlds of researchers, practitioners and policymakers.

Donna Scarboro, PhD, The George Washington University

I was raised in a semi-rural, monolingual environment. The most exciting travel of my youth was a car trip to Iowa to see friends of my parents. With six children packed into an old Nash Rambler, every trip was pretty wild. But travel by car was not my way into other worlds: my most vivid experiences of other places were in books and stories. When not biking around my small town or frequenting the backyards of my friends until dark, I was likely to be hidden away in a book. *The Secret Garden* particularly captured me, with images of India and England that took me far away and yet resonated with the culture and place I knew. I grew up in historic times in the South, with school desegregation coming to my town over the years I was in middle school and high school. Though it would be years before I would make the connection, I had become keenly aware of the costs of force-fitting two cultures, and of the price some in my community had paid when they were robbed of their cultural context, plunged into an unwelcoming one, and deprived of the education and resources to thrive in place.

Years later, teaching post-colonial approaches to the study of literature, my awareness of cultural appropriation and cultural annihilation surfaced. But as I've said, that would take a while. When I finished college in the mid-1970s, I asked for one thing for graduation: the chance to go to Europe. My family supported the request but perhaps

327

did not fully believe that I would put on a backpack and get on an airplane, to vanish again into a landscape of imagination. I traveled to five countries that summer, reading, counting pennies, absorbing every experience. I subsequently started my PhD program and moved at the dissertation stage to Washington, DC. After teaching for several years I was offered a full-time position combining teaching and administrative work. I found that I enjoyed the team work and accomplishment that came with being an administrator in complement to the privilege of leading students through deep analysis of challenging texts. My administrative role involved – among miscellaneous other duties – assisting faculty members who wanted to organize short-term study abroad during the summer. Soon, this and other assignments grew, and I eventually became responsible for a small study abroad office. That office tracked about 350 students. Over the years I served at GW, eventually as Associate Provost for International Programs, we had nearly 2000. Truth really is stranger than fiction, and my international experience, working with partners and associates in three dozen countries, has proven a happy substitute for bike rides and exciting books.

Richard Slimbach, PhD, Azusa Pacific University

Since high school days in Los Angeles I've been attracted to the unfamiliar. School breaks were opportunities to take to the road, the first being at age 16, as soon as my newly minted driver's license arrived in the mail. With only a sleeping bag and rucksack, I made a series of unannounced visits to different Native American communities throughout the southwest United States. This was a first taste of what would become a lifelong appetite for a special type of travel schooling. Although it wasn't clear to me at the time, these excursions into the unknown were teaching me *how to learn* from those who appear utterly different from me, and to allow *their* vision of life to revise *my* vision of life. Even the most confounding places (like Haiti and Ethiopia) would reveal a purposeful and priceless quality, something essentially sacred to receive and to cherish.

Following graduation from Humboldt State University, I affiliated with various international intentional communities and grassroots development organizations. They put me into direct relationship with migrant farmers (recounted in my chapter in this volume), homeless men (Fresno, California), border populations (Juárez, Mexico), and Vietnamese refugees (Pasadena, California). I encountered people who experienced more hardship in a single day than I had known my entire lifetime. Something of a 'conversion' took place. The question was no longer, 'How might intercultural experience gratify my wanderlust?' but rather, 'How might I use my privilege to serve the public good?'

Volunteer English tutoring led to graduate studies in TESOL and eventually to two years dedicated to occupational literacy program development among Muslim cycle rickshaw drivers in Hyderabad, India. Expulsion from India (a long story) provided the impetus to enroll in doctoral studies in international education. My research and writing was focused on non-formal educational development among politicized Baloch in Karachi, Pakistan.

All of these experiences solidified a personal commitment to global learning as both a personal passion and a professional responsibility. Before the ink on the doctoral diploma had dried, in 1990, I was hired to teach for the School of Education at Azusa Pacific University (APU). Two years later, during the Los Angeles Uprising, the APU's provost issued an invitation that would confirm the course of scholarly practice: to create campus-based courses and off-campus programs to help form a new generation of cultural mediators and peacemakers.

Over the next two decades, professional energies were dedicated to creating, teaching and managing three dozen courses in a portfolio of global learning programs: foreign language learning (Spanish), urban field study (LA Term), applied linguistics (graduate TESOL), full-immersion undergraduate education abroad (Global Learning Term), and graduate-level development practice (Master of Arts in Transformational Urban Leadership). Together, these programs have placed hundreds of students in study, service-learning and research projects in over 50 countries.

Bernhard Streitwieser, PhD, The George Washington University

I moved to the United States from Germany at age ten and in high school studied Spanish and spent the summer before college studying in Madrid. In college I majored in international relations and minored in Spanish – mostly because I liked 'international things' – and studied abroad for a semester in Salamanca. After college I worked briefly in Madrid and also in Washington, DC for a senator. I then spent several aimless months pursuing film work in Hollywood but soon realized that careers in politics and in acting – similar occupations – were not suited for me.

One day, while sitting in a library contemplating my future, I came across a line in *What Color Is Your Parachute* that struck a chord with me: 'When in doing that *thing* you lose all track of time, you know that is what you should be doing.' I remembered how happy I had been at the university, how I loved the calm of libraries and the satisfaction of finishing projects and papers. I enrolled in a graduate program in linguistics at Georgetown University to become an ESL teacher. Two years later I continued into a linguistics PhD program at Columbia University and that fall happened into a course in comparative education. Finding the perfect mix of 'international things' – education, language, the study of culture and history, critical inquiry, and the application of knowledge to real-world problems – I had found my passion. My advisor, Gita Steiner-Khamsi, also encouraged my interest in returning to Germany to write my dissertation on East German teachers and their transition to the unified German school system, so I spent two years at Berlin's Max Planck Institute funded by an Alexander von Humboldt Foundation Federal Chancellor Grant.

After graduation I took a job as an analyst at the American Institutes for Research in Washington, DC, but the constant proposal-writing-to-program-evaluation cycle bored me and again I yearned for the intellectual challenges at a university. I accepted a research position at Northwestern's Searle Center for Learning and Teaching, where Greg Light (who also has a chapter in this book) became a wonderful mentor to me for research, publishing and presenting. I also lectured in the German Department and the School of Education and Social Policy. For eight years I led Mellon Foundation– and NSF-funded studies and also worked for two years as the associate director of the university's Study Abroad Office. I left that office due to a lack of research opportunity and the frustrating dissonance between its activities and the developing field, where the most prominent voices, among them Hans de Wit and Brian Whalen (who are also involved in this book), were advocating for research to inform and improve practice. I returned to my research position at the Center for Teaching and secured internal seed funding from the Buffett Center for International and Comparative Studies to conduct a study on returning education abroad students, which became the basis for the Student Conceptions of International Experience project.

In 2010 I returned to Berlin (with my wife, Mary Beth, and our children, Max and Lena) as a Fulbright-funded guest professor at the Humboldt Universität, where I studied the European ERASMUS Mobility Programme and taught on international higher education and student mobility. With additional funding from the German Academic Exchange Service (DAAD) and an invitation to serve as interim chair of the Department of Comparative Education, I extended my time in Germany to 2014, when I accepted a tenure-track position in George Washington University's graduate International Education Program. The philosophy of scholars and practitioners informing each other's work has inspired me to assemble this collection of essays by colleagues in our field, who share my passion in constructively critiquing our livelihood and always looking for ways to make it better.

Brian Whalen, PhD, The Forum on Education Abroad

My academic training is in the field of cultural psychology, specifically in how American literature reflects distinctive characteristics of US culture, society and individuals. Professional experiences in which I worked as a counselor in a psychiatric hospital and a prison helped to shape my understanding of psychology. My dissertation, *Home and Homelessness in the American Imagination*, examined the psychological dimensions of feeling perpetually uprooted, including how this is reflected in travel to and from abroad.

It was shortly thereafter that I moved to Italy, one of my ancestral homelands, and began to work in education abroad as a teacher and administrator. I had very little preparation for what my responsibilities were, and yet directing programs and working closely with faculty and students for those five years was one of the most important and enjoyable experiences I have had in education abroad. My view of cultural psychology greatly expanded during this time, deepening my appreciation for the uniqueness of American culture and opening up my mind to Italian and other European cultures and their expressions. When I returned to the United States in the early 1990s I recognized, along with several other colleagues, that there was a need for a scholarly journal in education abroad that could encourage and provide research-based articles and thoughtful essays in order to advance the field. I remember thinking that there were very few writings in the field that tried to explore the essence of what it was that I had been doing in Italy, and what so many others were doing in their education abroad work. The result was the founding of *Frontiers: The Interdisciplinary Journal of Study Abroad*, which has been my main contribution to scholarship in the education abroad field over the past 20 years.

We always had in mind that *Frontiers* would attract scholar-practitioners who were trained in wide varieties of academic disciplines and would turn their attention to an education abroad topic or issue. For example, I wrote a piece years ago in which I analyzed student reflections on the meaning of their education abroad experience in light of literary intercultural journeys in order to understand the psychology at work when one crosses borders. For me, and I suspect for many scholar-practitioners, the pursuit of scholarship has many benefits, not the least of which is the way in which it provides greater meaning to one's work, and to the education abroad field as a whole. Now, through my work with the Forum on Education Abroad, I see the fruit of scholar-practitioner work on a daily basis as I help to encourage, foster and lead scholar-practitioner research to serve the education abroad field.

Taylor C. Woodman, PhD Candidate, University of Maryland

My first experience with border crossing began when I left my hometown for my undergraduate studies at Virginia Tech. During my time at Virginia Tech, I spent a semester in South Africa and Argentina. Upon my return I was hired to work as a peer advisor in my university's education abroad office. With a degree in hand, I moved to Washington, DC to pursue international education as a career. I worked in education abroad and in the Persian language flagship program at the University of Maryland while pursuing my master's. During my time at UMD, I participated in a short-term program to Senegal and a staff exchange with the University of Ghana. After UMD, I began working in the Office for Study Abroad at The George Washington University as an education abroad advisor. I eventually made my way back to UMD to pursue a PhD. I now serve on committees for NAFSA and Diversity Abroad in an effort to create access to international experiences. I have directed education abroad courses that have taken students to Cuba, the Dominican Republic, Brazil, Spain and the Netherlands. I strive to embody the scholar-practitioner mindset by applying my studies and research to my daily practice in education abroad.

Michael Woolf, PhD, CAPA, The Global Education Network

I graduated in 1968 with a BA in history and politics. My exam papers were described as 'elegantly vacuous'. It was, however, the '60s, when, as Wordsworth wrote of a different era, 'Bliss was it in that dawn to be alive/But to be young was very heaven.' With a single-minded sense of destiny, I went to Prague in pursuit of love, not revolution. Broken-hearted and broke, I slunk back to England and became a peculiarly inept school teacher in rural England. I tried to teach literature to a wonderfully tolerant and consistently uninterested student population until I applied for an MA programme in American literature at the University of East Anglia. My tutor, and later much-loved mentor, was Malcolm Bradbury. At my interview he pointed out that I was entirely unqualified but I displayed pitiful enthusiasm and neurotic dependency.

Malcolm eventually arranged a scholarship for me at Hull University. This was awarded by a mustard company, anxious to write off profits. I spent considerable time in New York 'working' on a thesis on Jewish-American writers. I focused upon a younger generation who had been entirely (justly?) ignored up to that point (and since). My doctorate was awarded because the panel couldn't agree on a reason to throw me out of the room.

So, I went to Italy to teach literature, at the universities of Padova and Venice. Mutual incomprehension, and a profound level of well-intentioned confusion, characterised my contributions, as did the interventions of the Brigata Rossa who, even in their more moderate paramilitary moments, did not encourage classroom scholarship. I was also blessed in meeting a great eccentric, Richard Creese-Parsons, in a bar in Campo St Angelo. On the basis of the fact that I was a Gemini, Richard offered me the post of senior consultant on the future of English language teaching in Italy: senior by default – I was the only consultant. The post was very attractive because: (a) I had more leisure time than the Doge of Venice; and (b) my salary at the university was, even by the standards of an unemployed gondolier, pitiful. At the beginning of my appointment I knew nothing about English language teaching in Italy. Two years later (when I limped back to England with what was left of my mind), I knew nothing about English language teaching in Italy.

In those marvellous dead days, there were two possibilities for neurotic dilettantes: university teaching and the BBC. I spent five years as a researcher and writer on documentaries for BBC radio – programmes statistically unheard by anybody – and periodically teaching at Middlesex University, Tottenham College and Holloway Women's Prison (where I was a slightly better option than solitary confinement). This was, of course, the perfect preparation for employment in international education. I worked for CIEE (twice), Syracuse University, FIE and now CAPA (my spiritual home). An odd characteristic of these posts is that they were all at relatively senior levels and I never made any kind of application or attended any interview. For one post, I was recruited on a street corner in Berlin; for another in a bar off the Cromwell Road. I was fired at the age of 14: a kosher café in London's East End found my chip-frying skills unacceptable even by the standards of an institution famed for outbreaks of salmonella.

Notes on Contributors

David B. Austell is Associate Provost and Director of the International Students and Scholars Office at Columbia University in New York City. He has undergraduate and graduate degrees in English Literature from the University of North Carolina at Chapel Hill, where he also completed his PhD in Higher Education, focusing on International Education; his doctoral dissertation, *The Birds in the Rich Forest*, concerned Chinese students in the United States during the Student Democracy Movement.

Louis ('Lou') Berends is currently University Relations Manager at the School for International Training (SIT). Berends completed his PhD in cultural and education policy studies with a concentration in comparative and international education at Loyola University Chicago (2011) and has lived, worked and traveled in more than 30 countries.

Giselda Beaudin is Director of International Programs at Rollins College in Winter Park, Florida. She earned her BA in Comparative Literature from Brown University and her MA in English and Creative Writing from Binghamton University.

Tamar Breslauer serves as the Senior Research Librarian for NAFSA: Association of International Educators. Breslauer received her bachelor's degree from Brandeis University in anthropology and her master's degree in library and information studies from the University of Michigan. Prior to her current position, Breslauer worked as a reference and instructional services librarian at several universities in the USA, as library director of a branch library in Madrid, Spain, and as a researcher for a public affairs radio program.

Elizabeth Brewer is Director of International Education at Beloit College, where her work has focused on strengthening student capacity to learn and develop from study abroad and increasing faculty and campus capacity for comprehensive internationalization. Brewer has written on study abroad integration and assessment, and on the opportunities institutional partnerships provide for strengthening student learning and institutional capacity. Her PhD is in Germanic languages and literatures, and she has worked in both public and private institutions.

David Comp serves as the Associate Director of International Programs at the University of Chicago Booth School of Business. Comp also serves as a study abroad research consultant for the Center for Global Education at the California State University, Dominguez Hills. Comp received his BA in Spanish and Latin American Studies from the University of Wisconsin-Eau Claire, his MS in Family Science from the University of Nebraska-Lincoln and his PhD in Cultural and Educational Policy Studies, Comparative and International Education from Loyola University Chicago.

Darla K. Deardorff is Executive Director of the Association of International Education Administrators, and is based at Duke University. She also holds faculty positions at numerous institutions around the world. Deardorff has published widely on intercultural and global education topics, including *The SAGE Handbook of Intercultural Competence* (SAGE, 2009), *The SAGE Handbook of International Higher Education* (SAGE, 2012) and *Building Cultural Competence* (Stylus, 2012). Deardorff holds a BA from Bridgewater College and an MA and EdD from North Carolina State University.

Hans de Wit is the director of the Center for International Higher Education at the Lynch School of Education at Boston College. Recent publications include *Possible Futures: the next 25 years of the internationalisation of higher education* (European Association for International Education, 2013) and *An Introduction to Higher Education Internationalisation* (Universita Cattolica University Press Vita e Pensiero, 2013). He is the Founding Editor of the *Journal of Studies in International Education*. He earned his bachelor's, master's and PhD degrees from the University of Amsterdam.

Jane Edwards has served as Dean of International and Professional Experience at Yale since 2006. She previously served in similar positions at Harvard and at Wesleyan University. Edwards holds a BA/MA from Cambridge University, and a PhD from the University of Pennsylvania. Edwards has taught throughout her career, and served in leadership roles for NAFSA, the Forum, CIEE and World Learning, and on the editorial board of the *Journal of Studies in International Education*.

John D. Heyl is founder of IELeaders.net, a website focusing on leadership issues in international education. He served as Senior International Officer (SIO) at the University of Missouri-Columbia and Old Dominion University (Norfolk, VA) and as Vice President for Global Education/Strategic Partnerships at CEA Study Abroad (Phoenix, AZ). Heyl authored *The Senior International Officer (SIO) as Change Agent* (AIEA, 2007) and co-edited *The SAGE Handbook of International Higher*

Education (SAGE, 2012). He holds a BA from Stanford University and a PhD in European history from Washington University-St. Louis.

John K. Hudzik was Vice President for Global Engagement and Strategic Projects at Michigan State University from 2006 to 2009 and is currently Professor of Criminal Justice, specializing in judicial systems. From 1995 to 2005, he was Dean of International Studies and Programs at Michigan State University and acting university provost in 2005. He is a past president of AIEA and a past president of NAFSA. His latest book is *Comprehensive Internationalization: institutional pathways to success* (Routledge, 2015). He earned three academic degrees from MSU: a bachelor of arts in economics, history and political science, a master's in political science, and a doctorate in political science. He is currently President of MUCIA (Midwest University Consortium for International Activity).

Fiona Hunter is based in Italy, where she works as Research Associate at the Centre for Higher Education Internationalisation (CHEI) at the Università Cattolica del Sacro Cuore in Milan. Hunter also works as a higher education consultant helping universities to think more strategically, either for organisational improvement in general or with a specific focus on internationalisation. She holds a Doctor of Business Administration (DBA) in higher education management from the University of Bath in the United Kingdom.

Bruce La Brack is Professor Emeritus, School of International Studies, University of the Pacific, Stockton, California, USA. For nearly forty years, La Brack served as an anthropologist and international studies professor, and founded and directed the University of the Pacific's cross-cultural training programs. La Brack earned his bachelor's degree (comparative literature) and master's degree (oriental studies and Asian language) from the University of Arizona, and an MPhil (Asian philosophy) and PhD (interdisciplinary social sciences) from the Maxwell School of Syracuse University.

Gregory Light recently retired as the director of the Searle Center for Advancing Learning and Teaching and as a professor in the School of Education and Social Policy at Northwestern University in Chicago. Prior to his time at Northwestern, Light was a faculty member of the Lifelong Learning and International Education Group in the Institute of Education (UCL) at the University of London, where he completed a PhD in student learning.

Anthony C. Ogden is Executive Director of Education Abroad and Exchanges and an adjunct assistant professor in educational policy and evaluation studies at the University of Kentucky. Ogden earned his bachelor's degree from Berea College, his master's degree in international and intercultural management at the SIT Graduate Institute, and his PhD at The Pennsylvania State University in educational theory and policy with a dual title in comparative and international education.

Katherine N. Punteney is Program Chair and Assistant Professor of the MA in International Education Management program at the Middlebury Institute of International Studies in Monterey, California, USA. Punteney earned her bachelor's degree from the University of Puget Sound, her master's degree in international education from the SIT Graduate Institute, and her EdD in educational leadership from California State University, Sacramento.

Rosalind Latiner Raby is Senior Lecturer in Educational Leadership and Policy Studies at California State University, Northridge and is affiliate faculty for the ELPS EdD Community College program. Raby is also director of California Colleges for International Education, a non-profit consortium of 91 California community colleges. Raby received her PhD in comparative and international education (UCLA) and since 1984 has worked with community colleges to internationalize curriculum and campuses. She has published widely in the field.

Mandy Reinig is Director of International Education at St Mary's College of Maryland. Reinig earned her bachelor's degree in international studies from Saginaw Valley State University, a master's degree in Latin American studies from Ohio University, and a second master's degree from The Pennsylvania State University in Teaching English as a Second Language.

Laura E. Rumbley is Associate Director of the Boston College Center for International Higher Education (CIHE). Rumbley is co-editor of the *Journal of Studies in International Education* and chair of the Publications Committee of the European Association for International Education (EAIE). Rumbley, who received her PhD from Boston College, served briefly as a US Foreign Service Officer and is also the former deputy director of the Brussels-based Academic Cooperation Association (ACA).

Donna Scarboro is Associate Provost for International Programs at George Washington University. She holds MA and PhD degrees in English Literature from Emory University (1982, 1989) and a BA from Guilford College. She joined the English Department of George Washington University in 1983, eventually moving to administration and assuming responsibility for study abroad, exchanges and overseas programs. She was the president of AIEA in 2012 and served on the board of Diversity Abroad from 2013 to 2015.

Richard Slimbach is Professor of Global Studies and Coordinator of the Global Studies Program at Azusa Pacific University. Slimbach founded APU's Los Angeles Term, Global Learning Term, and MA in Transformational Urban Leadership (MATUL) programs, the latter focused exclusively on the planet's one billion slum dwellers. Slimbach holds a PhD in comparative and international education from UCLA and is the author of *Becoming World Wise* (Stylus, 2010).

Bernhard Streitwieser is Assistant Professor of International Education at the George Washington University Graduate School of Education and Human Development. He earned his PhD in International and Comparative Education from Columbia University, Teachers College, his MS in Applied Linguistics from Georgetown University, and his BA in International Relations and minor in Spanish from the University of Virginia. He most recently published *Internationalisation of Higher Education and Global Mobility* in the series Oxford Studies in Comparative Education (Symposium Books, 2014).

Brian Whalen is the president and CEO of the Forum on Education Abroad. Until 2010 he was also Associate Provost, Associate Professor of International Studies and Executive Director of the Office of Global Education at Dickinson College in Carlisle, Pennsylvania, where the Forum continues to be housed. Brian is the founding editor of *Frontiers: The Interdisciplinary Journal of Study Abroad*, started in 1994 as the first academic journal devoted to study abroad, and he continues to serve as its editor. Brian holds BA, MA and PhD degrees in psychology with a focus on cultural psychology.

Taylor C. Woodman is a PhD student in international education policy at the University of Maryland and the Special Projects Manager for The George Washington Office for Study Abroad. Woodman serves as a lecturer in the international education policy programs at the University of Maryland and The George Washington University. Woodman earned his bachelor's degree in public and urban affairs with a concentration on global development from Virginia Tech and his master's degree in international education policy from the University of Maryland.

Michael Woolf is Deputy President for Strategic Development at CAPA Global Education Network. Woolf has had much of his career in an international context. Prior to working in mainstream international education, he taught American literature at the universities of Hull, Middlesex, Padova and Venice and worked as a researcher-writer for

BBC radio. Woolf has held leadership roles in international education for many years with, among others FIE, CIEE and Syracuse University. Woolf has written widely on international education and cultural studies.